THE LAW OF CONTRACT 1670–1870

The foundations for modern contract law were laid between 1670 and 1870. Rather than advancing a purely chronological account, this examination of the development of contract law doctrine in England during that time explores key themes in order to better understand the drivers of legal change. These themes include the relationship between lawyers and merchants, the role of equity, the place of statute, and the part played by legal literature. Developments are considered in the context of the legal system of the time and through those who were involved in litigation as lawyers, judges, jurors or litigants. It concludes that the way in which contract law developed was complex. Legal change was often uneven and slow, and some of the apparent changes had deep roots in the past. Clashes between conservative and more reformist tendencies were not uncommon.

WARREN SWAIN is an Associate Professor at the TC Beirne School of Law, University of Queensland, Australia.

CAMBRIDGE STUDIES IN ENGLISH LEGAL HISTORY

Edited by
J. H. Baker
Fellow of St Catharine's College, Cambridge

Recent series titles include

The Law of Contract 1670–1870
Warren Swain

A History of English Tort Law 1900–1950
Paul Mitchell

Sir Edward Coke and the Reformation of the Laws
Religion, Politics and Jurisprudence, 1578–1616
David Chan Smith

Medieval English Conveyances
John M. Kaye

Marriage Law and Practices in the Long Eighteenth Century
A Reassessment
Rebecca Probert

The Rise and Fall of the English Ecclesiastical Courts, 1500–1860
R. B. Outhwaite

Law Courts and Lawyers in the City of London, 1300–1550
Penny Tucker

Legal Foundations of Tribunals in Nineteenth Century England
Chantal Stebbings

Pettyfoggers and Vipers of the Commonwealth
The 'Lower Branch' of the Legal Profession In Early Modern England
C. W. Brooks

Roman Canon Law in Reformation England
R. H. Helmholz, Sir Henry Maine

A Study in Victorian Jurisprudence
R. C. J. Cocks, Sir William Scott, Lord Stowell

Judge of the High Court of Admiralty, 1798–1828
Henry J. Bourguignon

The Early History of the Law of Bills and Notes
A Study of the Origins of Anglo-American Commercial Law
James Steven Rogers

The Law of Treason in England in the Later Middle Ages
J. G. Bellamy

William Sheppard, Cromwell's Law Reformer
Nancy L. Matthews

THE LAW OF CONTRACT 1670–1870

WARREN SWAIN

CAMBRIDGE
UNIVERSITY PRESS

CAMBRIDGE
UNIVERSITY PRESS

University Printing House, Cambridge CB2 8BS, United Kingdom

Cambridge University Press is part of the University of Cambridge.

It furthers the University's mission by disseminating knowledge in the pursuit of education, learning and research at the highest international levels of excellence.

www.cambridge.org
Information on this title: www.cambridge.org/9781107040762

First published 2015

A catalogue record for this publication is available from the British Library

Library of Congress Cataloguing in Publication data
Swain, Warren, 1973– author.
The law of contract, 1670–1870 / Warren Swain.
pages cm. – (Cambridge studies in english legal history)
ISBN 978-1-107-04076-2 (hardback)
1. Contracts – England – History. I. Title.
KD1554.S93 2015
346.4202′20903–dc23
2014043957

ISBN 978-1-107-04076-2 Hardback

CONTENTS

ACKNOWLEDGMENTS

It was W.H. Auden who wrote that, 'In headaches and in worry vaguely life leaks away'. This is all the more true when writing a book. This book originated in an Oxford D.Phil, *Aspects of the Action of Assumpsit 1750–1855* (2003), only a fraction of which has survived into the current work. I should like to thank the examiners of that thesis, Professor Thomas Watkin and Professor John Cartwright, for their helpful comments and advice. I gratefully acknowledge the help and wise counsel of my supervisor and friend, Professor David Ibbetson. I should also like to thank two people who first kindled my interest in law and legal history respectively. The first, the late Roy Stuart, is rightly remembered with great fondness by generations of Hertford undergraduates. I only hope that I have pinned down the issues with sufficient clarity. The second, Jeffrey Hackney, encouraged my first faltering steps in legal history. I owe David, Roy and Jeffrey a huge intellectual debt.

This book has taken a long time to write, during which I have been a member of the law faculties at Oxford, Birmingham and Durham universities as well as the University of Queensland. Various friends have kept me going. It would be remiss not to mention Kenny, Jennean, Mick 'The Hat' and Jean, Tom, Paul, Tony and the late Julian Walters from the early years. In Birmingham I should like to thank my friends who took lunch on the bottom floor of staff house and could still remember a time when universities were fun places to work. Of my colleagues in Durham it suffices to say, along with Virgil, 'latet anguis in herba'. I would however like to thank the regulars in *The Shakespeare* for some happy memories from my time in Durham. During the crucial final stages my friends in Brisbane, Graeme, Kit and Dominic, have been more help than they know. Dave Campbell and the late Brian Simpson both provided encouragement and made helpful suggestions when the project was flagging. I should also like to thank my research assistant Joseph Clowes, whose role went way beyond proof reading, for his friendship and wisdom beyond his years. At various points my family has provided financial support. My father is my most loyal reader and I hope that he will find something here to enjoy. Finally and most importantly I should like to thank my former partner Karen Fairweather who lived with this book for many years. It is to her that it is dedicated with affection. Needless to say any errors remaining are my own.

Some of the material used in this book has appeared in different forms as: 'The Changing Nature of the Doctrine of Consideration 1750–1850' (2005) 26 *Journal of Legal History* 49–61; 'Moses v. Macferlan (1760)', in Charles Mitchell and Paul Mitchell (eds.), *Landmark Cases in the Law of Restitution* (Oxford: Hart, 2006), pp. 19–37; 'Da Costa v. Jones (1778)', in Charles Mitchell and Paul Mitchell (eds.), *Landmark Cases in the Law of Contract* (Oxford: Hart, 2008), pp. 119–34; 'The Classical Model of Contract: the Product of a Revolution in Legal Thought' (2010) 30 *Legal Studies* 513–32. I am grateful to John Wiley and Sons, Taylor and Francis, and Bloomsbury Publishing plc for permission to use this material.

TABLE OF CASES

TABLE OF STATUTES

1

Introduction

> Fundamental change [in the law] happens slowly and by stages so small that nobody at the time could see them as in any way important . . . legal history more than most kinds of history, depends upon the assumptions by which the materials are read . . . people do not formulate their assumptions for themselves, let alone spell them out for the benefit of future historians, and in the case of the law there is never the occasion to write down what everybody knows.[1]

This book is concerned with the history of contract law over a two hundred year period stretching between 1670 and 1870. Inevitably it is also about how the Common law and Equity develops and evolves during that time.[2] The period concerned witnessed profound political, economic, cultural and social change. It would be surprising if the law of contract was unaffected. Legal change cannot be reduced to statistics. It is extremely difficult to measure. Not least of these challenges is identifying what the law is at any given time. It is not uncommon for there to be different possible rules or formulations of rules operating at the same time.[3] The fact that a change has occurred at all is often only apparent later on. The law develops slowly. Rather than a sudden leap forward the law usually shifts by degrees, little by little. Sometimes these small shifts collectively alter the overall direction of contract law. This can be expressed in the idea of a 'tipping point'.[4] But things are not always

[1] S.F.C. Milsom, *The Natural History of the Common Law* (New York: Columbia University Press, 2003), pp. 75–6.

[2] For an excellent discussion of legal change viewed historically with a focus on the twentieth century, see Paul Mitchell, 'Patterns of Legal Change' (2012) 65 *Current Legal Problems* 177.

[3] David Ibbetson, 'What is Legal History a History of?', in Andrew Lewis and Michael Lobban (eds.), *Law and History* (Oxford: Oxford University Press, 2004), pp. 39–40.

[4] David Ibbetson, 'Comparative Legal History: A Methodology', in Anthony Musson and Chantal Stebbings (eds.), *Making Legal History* (Cambridge: Cambridge University Press, 2012), p. 140.

what they seem. Even apparently drastic shifts can take a while to bed in.[5] It is quite common for an apparent change in direction to occur which is then overturned by a reassertion of the *status quo*. The pull of the past is extremely strong in the psychological make-up of lawyers. At times it is sufficiently powerful to stifle innovation. There is often a tension between old and new. Nowhere is this better illustrated than by the survival of the old doctrine of consideration into modern times. Even when a very obvious and unequivocal adjustment has occurred, for example as the result of a statute, existing attitudes can be very difficult to shake off.[6]

Identifying the reasons behind those changes is even more difficult. Motives are usually, but not always, hidden. Throughout history, legal development has been a battle between conservative and reformist instincts. Lawyers during the period concerned, and indeed later, tend towards the former. Human nature tends to favour the familiar.[7] It is understandable that lawyers in particular should think like this. They are after all trying to win the case for their clients and not, unless it achieves this objective, to bring about changes in the law. Judges are not usually by inclination radical innovators. It is what makes those individual judges who are exceptions so remarkable and memorable. The law almost always evolves without any discernible pattern or master plan. Judges are not legal theorists, although they may on occasion be swayed by philosophical ideas.[8] This may just be a matter of rationalising an existing rule in a new way. Sometimes new ideas can have an impact but this should probably not be overstated. The intellectual climate generated by the Enlightenment may in part help to explain why lawyers were becoming more receptive to new ideas. By its nature such a claim about intellectual influence is always going to be a speculative one.

[5] A very good example is provided by the famous *Slade's Case* (1602) 4 Co Rep 92, David Ibbetson, 'Sixteenth Century Contract Law: Slade's Case in Context' (1984) 4 *Oxford Journal of Legal Studies* 295.

[6] Perhaps the best modern example of this is the way in which, despite the Land Registration Act 1925, a great deal of real property was still subject to the old unregistered regime for many decades. The survival of unregistered land was one of the factors behind the Land Registration Act 2002.

[7] This point need not be laboured to anyone who has spent a substantial amount of time in universities. These are institutions about which F.M. Cornford, *Microcosmographia Academica* (Cambridge: Bowes & Bowes, 1908), remains as relevant today as it ever was. The same point has been made in relation to working class culture, Richard Hoggart, *The Uses of Literacy* (London: Penguin, 2009).

[8] The precise role that theory ought to play remains contentious in the modern law. For a sophisticated defence of theory, see Ronald Dworkin, *Justice in Robes* (Cambridge, Mass.: Harvard University Press, 2006), pp. 49–74.

Lawyers operate within the constrictions of the legal system of their own times. Eighteenth century judges were not contained by the rigid system of precedent in the modern sense. There was still a very clear notion that previous cases mattered. Chief Justice Hale had talked about the notion of *stare decisis* as early as the 1670s.[9] Long before precedent in a strict sense became so important, lawyers were prepared to resort to the idea of common learning.[10] The past had political significance as well. Lawyers of the seventeenth century were keen to represent the Common law as such a venerable institution because this was the best way of consolidating their own professional position.[11] The idea that the Common law was an ancient institution continued to be influential. It represents a further reason for resisting change which only really began to unravel in the nineteenth century.

There were structural constraints on lawyers too. The legal system was still dominated by the forms of action and the old pleading rules. It was not until the end of the period discussed that fusion between the two jurisdictions, Chancery and the Common law, was a realistic prospect. Chancery was concerned with some matters which we now think of as contractual. This court played a significant role in loan transactions and elsewhere. But the relationship between Equity and the Common law is not entirely captured in the idea of two jurisdictions side-by-side. Equitable ideas and doctrine were taken up by Lord Mansfield and others and integrated into the Common law. There was no jury in the Court of Chancery. As a result it is often easier to identify substantive legal doctrine. The procedures of the central Common law courts were quite different. Before the nineteenth century, contract cases were decided by juries. Substantive questions were not, at least not very often, clearly enunciated. The jury also introduced an element of chance. It would be unrealistic to expect jurors to ignore their own past experiences. A juryman who has in the past bought a defective horse is unlikely to be sympathetic when a horse merchant finds himself a defendant in an action for breach of contract for selling a defective horse.[12] During the eighteenth century it became easier to challenge a jury verdict. The

[9] *Hanslap* v. *Carter* (1673) 1 Vent 243; *Kirkbright* v. *Curwin* (1676) 3 Keb 611.

[10] J.H. Baker, *The Law's Two Bodies* (Oxford: Oxford University Press, 2001), pp. 64–86.

[11] These ideas are fully explored in J.G.A. Pocock, *The Ancient Constitution and the Feudal Law: A Study of English Historical Thought in the Seventeenth Century*, 2nd edn (Cambridge: Cambridge University Press, 1987).

[12] Much in the manner of the old adage 'a conservative is just a liberal who has been mugged'.

process still took time and involved expense at the risk of an outcome that still might not be favourable.

Any work of history involves an effort of imagination. The legal historian of the eighteenth and nineteenth century is in an advantageous position. There is no lack of evidence. Printed reports of varying standards of reliability exist.[13] Cases are readily reported in newspapers. Some of the trial notes of judges and barristers survive. A few are readily accessible.[14] Many are not.[15] The emergence of a print culture in the eighteenth century saw a growing number of law books.[16] As the cost of production and paper fell in the nineteenth century the market was flooded with legal treatises.[17] The growth in law reports and literature in the nineteenth century presents its own challenges. The enormous increase in electronic resources has had a significant impact on legal historical research.[18] At times it is difficult not to feel overwhelmed. A great deal is still lost to us. For example, relatively little is known about the civil trial process. Nisi prius cases were not regularly reported until around 1800.[19] All we are left with are glimpses of the central, not always harmonious,[20] relationship between judge and jury but not much more. This can be frustrating.

[13] There are sometimes vital differences between reports. The most famous example in this period is the case of *Stilk* v. *Myrick* (1809) 2 Camp 317, 6 Esp 129.

[14] Most obviously some of Lord Mansfield's trial notes, James Oldham, *The Mansfield Manuscripts and the Growth of English Law in the Eighteenth Century*, 2 vols. (Chapel Hill: University of North Carolina Press, 1992).

[15] Extensive trial notes from the collection of Serjeant George Hill, nicknamed Serjeant Labyrinth, are preserved as LI MS Hill; for details, see J.H. Baker, *English Legal Manuscripts*, 2 vols. (London: Inter Documentation Co., 1978), vol. II, pp. 80–90. These are also available on microfiche. Lord Hardwicke's trial notes at nisi prius and in Chancery are another major collection which is not transcribed (BL Add MS 33935–36227). For a discussion of Lord Hardwicke's nisi prius papers, see Henry Horwitz, 'The Nisi Prius Trial Notes of Lord Chancellor Hardwicke' (2002) 23 *Journal of Legal History* 152.

[16] Roy Porter, *Enlightenment* (London: Penguin, 2000), pp. 72–95.

[17] S.H. Steinberg, *Five Hundred Years of Printing*, 3rd edn (London: Penguin, 1974), pp. 277–81.

[18] The electronic versions of the English Reports and the Making of Modern Law database are particularly significant. On the former, see James Oldham, 'Jury Research in the English Reports in CD-ROM', in John Cairns and Grant McLeod (eds.), *The Dearest Birth Right of the People of England: The Jury in the History of the Common Law* (Oxford: Hart, 2002), pp. 131–54.

[19] James Oldham, 'Law Making at Nisi Prius in the Early 1800s' (2004) 25 *Journal of Legal History* 221.

[20] Oldham, *Mansfield Manuscripts*, vol. I, p. 90.

The approach adopted in this book is unashamedly doctrinal. Some will find this 'excruciatingly tedious'.[21] Undoubtedly it cannot provide a full account. The emphasis is largely on the courts at Westminster. It was in these courts that contract doctrine was developed. In practice, the local courts of various kinds were much closer to the everyday experience of many litigants. The Courts of Requests, or Courts of Conscience as they were sometimes known, were popular in low value contract claims. In 1846 this court was replaced by the new County Court which was also very well used. Although records survive giving details of how many claims and what sort of claims were brought, how much was claimed and the nature of the decision-making process in these courts is lost to us. At best we can guess that there was some rough and ready justice.[22] Some litigation did not even get to trial. Arbitration was increasingly popular by the eighteenth century.[23] Once again, the principles that were applied are hidden from us and there is no way of finding out what they were. Despite these limitations, and others, doctrinal legal history does have considerable value. As the late Brian Simpson observed in his *History of the Common Law of Contract*:

> Doctrinal legal history ... is a special branch of the history of ideas, of their reception, evolution and interaction, and the study of these processes in the context of contract law has ... an importance wider than that of merely illustrating the detailed elaboration of the complex moral principles which underlie one particular legal institution. Additionally it contributes to an understanding of how a sophisticated legal system works and, at a more profound level, in what it consists.[24]

Writing just before he died, Simpson said of his earlier work that 'it belongs to a genre that has become unfashionable, and proceeds on the assumption that law can legitimately be studied as an autonomous discipline'.[25] The 'unfashionable' approach advocated by Simpson is often characterised as internal legal history. Legal development is

[21] William MacNeil, 'Living on: Borderlines – Law/History' (1995) 6 *Law and Critique* 167, 173.

[22] Some clues about the County Courts emerge from the 1850s from reports in local newspapers, see Patrick Polden, *A History of the County Court 1846–1971* (Cambridge: Cambridge University Press, 1999), p. 41.

[23] Henry Horwitz and James Oldham, 'John Locke, Lord Mansfield, and Arbitration During the Eighteenth Century' (1993) 36 *Historical Journal* 137.

[24] A.W. Brian Simpson, *A History of the Common Law of Contract: The Rise of the Action of Assumpsit*, pbk edn (Oxford: Oxford University Press, 1987), p. vii.

[25] A.W. Brian Simpson, *Reflections on the Concept of Law* (Oxford: Oxford University Press, 2011), p. 132.

examined from within the law from the perspective of those who are part of the legal process, namely, the litigants, lawyers, judges and legal writers. Internal legal history is sometimes contrasted with external legal history or that which looks at legal development from outside the legal system. This division is sometimes seen as reflecting a difference in the methodology between those who are trained historians and those who are trained lawyers.[26] The leading English legal historians from Maitland through to Milsom and Baker are almost exclusively in the second category.[27] Whether or not a legal historian is trained as a lawyer or a historian is bound to have a major influence on how the evidence is approached. All the same the division is never really an absolute one. Even legally trained legal historians are perfectly well aware that legal development occurs within a social context.[28]

A different sort of legal history began to emerge in the 1970s.[29] It went much further than anything that had been attempted before. Its supporters criticised the conservatism of traditional forms of legal history[30] and saw themselves as setting a new agenda.[31] It was argued that the law was not politically neutral. Rather, ideology drove legal change. It was contended that lawyers and judges were allies of the wealthy commercial elite. These works grew out of the Critical Legal Studies movement.[32] The most celebrated product of this period is Morton Horwitz's *The Transformation of American Law 1780–1860*.[33] It was followed a few

[26] David Sugarman, 'Great Beyond His Knowing: Morton Horwitz's Influence on Legal Education and Scholarship in England, Canada, and Australia', in Daniel Hamilton and Alfred Brophy (eds.), *Transformations in American Legal History: Law, Ideology and Methods. Essays in Honor of Morton J. Horwitz*, 2 vols. (Cambridge, Mass.: Harvard University Press, 2010), vol. II, p. 511.

[27] S.F.C. Milsom, 'Pollock and Maitland: A Lawyer's Retrospective', in John Hudson (ed.), *The History of English Law: Centenary Essays on Pollock and Maitland* (Oxford: Oxford University Press, 1996), pp. 243–59.

[28] For a brilliant example, see S.F.C. Milsom, *The Legal Framework of English Feudalism* (Cambridge: Cambridge University Press, 1976).

[29] For an account of the legal historiography of the last fifty years, see K.J.M. Smith and J.P.S. McLaren, 'History's Living Legacy: An Outline of Modern Historiography of the Common Law' (2001) 21 *Legal Studies* 251.

[30] Morton Horwitz, 'The Conservative Tradition in the Writing of American Legal History' (1973) 17 *American Journal of Legal History* 275.

[31] Robert Gordon, 'Historicism in Legal Scholarship' (1980–1981) 90 *Yale Law Journal* 1017; Robert Gordon, 'Critical Legal Histories' (1984) 36 *Stanford Law Review* 57.

[32] For a very useful overview, see Neil Duxbury, *Patterns of American Jurisprudence* (Oxford: Oxford University Press, 2001), pp. 421–510.

[33] (Cambridge, Mass.: Harvard University Press, 1977). This was not the only significant historical work from this period. Others include, Duncan Kennedy, 'The Structure of

years later by Patrick Atiyah's *The Rise and Fall of Freedom of Contract*[34] which focused on England and was not so overtly political. Atiyah was more contract theorist than legal historian.[35] He nevertheless accepted some of the premises of Horwitz's book.[36] The most important of these was the way in which contract law shifted away from an essentially equitable model around 1770. Whereas at one time judges had placed value on fairness, they now placed greater emphasis on freedom of contract and enforcing contracts. These works are broad in scope and ambitious in intent. They have influenced a whole generation of legal historians, particularly in the United States.

The Critical Legal Studies movement has never made any attempt to disguise the political sympathies of its adherents.[37] It is unlikely to include many cheerleaders for unrestrained free market economics.[38] Political partisanship aside, the significant methodological flaws in these works are well documented. The use of case law is patchy. Some of the arguments are supported by a handful of authorities which are often decades apart.[39] Facts were sometimes passed over in the cause of a good story. Horwitz would later concede that he paid insufficient attention to cultural factors.[40] By definition, if the law is being used covertly to further the interests of particularly powerful groups, then it is going to be difficult to find historical evidence that this is so.

The other main body of literature of external legal history grew out of the Law and Society movement. Writers like Willard Hurst regarded

Blackstone's Commentaries' (1979) 28 *Buffalo Law Review* 205; Duncan Kennedy, *The Rise and Fall of Classical Legal Thought* (Washington D.C.: Beard Books, 2006).

34 (Oxford: Oxford University Press, 1979).

35 Atiyah has produced two major volumes of contract theory: P.S. Atiyah, *Promises, Morals, And Law* (Oxford: Oxford University Press, 1981); P.S. Atiyah, *Essays on Contract* (Oxford: Oxford University Press, 1986).

36 Atiyah attended some of Horwitz's seminars at Harvard and has acknowledged his influence: Patrick Atiyah, 'An Autobiographical Fragment', in Geoffrey Wilson (ed.), *Frontiers of Legal Scholarship* (Chichester: Wiley, 1995), pp. 45–6.

37 Duxbury, *Patterns*, pp. 428–35; Mark Tushnet, 'Critical Legal Studies: A Political History' (1991) 100 *Yale Law Journal* 1515.

38 Such hostility to free market capitalism is not confined to those on the political left, at least in England, as convincingly demonstrated in Martin Weiner, *English Culture and the Decline of the Industrial Spirit 1850–1980*, 2nd edn (Cambridge: Cambridge University Press, 2004).

39 For a detailed refutation of Horwitz using the case law, see A.W.B. Simpson, 'The Horwitz Thesis and the History of Contracts' (1979) 46 *University of Chicago Law Review* 533.

40 Morton Horwitz, *The Transformation of American Law 1870–1960* (Oxford: Oxford University Press, 1992), p. vii.

legal history which focused on the courts as too narrow. It was necessary to look at a wider range of agencies. The relationship between law and society was a complex one, but a failure to address these issues was said to give an incomplete picture. Legal history of this sort works best on a small scale. Hurst's study of the lumber industry in Wisconsin is perhaps the most outstanding example.[41] This sort of history is nevertheless open to the objection that it fails to recognise the 'autonomous internal dynamics of the legal process'.[42]

This book is different. It attempts to examine the law of contract during this period through some key themes. It is not intended to be a comprehensive account of every aspect of contract doctrine during this period. In doing so, developments in contract are situated within wider debates including the supposed needs of merchants, the usury laws and the morality of gambling. These wider themes do not just reflect practical concerns. There are intellectual concerns too. The rise of contract theory can only be fully understood when set against the growth of interest in the works of the Natural lawyers across Europe in the eighteenth century.[43] By the nineteenth century this naturally leads to consideration of the role of legal writers in shaping the direction of legal doctrine. This is a question that still resonates today.[44]

The period under investigation is a significant one in the history of the law of contract. By the late nineteenth century a body of contract law doctrine had emerged which is still recognisable to modern lawyers. Rather than viewing this process as part of some master plan, whether conscious or not, it is better to see these changes as the product of numerous factors which are often pulling in different directions. Perhaps the most important of these was the decline of the jury. As judges wrestled control from the jury, issues of fact and law came into sharper focus. Questions which in earlier centuries fell to be decided by the jury in the guise of whether the parties had entered into an agreement came instead to be seen as matters of legal doctrine. The emergence of

[41] James Willard Hurst, *Law and Economic Growth: The Legal History of the Lumber Industry in Wisconsin 1836–1915* (Cambridge, Mass.: Harvard University Press, 1964).

[42] Mark Tushnet made these remarks in a review of another significant book to come out of the Wisconsin school, 'Perspectives on the Development of American Law: A Critical Review of Friedman's A History of American Law' [1977] *Wisconsin Law Review* 81, 83.

[43] This is itself part of an older tradition which can be traced back to Aristotle: James Gordley, *The Philosophical Origins of Modern Contract Doctrine* (Oxford: Oxford University Press, 1991).

[44] Warren Swain, 'Unjust Enrichment and the Role of Legal History in England and Australia' (2013) 36 *New South Wales Law Journal* 1030.

the rules about offer and acceptance, vitiating factors and even rules about contractual interpretation can all be explained in this way. This left a gap. Doctrine had to be formulated without any historical precedents. It was fortunate that there was a ready-made structure into which the law could be slotted. This was known as the Will Theory. It was built on the simple notion that contracts were formed from a meeting of wills. From this simple definition everything else flowed. The extent to which contract doctrine genuinely reflected these ideas is more dubious. There were many instances which could not fit into the new structure. The most obvious was the well-established doctrine of consideration. The Will Theory undoubtedly shaped the way that lawyers and legal writers thought about contract law. It also helped to give the law an appearance of coherence which it never entirely possessed. Other legal historians have placed too much weight on these changes. Rather than a revolution in the law of contract, the nineteenth century is better interpreted as an evolution on the law of an earlier period. There was certainly not the kind of major shift that writers like Horwitz and Atiyah claimed occurred.

Fifty years ago, in his Hamlyn Lecture *Judge and Jurist in the Reign of Victoria*, Cecil Fifoot argued that 'Law, no more, than any other human creation, is the automatic result of natural forces or intellectual movements. It is made by men . . . English lawyers of all men, should believe in the power of the great judge.'[45] History which recognises the contribution of individuals, and even legal biography, may just be starting to come back into favour after many years where it was unpopular.[46] Individuals can and do have a central role to play in legal development. This argument should not be pressed too hard however. Lord Mansfield was not always the reformer of popular perception. Judges, like everyone else, could be inconsistent. They often had to deal with heavy case-loads over relatively short periods of time which left little time for reflection. The emphasis on 'big' figures like Lord Mansfield should not mean that the role of others be overlooked. Many judges played significant parts in shaping contract doctrine. Those who resisted change are often overlooked, but they are just as important as those who urged reform.

Developments in the law of contract between 1670 and 1870 do not conform to any artificial model. There is no convincing evidence that

[45] (London: Sweet & Maxwell, 1959), p. 12.

[46] R. Gwynedd Parry, 'Is Legal Biography Really Legal Scholarship?' (2010) 30 *Legal Studies* 208.

judges were more or less inclined towards the interests of the individual or commercial parties in 1670 or 1870. In truth, at various times and in various ways, judges came to decisions which both served the interests of merchants and offered protection from exploitation. The idea that the law of contract was equitable before 1770 is particularly unconvincing. The law of contract did evolve. As the jury declined, legal doctrine became much more prominent. The chapters that follow will attempt to address such fundamental questions about cause and consequence. What occurred cannot be written off as a series of accidents,[47] but some of the developments were certainly the result of a serendipitous combination of factors and forces coming together at the same moment. This book explores some of them.

47 The role of 'accidents', and more broadly cause, in history is controversial, E.H. Carr, *What Is History?*, 2nd edn (London: Penguin, 1988), pp. 98–108; Richard Evans, *In Defence of History* (London: Granta, 1997), pp. 129–60.

2

The legal system and the law of contract

Writing in *The Critical Review* in early 1762, the editor and well-known novelist, Tobias Smollett, set down some thoughts on the state of English law:

> When we reflect into what a variety of departments the laws of England are divided, we shall find little cause to be astonished at the difficulty of obtaining justice, the opposition that appears between the several parts, and the flat contradiction which frequently occurs between law and equity. It is this immense variety, and contradictory spirit, that foils all attempts to reduce them to general principles, and to this we may ascribe the tediousness, the uncertainty, and expense of litigation . . . From the number and variety of laws it is frequently a problem, which the most able of the profession cannot solve, what really is the law. The common law, the statute law, the provincial customs, the crown law, the law custom of parliament, the reasonable customs, the canon law, the civil law, the forest law, the law of marquee and reprisals, the commercial laws, the martial laws, form such a vast chaos of jargon, absurdity, and contradiction . . . that the kingdom is deluged with pettifoggers and distributors and advocates of justice, almost equal in number to the clients.[1]

Given his own unhappy experiences, Smollett's rather jaundiced opinion of the legal system is quite understandable.[2] Many contemporaries would have agreed with his analysis.[3] The high cost of litigation was a constant source of complaint and with some justification. A rise in legal fees resulted in a doubling of the cost of litigation in the central courts between 1680 and 1750.[4] The 'vast chaos' described by Smollett was the

[1] 'The Frederician Code' (1762) 13 *The Critical Review Series I*, 1, 3.

[2] The legal system was mercilessly satirised in several of Smollett's novels, see Alice Parker, 'Tobias Smollett and the Law' (1942) 39 *Studies in Philology* 545.

[3] For a discussion of perceptions of law and lawyers, see Wilfrid Prest, 'The Experience of Litigation in Eighteenth-Century England', in David Lemmings (ed.), *The British and Their Laws in the Eighteenth Century* (Woodbridge: The Boydell Press, 2005), pp. 133–54.

[4] Christopher Brooks, *Lawyers, Litigation and English Society since 1450* (London: Hambledon Press, 1998), p. 47.

product of a legal system which had developed over many centuries[5] in a piecemeal and haphazard fashion.[6] The comprehensive reforms that finally arrived in the nineteenth century can be justly characterised as a 'mixture of continuity and change'.[7]

William Blackstone, who would later become a great defender of the *status quo*, in a letter written when still a student, shared some of the frustrations articulated by Smollett. Blackstone likened the Common law to a building which from a regular edifice of earlier times:

> is now, swollen, shrunk, curtailed, enlarged, altered & mangled by various contradictory Statutes &c; it resembles the same Edifice, with many of its most useful Parts pulled down, with preposterous Additions in other Places, of different Materials & coarse Workmanship according to Whim, or Prejudice, or private Convenience of the Builders.[8]

Whether because of its 'immense variety', 'vast chaos' or because it was a 'huge, irregular Pile', the way that the law of contract was conceptualised in 1700 justified all three labels.

Conceptualising contract

It is fair to say that most modern lawyers, at least traditionally minded ones, would see nothing controversial in the following statement taken from the opening paragraph of a leading contract textbook, 'A contract is an agreement giving rise to obligations which are enforced or recognised by law. The factor which distinguishes contractual from other legal obligations is that they are based on the agreement of the contracting parties.'[9]

5 William Blackstone described the 'little contrarieties, which the practice of many centuries will necessarily create in any human system', William Blackstone, *Commentaries on the Laws of England*, 4 vols. (Oxford, 1765), vol. I, p. 30.

6 The best introduction to these many centuries of developments in the legal system remains, J.H. Baker, *An Introduction to English Legal History*, 4th edn (London: Butterworths, 2002).

7 Patrick Polden, 'The Courts of Law', in William Cornish, Stuart Anderson, Raymond Cocks, Michael Lobban, Patrick Polden and Keith Smith, *The Oxford History of the Laws of England, Volume XI 1820–1914: English Legal System* (Oxford: Oxford University Press, 2010), p. 526.

8 W. Prest (ed.), *The Letters of Sir William Blackstone* (London: Selden Society, 2005), p. 4. On the influence of Blackstone's interest in architecture on his legal thought generally, see Carol Mathews, 'A Model of the Old House Architecture in Blackstone's Life and Commentaries', in Wilfrid Prest (ed.), *Blackstone and His Commentaries* (Oxford: Hart, 2009), pp. 15–34.

9 Edwin Peel (ed.), *Treitel The Law of Contract*, 13th edn (London: Sweet & Maxwell, 2011), p. 1. With a few minor changes the same definition has appeared since the first edition of the work, G.H. Treitel, *The Law of Contract* (London: Stevens & Sons, 1962), p. 1.

Treitel's definition emphasises the way that the law of contract is supposedly made up of a single coherent body of rules irrespective of the type of transaction and that it is grounded in the simple idea of a legally enforceable agreement. This depiction of the law of contract, whilst very well established, has not gone unchallenged by modern scholars.[10] It is usually associated with the so-called classical model of contract which was at its height in the nineteenth century. Lawyers a century before would certainly have been baffled by it.

The phrase a 'heap of good learning'[11] was used by Thomas Wood in order to describe the state of English law in the early eighteenth century. In fact, the Common law was less lacking in order than possessing an order derived from practice rather than theory.[12] The point can be illustrated by reference to the legal abridgments. Some of these works were vast and ambitious undertakings. Charles Viner's *A General Abridgement of Law and Equity*, published between 1741 and 1758, ran to more than twenty volumes.[13] When Viner did actually attempt a general definition of a contract, significantly he chose a passage from Justinian's *Institutes* rather than relying on an English source:

> A contract is an agreement entered into by several persons, inducing an obligation by its own nature, and the obligations arising from contracts are divided and distinguished according as they are perfected, either by sole consent of the contractors, or by the intervention or tradition of things, or lastly by word or writing . . . But as all obligations cannot be bound up under general and regular names of contracts, the law allows

[10] The literature is vast. Some examples of varying degrees of merit include, Hugh Collins, *The Law of Contract*, 4th edn (London: Lexis Nexis, 2003); David Campbell (ed.), Ian MacNeil, *The Relational Theory of Contract* (London: Sweet & Maxwell, 2001); Roger Brownsword, *Contract Law: Themes for the Twenty-First Century*, 2nd edn (Oxford: Oxford University Press, 2006); Linda Mulcahy and Sally Wheeler (eds.), *Feminist Perspectives on Contract Law* (London: Cavendish, 2005).

[11] *An Institute of the Laws of England in their Natural Order*, 2 vols. (London, 1720), vol. I, p. ii.

[12] This is not to say that no one had devised schemes other than those adopted by the writers of the abridgments. Nevertheless, most lawyers in contract disputes would have viewed the law in terms of forms of actions.

[13] The abridgment was published between 1741 and 1756, with an index added posthumously in 1758. Viner sold his work by subscription. Early subscribers included William Murray, later Lord Mansfield, and Dudley Ryder, the Attorney-General. After Viner's death one enterprising publisher offered the work in monthly instalments at a cost of 15s, Anon, *An address to the purchasers or subscribers to the General and complete abridgment of law and equity, by Charles Viner* (London, 1767). A full reprint appeared in the 1790s.

> some obligations to pass under the name of quasi-contracts, because they have some resemblance and are of the nature of contracts.[14]

Beneath the thin veneer of Roman learning the reality was rather different. Contracts in England were not 'distinguished according as they are perfected'. The modern division in English law between contract, tort and unjust enrichment would have appeared quite alien to Viner and his contemporaries.[15] Instead the abridgment writers worked according to the alphabet using main headings corresponding to the forms of action: Account, Action upon the case upon Assumpsit, Covenant and Debt.[16] The forms of action, a special form of words into which the claim at Common law had to be slotted, continued to exert a vice like hold over legal thinking.[17] Beneath the main headings Viner devised a series of sub-headings which went on to describe when the action could be brought and how it must be pleaded.[18] The majority of the text under the head of assumpsit was given over to examples of good consideration but there was little or no analysis.[19] Other matters relating to contracts were scattered throughout the twenty-three volumes: Baron and Feme, Bills of Exchange, Conditions, Consideration, Contract and Agreement, Covin, Deeds, Duress of Imprisonment, Enfant, Feme, Freight, Fraud, Guardian and Ward, Marriage, Master and Servant, Master of a ship, Parties, Pawn, Penalty, Sale, Surety, Vendor and Vendee, Usury, Wages.

The actions that Viner was describing were long established.[20] Debt was of sufficient antiquity to have featured in *Glanvill*, the twelfth

[14] *Abridgement* (Aldershot, 1751), vol. V, p. 504. The original passage can be found in: Thomas Sandars (trans.), *The Institutes of Justinian* (London: Longmans, 1948), 3.13.2.

[15] For a conventional outline of the modern division, see Andrew Burrows, *Understanding the Law of Obligations* (Oxford: Hart, 1998), pp. 1–15.

[16] In volume one of Viner, *Abridgement* (Aldershot, 1746), assumpsit took up one sixth of the volume.

[17] For background, see A.H. Chaytor and W.J. Whittaker (eds.), F.W. Maitland, *The Forms of Action at Common Law* (Cambridge: Cambridge University Press, 1948).

[18] This form of sub-division was more elaborate than in previous abridgments: A.W. B. Simpson, 'The Rise and Fall of the Legal Treatise: Legal Principles and the Forms of Legal Literature' (1981) 48 *University of Chicago Law Review* 632, 640.

[19] Viner, *Abridgement*, vol. I, pp. 279–333. In this respect, Viner's abridgment was dated in comparison to his contemporaries such as Bacon and Comyns, see W.S. Holdsworth, *Sources and Literature of English Law* (Oxford: Oxford University Press, 1925), pp. 109–11.

[20] For detailed discussion on the law of contract up until 1700, see J.H. Baker, *An Introduction to English Legal History*, 4th edn (London: Butterworths, 2002); David Ibbetson, *An Historical Introduction to the Law of Obligations* (Oxford: Oxford University Press, 1999); A.W. Brian Simpson, *A History of the Common Law of Contract: The Rise of the Action of Assumpsit*, pbk edn (Oxford: Oxford University Press, 1987).

century law treatise.[21] The action alleged that the plaintiff was entitled to a fixed sum of money owed by the defendant.[22] Where significant sums were involved the prudent used a deed. In these cases of debt on a bond, the contract derived its binding force from the deed itself.[23] The invention of bonds conditioned on performance meant that this remedy was extremely flexible.[24] Debt on a bond continued to be popular thereafter.[25] A deed was not however essential in order to bring a claim in debt. In debt on a contract the agreement was binding because of the presence of a *quid pro quo*.[26] By the fifteenth century *quid pro quo* had a precise technical meaning but it represented a simple idea that the binding force of the contract was derived from reciprocity or exchange.[27]

In the absence of a deed, assumpsit was a more attractive action than debt.[28] Assumpsit took its name from the allegation in the count that the defendant 'assumed and faithfully promised' – *assumpsit et fideliter promisit* – to do something for the plaintiff. The allegation of a wrongful breach, which concluded the count, was a reminder that assumpsit originated in trespass on the case – an action in tort. From around 1570, in order to bring a successful claim in assumpsit, the plaintiff was also required to prove that the promise was supported by good consideration.[29]

[21] G.D.G. Hall (ed.), *The Treatise on the Laws and Customs of the Realm of England Commonly Called Glanvill* (Oxford: Oxford University Press, 1965), book X.

[22] For a host of examples of declarations in debt, see John Wentworth, *A complete system of pleading: comprehending the most approved precedents and forms of practice*, 10 vols. (London, 1797–1799), vol. V.

[23] As a result there were a limited number of defences. Where the bond was unconditional these were confined to the validity of the bond, see Simpson, *Contract*, pp. 95–101.

[24] Simpson, *Contract*, pp. 101–13.

[25] In 1750, 32 per cent of actions in both the King's Bench and Common Pleas were in debt. The vast majority were probably debt on a bond, see Brooks, *Lawyers*, p. 52, table 3.8.

[26] Simpson, *Contract*, pp. 153–69.

[27] William McGovern, 'Contract in Medieval England: The Necessity for Quid Pro Quo and a Sum Certain' (1969) 13 *American Journal of Legal History* 173.

[28] In debt on a contract, wager of law rather than a jury could be used. Wager may have favoured defendants, see Simpson, *Contract*, pp. 137–41. Because debt was a claim for a fixed sum, the fact that the plaintiff could only prove a smaller sum was due also meant that the claim failed in its entirety. In assumpsit the plaintiff could recover the amount of loss that was proved even if this was less than the sum in the declaration.

[29] The literature on consideration is vast, but for an overview of the main features during the crucial formative period of the doctrine and just before, see David Ibbetson, 'Consideration and the Theory of Contract in the Sixteenth Century Common Law', in John Barton (ed.), *Towards a General Law of Contract* (Berlin: Duncker & Humblot, 1990), pp. 67–123; J.H. Baker, 'Origins of the "Doctrine" of Consideration, 1535–1585', in Morris Arnold *et al.* (eds.), *On The Laws and Customs of England: Essays in Honor of Samuel E. Thorne* (Chapel Hill: University of North Carolina Press, 1981), pp. 336–58;

Consideration was founded on the idea of exchange for the promise. It consisted of a benefit to the promisor in exchange for the promise, or for the promisee to suffer a detriment.

Assumpsits fell into two broad categories. In its earliest form assumpsit plugged gaps in the older actions of debt and covenant.[30] Around 1600 it was finally settled that the availability of debt on the same facts was no bar to a claim.[31] This result was achieved using a form of pleading known as indebitatus assumpsit which alleged that the defendant was indebted to the plaintiff and had promised to pay. To begin with indebitatus assumpsit was just a term used to describe a situation where assumpsit was brought in place of debt. By the seventeenth century it had a more technical meaning as a form of count[32] which was distinct from special assumpsit. Instead of alleging an underlying debt, special assumpsit set out the alleged agreement in greater detail. The plaintiff ran the risk that if they were unable to prove one of the material details the claim would fail for a material variance. In order to counter this danger, the early nineteenth century authority on pleading, Edward Lawes, advised pleaders to include several different special counts on the same claim and to join an indebitatus count as an additional insurance.[33]

The standard system of classification using the forms of action was a formidable barrier to any attempts to construct a unified law of contract built around shared substantive principles. This did not mean that no substantive ideas existed. Although expressed in different ways, the idea of reciprocity or exchange underpinned both the actions of assumpsit

J.H. Baker, *The Oxford History of the Laws of England Volume VI 1483–1558* (Oxford: Oxford University Press, 2003), pp. 862–8.

30 Simpson, *Contract*, pp. 248–75.

31 There is a considerable literature surrounding this development, see J.H. Baker, 'New Light on Slade's Case' (1971) 29 *Cambridge Law Journal* 51; David Ibbetson, 'Assumpsit and Debt in the Early Sixteenth Century: The Origins of the Indebitatus Count' (1982) 41 *Cambridge Law Journal* 142; David Ibbetson, 'Sixteenth Century Contract Law: Slade's Case in Context' (1984) 4 *Oxford Journal of Legal Studies* 295.

32 Ibbetson, *Historical Introduction*, p. 148; Simpson, *Contract*, p. 307.

33 Edward Lawes, *A Practical Treatise on Pleading in Assumpsit* (London: W. Reed, 1810), pp. 26–7. For examples of special and indebitatus assumpsits in specimen declarations, see Wentworth, *Pleading*, vol. I, pp. 186–214. For early examples in practice, see *Widdrington* v. *Goddard* (1664), in J.H. Baker, *Baker and Milsom Sources of English Legal History Private Law to 1750*, 2nd edn (Oxford: Oxford University Press, 2010), pp. 511–13; *R* v. *W* (c. 1670), *Baker and Milsom*, pp. 513–14. Difficulties might arise if the counts had failed to conceal that the plaintiff was claiming exactly the same sum on different counts: *Weaver* v. *Boroughs* (1726) 1 Stra 648.

and debt on a contract.[34] Paradoxically, as well as stifling legal development, the forms of action may on occasion have actually helped to make it possible. There is no clearer example than the non-contractual assumpsits which for a time were able to flourish behind the cloak of the forms of action.

The word 'contract' has a long history. In the Middle Ages it simply meant agreement.[35] Hamburger has suggested that by the 'late sixteenth century ... contract had become a legally significant concept which influenced and was influenced by judicial decisions'.[36] Edward Coke's commonplace book, rather than having separate headings representing different actions, preferred 'Contract Bargain &c'.[37] The term 'contract' had certainly evolved but Hamburger overstates his case.[38] Whilst 'contract' in the sense of the social contract played a prominent role in political theory from the seventeenth century,[39] its legal role, with one exception, continued to remain more peripheral. That exception was the rule against joining contract and tort in the same action.[40]

Lawyers were only slowly beginning to think in terms of contracts rather than forms of action even as late as the eighteenth century. When a sealed instrument was used, debt on a bond remained the action of choice into the nineteenth century. Debt on a bond remained so popular because of the ease of proof and the fact that debt on a bond took priority over simple contract debts in the administration of estates.[41] Informal contracts were different. Assumpsit had eclipsed the other forms of

34 Ibbetson, *Historical Introduction*, pp. 80–3, 141–5.

35 R.M. Jackson, 'The Scope of the Term "Contract"' (1937) 53 *Law Quarterly Review* 535; Simpson, *Contract*, pp. 187–90.

36 Philip Hamburger, 'The Development of the Nineteenth-Century Consensus Theory of Contract' (1989) 7 *Law and History Review* 241, 253.

37 Ian Williams, 'Early Modern Judges and the Practice of Precedent', in Paul Brand and Joshua Getzler (eds.), *Judges and Judging in the History of the Common Law and Civil Law* (Cambridge: Cambridge University Press, 2012), p. 55.

38 For a contrary view, see Tariq Baloch, *Unjust Enrichment and Contract* (Oxford: Hart, 2009), p. 11.

39 Most famously by Thomas Hobbes, see Richard Tuck (ed.), Thomas Hobbes, *Leviathan* (Cambridge: Cambridge University Press, 1991). Hobbes in turn was influenced by the Common law of contract, see Robinson Grover, 'The Legal Origins of Thomas Hobbes's Doctrine of Contract' (1980) 18 *Journal of the History of Philosophy* 177.

40 *Denison* v. *Ralphson* (1682) 1 Vent 365; *Dalston* v. *Janson* (1695) 5 Mod 90, Holt 7, 1 Ld Raym 584.

41 The priority rule was described by Chitty as the main attraction of debt on a bond: Joseph Chitty, *The Practice of the Law in all its Departments*, 2nd edn, 2 vols. (London: S. Sweet, 1834), vol. I, p. 114. This rule was abolished by (1869) 32 & 33 Vict c. 46.

action by the 1750s.[42] In these circumstances, no great leap of imagination was needed before assumpsit and 'contract' were, at least some of the time, treated as synonymous.[43] By the end of the eighteenth century the term 'contract' was also starting to be used more widely as a tool of classification. For example, in resisting attempts to undermine the doctrine of consideration, Lord Chief Baron Skynner stated that 'All contracts are by the laws of England distinguished into agreements by speciality, and agreements by parol'.[44]

Despite the emergence of new ways of thinking about contract in the eighteenth century, most lawyers, for the most part, continued to visualise the law of contract through the prism of the forms of action. That was their everyday experience because that was how claims were framed. Even those like Blackstone who were willing to think in more abstract terms were uneasy about jettisoning such long established modes of thinking. By the early nineteenth century these old certainties began to break down. There were two reasons for this; one practical and one intellectual. Even with the demise of the original writs, which in personal actions were only exceptionally required to instigate a suit in the Common law courts,[45] the precise form still determined the procedures that could be used. Differences in form determined whether it was possible to secure the defendant's appearance through imprisonment or bail.[46] Although a uniform writ of summons was introduced in 1832,[47] it remained necessary to identify a form of action in the

[42] Wilmot C.J. would express surprise when faced with an action of account: *Godfrey* v. *Saunders* (1770) 3 Wils KB 94. For a similar view, see Matthew Bacon, *A New Abridgment of the Law*, 5 vols. (London, 1736), vol. I, p. 16. Covenant was largely confined to real property transactions. Debt on a contract as opposed to debt on a bond was also described by Blackstone as 'seldom brought', William Blackstone, *Commentaries on the Laws of England*, 4 vols. (Oxford, 1768), vol. III, p. 154. Later on it would enjoy a brief revival: Joseph Chitty, *A Treatise on the Parties to Actions, the Forms of Action and on Pleading*, 2 vols. (London: J. Butterworth & W. Clark, 1809), vol. I, p. 107.

[43] Francis Buller, *An Introduction to the Law Relative to Trials at Nisi Prius* (London, 1767), p. 120; Isaac Espinasse, *A Digest of the Law of Actions at Nisi Prius*, 2 vols. (Dublin, 1790), vol. I, p. iii. An even earlier example can be found in William Sheppard, *Actions Upon the Case for Deeds viz Contracts, Assumpsits, Deceits, Nuisances, Trover and Conversion*, 2nd edn (London, 1675), p. 35.

[44] *Rann* v. *Hughes* (1778) 7 TR 350, fn. (a), LI MS Misc. 130 f. 74.

[45] William Tidd, *The practice of the Court of King's Bench in personal actions*, 2 vols. (London, 1790), vol. I, p. 2.

[46] For a description of the whole process of initiating proceedings, see Polden, 'Courts of Law', in Cornish *et al.*, *Oxford History XI*, pp. 569–80.

[47] (1832) 2 & 3 Will IV c. 39 s. 1.

summons until 1852,[48] from which point the forms of action continued to exist in name only.[49]

The intellectual shift was almost as tortuous. Sir Frederick Pollock, perhaps the most thoughtful of the nineteenth century contract writers, noted in the first edition of his textbook that 'It is somewhat curious that no such thing as a satisfactory definition of contract is to be found in our books'.[50] Writers before Pollock made little progress in this regard. Joseph Chitty used 'contract' and 'agreement' interchangeably.[51] Following a discussion of different sorts of rights, Stephen Leake was content to claim that simple contracts were of two sorts, those arising from agreements and those that were independent of it.[52] Pollock's treatment was more sophisticated.[53] He went to considerable lengths to explore the relationship between the 'contract' and 'agreement' and to consider the main features of each. In the absence of English authority he turned to the German jurist Von Savigny, a man whom he regarded as a 'true scientific genius'.[54] Pollock referred to Von Savigny's *System des heutigen römischen Rechts* in order to claim that it was possible to distinguish a contract and an 'agreement in a wider sense' or a 'legal agreement'.[55] The crucial passage was followed 'almost literally' by Pollock.[56] Whether it supports the conclusions that he purported to draw is more doubtful. Von Savigny conceded that *vertrag*, or 'contract', was sometimes used imprecisely.[57] But his discussion of a 'contract of sale', at its heart, pertains more to contract in its narrowest sense than what Pollock

48 (1852) 15 & 16 Vict c. 76 s. 3.

49 *1st Report of Her Majesty's Commissioners for Inquiring into the Process, Practice, and System of Pleading in the Superior Courts of Common Law* (1851) [1389] PP vol. XXII, 567. Even so, the influence of the forms of action did not die out entirely, see Lord Atkin in *United Australia Ltd* v. *Barclays Bank Ltd* [1943] 1 AC 1, 29.

50 Frederick Pollock, *Principles of Contract at Law and in Equity* (London: Stevens & Sons, 1876), p. 1.

51 Joseph Chitty, *A Practical Treatise on the Law of Contracts Not Under Seal* (London: S. Sweet, 1826), p. 1.

52 Stephen Leake, *The Elements of the Law of Contracts* (London: Stevens & Sons, 1867), pp. 1–7.

53 For a more general discussion, see Neil Duxbury, *Frederick Pollock and the English Juristic Tradition* (Oxford: Oxford University Press, 2004), pp. 191–2.

54 Pollock, *Contract*, 1st edn, p. 2, fn. b.

55 He summarised this position in a footnote, Pollock, *Contract*, 1st edn, p. 7, fn. (a) 'Agreement = Vertrag, wodurch eine Obligation entstehen soll. Contract = Vertrag, wodurch eine klagbare Obligation entsteht'. That is the difference between an obligation and a legally enforceable obligation.

56 In Friedrich von Savigny, *System des heutigen römischen Rechts*, 9 vols. (Berlin: Veit und Comp, 1840), vol. III, § 140.

57 *Ibid.*

called 'agreement in a wider sense'. In a marginal note Pollock conceded that 'contract [was a] special and complex conception' which early versions of his treatise did little to dispel. The whole approach would be abandoned in the third edition on the grounds that it was, in the author's view, in 'sundry respects inadequate'.[58]

The eighteenth century evidence is a long way from a unified law of contract. That would emerge later on, but all the same this way of thinking long pre-dated the abolition of the forms of action. There was no sudden shift. Even when a unified concept of contract became more established, English writers, even one as influential as Pollock, struggled to provide a clear sighted justification. Even today no one school of contract theory seems to hold all the answers.[59] Litigants care nothing for such matters. They are only concerned with ensuring a successful outcome of their cause. Here the picture is equally diffuse.

Litigating claims in contract

In the eighteenth and nineteenth centuries contract disputes were litigated in all sorts of different forums. At the pinnacle were the three superior Common law courts at Westminster, the King's Bench, the Common Pleas, and the Exchequer Pleas.[60] The King's Bench replaced the Common Pleas as the primary venue for civil litigation during the great litigation slump which occurred between 1680 and the 1750s.[61] It remained dominant

[58] Frederick Pollock, *Principles of Contract at Law and in Equity*, 3rd edn (London: Stevens & Sons, 1881), p. vi.

[59] For an introduction to some of the various approaches, see Stephen Smith, *Contract Theory* (Oxford: Oxford University Press, 2004).

[60] Brooks has surveyed the business of the King's Bench and Common Pleas in 1640 and 1750. His evidence shows that contract claims made up a significant percentage of both courts' business, but that actions of debt had declined significantly in percentage terms by 1750. There was a corresponding rise in actions on the case which in the guise of assumpsit included contract actions, see Brooks, *Lawyers*, p. 52. David Lemmings, *Professors of the Law* (Oxford: Oxford University Press, 2000), p. 98, also argues that there was a significant decline in debt. A study by Francis shows a slightly different picture in which debt is still significant in the central courts into the late eighteenth century. Debt is the dominant action in the King's Bench during the sample year (1790), with debt accounting for 52.2 per cent in total, of which debt on a bond accounts for 36.6 per cent of all actions, see Clinton Francis, 'Practice, Strategy, and Institution: Debt Collection in the English Common-Law Courts, 1740–1840' (1985–1986) 80 *Northwestern University Law Review* 807, 913, 915, 917.

[61] Brooks, *Lawyers*, p. 68. The slump in litigation touched all of the central courts and also the local ones. For a discussion of the literature on this subject and some speculation on the reasons for the slump, see Henry Horwitz, 'Changes in the Law and Reform of the Legal Order: England (and Wales) 1689–1760' (2002) 21 *Parliamentary History* 301, 306–11.

thereafter and had the largest role in contract disputes of the three central courts. Contracts of various descriptions also found a way into the Court of Chancery.[62] In a society in which wealth was still largely represented in real property, agreements relating to land were a staple of Chancery business.[63] Chancery also played an important role in regulating unfair bargains. For a time, equitable doctrine went beyond its own borders as it was taken up by Common law judges. The printed reports preserve a clear, if often incomplete, picture of contract law in all four of these courts.[64] A number of smaller jurisdictions are less well documented but were significant in practice.

The judge and jurist, Sir Matthew Hale, explained in the late seventeenth century that 'The Court of Admiralty claim a Jurisdiction touching Contracts or Injuries made or done entirely upon the high Sea and out of other Bodies of English Counties'.[65] At the time Hale was writing, the Admiralty Court was in a terminal decline.[66] The process continued into the eighteenth century despite the rapid expansion of the merchant navy.[67] The Common law courts, which enjoyed a concurrent jurisdiction, in many instances of maritime contracts, absorbed much of this business, although there continued to be some very public jurisdictional squabbles, especially in relation to sailors' wages.[68] Although much diminished, the Admiralty

62 Henry Horwitz and Patrick Polden, 'Continuity or Change in the Court of Chancery in the Seventeenth and Eighteenth Centuries?' (1996) 35 *Journal of British Studies* 24, 35.

63 *Ibid.*, p. 35.

64 There was a steady increase in the number of printed reports over the course of the eighteenth century. The numbers were not vast. Chancery was particularly poorly served by the printed reports. There were no nisi prius reports until the end of the century. The printed reports can sometimes be supplemented by barristers' and judges' notebooks which contain manuscript reports. Judges of the time were prepared to use manuscript reports. For example, *Smith* v. *Parkhurst* (1739) Andr 315, 324.

65 M.J. Prichard and D.E.C. Yale (eds.), *Hale and Fleetwood on Admiralty Jurisdiction* (London: Selden Society, 1993), p. 13.

66 D.E.C. Yale, 'A View of the Admiralty Jurisdiction: Sir Mathew Hale and the Civilians', in Dafydd Jenkins (ed.), *Legal History Studies 1972* (Cardiff: University of Wales Press, 1972), pp. 87–109. For the important role of the Admiralty Court in the seventeenth century, see George Steckley, 'Collisions, Prohibitions and the Admiralty Court in Seventeenth Century London' (2003) 21 *Law and History Review* 41.

67 E.E. Rich and C.H. Wilson (eds.), *The Cambridge Economic History of Europe*, 8 vols. (Cambridge: Cambridge University Press, 1977), vol. V, p. 530. Merchant ships had a total tonnage of 421,000 tonnes in 1751 compared with 115,000 tonnes in 1630. By 1760 there were 7,081 merchant ships with a tonnage of 486,740 tonnes.

68 Examples include: *Bayly* v. *Grant* (1699) Holt 48, 1 Salk 33; *Gawne* v. *Grandee* (1706) Holt 49; *Ragg* v. *King* (1729) 1 Barn KB 297; *Reed* v. *Chapman* (1732) 2 Barn KB 160. For the role of the Admiralty Court in the case of sailors' wages, see George Steckley,

Court remained a significant presence in a few areas, of which prize money was one of the most significant, especially in wartime.[69] Into the nineteenth century the Admiralty Court actually increased the scope of its jurisdiction without too much objection from the Common lawyers,[70] before it finally ceased to be an independent court on becoming part of one division of the High Court.[71]

Various local courts heard small contract disputes. Comparatively little is known about the way these tribunals operated.[72] The Courts of Conscience,[73] which were found in some larger urban centres,[74] were popular in the eighteenth century.[75] William Hutton, a Commissioner in the Birmingham Court, in his court guidebook,[76] was well placed to describe the rapid turnover of business,[77] much of which was low value contract litigation.[78] Hutton was a great champion of the court,

'Litigious Mariners: Wage Cases in the Seventeenth Century Admiralty Court' (1999) 42 *Historical Journal* 315.

69 For some indication of the scope of the jurisdiction in the late eighteenth century, see Arthur Browne, *A Compendious View of the Civil Law*, 2 vols. (London, 1798), vol. II, pp. 147–200.

70 F. Wiswall, *The Development of Admiralty Jurisdiction and Practice since 1800* (Cambridge: Cambridge University Press, 1970), p. 26; Polden, 'Courts of Law', in Cornish *et al.*, *Oxford History XI*, pp. 714–19.

71 Wiswall, *Admiralty Jurisdiction*, pp. 102–15.

72 For a summary of some of these courts, see A.H. Manchester, *Modern Legal History* (London: Butterworths, 1980), pp. 112–14. For a discussion of the Mayor's and Sherriff's courts, see Brooks, *Lawyers*, pp. 40–1. For a discussion of the role of local courts in contract disputes in the previous century, see Craig Muldrew, *The Economy of Obligation* (Basingstoke: MacMillan, 1998), pp. 199–271.

73 On the Courts of Conscience, see W.S. Holdsworth, *A History of English Law*, 17 vols. (London: Methuen, 1922), vol. I, pp. 190–1; Margot Finn, *The Character of Credit* (Cambridge: Cambridge University Press, 2003), pp. 197–235. The Court of Conscience was still sometimes called the Court of Requests in recognition of its origins, see W.H. D. Winder, 'The Courts of Requests' (1936) 52 *Law Quarterly Review* 369.

74 Which included London, Birmingham, Newcastle and other urban centres listed by Blackstone, Blackstone, *Commentaries*, vol. III, p. 82.

75 Its popularity may have varied. Brooks, *Lawyers*, pp. 40–1 shows that there were 3,921 actions in the Newcastle Court of Conscience in 1829–30 from a low point of 378 in 1804–5. The previous high was 1,826 in 1697–8.

76 *Courts of Requests: Their Nature, Utility and Powers Described* (Birmingham, 1787).

77 *Ibid.*, p. 11, Hutton claimed that he heard 150 cases a week. The rapid turnover may have been assisted by the fact that many of the parties settled prior to the hearing, Margot Finn, 'Debt and Credit in Bath's Court of Requests 1829–39' (1994) 21 *Urban History* 211, 218.

78 This was mirrored elsewhere: on London in 1799, see Brooks, *Lawyers*, pp. 73–4; on Norwich, see Michele Slatter, 'The Norwich Court of Requests – A Tradition Continued' (1984) 5 *Journal of Legal History* 97. These courts continued to be a popular forum for

believing it to be close to perfection.[79] Sir William Blackstone conceded that the Court of Conscience involved 'very little trouble and expense' but thought that in the absence of a jury, it allowed the Commissioners a 'petty tyranny'.[80] He was not alone in this view. By the early nineteenth century there was a growing sense of dissatisfaction with the lay Commissioners, whether justified or not, and in 1846 the court was replaced by the new County Court.[81] The County Court proved to be equally popular for low value claims.[82]

That Blackstone should single out the absence of a jury is not surprising.[83] The jury continued to be central to the way that many in England thought about their legal system.[84] As one writer of the 1740s explained, 'They are incorporated with our Constitution and are the most valuable part of it; nay, may be termed the very vitals of it; without them no man's life can be impeached, no man's liberty or property ought to be taken from him'.[85] Outside of the Court of Chancery, which operated without jurors, the civil jury remained in rude health throughout the eighteenth century. But perceptions of the jury were not always favourable,[86] and real reform would eventually have serious implications for the law of contract.

The jury's role was to answer the question or issue put to them after pleading was finished and issue joined.[87] Pleading was a paper exercise

contract litigation into the nineteenth century, see H.W. Arthurs, 'Without the Law: Courts of Local and Special Jurisdiction in Nineteenth Century England' (1984) 5 *Journal of Legal History* 130, 132–7; H.W. Arthurs, *Without the Law* (Toronto: University of Toronto Press, 1985), pp. 25–34.

79 Hutton, *Courts of Requests*, p. v.

80 Blackstone, *Commentaries*, vol. III, p. 82.

81 County Courts (England) Act (1846) 9 & 10 Vict c. 95; Patrick Polden, *A History of the County Court, 1846–1971* (Cambridge: Cambridge University Press, 1999), pp. 22–3.

82 Paul Johnson, 'Small Debts and Economic Distress in England and Wales, 1857–1913' (1993) 46 *Economic History Review (NS)* 65.

83 In his response, Hutton recognised the importance of juries but said that he did not regard juries to be necessary in the kind of minor disputes heard in the Court of Conscience: William Hutton, *A Dissertation on Juries* (Birmingham, 1789).

84 The Declaration of Rights of 1689 contained a clause on juries, see Julian Hoppit, *A Land of Liberty? England 1689–1727* (Oxford: Oxford University Press, 2000), p. 24.

85 Anon, *A Compendious Library of the Law* (London, 1740), p. 122.

86 There was a good deal of complaining about how the jury operated and particularly about the poor calibre of jurors, see James Oldham, 'The Origins of the Special Jury' (1983) 50 *University of Chicago Law Review* 137, 141–4. Some of this criticism was quite specific, for example Anon, *The Advantages of Settling Disputes by Arbitration* (Carlisle, 1795), p. 9, 'the want of local knowledge in jurors, is an evil of no small magnitude'. These sorts of complaints were still around fifty years later: (1848) 11 *Law Times* 425; I am grateful to Mr John Hajek for this reference.

87 For an overview of the pleading process and the jury, see Baker, *Introduction*, pp. 71–96.

by this stage. The process attracted admirers[88] and detractors[89] alike, but required a degree of skill and was sometimes devolved to a group of lawyers known as 'special pleaders'.[90] In contract actions, joinder of issue was usually reached when the defence submitted a general blanket denial of liability. In the case of assumpsit, the form of words deployed was 'non assumpsit'. The actual hearing, where evidence was presented, usually took place at nisi prius before a judge on circuit in a county close to where the action arose.[91] In some respects the rules of evidence were not always as strict as they later became. In other ways they were very restricted. Crucially, in the superior Common law courts, parties with an interest in the suit could not give evidence until 1843, and actual parties were not competent witnesses until even later.[92]

By 1700 the jury was an impartial tribunal of fact along modern lines,[93] but very little is known about how the jurors actually went about reaching a decision.[94] The process was not recorded and reasons were not given.[95] A ballad of the period advised jurors to 'be judges of

[88] Richard Wooddeson, *Elements of Jurisprudence Treated of in the Preliminary Part of a Course of Lectures on the Laws of England* (London, 1783), p. 107, 'a science which hath always been spoken of with high encomiums by the greatest proficients in legal learning'. For a discussion of the eighteenth century literature on pleading, see Michael Lobban, *The Common Law and English Jurisprudence 1760–1850* (Oxford: Oxford University Press, 1991), pp. 61–7.

[89] Richard Boote, *An Historical Treatise of an Action or Suit at Law* (London, 1766). Jeremy Bentham was a predictable and vociferous critic.

[90] Lemmings, *Professors*, pp. 33–4. Some judges may also have found the mechanics of pleading difficult to grasp. There is evidence that on becoming a Chief Justice of the Common Pleas, William De Grey went to a considerable effort to familiarise himself with the rules of procedure and pleading, Emily Kadens, 'The Puzzle of Judicial Education: The Case of Chief Justice William De Grey' (2009–2010) 75 *Brooklyn Law Review* 143, 169–77.

[91] Trials at Bar required leave of the court and were the exception rather than the rule. Some of the factors to be considered were set out in argument in *Brown* v. *Brown* (1780) 2 Doug 437. The London equivalent to nisi prius was the court at Guildhall in Middlesex.

[92] (1843) 6 & 7 Vict c. 85; (1851) 14 & 15 Vict c. 99. C.J.W. Allen, *The Law of Evidence in Victorian England* (Cambridge: Cambridge University Press, 1997), pp. 96–8, 100–10.

[93] Earlier jurors had been more like witnesses: John Mitnick, 'From Neighbor-Witness to Judge of Proofs: The Transformation of the English Civil Juror' (1988) 32 *American Journal of Legal History* 201.

[94] The way in which juries reach verdicts continues to be debated at great length in modern times. The literature on the subject is vast, particularly in the United States. For an overview, see Dennis Devine *et al.*, 'Jury Decision Making: 45 Years of Empirical Research on Deliberating Groups' (2001) 7 *Psychology Public Policy and Law* 622.

[95] Sometimes a sense of the process can be gained from judges' notebooks.

fact, though not judges of laws'.[96] Although a distinction between law and fact was firmly established by the sixteenth century,[97] applying the division in practice was not always so easy. As the barrister in Sir John Hawles's *The English-mans right a dialogue between a barrister at law and a jury-man* explained, 'yet must your jury apply matter of fact and law together and from their consideration of, and a right of judgment upon both, bring forth their verdict'.[98]

Hawles illustrated his point with reference to the general issue.[99] In his day, and for a long time afterwards, many issues that came to be expressed as clear legal rules remained bundled up with the facts and hidden behind a blank jury verdict. The point can be illustrated with a simple example. In a straightforward contract dispute the most obvious strategy for a defendant is to give reasons for the non-existence of the contract, for example, through mistake, fraud, lack of intention, or failure to reach an agreement. In 1700 these were largely issues that could be raised in evidence, the general issue of 'non-assumpsit' having been pleaded. For much of the time, clear judicial definitions of mistake etc. were absent.[100] This came later. What Barton has called 'nisi prius law'[101] gave some guidance, but it was not law as understood in the modern sense. As Milsom has explained, 'the most such dialogues can have done was to contribute to professional tradition among lawyers. They could not create law until they could formally be the basis of a judgment by the full court; and it was not until the seventeenth century that it became regularly possible.'[102]

In determining the existence and content of a contract, jurors were allowed and even encouraged to bring their own expertise to bear. The mercantile juries, which flourished under the gaze of Lord Mansfield and which continued into the nineteenth century, are the most obvious example.[103] This is not to say that the relationship between judge and

[96] William Pulteney, *The honest jury or Caleb triumphant. A new ballad* (London, 1729), p. 3.

[97] Barbara Shapiro, *A Culture of Fact: England 1550–1720* (Ithaca: Cornell University Press, 2003), pp. 10–11; Morris Arnold, 'Law and Fact in the Medieval Jury Trial: Out of Sight, Out of Mind' (1974) 18 *American Journal of Legal History* 267.

[98] (London, 1680), p. 11. [99] *Ibid.*

[100] For a rare example of fraud bubbling to the surface, see *Bright* v. *Eynon* (1757) 1 Burr 390.

[101] J.L. Barton, 'Review of AWB Simpson, A History of the Common Law of Contract' (1977) 27 *University of Toronto Law Journal* 373, 375.

[102] S.F.C. Milsom, 'The Past and the Future of Judge-Made Law' (1981–1982) 8 *Monash University Law Review* 1, 7.

[103] James Oldham, *The Varied Life of the Self-Informing Jury* (London: Selden Society, 2005), pp. 24–31.

jurors was never strained. Lord Mansfield supposedly told James Boswell that juries always followed his directions except in 'political causes'.[104] He overstates the case, as *Hollingsworth* v. *Tattersall*[105] shows. Judges did give directions and these were often very intrusive in instructing the jury to find one way or the other.[106] To some extent a successful system also relied on the good sense of jurors.[107] But judges were also increasingly watchful. Holt C.J. explained in *Ash* v. *Ash* that:

> The jury were very shy of giving a reason of their verdict, thinking that they had an absolute despotick power, but I did rectify that mistake; for the jury are to try causes with the assistance of the judges; and ought to give reasons when required; that if they go on any mistake, they may be set right.[108]

At the same time, matters of contract doctrine were becoming more visible than in the earlier centuries, where the nature of litigation had placed an emphasis on pleading and law reporting was a comparatively hit and miss affair. The vehicle for these changes was the transformation of the civil jury. Its origins can be traced to the mid-seventeenth century.[109] First, and very gradually, judges began to wrestle control from the jury on the back of procedural reforms. The motion for new trial began to be used for matters which appeared off as well as on the record.[110] As a result of apparently technical change, it became easier for the losing party to mount a challenge to the jury's verdict than had been possible using the old action of attaint.[111] The motion was heard

104 Oldham, *Mansfield Manuscripts*, vol. I, p. 206.

105 (1778). The case is overlooked by the nominate reports. As a decision at Guildhall rather than in banc this is not surprising. Lord Mansfield's note of the trial survives: Oldham, *Mansfield Manuscripts*, vol. I, pp. 332–3. Two different newspaper reports have also been located: *London Chronicle*, 30 May 1778; *Morning Post*, 1 June 1778.

106 For examples from the notebooks of Dudley Ryder, see John Langbein, 'Historical Foundations of the Law of Evidence: A View from the Ryder Sources' (1996) 96 *Columbia Law Review* 1168, 1190–3.

107 J.H. Baker, *The Law's Two Bodies* (Oxford: Oxford University Press, 2001), p. 63.

108 (1696) Holt 701, 702.

109 Baker, *Introduction*, pp. 81–5.

110 *Wood* v. *Gunston* (1655) Style 462, 466. For a flavour of the content of court records, see J.H. Baker, 'Records, Reports and the Origins of Case Law in England', in John Baker (ed.), *Judicial Records, Law Reports, and the Growth of Case Law* (Berlin: Duncker & Humblot, 1989), pp. 34–6.

111 B.J. Sellon, *The Practice of the Courts of King's Bench and Common Pleas*, 2 vols. (London, 1792), vol. I, p. 502, 'the writ of attaint is now a sound in every case it does not pretend to be a remedy'. Though not used it was not formally abolished until 1825: (1825) 6 Geo IV c. 50 s. 60.

before judges in banc at Westminster in reliance on an account in the trial judge's notebook.[112]

A verdict could be challenged if the jury had failed to follow a judge's direction. By the early eighteenth century the scope of the motion for new trial was further expanded to include situations where the judge had erred in his direction.[113] In these cases the judges sitting in banc were essentially asked to consider whether the trial judge, in his direction to the jury, had got the law right. Questions of law could also be raised in banc more directly and effectively than the old special verdict had allowed,[114] by reserving points of law[115] and case stated.[116] Taken together, greater control of juries and the relative ease of extracting issues of law for deliberation helped to firm up the roles of judge and jury and the line between law and fact.[117] In the 1760s Wilmot J. had stated that:

> For, though when facts and law happened to be so complicated and intermixed that a jury can not help taking both into their consideration,

112 Sellon, *Practice*, vol. I, p. 504; John Archbold, *The Practice of the Court of King's Bench*, 2 vols. (London: J. Butterworth, 1819), vol. II, p. 227. In *Atkins* v. *Drake* (1824) M'Cle & Yo 213, 229, Chief Baron Alexander described the process of reading the notes of the trial judge in the case of a motion for new trial.

113 For a complete list of situations where the motion could be used, see John Morgan, *Essays Upon the Law of Evidence, New Trials, Special Verdicts, Trials at Bar and Repleaders*, 3 vols. (London, 1789), vol. II, p. 1 sets out the various grounds: 1. misbehaviour of a party towards the jury; 2. a verdict obtained by fraud, stratagem or inequitable means; 3. gross misbehaviour of the jury; 4. a verdict contrary to the evidence, or a hard action; 5. a verdict against record, or against law; 6. for excessive damages; 7. for insufficient damages; 8. for refusing evidence by, or misdirection or non-direction of the judge; 9. and other causes as irregularity. For an example of a motion, see *Bowen* v. *Proctor* (1715) in W. Hamilton Bryson (ed.), *Sir John Randolph's King's Bench Reports 1715–1716* (New York: Hein, 1996) [74].

114 For a summary of the operation of the special verdict, see Tidd, *Practice*, vol. I, pp. 595–6; Sellon, *Practice*, vol. II, pp. 50–60.

115 M.J. Prichard, 'Non-Suit: A Premature Obituary' (1960) 18 *Cambridge Law Journal* 88; *Baskerville* v. *Brown* (1761) 2 Burr 1229; *Dally* v. *Smith* (1771) 4 Burr 2148; *Clay* v. *Willan* (1789) 1 H Bla 298.

116 This method was particularly favoured by Lord Mansfield, see James Oldham, 'The Seventh Amendment Right to Jury Trial: Late Eighteenth Century Practice Reconsidered', in Katherine O'Donovan and Gerry Rubin (eds.), *Human Rights and Legal History: Essays in Honour of Brian Simpson* (Oxford: Oxford University Press, 2000), p. 235. Tidd was also an admirer, Tidd, *Practice*, vol. I, pp. 597–8. The case stated worked by giving a general verdict, usually for the plaintiff, subject to an opinion of the court in banc on a question drawn up by counsel on both sides on a point of law.

117 Judges were still reluctant to intervene in relation to findings of fact, see *Smith* v. *Frampton* (1695) 1 Ld Raym 62.

> it may be difficult or even impossible for them to avoid founding their verdict upon both; yet they are not at liberty to determine contrary to the law: they ought to take their notion of law, from the direction of the Judge who tries the cause.[118]

A mere twenty years later, Buller J. was adopting a more robust approach: 'In a question of law however unpleasant it may be to us, we must not yield to the decision of a jury.'[119] Earlier decisions also began to exert greater force on judges.[120] By the middle of the nineteenth century the boundary between law and fact had become absolutely distinct in both theory and practice.[121] There were two main catalysts for this shift. The rise of special pleading in the 1830s lifted the veil on the general issue,[122] especially highlighted in the discussion of fraud.[123] The practical consequence of this change was that juries were no longer presented with a broad general issue. The plea 'non-assumpsit' could only be used to deny the existence of a promise. All those other matters which could in the past have been raised by this plea had to be pleaded specially, that is specifically identified. The rise of special pleading was not without problems,[124] but the impact on the law of contract was enormous.

118 *Grant* v. *Vaughan* (1764) 3 Burr 1516, 1526.

119 *Appleton* v. *Sweetapple* (1782) 3 Doug 137, 140. For similar remarks elsewhere, see *Tindal* v. *Brown* (1786) 1 TR 167, 169; *Sproat* v. *Matthews* (1786) 1 TR 182, 187.

120 Harold Berman and Charles Reid, 'The Transformation of English Legal Science from Hale to Blackstone' (1996) 45 *Emory Law Journal* 437, 444–51.

121 Anon, 'Of the Distinction between Law and Fact' (1844) 1 *Law Review* 37.

122 These reforms were known as the Hilary Rules Reg Gen HT 4 Will IV. They are reproduced in (1834) LJ Repts KB 5. When Henry Brougham, in his famous speech on law reform, came to criticise the wide general issue he used assumpsit as one of his examples: (1828) 18 HC Deb 127, 201. The expert on pleading in assumpsit, Edward Lawes, writing a few years earlier, pointed out that 'almost every sort of defence might be given in evidence' under the general issue in assumpsit: Lawes, *Pleading*, p. 520. By this he presumably meant anything which the law recognised as a valid defence to an action of assumpsit. For example, duress to the person was a valid defence whereas what is now termed economic duress was not.

123 As part of the reforms, fraud had to be pleaded specially which meant that it had to be specifically identified. In his evidence to the commission which preceded these reforms, Chitty explained that fraud was currently pleaded under the general issue: *2nd Report into the Practice and Proceedings of the Superior Courts of Common Law* (1830) [123] PP vol. XI, 547, 11 App B No. 4 § 56.

124 It encouraged formal objections as a delaying tactic, as noted in the *1st Report of Her Majesty's Commissioners for Inquiring into the Process, Practice and System of Pleading in the Superior Courts of the Common law* (1851) [1389] PP vol. XII, 567 and satirised in *Crogate's Case: A Dialogue in Ye Shades on Special Pleading Reform* which is reproduced in W.S. Holdsworth, *A History of English Law*, 17 vols. (London: Methuen, 1944), vol. IX, pp. 417–31.

When combined with the process of the emasculation of the jury,[125] which still gathered pace, it completely changed the way that contract litigation was structured. The trial process was no longer quite so hidden from view. Judges began to give definitions in law for those matters that were identified by the plea. By the mid-nineteenth century matters which in the past had been addressed under the general issue, came to be expressed as clear, distinct and carefully defined legal doctrines. The role of the jury was confined to applying the facts to the legal definition provided by the judge. As part of this process judges began to articulate general principles of contractual liability. These would form the basis of the classical model of contract. This most emphatically does not mean that the principles were novel. Some had very deep roots but had simply not been (fully) articulated as legal rules.

Legal literature and the law of contract

From the late nineteenth century a good deal of the contract literature was written specifically with the law student in mind. William Anson, in the preface to the first edition of his treatise *Principles of the English Law of Contract*, stated that 'This book is an attempt to draw such an outline of the principles of the law of Contract as may be useful to students, and, perhaps, convenient to those who are engaged in the teaching of law.'[126]

At the time Anson was writing in 1879, the Common law had only been taught as a separate subject for less than a decade at Oxford, his own university.[127] The law of contract had only just begun to be

[125] This was not just a matter of the frequency with which civil juries were utilised, which did decline significantly from the 1880s, but a question of where the balance of power between juries and judges lay. On the issue of usage, see Michael Lobban, 'The Strange Life of the English Civil Jury, 1837–1914', in John Cairns and Grant McLeod (eds.), *The Dearest Birth Right of the People of England* (Oxford: Hart, 2002), pp. 173–209; Conor Hanly, 'The Decline of Civil Jury Trial in Nineteenth-Century England' (2005) 26 *Journal of Legal History* 253.

[126] William Anson, *Principles of the English Law of Contract* (Oxford: Clarendon Press, 1879), p. v. Anson is sometimes identified as the first author of a contract book written for students, for example A.V. Dicey, 'Law-Teaching, Oral and Written', in Herbert Henson (ed.), *A Memoir of the Right Honourable Sir William Anson* (Oxford: Oxford University Press, 1920), p. 92. This statement ignores the claims of John Smith, *The Law of Contracts* (London: William Benning, 1847).

[127] A joint degree with Modern History had begun in 1850. For the early history, see F.H. Lawson, *The Oxford Law School 1850–1965* (Oxford: Oxford University Press, 1968), pp. 34–60; Barry Nicholas, 'Jurisprudence', in M.G. Brock and M.C. Curthoys

examined.[128] By the mid-nineteenth century the Common law was also being taught at Cambridge and in London.[129] It could not really be said that legal education was in very good health at this time.[130] For many decades yet, the impact of these degrees and those who read for them on the legal profession was not as great as it later became.[131] Anson was not the only academic lawyer producing important treatises, but writers like him were still the exception.[132] The impetus for most legal writing still came from the legal profession rather than universities.[133] The publication of a legal treatise was one of the ways in which a young barrister might establish a career.[134] Much of the writing about contract reflected these trends, although some significant writers defy easy classification.[135]

Writing in the mid-eighteenth century, one observer made the point that 'there is scarce a thing of greater importance to a student than a proper choice of book'.[136] There was certainly a sizable body of legal literature in existence by 1700. *Littleton's Tenures*,[137] along with Coke's

(eds.), *The History of the University of Oxford*, 8 vols. (Oxford: Oxford University Press, 2000), vol. VII, pp. 385–96.

128 Nicholas, *ibid.*, p. 394.

129 For a very useful discussion of legal education in the nineteenth century, see Michael Lobban, 'The Education of Lawyers', in Cornish *et al.*, *Oxford History XI*, pp. 1175–1201. On London, see J.H. Baker, 'University College and Legal Education 1826–1976' (1977) 30 *Current Legal Problems* 1, 1–7.

130 A Select Committee Report did not paint a very encouraging picture: *Report of the Select Committee on Legal Education* (1846) [686] PP vol. X, 1.

131 Raymond Cocks, *Foundations of the Modern Bar* (London: Sweet & Maxwell, 1983), p. 186.

132 Other obvious exceptions include Frederic Maitland, Sir Henry Maine, Sir William Markby, Albert Venn Dicey and Sir Thomas Erskine Holland.

133 In America the exact opposite was the case. Legal writers were mainly products of the universities, see Michael Hoeflich, *Legal Publishing in Antebellum America* (New York: Cambridge University Press, 2010), p. 17.

134 Patrick Polden, 'Barristers', in Cornish *et al.*, *Oxford History XI*, pp. 1017, 1035–6.

135 Those who defy classification include the Anglo-Indian writers Sir William Jones and Henry Colebrooke. On the former, see Michael Franklin, *Orientalist Jones* (Oxford: Oxford University Press, 2011); Alexander Murray (ed.), *Sir William Jones 1746–94: A Commemoration* (Oxford: Oxford University Press, 1998). On the latter, see Rosane Rocher and Ludo Rocher, *The Making of Western Indology* (Abingdon: Routledge, 2012).

136 Joseph Simpson, *Reflections on the Natural and Acquired Endowments Requisite for the Study of Law* (London, 1764).

137 Roger North, *A Discourse on the Study of the Laws* (London: C. Baldwyn, 1824), pp. 9–10. See also, Anon, *A Treatise on the Study of the Law* (London, 1797), p. 55, a letter supposedly written by Lord Ashburton. Thomas Littleton's *New Tenures* of 1481 was the first English

works,[138] were likely to have been the works most familiar to law students.[139] Although contract law can be found in the very earliest law books,[140] and appears with some regularity thereafter,[141] anything approaching a contractual equivalent to *Littleton* took a long time to emerge.

A steady flow of writers attempted to systematise the Common law.[142] Some progress was made in fitting the law of contract within an alternative structure to that provided by the forms of action. Perhaps the most striking thing about these works was not the presence of contract law, but its relative absence. Thomas Wood in his *An Institute of the Laws of England in their Natural Order*[143] followed the Roman division[144] between persons, things and actions, to which he added a Common law gloss.[145] Contracts were treated as a species of personal property,[146] although his actual discussion is largely confined to the

printed law book and one which in the words of Baker, *Introduction*, p. 188, possessed of the authority 'enjoyed by no other legal author before or since'.

138 On Coke's writings, see William Holdsworth, *Some Makers of English Law*, pbk edn (Cambridge: Cambridge University Press, 1966), pp. 120–7.

139 Sir Thomas Reeve singled out both authors, see 'Lord Chief Justice Reeve's Instructions to his Nephew Concerning the Study of the Law', in Francis Hargrave, *Collectanea Juridica*, 2 vols. (London: E. Brooke, 1840), vol. I, p. 79. Dudley Ryder, in William Matthews (ed.), *The Diary of Dudley Ryder 1715–1716* (London: Methuen, 1939), p. 49 and William Blackstone, Prest, *Letters*, p. 3 evidently read Coke and Littleton as students. The extent to which these men were representative of law students is more doubtful. There may be more truth in the quip in *The Spectator* in 1711 that 'Aristotle and Longinus are better understood . . . than Littleton and Cooke [*sic*]', reproduced in Erin Mackie, *The Commerce of Everyday Life* (London: Palgrave, 1998), p. 84.

140 *Glanvill* dates from the late 1180s. The other major medieval law book is *Bracton* which has been dated to the 1220s and 1230s. The standard modern edition is: S. Thorne (ed.), *Bracton On the Laws and Customs of England*, 4 vols. (Cambridge, Mass.: Harvard University Press, 1968).

141 Even in a quite abstract manner. For example, St German's, *Doctor and Student* which appeared in the early sixteenth century contained a discussion on the nature of enforceability of promises, see T.F.T. Plucknett and J.L. Barton (eds.), *St German's Doctor and Student* (London: Selden Society, 1974), pp. 228–33.

142 Matthew Hale, *The Analysis of the Law* (London, 1713); Henry Finch, *English Law, or, A Discourse Thereof* (London, 1627). On Hale, see Berman and Reid, 'English Legal Science', pp. 444–51. On Finch, see Wilfrid Prest, 'Dialectical Origins of Finch's Law' (1977) 36 *Cambridge Law Journal* 326; Robert Robinson, 'A Study in Eighteenth Century Legal Scholarship' (1991) 35 *American Journal of Legal History* 432, 454.

143 2 vols. (London, 1720).

144 Wood was, after all, a Civilian whose other major work was *A New Institute of Imperial or Civil Law* (London, 1704).

145 Wood used a four-fold division: of Persons, Of Estates, Of Crimes and Misdemeanours, Of the Courts of Justice. On Wood generally, see Daniel Coquillette, *The Civilian Writers of Doctors' Commons* (Berlin: Duncker & Humblot, 1988), pp. 198–203.

146 Wood, *Institute*, vol. II, ch. 5 'Of Estates in Goods and Chattels Personal'.

contract of sale.[147] Given his *Institute* was intend as an introductory text written for the 'the youth in our universities',[148] who Wood believed should receive instruction in the Common law, the fact that he chose to concentrate on real property is understandable.

Sir William Blackstone was the most well-known member of the systematisers.[149] Blackstone devoted a good deal of thought to the organisation of English Law beginning with his brief *Analysis of The Laws of England*, published in 1756,[150] through to his famous *Commentaries on the Laws of England* a few years later. By utilising Hale's distinction between 'rights' and 'wrongs',[151] Blackstone presented contracts as a means of creating a personal property right. These property rights were described in Book Two, 'Rights of Things'.[152] The failure to perform the contract was classified as a wrong and described in Book Three, 'Private Wrongs'.[153] Despite abandoning the forms of action in his classificatory scheme, Blackstone was still unable to shake them off entirely. Because his description of a contract as an 'agreement upon sufficient consideration'[154] appeared alongside the various forms of action, namely, debt, covenant and assumpsit, it was one that the most conservative Common lawyer could feel at ease with. Not that the law of contract was a major component of the *Commentaries*, an omission which his contemporary Sir William Jones did not believe detracted much from the 'merit of his [Blackstone's] incomparable work'.[155] Jones was probably right not to read too much into Blackstone's relatively thin treatment of contract generally and bailment in particular. It

[147] There is a brief discussion of the contract of sale in Wood, *Institute*, vol. II, ch. 6.

[148] Wood, *Institute*, vol. I, p. viii.

[149] Simpson, 'Legal Treatise', 652, 'The great legal publishing event of the century was of course the appearance of Blackstone's Commentaries.'

[150] (Oxford, 1756), pp. v–vii. The first edition of 1756 had a print run of 1,000 copies, see Wilfrid Prest, *William Blackstone Law and Letters in the Eighteenth Century* (Oxford: Oxford University Press, 2008), p. 142. The seventh and final edition was published in 1771.

[151] John Austin rather unkindly called Blackstone's scheme a 'slavish and blundering copy': Robert Campbell (ed.), John Austin, *Lectures on Jurisprudence or the Philosophy of Positive Law*, 2 vols. (London: John Murray, 1869), vol. I, p. 71.

[152] William Blackstone, *Commentaries on the Laws of England*, 4 vols. (Oxford, 1766), vol. II, pp. 396–8 (chose in action); vol. II, pp. 442–70 (acquisition of property by contract); vol. II, pp. 471–88 (bankruptcy).

[153] Blackstone, *Commentaries*, vol. III, pp. 153–66 (injuries to personal property).

[154] Blackstone, *Commentaries*, vol. II, p. 442.

[155] David Ibbetson (ed.), William Jones, *An Essay on the Law of Bailments* (Bangor: Welsh Legal History Society, 2004), pp. 3–4.

is not necessarily an indication of the insignificance of contracts in the minds of lawyers in the 1750s.[156] Blackstone had no need to be comprehensive. His lectures, on which the *Commentaries* were based, no doubt reflected the interests of his audience of 'gentleman of independent estates and fortunes' who paid a fee to attend.[157]

Blackstone's *Commentaries* were a best-seller during his own life time[158] and twenty-three English and Irish editions had appeared by the mid-nineteen century. The *Commentaries* had an appeal beyond the legal profession.[159] As well as rendering the law accessible to the general reader, Blackstone's writing was also part of the trend towards a more ordered and scientific method. Jones wrote that the 'Commentaries are the most correct and beautiful outline, that ever was exhibited of any human science'.[160] Nevertheless, his attempt to reshape the structure of English law ended in failure for a very simple reason: the Common law continued to be ordered around remedies rather than rights. It was almost inevitable that the forms of action would keep intruding, placing a strain on the whole scheme.[161] The scale of Blackstone's achievement and the obstacles in the way of an analytical scheme are all too obvious from the fate of his two successors as Vinerian Professors.[162] One, Robert Chambers,[163] was content to plagiarise his predecessor, whilst the other,

156 For a contrary view, see David Lieberman, 'Contract before Freedom of Contract', in Harry Scheiber (ed.), *The State and Freedom of Contract* (Stanford, Calif.: Stanford University Press, 1998), p. 90.

157 Blackstone, *Commentaries*, vol. I, p. 7. For the details of Blackstone's lectures, see Prest, *Law and Letters*, pp. 112–18.

158 Tariq Baloch, 'Law Booksellers and Printers as Agents of Unchange' (2007) 66 *Cambridge Law Journal* 389, 405, shows that nearly 13,000 copies were sold between 1773 and 1787.

159 Edward Gibbon described Blackstone's 'excellent Commentaries' and wrote that the law was 'the first science of an Englishman of rank and fortune', Edward Gibbon, *Memoirs of My Life* (London: Penguin, 1990), p. 90. Blackstone's work was certainly read by judges, see Prest, *Letters*, pp. 112–13, which shows that Lord Mansfield and Wilmot J. drew Blackstone's attention to errors in the *Commentaries*.

160 Jones, *Bailment*, pp. 3–4. 161 Blackstone, *Commentaries*, vol. II, pp. 153–66.

162 Harold Hanbury, *The Vinerian Chair and Legal Education* (Oxford: Blackwell, 1958), pp. 52–78.

163 Chambers's lectures remained unpublished until more than 200 years after his death: Thomas Curley (ed.), Robert Chambers, *A Course of Lectures on English Law Delivered at the University of Oxford 1767–73*, 2 vols. (Oxford: Oxford University Press, 1986), vol. II, pp. 209–17, 221–5. On the structure of Chambers's lectures, see John Cairns, 'Eighteenth Century Professorial Classification of English Common Law' (1987–1988) 33 *McGill Law Journal* 226. Chambers's lectures were produced in collaboration with Samuel Johnson, see Thomas Curley, *Sir Robert Chambers Law, Literature, and Empire in the Age of Johnson* (Madison: Wis.: University of Wisconsin Press, 1998), pp. 82–127.

Richard Wooddeson,[164] abandoned the analytical division between 'rights' and 'wrongs' altogether in favour of a simple description of the forms of action.[165]

The influence of Civilian literature on the Common law in the eighteenth century is more difficult to fathom.[166] Classical learning of all types was highly regarded,[167] and whilst it might be expected that a seventeenth century Civilian like Robert Wiseman would heap praise on Roman and Civil law,[168] both had an appeal beyond eighteenth century Civilian circles.[169] Common lawyers like Roger North also saw the value of Civilian learning.[170] At the same time, it is difficult to argue that there was any continuous, systematic borrowing from Roman or Civilian law by Common law judges as opposed to more isolated examples. When faced with the arduous task of imposing some kind of structure on the previously incoherent law of bailment, Holt C.J. turned to Roman law in *Coggs* v. *Barnard*.[171] In *Clement* v. *Scudamore*,[172] a decision concerned with gavelkind,[173] the same judge cast his net even wider. Alongside Coke, there was a discussion of the law of ancient Israel, Greece and Rome. But these occasions provide rare instances where Roman law could be used to good effect when dealing with particularly intractable

[164] Richard Wooddeson, *A Systematical View of the Laws of England as Treated of in a Course of Vinerian Lectures*, 3 vols. (London, 1792–1793).

[165] Wooddeson, *ibid.*, vol. III, pp. 78, 81–3 (annuity); pp. 83–5 (account), pp. 85–95 (covenant), pp. 95–104 (debt), pp. 104–7 (detinue). The coverage of assumpsit in lectures 46 and 47 was more comprehensive.

[166] M.H. Hoeflich, *Roman and Civil Law and the Development of Anglo-American Jurisprudence in the Nineteenth Century* (Athens, Ga: University of Georgia Press, 1997), p. 4: 'there was little activity to be discerned in Roman and civil law'. Roman law had always had some influence on English law. This is traced in David Siepp, 'Roman Legal Categories in the Early Common Law', in Thomas Watkin (ed.), *Legal Record and Historical Reality* (London: Hambledon Press, 1989), pp. 9–36.

[167] R.M. Ogilvie, *Latin and Greek: A History of the Influence of Classics on English Life from 1600 to 1918* (London: Routledge & Kegan Paul, 1964), pp. 34–73.

[168] Robert Wiseman, *The Law of Laws, or The Excellency of the Civil Law Above All Humane Laws Whatsoever* (London, 1654).

[169] On the Civilians of the period, see H.F. Jolowicz, 'Some English Civilians' (1949) 2 *Current Legal Problems* 139; Coquillette, *Civilian Writers*, pp. 209–14.

[170] North, *Study of the Laws*, pp. 8–9.

[171] (1703) 2 Ld Raym 909; 3 Ld Raym 163; 1 Salk 26, 2 Salk 735, 3 Salk 11, 268; 1 Com 133; Holt 13, 131, 528.

[172] (1703) 6 Mod 120; Holt 124.

[173] Gavelkind was a special type of land tenure, largely confined to Kent, see A.W. B. Simpson, *A History of the Land Law*, 2nd edn (Oxford: Oxford University Press, 1986), p. 21.

contemporary problems.[174] This trend continued for the rest of the century, although undoubtedly some judges were more receptive to sources from outside the Common law than others.

Richard Campbell offered the following advice to those beginning their study of law: 'A few well-chosen authors will suffice, and give the student a clearer idea of this too much perplexed study than if he was to read the whole heap of rubbish that has been writ upon the subject.'[175] His 'well-chosen authors' included Pufendorf and Grotius. Campbell explained that 'Knowledge in the Law of Nature and Nations, the Civil Law, will very much contribute to his knowledge of the law in general and . . . of particular laws of other countries.'[176]

Campbell made these remarks at a time when Natural law ideas were popular across Europe.[177] The period also saw the first flowering of contract theory in England. These events are probably not unrelated. Barbeyrac, who edited Pufendorf's *De iure naturae et gentium* and added a commentary, was Pufendorf's great populariser,[178] and both Grotius and Pufendorf were readily accessible in English translations.[179] The Natural lawyers' analysis of contracts would attract English imitators for the next few hundred years. It was based on an apparently simple proposition, that a contract was binding because it arose from an agreement formed by promising.[180] The significance of promising had long been recognised.[181] Aristotle, Thomas Aquinas and the Neo-Scholastics had all, by different routes, come to a similar

[174] The doctrine of restraint of trade was not that far away from bailment, in the sense that the subject lacked a coherent order. In *Mitchell* v. *Reynolds* (1711) 1 P Wms 181, 191, where Parker C.J. also made use of Roman law.

[175] R. Campbell, *The London Tradesman* (London, 1747), p. 75. [176] *Ibid.*

[177] Knud Haakonssen, *Natural Law and Moral Philosophy* (Cambridge: Cambridge University Press, 1996); T.J. Hochstrasser, *Natural Law Theories in the Early Enlightenment* (Cambridge: Cambridge University Press, 2000).

[178] James Gordley, *The Philosophical Origins of Modern Contract Doctrine* (Oxford: Oxford University Press, 1991), pp. 129–30.

[179] H. Grotius, *Of the Rights of War and Peace*, 3 vols. (London, 1715). An even earlier translation appeared in 1654: Samuel Pufendorf, *Of the Law of Nature and Nations* (Oxford, 1703). Reference is to the modern translations: F. Kelsey (trans.) Hugo Grotius, *The Rights of War and Peace (1646 edn)* (Oxford: Oxford University Press, 1925); Charles and William Oldfather (trans.), Samuel Pufendorf, *Of the Law of Nature and Nations (1688 edn)* (Oxford: Oxford University Press, 1934).

[180] Pufendorf, *Nature and Nations*, 3.5–6. Grotius certainly accepted the binding force of promises, but contracts were also described as acts which are 'advantageous to other men', *Rights of War and Peace*, 2.11.4, 2.12.1.

[181] For broader discussion, see Martin Hogg, *Promises and Contract Law* (Cambridge: Cambridge University Press, 2011); Warren Swain, 'Contract as Promise: The Role of

conclusion.[182] What was new was the way that the Natural lawyers were prepared to use these insights in order to construct a detailed framework which addressed the nuts and bolts of the contracting process. It was very much applied theory. From an analytical point of view this was an enormous advance on most English writers who continued to rely on the forms of action or conceptualised contracts as a form of personal property. For Natural lawyers, consent was the key organising principle. Pufendorf explained why:

> Since promises and pacts regularly limit our liberty and lay upon us some burden in that we must now of necessity do something, the performance or omission of which lay before entirely within our own decision, no more pertinent reason can be advanced, whereby a man can be prevented from complaining hereafter of having to carry such a burden that he agreed to it of his own accord, and sought on his own judgement what he had full power to refuse.[183]

Natural law principles may have contributed to substantive legal doctrine in the law of contract and elsewhere quite early on.[184] The influence was felt most keenly once Natural law principles were incorporated into the English literature through the medium of the Will Theory a century later.

The first English writer to provide a detailed treatment of the law of contract was Sir Jeffrey Gilbert, who died in 1724.[185] Gilbert seems to have intended to write an institutional work structured according to persons, things and actions.[186] Contracts were presented as a species of personal property. A contract, he wrote, is 'the act of two or more persons concurring, the one in parting with and the other in receiving some property, right or benefit'.[187] His definition was borrowed from

Promising in the Law of Contract. An Historical Account' (2013) 17 *Edinburgh Law Review* 1.

182 The history of these ideas is traced by James Gordley, *Modern Contract Doctrine*, and in summary in James Gordley, *Foundations of Private Law* (Oxford: Oxford University Press, 2006), pp. 292–3.

183 Pufendorf, *Nature and Nations*, 3.6.1.

184 D. Ibbetson, 'Natural Law and Common Law' (2001) 5 *Edinburgh Law Review* 4.

185 Michael Macnair, 'Sir Jeffrey Gilbert and His Treatises' (1994) 15 *Journal of Legal History* 252.

186 Part of the surviving manuscript is held at Columbia University, Singleton MS: J.H. Baker, *English Legal Manuscripts in the United States of America: A Descriptive List*, 2 vols. (London: Selden Society, 1985), vol. II, pp. 46–7. A copy of the section of the manuscript concerned with contract is available in the British Library as BL MS Hargrave 265, 266.

187 BL MS Hargrave 265 f. 39.

Thomas Hobbes[188] but his approach was more novel in other respects. The fact that he portrayed contract as a coherent whole, with a distinct theoretical rationale comprised of detailed rules, was a significant step forward. He rejected the view of Natural lawyers that a mutual declaration of promises was enough to create a contract. A serious intent as evidenced by consideration was also required.[189] In this respect, Gilbert's analysis could be reconciled with the Common law of the time.

Gilbert's work on contract was never published. The first published treatise was the misleadingly titled *Treatise of Equity*[190] of 1737 which is attributed to Henry Ballow.[191] A further edition, edited by John Fonblanque, who added extensive notes,[192] ran to five further editions, the last of which was published in 1820.[193] Dr Johnson described Ballow as a 'very able man',[194] but like Gilbert, he was to some extent happy to copy from others. Whilst his attempts to blend Pufendorf's version of Natural law and the Common law cannot be regarded as an unqualified success,[195] Ballow would not be the last English writer to struggle to reconcile a theoretical framework with the realities of the Common law, but it did show that Gilbert was not a one off.

From a position where it was largely ignored fifty years previously, the subject of contract began to attract attention from a whole range of people. The philosopher and theologian Joseph Priestley delivered lectures on law at the Dissenting Warrington Academy. An outline survives.[196] Priestley wanted to provide a practical education and the fact that he concentrated on sale, bailment, hire, usury and insurance reflects

188 Ibbetson, *Historical Introduction*, pp. 216–17. For Hobbes's views on contract, see J.C. A. Gaskin (ed.), Thomas Hobbes, *The Elements of Law* (Oxford: Oxford University Press, 1999), book 1, ch. 15.

189 BL MS Hargrave 265, ff. 39–40, 43. 190 (London, 1737).

191 Neil Jones, 'Ballow (Bellewe), Henry', *Oxford Dictionary of National Biography*, discusses the question of authorship.

192 In an edition published in 1793–4. For some biographical information on Fonblanque, see Raymond Cocks, 'The Middle Temple in the 19th Century', in Richard Harvery (ed.), *History of the Middle Temple* (Oxford: Hart, 2011), p. 295.

193 *A Treatise of Equity*, 5th edn (London: Clarke, 1820).

194 Marshall Waingrow, Bruce Redford and Elizabeth Goldring (eds.), James Boswell, *The Life of Samuel Johnson*, 4 vols. (Edinburgh: Edinburgh University Press, 1999), vol. II, p. 294, which is cited by Jones, 'Ballow'. Johnson also confided that 'I learned what I know of law chiefly from Mr Ballow', though he admitted that since that time he had only met Ballow just once.

195 Ibbetson, *Historical Introduction*, pp. 218–19.

196 Joseph Priestley, *An Essay on the Course of Liberal Education* (London, 1765).

that desire.[197] Other leading thinkers like Adam Smith,[198] and the English clergyman William Paley,[199] were more interested in explaining why contracts were binding. In the hands of Smith and Paley it was not the promise or consent that generated a binding obligation, but the expectations both engendered. In an unpublished lecture delivered in the mid-1760s, Smith explained, 'That obligation to performance which arises from contract is founded on the reasonable expectation produced by a promise, which considerably differs from a mere declaration of intention.'[200] In adopting this argument, Smith was quite deliberately seeking to undermine the Natural lawyers.[201] Paley favoured a similar approach, seeing expectations as fundamental to the operation of society as a whole, because 'Men act from their expectations'.[202]

As well as Adam Smith, the Scottish Enlightenment produced several noteworthy legal thinkers who took an interest in the law of contract.[203] John Millar, the Regius Chair of Civil Law at Glasgow University for forty years after 1761, gave lectures on English Law.[204] Millar's mentor, Lord Kames, discussed the nature of contracts in some detail in his *Principles of Equity*.[205] Consent was a central theme: 'That particular

197 *Ibid.*, pp. 122–3.

198 For a summary of Adam Smith's work on law, see David Lieberman, 'Adam Smith on Justice, Rights and Law', in Knud Haakonssen (ed.), *The Cambridge Companion to Adam Smith* (Cambridge: Cambridge University Press, 2006), pp. 214–45.

199 Paley was a theologian but he often attended the law courts in his youth and it is said that a 'legalistic approach' was evident in the 'method and literary style of his biblical criticism', see D.L. Le Mahieu, *The Mind of William Paley* (Lincoln, Nebr.: University of Nebraska Press, 1976), p. 26.

200 Ronald Meek, D.D. Raphael and Peter Stein (eds.), Adam Smith, *Lectures on Jurisprudence* (Oxford: Oxford University Press, 1978), p. 472.

201 Lieberman, 'Adam Smith', p. 222.

202 William Paley, *The Principles of Moral and Political Philosophy* (London, 1785), p. 105. This work was adopted for use at Cambridge University shortly after it was published, see Le Mahieu, *Paley*, p. 23. The book seems to have enjoyed a wide readership. In a letter written by George Wilson and sent to Jeremy Bentham on 24 September 1786, he observed that 'it has gone through two editions, with prodigious applause'.

203 John Cairns, 'Legal Theory', in Alexander Broadie (ed.), *The Cambridge Companion to the Scottish Enlightenment* (Cambridge: Cambridge University Press, 2003), pp. 222–42.

204 On Millar and his lectures, see John Cairns, 'Famous as a School for Law, as Edinburgh . . . for Medicine: Legal Education in Glasgow, 1761–1801', in Andrew Hook and Richard Sher (eds.), *The Glasgow Enlightenment* (East Linton: Tuckwell Press, 1995), p. 133; W. Lehman, 'Some Observations on the Law Lectures of Professor Millar at the University of Glasgow (1761–1801)' (1970) 15 *NS Juridical Review* 56.

205 2nd edn (Edinburgh, 1767). For a discussion, see Michael Lobban, 'The Ambition of Lord Kame's Equity', in Andrew Lewis and Michael Lobban (eds.), *Law and History* (Oxford: Oxford University Press, 2003), pp. 115–18.

act of the will which binds us whether in promising or in contracting, is termed consent.'[206] There was one important difference between Kames and the Natural lawyers. Kames used consent in order to explain why a contract was binding. In Natural law, consent was a condition for, rather than an explanation of, the binding force of contracts. For the Natural lawyers, contracts were binding because they were derived from promises. Promises were binding because promises had moral force. Within a century Kames's version, later given the name Will Theory, would come to be the dominant justification for contractual liability.

Brian Simpson has argued that 'the most striking feature of pre-nineteenth century contract is the dearth of treatise dealing with the subject'.[207] James Gordley is equally unenthusiastic about the state of the literature: 'Before the nineteenth century, with the exception of a few pages in Blackstone, the Common lawyers did not think in terms of contracts, let alone in terms of contract theory. They thought in terms of writs or forms of actions.'[208] In numerical terms, the size of the eighteenth century contract literature was puny by comparison with the nineteenth. But it was increasing in range and sophistication all of the time. It ran from the theoretical to the practical, giving basic advice on aspects of contracting through specialist works on particular types of contract.[209] Contract also featured in the burgeoning mercantile literature.

The growth of contract literature in the eighteenth century was one part of the phenomena of the 'complex penetration of print'[210] and the 'culture of improvement'.[211] Monopolistic practices in the book trade aided by perpetual copyright and the law patent which had so stifled

206 Kames, *Equity*, p. 119.

207 A.W.B. Simpson, 'Innovation in Nineteenth Century Contract Law' (1975) 91 *Law Quarterly Review* 247, 250.

208 Gordley, *Foundations*, p. 288.

209 Michael Lobban, 'The English Legal Treatise and English Law in the Eighteenth Century' (1997) 13 *Iuris Scripta Historica* 69. These works were becoming better organised and indexed which in turn increased their usefulness to practitioners, see Simon Stern, 'The Case and the Exceptions: Creating Instrumental Texts in Law and Literature', in Laura Runge and Pat Rogers (eds.), *Producing the Eighteenth Century Book: Writers and Publishers in England 1650–1800* (Newark, Del.: University of Delaware Press, 2009), pp. 95–116.

210 James Raven, 'The Book Trades', in Isabel Rivers (ed.), *Books and Their Readers in Eighteenth Century England: New Essays* (London: Continuum, 2001), pp. 1–34; James Raven, *Judging New Wealth* (Oxford: Oxford University Press, 1992), pp. 31–41.

211 Peter Borsay, 'The Culture of Improvement', in Paul Langford (ed.), *The Eighteenth Century* (Oxford University Press, 2002), pp. 183–212.

innovative legal writing, came to an end.[212] In the vibrant print culture of the English Enlightenment,[213] legal literature began to enter a more fruitful phase. In the first line of his treatise, Ballow explained that, 'It is plain that Law is a moral science'.[214] Rational or scientific approaches to legal reasoning were nothing new. Lawyers like Hale and Nottingham had advocated something similar a century earlier.[215] But these modes of thought became more ubiquitous. Natural lawyers who also viewed law as a science were one obvious direct source of inspiration.[216] The emergence of a self-confessed 'scientific' approach to legal writing also continued to mirror what was going on outside the law, particularly in the natural sciences. The work of the Swedish botanist Linnaeus was enormously influential in England.[217] Linnaeus and his followers promoted a methodical and taxonomical approach to the classification of plants which was equally well suited to legal analysis. Gilbert in particular may have been influenced by new directions in scientific thought.[218] Even a popular practitioner's work like Giles Jacob's *New Law Dictionary* can be seen as 'part of new Enlightenment approaches to the mastery, communication, and progress of knowledge'.[219]

Sir William Jones's *Essay on the Law of Bailments*, published in 1781, provides an early example of the type of more sophisticated and theoretical expositions of contract law which became popular in the following century and beyond. Jones wrote that 'If law be a science, and really deserve so sublime a name, it must be founded on principle, and claim an exalted rank in the empire of reason'.[220] This approach put him firmly

212 Baloch, 'Law Booksellers', pp. 409–14.

213 J.C.D. Clark, *English Society 1660–1832* (Cambridge: Cambridge University Press, 2000), p. 9: 'it was only . . . in the mid-nineteenth century that it was reified as the "Enlightenment"'; cf. Roy Porter, *Enlightenment* (London: Penguin, 2001), p. 5. On the print culture and the Enlightenment, see Porter, *ibid.*, pp. 72–95.

214 Ballow, *Equity*, p. 1.

215 Dennis Klinck, 'Lord Nottingham's "Certain Measures"'(2010) 28 *Law and History Review* 711. For the influence of scientific thought on legal thought more generally, see Barbara Shapiro, 'Law and Science in Seventeenth Century England' (1968–1969) 21 *Stanford Law Review* 727.

216 Jones, *Bailment*, pp. 26–7.

217 Richard Holmes, *The Age of Wonder* (London: Harper Collins, 2008), p. 11.

218 Shapiro, 'Law and Science', p. 738, suggests that Gilbert's mathematical interests may have influenced his legal writing.

219 Julia Rudolph, 'That "Blunderbuss of Law": Giles Jacob, Abridgment, and Print Culture' (2008) 37 *Studies in Eighteenth Century Culture* 197, 208.

220 Jones, *Bailment*, p. 123.

within the Natural law tradition.[221] Jones was only concerned with the contract of bailment. In the next generation a scientific method was applied to the law of contract as a whole. But the achievements of the early contract writers should not be underestimated. Gilbert and Ballow made significant progress in presenting the law of contract in a systematic way. That Ballow used a Natural lawyer's analysis was an achievement in itself. He also deserves to be credited with introducing a version of the consensual analysis of contracting into the mainstream English legal writing where it has remained, largely unchallenged, until the twentieth century. There were no eighteenth century equivalents to the great nineteenth century contract treatise. But in many ways the earlier writers paved the way for what came later. As with the changes in legal procedure and the jury, nineteenth century developments had very deep roots.

[221] For the place of Jones within the tradition, see David Lieberman, *The Province of Legislation Determined: Legal Theory in Eighteenth Century Britain* (Cambridge: Cambridge University Press, 1989), p. 34, and Jones, *Bailment*, p. 26. For Jones and his debt to Natural law in his own words, see Jones, *Bailment*, p. 116.

3

Lawyers and merchants I

It is impossible to read Daniel Defoe's *A Tour Through the Whole Island of Great Britain*[1] and not be struck by the vitality and variety of commercial activity in Britain in the 1720s.[2] A more recent summary of the state of the economy around 1700 has argued that 'In many respects England's economy in 1689 was surprisingly modern in form. But if industry, services, and trade also grew, such growth was undeniably slow, erratic, and unstable.'[3]

There was more than national pride behind Defoe's claim that England was 'not only a trading country, but the greatest trading country in the World'.[4] It was a view shared by foreign observers such as Voltaire[5] and La Rochefoucauld.[6] The growth in trade was fed by an expanding manufacturing base.[7] The rise of a commercial economy was

1 Pat Rogers (ed.), Daniel Defoe, *A Tour Through the Whole Island of Great Britain* (London: Penguin, 1986).

2 In recent times economic historians have argued that the Industrial Revolution, rather than a sudden leap forward, was part of a continual process: Jeffrey Williamson, 'Why Was British Economic Growth So Slow During the Industrial Revolution' (1984) 44 *Journal of Economic History* 687; N.F.R. Crafts, *British Economic Growth During the Industrial Revolution* (Oxford: Oxford University Press, 1985); Maxine Berg and Pat Hudson, 'Rehabilitating the Industrial Revolution' (1992) 45 *Economic History Review (NS)* 24. For a summary of the literature, see David Cannadine, 'The Present and the Past in the English Industrial Revolution 1880–1980' (1984) 103 *Past and Present* 131.

3 Julian Hoppit, *A Land of Liberty? England 1689–1727* (Oxford: Oxford University Press, 2000), p. 313.

4 Daniel Defoe, *The Complete English Tradesman*, 2 vols. (London, 1727), vol. I, p. 204. Total exports rose from £4.1 million in the 1660s to £6.4 million in 1700, see Peter Mathias, *The First Industrial Nation*, 2nd edn (London: Methuen, 1995), p. 84. The variety of trade also increased from a position as late as the 1640s when over 80 per cent of exports from London consisted of woollen cloth: Ralph Davis, 'English Foreign Trade, 1660–1700' (1954) 7 *Economic History Review (NS)* 150.

5 Leonard Tancock (trans.), Voltaire, *Letters on England* (London: Penguin, 2005), p. 51.

6 S.C. Roberts (trans.), F. De La Rochefoucauld, *A Frenchman in England 1700–1850* (Cambridge: Cambridge University Press, 1933), p. 198.

7 Keith Wrightson, *Earthly Necessities* (London: Penguin, 2002), pp. 240–5.

accompanied by a growing body of mercantile literature, some of which touched on legal topics.[8] By the early eighteenth century the 'cult of trade' had become a central tenet of national identity[9] and found expression in William Blackstone's use of the term a 'polite and commercial people' to describe his fellow countrymen.[10]

It has been claimed that for most of the seventeenth century, 'the law fell far short of business needs'.[11] Reform was never going to be easy. The pace and magnitude of economic developments generated very profound tensions within the established social order. Some of these were articulated in the literature of the period.[12] The same frictions were also evident in the legal system. The Common law could sometimes appear conservative in the face of these pressures. These issues were debated in the mercantile literature and reflected in the development of contract doctrine and the way in which the legal system attempted to come to terms with economic change.

Even before the South Sea Bubble disaster,[13] the more perceptive mercantile writers recognised that economic growth was fragile.[14] The

[8] Joyce Appleby, *Economic Thought and Ideology in Seventeenth-Century England* (Princeton: Princeton University Press, 1980).

[9] Linda Colley, *Britons Forging the Nation 1707–1837* (London: Pimlico, 1994), p. 60.

[10] William Blackstone, *Commentaries on the Laws of England*, 4 vols. (Oxford, 1768), vol. III, p. 326. Behind the terminology, Blackstone was less concerned with matters like negotiable instruments than he was with the influence of commerce on real property, see David Lieberman, 'Property, Commerce, and the Common Law', in John Brewer and Susan Staves (eds.), *Early Modern Conceptions of Property* (London: Routledge, 1996), p. 149.

[11] Richard Grassby, *The Business Community of Seventeenth-Century England* (Cambridge: Cambridge University Press, 2002), p. 215. Merchants could hardly be the only powerful group who felt dissatisfied with the state of the law in so far as it affected them. The large landowners expressed similar sentiments, Paul Langford, *Public Life and the Propertied Englishman 1689–1798* (Oxford: Oxford University Press, 1994), pp. 35–51. For a discussion relating some of the case law to commercial interests, see Clinton Francis, 'The Structure of Judicial Administration and the Development of Contract Law in Seventeenth-Century England' (1983) 83 *Columbia Law Review* 35, 120–7.

[12] John McVeagh, *Tradefull Merchants* (London: Routledge, 1981); James Raven, *Judging New Wealth* (Oxford: Oxford University Press, 2001); Liz Bellamy, *Commerce, Morality and the Eighteenth-Century Novel* (Cambridge: Cambridge University Press, 1998). These scholars show how popular attitudes towards commerce, as reflected in contemporary literature, became more hostile as the eighteenth century progressed.

[13] Malcolm Balen, *A Very English Deceit: The South Sea Bubble and the World's First Great Financial Scandal* (London: Fourth Estate, 2002).

[14] For a host of examples, see J.R. McCulloch, *Early English Tracts on Commerce* (Cambridge: Economic History Society, 1952). Other examples include: Gerard Malynes, *The center of the circle of commerce* (London, 1623); Charles King, *The British Merchant; or, Commerce Preserv'd*, 3 vols. (London, 1721).

spirit of competition with other nations, especially Holland,[15] generated some unfavourable comparisons between the two legal systems. William Petyt contrasted the English with the Dutch and 'their Register of Titles and Contracts, and their cheap and easie decision of Law-Suits'.[16] Sir Josiah Child made much the same points before grumbling that:

> The law that is in use among them for transference of bills for debt from one man to another: this is of extraordinary advantage to them in their commerce; by means whereof they can turn their stocks, twice or thrice in trade, for once that we can in England.[17]

Child touched on something that would come to dominate the law reports in the decades around 1700: the status and operation of bills of exchange and promissory notes. The issue was important on its own terms, but it also raised wider questions about the nature of the relationship between lawyers and merchants and between the Common law and Law Merchant.

Merchants and lawyers

Throughout the Middle Ages the mercantile courts performed a vital function.[18] The way that these bodies operated is described in the thirteenth century treatise *Lex Mercatoria*. Within its pages the Common law was described as the 'mother' of mercantile law.[19] In practice, the difference between mercantile law, which applied to merchants, and Common law, which applied to everyone, was less one of substance than procedure.[20] The mercantile courts were speedier and used different modes of

[15] In his *Brief Observations Concerning Trade and Interest of Money* (London, 1668), p. 3, Sir Josiah Child wrote that 'The prodigious increase of the Netherlands in their domestick and sovereign trade riches, and multitude of shipping is the envy of the present, and may be the wonder of all future generations.'

[16] *Britannia Languens, or A Discourse of Trade* (London, 1680), p. 4.

[17] Child, *Brief Observations*, p. 6. For a discussion of Sir Josiah Child with some context, see William Letwin, *The Origins of Scientific Economics* (London: Routledge, 2003), pp. 3–47.

[18] There were various mercantile courts including the Fair Courts, Borough Courts and Courts Staple. For the details, see W.S. Holdsworth, *A History of English Law*, 17 vols. (London: Methuen, 1922), vol. I, pp. 535–44.

[19] Mary Basile, Jane Bestor, Daniel Coquillette and Charles Donahue (eds.), *Lex Mercatoria and Legal Pluralism: A Late Thirteenth-Century Treatise and Its Afterlife* (Cambridge, Mass.: Ames Foundation, 1998), ch. 9. For the implications of this statement, see pp. 27–34.

[20] J.H. Baker, 'The Law Merchant and the Common Law Before 1700' (1979) 38 *Cambridge Law Journal* 295, 299–302.

proof.[21] This made them attractive to commercial parties. The exact relationship between Common law and mercantile law was thrust into the spot light by the jurisdictional conflicts of the sixteenth and early seventeenth centuries.[22] This resulted in a relative decline in importance of the Admiralty Court, but the precise nature of the relationship between law and commerce was not yet determined. By the second half of the seventeenth century the debate had moved on. The main question by this time was the extent to which mercantile custom could be integrated into the Common law, and on a more general level, the extent to which Common lawyers were sufficiently receptive to mercantile needs.

It is sometimes assumed that Common lawyers had little interest in the needs of commerce before Lord Mansfield's time, or even worse, that 'contract law was essentially antagonistic to the interests of commercial classes'.[23] Some contemporaries certainly thought so and a degree of mistrust existed between merchants and lawyers. Marius counselled that 'the right dealing merchant doth not care how little he hath to do in the Common law'.[24] Seventy years later, in *The Complete English Tradesman*, Daniel Defoe described law-suits as the 'plagues of a tradesman's life'.[25] Following his own unhappy experiences,[26] Defoe was not an impartial observer, but commercial men must often have viewed the law courts as a forum of last resort after other methods like informal pressure[27] and arbitration had failed. The decision to involve lawyers was certainly not to be taken lightly.[28] Thomas Turner, a Sussex shopkeeper, confided to his diary in 1758:

> Oh, what a confusion and tumult there is in my breast about this affair! To think what a terrible thing it is to arrest a person, for by these means

[21] Basile *et al.*, *Lex Mercatoria*, ch. 6. [22] *Ibid.*, pp. 128–46.

[23] Morton Horwitz, *The Transformation of American Law 1780–1860* (Cambridge, Mass.: Harvard University Press, 1977), p. 167.

[24] John Marius, *Advice Concerning Bills of Exchange*, 2nd edn (London, 1655), preface. These remarks did not appear in the first edition of 1651.

[25] *The complete English tradesman* (London, 1727), p. 344.

[26] His problems extended to both the Civil and Criminal law. For details of these episodes, see Paula Backscheider, *Daniel Defoe: His Life* (Baltimore: Johns Hopkins University Press, 1989).

[27] For an example of this sort of informal pressure, see Jacob Price (ed.), *Joshua Johnson's Letterbook, 1771–1774* (London: London Record Society, 1979), [90], [93].

[28] A significant number may still have litigated in the central courts over relatively small claims, Henry Horwitz, 'The Nisi Prius Trial Notes of Lord Chancellor Hardwicke' (2002) 23 *Journal of Legal History* 152, 161. A number of these parties may not have been legally represented.

> he may be entirely torn to pieces; but, on the other hand, this debt hath been standing above four years . . . and I am so oppressed for want of money that I know not which way to turn.[29]

Josiah Child's complaint was more specific. He wrote that, 'After great expences of time and money, it is as well if we can make our own council (being common lawyers) understand one half our case, we being amongst them as in a foreign country, our language strange to them, and theirs strange to us.'[30]

It is difficult to believe that lawyers were as completely insulated from commercial realities as Child claimed. Before the nineteenth century, few judges came from mercantile backgrounds.[31] But not only were lawyers more sensitive to market forces than the other professions,[32] there were numerous ways for them to come into contact with merchants and mercantile practice. The lower branch of the legal profession, the attorneys, performed various business functions, including acting as stewards through to sitting on corporate bodies and lending money.[33] Barristers were also increasingly involved in business, not just as advocates but as advisers and standing counsel to commercial bodies.[34] These activities gave lawyers 'extensive knowledge of the world'.[35] The flourishing coffee house culture of the eighteenth century provided lawyers with

[29] R.W. Blencowe and M.A. Lower (eds.), Thomas Turner, *The Diary of a Georgian Shopkeeper* (Oxford: Oxford University Press, 1979), p. 26.

[30] Josiah Child, *A Discourse about Trade* (London, 1690), pp. 113–14.

[31] Daniel Duman, *The Judicial Bench in England 1727–1875* (London: Royal Historical Society, 1982), p. 51. Between 1727 and 1760 the percentage of judges whose father was a merchant was less than 10 per cent. By 1850 it had risen to nearly 30 per cent.

[32] David Lemmings, *Gentlemen and Barristers* (Oxford: Oxford University Press, 1990), p. 176.

[33] Peter Mathias, 'The Lawyer as Businessman in Eighteenth-Century England', in Peter Mathias and D.C. Coleman (eds.), *Enterprise and History* (Cambridge: Cambridge University Press, 1984), pp. 151–70; C. Brooks, *Pettyfoggers and Vipers of the Commonwealth: The 'Lower Branch' of the Legal Profession in Early Modern England* (Cambridge: Cambridge University Press, 2004), pp. 196–203. As the century progressed these sorts of activities became more numerous: M. Miles, '"Eminent Practitioners": The New Visage of Country Attorneys c.1750–1800', in G.R. Rubin and David Sugarman (eds.), *Law, Economy and Society, 1750–1914: Essays in the History of English Law* (Abingdon: Professional Books, 1984), pp. 470–503.

[34] Lemmings, *Gentlemen and Barristers*, pp. 173–5. William Blackstone acted as Bursar for All Souls College Oxford in the 1740s, Wilfrid Prest, *William Blackstone: Law and Letters in the Eighteenth Century* (Oxford: Oxford University Press, 2008), pp. 75–95.

[35] P.J. Corfield, *Power and the Professions in Britain 1700–1850* (London: Routledge, 1995), p. 73.

opportunities for social interaction with merchants.[36] There was a growing body of literature which a lawyer who wanted to know about mercantile law and practice might consult, including Giles Jacob's *Lex Mercatoria or the Merchant's Companion*,[37] Wyndam Beawes's *Lex Mercatoria Rediviva or the Merchant's Directory*,[38] as well as a host of other smaller works.

The Common law courts had various more formal ways for ascertaining mercantile custom. These were listed in the 1670s by Sir Mathew Hale:

> The court use to ascertain themselves by Speech with Merchants or Civilians, or else it comes in question upon the general Issue; and then if it be a question touching the Customes of Merchants, Merchants are usually Jurors at the request of either party, and Merchants produced on either side are produced to ascertaine the Court and Jury touching the Custome of Merchants; and if it be a question touching the Marine Law, Merchants, Mariners and Civilians are heard.[39]

Mercantile custom might typically be raised in evidence during the course of a trial.[40] It was also possible to canvass mercantile opinion outside the court room.[41] On one occasion Holt C.J. is reported to have said that, 'he had all the eminent merchants in London with him at his chambers . . . and they all held it to be very common, and usual and very good practice'.[42] The mercantile special jury was at the hub of commercial contract litigation and, as James Oldham shows, mercantile jurors were highly influential in the development of legal doctrine.[43] Contact with mercantile jurors was a particularly effective way for a judge to

[36] Brian Cowan, *The Social Life of Coffee: The Emergence of the British Coffee House* (New Haven, Conn: Yale University Press, 2005), pp. 104–5; Peter Earle, *The Making of the English Middle Class* (London: Methuen, 1991), p. 54.

[37] (London, 1718). [38] (London, 1751).

[39] M.J. Prichard and D.E.C. Yale, *Hale and Fleetwood on Admiralty Jurisdiction* (London: Selden Society, 1992), p. 57.

[40] *Dehers* v. *Harriot* (1691) 1 Show 163, 164; *Tassell* v. *Lewis* (1695) 1 Ld Raym 743.

[41] This practice was a very old one, see J.H. Baker, 'Custom and Usage', in *Halsbury's Laws of England* (London: Butterworths, 1998), vol. XII (I), para. 663, fn. 3. Authorities include, *Vanheath* v. *Turner* (1621) Win Ch 24; *Pickering* v. *Barkley* (1649) 2 Rolle Abr 248, pl 10. For an early example, see *Dederit* v. *Abbot of Ramsey* (1315), Charles Gross and Hubert Hall (eds.), *Select Cases Concerning the Law Merchant* (London: Selden Society, 1929), p. 86.

[42] *Mutford* v. *Walcot* (1700) 1 Ld Raym 574, 575.

[43] James Oldham, *The Varied Life of the Self-Informing Jury* (London: Selden Society, 2005), pp. 23–4; James Oldham, 'The Origins of the Special Jury' (1983) 50 *University of Chicago Law Review* 137, 173–5.

build up a body of knowledge on mercantile practice over a long period of time.[44]

Explicit references to the mercantile literature also began to be made on the floor of the court. In *Ward* v. *Evans*,[45] Serjeant Darnall referred to Malynes's *Lex Mercatoria*[46] and John Marius's *Advice Concerning Bills of Exchange*[47] in order to support his argument that a servant's acceptance of a bill of exchange was capable of binding his master. Examples of this sort are fairly unusual in the first half of the eighteenth century.[48] Marius, although described by Strange[49] as 'esteemed by those who are most conversant in these affairs',[50] and Malynes, were merchants rather than lawyers. As the century went on, references to mercantile literature became more and more commonplace and the practice was seen as quite unexceptional. In *Dawkes* v. *De Lorane*, Gould J. was quite prepared to defend the use of Cunningham's rather workmanlike treatise on bills of exchange by counsel with the retort that 'Mr Cunningham's book was a very good book'.[51] Law and business also intermingled more indirectly through arbitration. Commercial parties had resorted to arbitration since the Middle Ages[52] and it remained a popular method of settling commercial disputes.[53] The century following the Arbitration Act of

44 In *Thwaits* v. *Angerstein*, *The Times*, 14 November 1798, Kenyon C.J., 'professed himself totally ignorant of navigation, except in so far as he had learned it from his apprenticeship in his judicial office. He had received a great deal of information from the different classes of merchants by whom he had the honour of being assisted in the administration of justice', cited by Emily Kadens, 'The Puzzle of Judicial Education: The Case of Chief Justice William De Grey' (2009) 79 *Brooklyn Law Review* 143, 159, fn. 82.

45 (1702) 2 Ld Raym 928.

46 (London, 1686), p. 271 (wrongly stated as p. 265 in the law report).

47 3rd edn (London, 1674), p. 47.

48 James Rogers, *The Early History of the Law of Bills and Notes* (Cambridge: Cambridge University Press, 1995), p. 153 citing, *Thorold* v. *Smith* (1706) Holt 462, 463; *Wegersloffe* v. *Keene* (1719) 1 Str 214, 217; *Lumley* v. *Palmer* (1734) Cas t Hard 74, 75; *Colehan* v. *Cooke* (1743) Willes 393; *Simmonds* v. *Parminter* (1747) 1 Wils KB 185.

49 Strange was counsel at the time. He would later become Master of the Rolls.

50 *Wegersloffe* v. *Keene* (1719) 1 Stra 214, 217.

51 (1771) 3 Wils KB 207, 212.

52 Edward Powell, 'Arbitration and the Law in England in the Late Middle Ages' (1983) 32 *5th Series Transactions of the Royal Historical Society* 49; Anthony Musson, 'Arbitration and the Legal Profession in Late Medieval England', in Matthew Dyson and David Ibbetson (eds.), *Law and the Legal Process* (Cambridge: Cambridge University Press, 2013), pp. 56–76.

53 For some explanations for the popularity of arbitration, see Anon, *The Advantages of Settling Disputes by Arbitration* (Carlisle, 1795); Anon, *Arbitrium Redivivum: Or The Law of Arbitration* (London, 1694). For an account of an unhappy experience of arbitration, see Anthony Da Costa, *The case of Mr Da Costa with Mr Monmartel, relating to a bill of exchange* (London, 1736).

1689 witnessed a significant change in the character of arbitration, with the process becoming much more 'legalised' and formal.[54] Barristers began to play a much larger role as arbitrators,[55] and the central courts began enforcing arbitration agreements.[56]

The fact that a particular mercantile practice could be proved to exist did not necessarily mean that the Common law would accommodate it. Inevitably different judges came to slightly different conclusions about where the balance between commercial convenience and Common law ought to lie. Willes C.J. explained in the 1740s, 'Courts of Law have always in mercantile affairs endeavoured to adapt the rules of law to the course and method of trade in order to promote trade and commerce instead of doing it any hurt.'[57] Willes C.J.'s remarks suggest that there was a longstanding willingness to consider the needs of merchants, but he was anxious that judges should be sensitive to mercantile needs rather than advocating a wholesale adoption of mercantile practice.[58] Tellingly, when faced with one particularly tricky question, Holt C.J., having consulted 'two of the most famous merchants in London',[59] still reached the opposite conclusion. Even where the witness was as authoritative as Malynes, there was no guarantee that the mercantile practice would be adopted as part of the Common law. As Holt C.J. made clear, it was not the existence of the practice that he doubted but whether it should be applied. He held that 'I am of opinion, and always was (notwithstanding the noise and cry, that it is the use of Lombard Street, as if the contrary opinion would blow up Lombard Street) that acceptance of such a note is not actual payment'.[60] Holt C.J. was referring to a negotiable instrument and these proved to be the main threat to a harmonious relationship between lawyers and merchants around 1700.

Negotiable instruments

Bills of exchange had been used by merchants since the Middle Ages.[61] In the early years of the eighteenth century, William Forbes began his

[54] Henry Horwitz and James Oldham, 'John Locke, Lord Mansfield, and Arbitration During the Eighteenth Century' (1993) 36 *Historical Journal* 137.

[55] *Ibid.*, p. 154. [56] *Ibid.*, p. 155. [57] *Stone* v. *Rawlinson* (1745) Willes 559, 561.

[58] J.H. Baker, 'The Law Merchant as a Source of English Law', in William Swadling and Gareth Jones (eds.), *The Search for Principle: Essays for Lord Goff of Chieveley* (Oxford: Oxford University Press, 2000), p. 88.

[59] *Buller* v. *Crips* (1703) 6 Mod 29, 30. [60] *Ward* v. *Evans* (1702) 2 Ld Raym 928, 930.

[61] M. Postan, *Medieval Trade and Finance* (Cambridge: Cambridge University Press, 1973), pp. 58–64; Edwin Hunt, *A History of Business 1200–1550* (Cambridge: Cambridge University Press, 1999), pp. 65–6.

book on the subject with a comment on the benefits of bills of exchange along traditional lines:

> Those short circular, letters or orders given by bankers and trading people, to furnish to others certain sums of money (commonly called bills of exchange) are of great use and advantage to trade, because money for carrying it on, is more speedily, conveniently, and safely remitted in bills than in specie.[62]

The way in which bills operated was straightforward enough. One merchant, A (the drawer), who wished to buy the goods of another merchant, B (the payee), in a different location, drew a bill on a third person in that location, C (the drawee). C was liable to pay the sum due for the goods to B.[63] Bills of exchange were written but not sealed, which meant that they were not traditionally recognised as a source of obligation in Common law, but instead were valuable evidence when it came to proving an underlying obligation in, for example, an action of debt on a contract.[64] By the mid-sixteenth century, bills of exchange had come to be enforced in the action of assumpsit on a regular basis.[65] Parol agreements were recognised in assumpsit actions and hence the absence of a deed was no bar. Assumpsit was also sufficiently adaptable to be able to accommodate all the multiple parties present in many bill transactions. Inland bills of exchange, which appeared in the early seventeenth century,[66] operated in the same way as foreign bills as a means of transferring funds from one part of England to another. Both sorts of bill could be indorsed. When the drawee accepted the bill he became liable to the payee. The payee, in turn, was permitted to indorse

[62] William Forbes, *A Methodical Treatise Concerning Bills of Exchange* (Edinburgh, 1718), p. i.

[63] The process is described in detail by J. Milnes Holden, *The History of Negotiable Instruments in English Law* (London: Athlone Press, 1955), pp. 21–9; Rogers, *Bills and Notes*, pp. 32–43.

[64] Baker, 'The Law Merchant', pp. 304–6.

[65] For early examples, see Baker, 'The Law Merchant', pp. 311–12; Rogers, *Bills and Notes*, pp. 57–60. J.H. Baker, *The Oxford History of the Laws of England Volume VI 1483–1558* (Oxford: Oxford University Press, 2003), p. 859, fn.120, cites authorities from the 1540s.

[66] In *Buller* v. *Crips* (1703) 6 Mod 29, Holt C.J. claimed to remember when actions on inland bills first began in a case before Hale C.J. (who was Chief Justice between 1671–1676). He made the same point in *Carter* v. *Palmer* (1713) 12 Mod 380. There is some evidence that inland bills were in use before this date, see Rogers, *Bills and Notes*, p. 101. The earliest reported case is *Edgar* v. *Chut* (1663) 1 Keb 592, 636.

the bill. This is known as the principle of negotiability.[67] The current holder was able to realise the value of the bill in the same way as the original payee. He could indorse the bill to another party and so on through a chain. Bills of exchange could also be traded for cash through a process known as discounting.[68]

By the end of the seventeenth century the pretence that bills of exchange were confined to transactions between merchants was gone.[69] Bills of exchange were increasingly important, not just as a way of trading overseas but as a way of raising credit.[70] This aspect of bills was vital given the absence of modern banking practices, the severe shortage of coinage,[71] and the slow rate of financial return on goods sent to market.[72] The changing character of bills was not welcomed by everyone,[73] but it was a fact of life. One mid-eighteenth century author made the point that, 'There is scarce any person either gentleman, tradesman, or farmer, but what must, at some times, have occasion for bills of exchange.'[74] In these circumstances, it wasn't just lawyers and merchants who needed to be able to draw up bills of exchange. *The Secretary's Guide*, published around the turn of the century, contained templates of bills of exchange which, according to the author, would enable 'a person of an ordinary capacity may make any writing of this nature, that shall be authentick, as if written by the most celebrated clerks'.[75]

67 The importance and extent of negotiability is considered by James Rogers, 'The Myth of Negotiability' (1989–1990) 31 *Boston College Law Review* 265.

68 Rogers, *Bills and Notes*, pp. 121–2. This process was described by Malynes, *Lex Mercatoria*, p. 99, cited by Holden, *Negotiable Instruments*, p. 69.

69 *Bromwich* v. *Loyd* (1697) 2 Lutw 1582, 1585. To begin with a fiction that the drawer was a 'trader for that purpose' was used: *Sarsfield* v. *Witherly* (1689) 1 Show 125, 2 Vent 292, Holt 112, Carth 82, Comb 45, 152.

70 Rogers, *Bills and Notes*, pp. 112–16.

71 Widespread forgery meant that the cash in circulation was not always authentic. For a discussion of the various coining offences of the eighteen century, see John Styles, 'Our Traitorous Money Makers: The Yorkshire Coiners and the Law, 1760–83', in John Brewer and John Styles (eds.), *An Ungovernable People* (London: Hutchinson, 1980), pp. 172–249.

72 Julian Hoppit, 'Financial Crisis in Eighteenth Century England' (1986) 39 *Economic History Review (NS)* 39, 43; T.S. Ashton, 'The Bill of Exchange and Private Banks 1790–1830' (1945) 15 *Economic History Review* 25; B.L. Anderson, 'Money and the Structure of Credit in the Eighteenth Century' (1970) 12 *Business History* 85; T.S. Ashton, *An Economic History of England: The 18th Century* (London: Methuen, 1959), pp. 167–200.

73 Anon, *A true state of publick credit* (London, 1721), p. 6, in the context of the difficulties of raising credit in the aftermath of the South Sea Bubble.

74 George Crooke, *The Merchant, Tradesman and Farmer's Director* (Lincoln, 1778), p. iii.

75 G.F., *The Secretary's Guide* (London, 1705), pp. v, 110.

Bills of exchange were to become a familiar feature of the law reports in the decades either side of 1700 and many of the principles which would be most associated with their operation in the future were worked out during this period. These included rules concerning the acceptance of bills,[76] the drawer's liability to a payee,[77] and the operation of indorsement.[78] But not every aspect of bills was easily or categorically settled.[79] The process by which these issues were resolved, and which saw a body of law grow up around bills of exchange and promissory notes, sheds some light on wider issues. These issues include the relationship between mercantile practice, custom and the Common law, along with the vexed question of the extent to which these devices should be allowed to encroach on the territory of mainstream contract law.

Holdsworth and others have described the process by which bills of exchange developed in the Common law as amounting to a 'reception' of law from the Continent under the guise of mercantile custom.[80] As Baker has pointed out, the assumption that 'the law of merchant at some time had an autonomous existence as a body of legal principles applicable everywhere' is historically unsound,[81] even if the seventeenth century did witness a 'growingly powerful and systematic expression of mercantile customs'.[82] The nature of the relationship between custom of any sort and the Common law was far from straightforward and this would have made any reception of this sort extremely difficult.[83] The mere existence of a custom has never been a guarantee that it would be

[76] *Anon* (1700) 12 Mod 345, Holt KB 296; *Jackson* v. *Piggot* (1698) 1 Ld Raym 364, 1 Salk 127, Carth 459, 12 Mod 211.

[77] *Woodward* v. *Rowe* (1666) 2 Keb 105, 132; *Starke* v. *Cheeseman* (1700) 1 Ld Raym 538.

[78] Rogers, *Bills and Notes*, pp. 170–3. Rogers argues that 'the practice of transferring bills seems to have been accommodated with relatively little difficulty'. He draws attention to the fact that Malynes, *Lex Mercatoria*, does not mention indorsement but nearly thirty years before it was mentioned by Marius, *Bills of Exchange*. Authorities include: *Dashwood* v. *Lee* (1667) 2 Keb 303; *Claxton* v. *Swift* (1686) 2 Show 441, 494, Comb 4, 3 Mod 86, 1 Lutw 878.

[79] For example, the position between drawer and indorsee was more difficult. For this and other examples, see Holden, *Negotiable Instruments*, pp. 56–63.

[80] W.S. Holdsworth, *A History of English Law*, 17 vols. (London: Methuen, 1937), vol. VIII, p. 151. For a broadly similar treatment, see L.S. Sutherland, 'The Law Merchant in the Seventeenth and Eighteenth Centuries' (1934) 17 *4th Series, Transactions of the Royal Historical Society* 149.

[81] Baker, 'The Law Merchant as a Source', p. 83.

[82] Sutherland, 'The Law Merchant', p. 157.

[83] Even Holdsworth, *English Law*, vol. VIII, p. 151, admitted that the process was 'no wholesale or slavish reception' but made no attempt to develop his insight.

adopted by the Common law.[84] Custom was not reflected in a single idea but was used in more than one way, a fact that would be critical in helping to account for the rise of bills of exchange.

Allegations of mercantile custom appeared in assumpsit actions on bills of exchange from the early seventeenth century[85] and quickly became the norm. For the purposes of pleading and proof, custom was either general or special. General custom was covered by judicial notice and did not need to be proved. Holt C.J. explained: 'We take notice of the laws of merchants that are general, not those that are particular usages.'[86] When Holt C.J. referred to 'particular usages' he was alluding to special custom which had to be pleaded and proved.[87] Different consequences flowed from each sort of custom. Special custom was capable of contradicting the Common law. General custom was an integral part of it.

There was relatively little Common law authority on the operation of bills of exchange in the first half of the seventeenth century.[88] In these circumstances, as Baker has explained, custom was 'a particularly useful device in framing extensions of the law'.[89] But what sort of custom? Blackstone treated mercantile law as a species of special custom.[90] Special custom was normally understood as pertaining to a particular geographical location.[91] Mercantile custom had no such limits. In those cases where mercantile custom was treated as *ius gentium*, the contrast could hardly be greater. For example, in *Mogadara* v. *Holt*, it was said that 'it is no more than the law of merchants, and that is *ius gentium*, and we are to take notice of it'.[92] But even where mercantile custom was not treated as general custom which the court was bound to take notice of, it was special custom of a very unusual sort. Pleas on bills of exchange were often what Baker has termed 'bi-local' or pertaining to two different cities.[93] Whilst not quite as

[84] Judges had shown a willingness to assess the value of customs of all types since the Middle Ages, see David Ibbetson, 'Custom in Medieval Law', in Amanda Perreau-Saussine and James Murphy (eds.), *The Nature of Customary Law* (Cambridge: Cambridge University Press, 2007), p. 174.

[85] Baker, 'The Law Merchant', pp. 312–13.

[86] *Lethulier's Case* (1692) 2 Salk 443.

[87] *Bellasis* v. *Hester* (1697) 1 Ld Raym 281.

[88] For some examples, see Baker, 'The Law Merchant', pp. 310–13.

[89] *Ibid.*, p. 317.

[90] William Blackstone, *Commentaries on the Laws of England*, 4 vols. (Oxford, 1765), vol. I, p. 75.

[91] This requirement is discussed in detail by Baker, *Halsbury's*, para. 616.

[92] (1691) 1 Show 317, 318.

[93] It was easy to see how this might slip into something broader. For examples, see Baker, *Halsbury's*, para. 602; *Claxton* v. *Swift* (1686) 1 Lutw 878; *Death* v. *Serwonters* (1686) 1 Lutw 885.

wide in scope as general custom, the allegation of special custom was broad enough to encompass the majority of such transactions.[94] Provided that the pleader stretched the rules rather than broke them, judges were largely untroubled before the 1690s. Perhaps fictions were deployed. In *Buller* v. *Crips*[95] it was noted that it was usual to allege 'a particular custom between London and Bristol'. The existence of special custom was a matter for a jury. Because jurors were often fellow merchants, they may have been more inclined to find in favour of a custom than judges, who would be inclined to take judicial notice.[96]

At a time when the Common law relating to bills of exchange was evolving in line with mercantile needs, this approach was all well and good, but by the end of the century the situation had changed. There was now a settled body of Common law rules. The period of development had passed. Unless custom was carefully handled, it had the potential to destabilise the Common law. In these circumstances, judges were anxious to draw mercantile practice into the Common law, probably not so much from a desire to encourage a reception of a body of mercantile law, but because it represented a threat. This was achieved by treating mercantile custom as general custom. The process put judges back in control.

Powell J. drew a distinction between *lex mercatoria* and special custom: 'The Court would take notice of the *lex mercatoria* . . . but that such special custom as this here ought to be pleaded'.[97] Once mercantile custom and Common law were one and the same, the possibility of conflict was removed at a stroke. In *Hawkins* v. *Cardy*,[98] having alleged the custom of merchants, the declaration stated that a drawer was liable on a bill that was partially indorsed so that only part of the sum due was payable to the indorsee. This ran up against the rule that Common law did not allow apportionment and the plaintiff's case was rejected. Holt C.J. held that 'This is not a particular local custom, but the common custom of merchants, of which the law takes notice; and therefore the Court cannot take the custom to be so'.[99]

The same technique was used in the face of the restrictions on gaming contracts[100] and contracts with infants,[101] although sometimes, as with a

[94] Baker, 'The Law Merchant', pp. 319–20. [95] (1703) 6 Mod 29.
[96] Baker, 'The Law Merchant', p. 320.
[97] *Bellasis* v. *Hester* (1697) 1 Ld Raym 280, 281. Another example includes, *Hodges* v. *Steward* (1695) 3 Salk 68, 69.
[98] (1698) 1 Ld Raym 360; Carth 466, 1 Salk 65, 12 Mod 213. [99] (1698) 1 Ld Raym 360.
[100] *Hussey* v. *Jacob* (1696) 1 Ld Raym 87, 88: 'this custom is properly the common law'.
[101] *Williams* v. *Harrison* (1690) Carth 160.

number of decisions relating to limitations of action, the Common law, rather than customary rules, was applied without comment or justification.[102] This is not to say that the way in which bills of exchange developed did not sometimes appear to be at odds with the Common law of contract. By the end of the seventeenth century judges were accepting actions by indorsees without question. This position appeared to clash with the Common law rule that only those who were parties had a right of action,[103] according to which claims by someone other than the original payee should fail. Conflict was only avoided by treating the indorsee as an assignee regardless of whether he brought the claim in his own name or in that of the initial payee.[104] *Hodges* v. *Steward* distinguished this situation from a bill of exchange made out to a named party or bearer:

> For a bill payable to J.S. or bearer is not assignable by the contract so as to enable the indorsee to bring an action, if the drawer refuse to pay because there is no such authority given to the party by the first contract, and the effect is only to discharge the drawee, if he pays it to the bearer, though he comes to it by trover, theft or otherwise. But when the bill is payable to J.S. or order, there an express power is given to the party to assign, and the indorsee may maintain an action.[105]

No indorsement by the nominal payee was required. It followed from this that the bearer's claim was independent of the payee and he could not be considered an assignee. The rule for assignees mirrored the position in mercantile law where bearers had a right of action. Although Mayles warned that the rule was a 'derogation of the nobleness of the said Bill of Exchange',[106] and Marius called them 'very dangerous',[107] arguing that there was a risk that the bill 'may come to a wrong man's hands'.[108]

The Common law courts were unwilling to give a bearer an action in his own name,[109] though it was sometimes hinted that it may have been

[102] *Renew* v. *Aston* (1687) Carth 3; *Chievely* v. *Bond* (1691) Carth 226, 4 Mod 105, 1 Show 341, Holt 427. For these and other examples, see Rogers, *Bills and Notes*, p. 167.

[103] David Ibbetson and Warren Swain, 'Third Party Beneficiaries in English Law: From Dutton v. Poole to Tweddle v. Atkinson', in Eltjo Schrage (ed.), *Ius Quaesitum Tertio* (Berlin: Duncker & Humblot, 2008), pp. 200–1.

[104] The solution arguably undermined the Common law rule against assigning a chose in action: Matthew Dylag, 'The Negotiability of Promissory Notes and Bills of Exchange in the Time of Chief Justice Holt' (2010) 31 *Journal of Legal History* 149, 152–3, 158–60.

[105] (1692) 1 Salk 125.

[106] Malynes, *Lex Mercatoria*, p. 394.

[107] Marius, *Bills of Exchange*, p. 14.

[108] *Ibid.*, p. 14.

[109] *Horton* v. *Coggs* (1691) 3 Lev 299; *Carter* v. *Palmer* (1700) 12 Mod 380; *Jordan* v. *Barloe* (1700) 3 Salk 67.

possible for him to bring an action in the name of the original payee.[110] A bearer might be a finder, in which case Marius's concerns were equally valid at Common law,[111] or seeking to recover when the original payee had already received payment on the bill.[112] Rogers has suggested that the courts were anxious about the operation of goldsmiths' notes.[113] In time such actions were permitted,[114] but statute had intervened by this point, fixing bills of exchange within a special regime and neutralising any threat that they might pose to general Common law principles.[115]

Once bills and notes were part of the Common law, a way of reconciling the requirement of consideration with the operation of bills of exchange needed to be found. As a result consideration was presumed.[116] The defendant could still show that good consideration was absent, including significantly where the bill had been lost or stolen.[117] Striking a balance between mercantile convenience and the Common law saw consideration downgraded in importance within this particular context. There was resistance, however, to going further and treating bills of exchange as a new sort of formal contract deriving binding force from the fact that it was in writing. Holt C.J. bluntly stated that, 'a bill of exchange is in law no specialty'.[118]

Promissory notes consisted of a promise to pay a particular sum at a particular time. They were, like bills of exchange, in writing, but not under seal. A promissory note could be used in evidence in an action of assumpsit. The ability of a promissory note to generate a cause of action in its own right at Common law was more problematic. In *Woolvil* v. *Young*[119] the court refused to accept a declaration on bill upon the 'custom of England'. It was necessary to either bring the case within the general custom of merchants or show that it was a bill of exchange. Otherwise, consideration was required. Promissory notes were an even greater threat to mainstream contract law than bills of exchange because

110 *Hodges* v. *Steward* (1692) 1 Salk 125, referring to a manuscript report of *Nicholson* v. *Sedgwick* (1697) discussed in Rogers, *Bills and Notes*, p. 174, fn. 14.

111 *Nicholson* v. *Sedgwick* (1697) 1 Ld Raym 180, 3 Salk 67.

112 *Horton* v. *Coggs* (1691) 3 Lev 299. 113 Rogers, *Bills and Notes*, p. 175, fn. 17.

114 *Grant* v. *Vaughan* (1764) 3 Burr 1516. 115 (1704) 3 & 4 Anne c. 9.

116 Holden, *Negotiable Instruments*, p. 102; *Josceline* v. *Lassere* (1715) Fort 281, 10 Mod 294, 316. The decision was also preserved in manuscript, see W. Hamilton Bryson, *Sir John Randolph's King's Bench Reports 1715 to 1716* (Buffalo: Hein, 1996), [14].

117 *Hinton's Case* (1682) 2 Show KB 235.

118 *Anon* (1694) Holt KB 115. For a discussion, see Holden, *Negotiable Instruments*, p. 62.

119 (1697) 5 Mod 367.

there was so little to distinguish them in appearance from a simple written contract. This was used as an argument for restricting the custom of merchants. In *Pearson* v. *Garrett*[120] counsel argued that, 'if such should be allowed to be within the custom of merchants, then every thing which is given without consideration may be as well within the custom, which would quite change the law'.[121] As a non-commercial transaction it was outside the custom of merchants and the claim failed. Even setting aside non-commercial transactions there was still a serious danger that promissory notes would undermine the requirement of consideration.[122] Entering into a binding contract would be as easy as reducing an agreement into writing.

In *Carter* v. *Palmer*[123] Holt C.J. warned that, 'we must take care that by such a drift the law of England be not changed by making all notes, bills of exchange'. Not long afterwards Sir Bartholomew Shower, as counsel in *Clerke* v. *Martin*,[124] met this statement head on by arguing that a promissory note payable to the plaintiff or his order was a bill of exchange within the custom of merchants.[125] Gould J. was receptive to this argument but Holt C.J. responded by citing *Horton* v. *Coggs*,[126] which had held that an action on a bearer bill was not within the custom of merchants.[127] He was less concerned to distinguish between different sorts of notes than to limit promissory notes altogether:

> The maintaining of these actions upon such notes, were innovations on the rules of the common law; and that it amounted to setting up a new sort of specialty, unknown to the common law, and invented in Lombard Street, which attempted in these matters of bills of exchange to give laws to Westminster Hall.[128]

In the absence of a deed, the term 'specialty' was being used loosely. But Holt C.J. was making the point that he was not prepared to allow written contracts to be enforced without consideration. The following year in *Cutting* v. *Williams*,[129] he claimed that this restrictive approach had unanimous support amongst his fellow judges. An allegation of the custom of merchants was not enough to take notes outside of the Common law. Alleging a special custom of London was no answer either,

[120] (1693) 4 Mod 242, Skin 398, Comb 227. [121] (1693) 4 Mod 242, 244.
[122] Dylag has made much the same point: 'Negotiability of Promissory Notes', pp. 164–5.
[123] (1700) 12 Mod 380. [124] (1702) 2 Ld Raym 757, 1 Salk 129, 364.
[125] (1702) 2 Ld Raym 757–8. [126] (1691) 3 Lev 296, 299.
[127] (1702) 2 Ld Raym 757, 758. [128] (1702) 2 Ld Raym 757, 758. [129] (1703) 7 Mod 154.

as *Potter* v. *Pearson*[130] made clear, the doctrine of consideration would not be sacrificed on the altar of commercial convenience: 'it is a void custom, since it binds a man to pay money without any consideration'. For the rule is, *ex nudo pacto non oritur actio.*[131] In *Buller* v. *Crips,*[132] Holt C.J. repeated his familiar objections:

> And the notes in question are only an invention of the goldsmiths in Lombard Street, who had in mind to make a law to bind all those who that did deal with them: and sure to allow such a note to carry any lien with it were to turn a piece of paper, which is in law but evidence of a parol contract, into a specialty: and besides, it would impower one to assign that to another which he could not have himself.[133]

As Lord Kenyon would later explain, Holt C.J. took the view that 'no action could be maintained on promissory notes as instruments, but they were only to be considered as evidence of the debt'.[134] This would place a significant limit on promissory notes, and another successor, Cockburn C.J., would accuse him of adopting a 'narrow-minded view of the matter'.[135] It is unlikely that Holt C.J. came to this conclusion lightly. Having consulted 'two of the most famous merchants in London' who had advised of the 'ill consequences' of his course of action, he could hardly have been unaware of the potential impact of his decision on the mercantile community. His stand against the march of promissory notes had been thought through over a period of time. It was also perfectly understandable. As other eighteenth century judges would find out, the doctrine of consideration was too central to be cast aside in quite such a brutal and obvious manner. Holt C.J.'s caution can be justified by the risk that contracts could be entered into without the reflection engendered by a deed or the reciprocity provided by consideration.[136] He was certainly not prejudiced against merchants.[137] Formal appearances were all important. In this spirit Holt C.J. was quite willing to suggest an alternative. In *Buller* v. *Crips*, he would suggest that bills of exchange between

130 (1703) 2 Ld Raym 759, 1 Salk 129, Holt 33. 131 (1703) 2 Ld Raym 759.

132 (1703) 6 Mod 29. Discussed by Rogers, *Bills and Notes*, pp. 177–86; Holden, *Negotiable Instruments*, p. 79.

133 (1703) 6 Mod 29. 134 *Brown* v. *Harraden* (1791) 4 TR 148, 151.

135 *Goodwin* v. *Robarts* (1875) LR 10 Ex 337, 349.

136 Baker, 'The Law Merchant as a Source', p. 93, Rogers, *Bills and Notes*, p. 184 described Holt C.J.'s attitude as 'entirely understandable'.

137 For a clear expression of pro-mercantile sentiments in the context of a bill of exchange, see *Anon* (1698) Holt 296, 297: 'that would destroy commerce and publick transactions of this nature'.

two rather than three persons could fill the gap and 'if there be such a necessity of dealing that way, why do not dealers use that way which is legal?'[138]

Passed in response to *Buller* v. *Crips* and *Clerke* v. *Martin*, the Promissory Notes Act became law in 1704[139] and was made perpetual four years later.[140] The purpose and effect of the Act is set out in the preamble: 'the intent to encourage trade and commerce which will be much advanced if such notes have the same effect as inland bills of exchange and shall be negotiated in like manner'.[141] From henceforth promissory notes were unequivocally actionable in assumpsit, but the exact role of consideration was still left open. When this question was addressed in *Brown* v. *Marsh*,[142] opinion was divided. Two of the judges were prepared to treat a promissory note as a form of specialty, in which case the absence of consideration was not relevant evidence. The two other judges, with whom Lord Chancellor King agreed, insisted that there was a 'great difference between a note and a bond':

> For in the case of a bond, where there were solemnities of contracting, *viz* the sealing and delivery, if there was no consideration, yet if there was no fraud in obtaining the bond, the money was a gift in law to the obligee; but the note was no more than a simple contract, and notwithstanding the statute says, that the money shall be due and payable by virtue of the note, that only makes the note itself evidence of the consideration, which it was not before the statute.[143]

Because the note was not conclusive evidence of consideration, the defendant was able to show that consideration was absent.[144] This point of view mirrored the position of bills of exchange. It was still a relatively short step to the position of the minority in *Brown* v. *Marsh*. In *Barnesly* v. *Baldwyn*,[145] for example, Lee C.J. would distinguish a note under the statute from one where consideration needed to be proved.[146] At the very least consideration was downgraded in importance. Holt C.J.'s concerns proved prophetic in other ways too.

Alongside these attempts to rationalise consideration, the courts adopted a deliberate policy of interpreting the legislation as broadly as

[138] (1703) 6 Mod 29, 30. [139] (1704) 3 & 4 Anne c. 9. [140] (1708) 7 Anne c. 25 s. 3.

[141] For further discussion of the early cases under the legislation, see Dylag, 'Negotiability of Promissory Notes', pp. 165–8.

[142] (1721) Gilb Rep 154. [143] *Ibid.*

[144] *Jefferies* v. *Austin* (1725) 1 Str 674 adopted the same rule but no reasons were given. A fuller report is available in manuscript, HLS MS 4062.

[145] (1741) 7 Mod 417. [146] *Ibid.*, p. 418.

possible. Raymond C.J. explained that 'The Act . . . is a remedial law, and to be extended in construction as far as in reason we can . . . It is sufficient if the substance of the note is a promise to pay money.'[147] This approach could be defended on the grounds that it ensured harmony between the Common law and commercial practice. In *Rawlinson* v. *Stone*, Denison J. justified the right of a personal representative of a deceased holder of a note to indorse it on his behalf on the grounds that the Act deserved a liberal interpretation for the 'benefit of trade and commerce', and observed that this was standard practice amongst merchants.[148] But this way of interpreting the legislation also encouraged numerous attempts to bring claims in situations that were a long way removed from mercantile transactions, even if most were unsuccessful.[149] As promissory notes became more familiar, the device appeared in popular culture[150] and even a church sermon.[151] In the end the legislation of 1704 did not bring about the destruction of assumpsit and a realignment of contract law; though it was not the end of attempts to undermine consideration. Promissory notes, like bills of exchange, could be seen as a class apart from mainstream contracts.

The scope of contractual obligations

Negotiable instruments were not the only sort of commercial contract to attract attention around 1700. In *Coggs* v. *Barnard*,[152] Holt C.J. delivered 'the first well ordered exposition of the English law of bailments'.[153] Holt C.J.'s scheme, which drew heavily on Roman law, sought to impose a structure on a jumble of authorities. Aspects of his analysis have proved

147 *Morice* v. *Lee* (1725) 8 Mod 362, 363. 148 (1746) 3 Wils KB 1, 4.

149 For examples, see *Garnet* v. *Clarke* (1709) 11 Mod 226; Rogers, *Bills and Notes*, pp. 185–6.

150 For example: Anon, *The Inconsolable: or the contented cuckold. A dramatic farce in three Acts* (London, 1738), p. 32; Arthur Friedman (ed.), Oliver Goldsmith, *The Vicar of Wakefield* (Oxford: Oxford University Press, 2006), p. 63. The novel was first published in 1766.

151 Charles Brent, *Money essay'd or the time value of it tryed* (London, 1728), p. 32 'for which you have this promissory note of the Gospel'. Brent was preaching to the merchants of Bristol at the time.

152 (1703) 2 Ld Raym 909; 3 Ld Raym 163; 1 Salk 26, 2 Salk 735, 3 Salk 11, 268; 1 Com 133; Holt 13, 131, 528. For a detailed discussion of the decision, see David Ibbetson, 'Coggs v. Barnard (1703)', in Charles Mitchell and Paul Mitchell (eds.), *Landmark Cases in the Law of Contract* (Oxford: Hart, 2008), pp. 1–22.

153 John Smith, *A Selection of Leading Cases on Various Branches of the Law*, 2 vols. (London: A. Maxwell, 1837), vol. I, p. 96.

to be extremely durable.[154] Holt C.J. also devoted some attention to maritime contracts, including an early decision on the operation of bills of lading.[155] Marine insurance was a 'matter of routine'[156] and, from the late sixteenth century, policies were drawn in a standard form.[157] There was a significant amount of insurance litigation from around the mid-sixteenth century.[158] In comparison to the mid-eighteenth century the body of reported authority on insurance remained fairly small, but it was starting to grow.[159]

The principal difficulty caused by bills of exchange, and particularly promissory notes, was the threat that they posed to existing notions about when the Common law would impose contractual obligations. The danger only passed once custom was under judicial control and negotiable instruments were securely locked in place by statute. The remit of negotiable instruments was part of a bigger concern which dominated the law reports in the last few decades of the seventeenth century and the

154 For example, the analysis of pawned goods which depended on a distinction between general and special property: William Blackstone, *Commentaries on the Laws of England*, 4 vols. (Oxford, 1766), vol. II, pp. 452–3; Francis Turner, *The Contract of Pawn* (London: Stevens, 1866), p. 61; *Donald* v. *Suckling* (1866) LR 1 QB 585, 595; *Mathew* v. *TM Sutton* [1994] 4 All ER 793, 800; N. Palmer (ed.), *Palmer on Bailment*, 3rd edn (London: Sweet & Maxwell, 2009), para. 22-004. For a more critical view of this terminology, see *The Odessa* [1916] AC 145, 159. For more detail on Holt C.J.'s analysis of pawnbroking, see Warren Swain and Karen Fairweather, 'The Legal Regulation of Pawnbroking in England, A Brief History', in James Devenney and Mel Kenny (eds.), *Consumer Credit, Debt and Investment in Europe* (Cambridge: Cambridge University Press, 2011), pp. 144–8.

155 *Evans* v. *Marlett* (1697) 1 Ld Raym 271. This decision has been described as 'the first definite pronouncement on the law of bills of lading from a common law court' by W.P. Bennett, *The History and Present Position of the Bill of Lading as a Document of Title to Goods* (Cambridge: Cambridge University Press, 1914), p. 13. There was also some discussion on the correct interpretation of charter-parties: *Wynne* v. *Fellowes* (1691) 1 Show 334.

156 C.G. Lewin, *Pensions and Insurance Before 1800* (East Linton: Tuckwell Press, 2003), p. 115.

157 Harold Raynes, *A History of British Assurance*, 2nd edn (London: Pitman, 1964), pp. 59–68.

158 David Ibbetson, 'Law and Custom: Insurance in Sixteenth Century England' (2008) 29 *Journal of Legal History* 291, 292–5.

159 These are discussed by W.S. Holdsworth, 'Early History of the Contract of Insurance' (1917) 17 *Columbia Law Review* 85, 105–6. The growth of insurance litigation is also evident from the manuscript reports of the period, see James Oldham, 'Underreported and Underrated: The Court of Common Pleas in the Eighteenth Century', in Hendrik Hartog *et al.* (eds.), *Law as Culture and Culture as Law* (Madison, Wis.: Madison House, 2000), pp. 119, 134–8.

early decades of the eighteenth century, namely, the proper scope of contractual obligations.

When taken together with negotiable instruments, a good case can be made for saying that these developments were the most significant group of authorities since *Slade's Case*.[160] At the end of the seventeenth century a number of decisions concerned the claims of third party beneficiaries.[161] The rule for sealed instruments was clear enough.[162] Only parties to the deed could maintain an action. Being named as a party was conclusive.[163] The rule was, occasionally, problematic to apply.[164] Different rules applied where a deed poll was used so that the agreement took effect unilaterally rather than *inter partes*. Any person named as a beneficiary could sue even though not a party to the original deed, a fact that would be of crucial importance in insurance contracts.[165] The situation relating to informal contracts was infinitely more complex. There are traces of a parties-only rule in assumpsit at the end of the sixteenth century, but such a substantive rule that the action must be brought by the promisee must have had relatively little weight, and always at risk of degenerating into a pleading rule requiring it to be alleged that the promise had been made to the plaintiff.[166]

Alongside this weak parties-only rule in assumpsit, a stronger rule emerged out of the doctrine of consideration. By the late seventeenth century the focus was less on why the promisor should be held to his promise than why the promisee should be entitled to receive the benefit. In *Bourne* v. *Mason and Robinson*,[167] a promise made to a debtor (who had provided consideration) to pay off his creditor was held not to give the creditor a right of action against the promisor. The creditor was, in the words of the report, a stranger to the consideration.[168] In the famous

[160] (1602) 4 Co Rept 91a, Yelv 20, Moo KB 433.

[161] The material that follows is discussed in greater detail in Ibbetson and Swain, 'Third Party Beneficiaries'. For further analysis, see Vernon Palmer, *The Paths to Privity* (Clark, N.J.: The Lawbook Exchange, 2006).

[162] Deeds were necessary for actions in covenant and debt on a bond.

[163] *Scudamore* v. *Vandenstene* (1587) Cro Eliz 56; *Gilby* v. *Copley* (1683) 3 Lev 138, 139; *Vernon* v. *Jefferys* (1740) 2 Str 1146, 7 Mod 358.

[164] *Salter* v. *Kidgley* (1689) Carth 76.

[165] *Scudamore* v. *Vandenstene* (1587) Cro Eliz 56; *Cooker* v. *Child* (1673) 2 Lev 74, 3 Keb 115; *Green* v. *Horne* (1694) Comb 219, 1 Salk 197.

[166] John Baker, 'Privity of Contract in the Common Law before 1680', in Eltjo Schrage (ed.), *Ius Quaesitum Tertio* (Berlin: Duncker & Humblot, 2008), pp. 41–57.

[167] (1670) 1 Vent 6, 2 Keb 454, 457, 527.

[168] 1 Vent 6. This case is discussed in detail by Baker, 'Privity of Contract', pp. 51–2.

case of *Dutton* v. *Poole*[169] the facts were found to fall inside an exception, but at the same time the decision succeeded in reinforcing the rule. By the early eighteenth century the rule that a stranger to the consideration had no action had completely supplanted the older and less resilient parties-only rule in assumpsit.[170]

Following *Crow* v. *Rogers*,[171] which restated the rule that consideration must move from the promisee, there was a long period of silence which was only broken in the early nineteenth century. In part this can be attributed to the law having reached a point of stability. The restriction on claims may also have been largely unproblematic because if consideration had been provided by somebody, the rules were sufficiently flexible to ensure that person could be regarded as the promisee and the contract enforced.[172] This still excluded the situation where the promisee had provided the consideration, but the promise had been made for the benefit of a third party, who was a volunteer. The intended beneficiary, having not provided any consideration, was refused an action. It was not the fact that the beneficiary was a third party that barred the claim, but rather the restrictive Common law doctrine of consideration. Whilst there is no evidence of general pressure to change the law, there are situations in which actions were allowed to be brought falling outside the mainstream Common law rules. Mercantile instruments were one example. The Court of Chancery was increasingly concerned with situations involving third party beneficiaries. This occurred by channelling cases involving promises of gifts, especially gifts on marriage, into the emerging law of trusts; the provision of equitable remedies in 'Dutton v. Poole' type cases involving death bed promises; and through suits in Equity by beneficiaries.[173]

The rationalisation of the rules relating to third party beneficiaries was not the only time that the doctrine of consideration came under scrutiny.

[169] (1679) 3 Keb 786, 814, 830, 836, 1 Freem 471, 1 Vent 318, 1 Vent 332, 2 Lev 210, T Jones 102, T Raym 302, BL MS Add 32521 f. 28 (from the notes of Lord Guilford).

[170] *Mayor and Aldermen of London* v. *Brasier* (1711) HLS MS 1142 f. 458.

[171] (1724) 1 Stra 592.

[172] If any doubt about this arose on the evidence the court would be astute to suppose that the recipient of the promise was an agent or attorney or to infer a second promise to the person providing the consideration: *Sadler* v. *Paine* (1582) Sav 23, 24; *Delabar* v. *Gould* (1661) 1 Keb 121, 122; *Starkey* v. *Mill* (1651) Style 296; *Martyn* v. *Hind* (1779) 2 Cowp 437, 1 Doug 142; *Master, Wardens, and Commonalty of Feltmakers* v. *Davis* (1797) 1 B & P 98, 102.

[173] Ibbetson and Swain, 'Third Party Beneficiaries', pp. 201–5.

Cumber v. *Wane*[174] was sufficiently notorious to be chosen to feature in *A Selection of Leading Cases on Various Branches of the Law*,[175] and sufficiently durable to appear in the law reports in modern times.[176] The factual context on the other hand was completely unremarkable. A creditor promised to discharge the debt of a debtor in consideration of payment of a sum smaller than that due. The rule in debt was well settled by *Pinnel's Case*,[177] which held that 'payment of a lesser sum on the day in satisfaction for a greater cannot be any satisfaction for the whole'.[178] Where payment was made before the date that the debt fell due the outcome was different. The payment was treated as satisfaction.[179] *Pinnel's Case* was concerned with the rules of accord and satisfaction in debt. The same result need not inevitably follow in the closely analogous circumstances in the action of assumpsit. Indeed, a series of decisions from *Cooke* v. *Hawke*[180] onwards held that that payment of a lesser sum did amount to good consideration for a promise to discharge a debt.[181]

In *Cumber* v. *Wane*[182] the plaintiff brought a claim in indebitatus assumpsit for £15. The defendant pleaded that he had given a promissory note to the value of £5 in satisfaction. The plaintiff argued that the note did not amount to satisfaction because it was a promise to pay in the future rather than an actual payment before the debt fell due. One way that this argument could be countered was to argue that the receipt of the note, just like the receipt of a lesser sum,[183] could, in practical terms, be advantageous. As Fortescue J. explained:

174 (1719) 11 Mod 342, 1 Stra 426.

175 The case did not feature in Smith's early editions. It first featured in the fourth edition, James Willes and Henry Keating (eds.), John Smith, *A Selection of Leading Cases on Various Branches of the Law*, 2 vols. (London: William Maxwell, 1856), vol. I, p. 252.

176 *D & C Builders* v. *Rees* [1966] 2 QB 617, 623 where Lord Denning said of the decision that it has 'suffered many vicissitudes but was, I think, rightly decided in point of law'.

177 (1602) 5 Co Rep 117 a.

178 A.W. Brian Simpson, *A History of the Common Law of Contract: The Rise of the Action of Assumpsit*, pbk edn (Oxford: Oxford University Press, 1987), pp. 103–7 makes the important point that these remarks were both *obiter* and capable of two interpretations.

179 The importance of this aspect of the decision is brought out particularly clearly in manuscript reports of the case, see John Baker, *Baker and Milsom Sources of English Legal History*, 2nd edn (Oxford: Oxford University Press, 2010), pp. 286–9.

180 Cited by David Ibbetson, 'Consideration and the Theory of Contract in Sixteenth Century Common Law', in John Barton (ed.), *Towards a General Law of Contract* (Berlin: Duncker & Humblot, 1990), p. 78 (1578) referred to from the plea roll in *Bosome* v. *Paine* HLS 1058 f. 18.

181 *Ibid.* 182 (1719) 11 Mod 342, 1 Stra 426.

183 For example, in *Reynolds* v. *Pinhowe* (1595) Cro Eliz 429 where £4 was given in respect of £5 owed it was held that 'it is a benefit to him to have it without suit or charge'.

> As to five pounds for fifteen pounds, the jury might not give two pounds damages; then reducing this to a certainty puts him in a better condition. A bond payable before the day of a former bond, is satisfaction. Why? Not because it extinguishes the debt, but because it puts the plaintiff into a better condition.[184]

The case came before the courts a second time and Pratt C.J., speaking for the whole of the court, found for the plaintiff:

> It must appear to . . . be a reasonable satisfaction; or at least the contrary must not appear, as it does in this case. If £5 be (as is admitted) no satisfaction for £15 why is a simple contract to pay £5 a satisfaction for another simple contract of three times the value?[185]

Pratt C.J.'s conclusions would receive plenty of criticism later on.[186] His analysis was surprising in light of earlier authority and because of the suggestion that the consideration in the form of the satisfaction must be reasonable.[187] The strict rule would be eroded through composition agreements.[188] It was also possible that juries, when faced with determining whether there was sufficient consideration, took a fairly relaxed view, hence the apparent absence of criticism of the decision before the nineteenth century.[189]

Cumber v. *Wane* can be seen as an attempt, in one particular context at least, to impose limits on enforceability which in other contexts were in the process of being relaxed. Contracts with infants for necessaries were binding.[190] The rest were void and lacking good consideration.[191] This strict position began to change. In *Ball* v. *Hesketh*[192] Holt C.J. ruled that

184 (1719) 11 Mod 342, 343. 185 1 Stra 426, 427.

186 Kevin Teeven, *Promises on Prior Obligations at Common Law* (Westport: Greenwood, 1998), p. 22, has called the judgment 'muddled'.

187 Though this situation was quite close to that where the courts *had* derogated from the principle that they would not inquire into the adequacy of the consideration, see Ibbetson, 'Consideration', p. 73 where the consideration and promise had some fixed value with respect to each other.

188 Michael Lobban, 'Foakes v. Beer (1884)', in Charles Mitchell and Paul Mitchell (eds.), *Landmark Cases in the Law of Contract* (Oxford: Hart, 2008), pp. 230–5.

189 In *Heathcote* v. *Crookshanks* (1787) 2 TR 24, 25 where Law, who would later become Lord Ellenborough, said in the course of argument that *Cumber* v. *Wane* had 'been repeatedly denied by this court to be law'.

190 A contract to borrow money to buy the necessities of life, on the other hand, was not binding, see *Earle* v. *Peale* (1711) Salk 386, 10 Mod 66. Parker C.J. made the point that 'it may be borrowed for necessaries, but laid out and spent at a tavern'.

191 *Stone* v. *Withipole* (1589) 1 Leon 113; Owen 94; Cro Eliz 126; Dyer 272; Yale MS GR 29.6 f. 81, *Baker and Milsom*, pp. 533–5.

192 (1697) Comb 381.

where an infant had borrowed money and on reaching maturity had promised to pay, the subsequent agreement was binding and could be enforced. The same outcome was reached in *Southerton* v. *Whitlock*[193] when an infant had purchased goods which were not necessaries and on reaching his majority promised to pay. The subsequent promise could be enforced.[194]

Ball v. *Hesketh* and *Southerton* v. *Whitlock* only ran to a handful of lines in the law reports and no attempt was made to explain why on reaching their majority the promises were binding when an infant's contract was not. There was no mention of the consideration necessary to support the agreement. Promises to pay in cases where the action on the original contract was time barred by the Statute of Limitations had some features in common with contracts with infants.[195] Holt C.J. consulted ten of his fellow judges in *Heyling* v. *Hastings*[196] before enforcing the contract.[197] In the first hearing Holt C.J. suggested that a promise revived the debt and drew parallels with the cases on infants.[198] In the final ruling he explained that 'the defendant has waved the benefit of the statute'.[199] It was necessary to consult all of the judges again within a decade in *Dean* v. *Crane*,[200] in which it was decided that there was insufficient evidence to support the declaration. If the reports are anything to go by, the nature of consideration was not discussed in any great detail in these decisions either.[201] There was certainly no attempt to rationalise liability in terms of moral consideration – that would come later.

The rules relating to third parties and satisfaction by payment of a smaller sum seem to restrict the scope of contractual obligations, but in practice both could be sidestepped. In a few cases, rather than becoming more restrictive, the law of contract broadened. But it was another category of legal obligations where growth was most significant. Precise

193 (1726) 2 Stra 690. 194 *Southerton* v. *Whitlock* (1726) 2 Stra 690.

195 Statute of Limitations (1623) 21 Jac I c. 16. Although analogous, there was the important difference that the contract had once been valid and actionable.

196 (1698) 1 Ld Raym 389, 1 Ld Raym 421; 5 Mod 425. The figure of ten is taken from the report at (1698) 1 Salk 29. For earlier authority which had suggested that such promises were actionable, see *Anon* (1674) 1 Vent 258.

197 The fact that the promise on the facts was conditional was said to make no difference.

198 (1698) 1 Ld Raym 389. 199 (1698) 1 Ld Raym 421.

200 (1704) 6 Mod 309, 1 Salk 28.

201 These decisions also show a change in perceptions of a pre-existing duty so far as it relates to consideration from the sixteenth century cases, see David Ibbetson, *A Historical Introduction to the Law of Obligations* (Oxford: Oxford University Press, 1999), p. 204, fn. 7.

classification of this area is difficult. Modern lawyers settle for unjust enrichment or restitution. Formally these were actions of assumpsit. But they were assumpsit of a special kind. Unlike the well-established form, no agreement was required. It meant that non-contractual claims developed outwards from the contractual core of the standard assumpsit actions. Money had and received was an exception. It was one action which, whilst formally an assumpsit, had no contractual core. This method of accommodating non-contractual claims was nothing new. Before the emergence of assumpsit the actions of account and debt had fulfilled a similar function. Both were sufficiently flexible to allow money to be recovered in the absence of an agreement because justice demanded that it should be returned.[202]

Because the appearance of a claim was the same whether in contract or not, the law was able to develop unhindered without the risk of a challenge on the grounds of formal error.[203] By the sixteenth century it was also straightforward to plead. Standard allegations known as the 'common counts' were used. Two of the common counts, *quantum valebant* for goods sold and delivered and the *quantum meruit* for work done, were formally varieties of special assumpsit. The remaining common counts were types of indebitatus assumpsit: 'money laid out',[204] 'money had and received',[205] 'money lent',[206] and 'account stated'.[207]

The difference between a situation where A promised to pay B a certain sum for his labour and a *quantum meruit* was that the parties did not fix a value on the labour in advance. Both were equally contractual. The history of these claims outside the contractual core is difficult to disentangle. The first definitive non-contractual use of *quantum meruit*, identified by Baker, concerned a contract that had failed or was unenforceable because the 'specific contract militates against genuine implication'.[208] He also

[202] R.M. Jackson, *The History of Quasi-Contract in English Law* (Cambridge: Cambridge University Press, 1936), pp. 32–6; David Ibbetson, 'Unjust Enrichment in England before 1600', in Eltjo Schrage (ed.), *Unjust Enrichment. The Comparative Legal History of the Law of Restitution* (Berlin: Duncker & Humblot, 1995), pp. 121–48; Ibbetson, *Historical Introduction*, pp. 265–8.

[203] For example, by raising a demurrer on formal grounds, see Henry Stephen, *A Treatise on Pleading in Civil Actions* (London: Butterworth, 1824), pp. 61–2.

[204] John Wentworth, *A Complete System of Pleading Comprehending the Most Approved Precedents and Forms of Practice*, 10 vols. (London, 1797), vol. III, p. 55.

[205] *Ibid.*, vol. III, pp. 55–6. [206] *Ibid.*, vol. III, p. 55. [207] *Ibid.*, vol. III, p. 56.

[208] J.H. Baker, 'The Use of Assumpsit for Restitutionary Money Claims 1600–1800', in Schrage (ed.), *Unjust Enrichment*, pp. 38–9. The essay is reproduced in J.H. Baker, *The Common Law Tradition* (London: Hambledon, 2000).

suggests that a claim against an infant for necessities may have arisen even earlier, though he concedes that the evidence is 'inconclusive'.[209]

At the end of the century, in *Cutter* v. *Powell*,[210] the relationship between contractual and non-contractual assumpsits would attract a good deal of attention. The first stirrings of this debate can be found seventy years before.[211] In *Weaver* v. *Buroughs*,[212] the plaintiff declared on a special assumpsit for the hire of a horse at 2s 6d per day for so many days, and to return the horse safe at the end of the period, and an indebitatus assumpsit for hire. Raymond C.J. refused to allow the claim for hire when the plaintiff had failed to prove the special count on the contract as laid. He also gave a further example, 'he put the case of a contract for goods at a certain price, where the plaintiff is never suffered to recover upon a *quantum meruit*, if he fails to prove the particular price agreed on'.[213]

Weaver v. *Buroughs* is explicable on the grounds that the plaintiff was trying to plead two contradictory things, that the hire at the rate of 2s 6d a day was agreed and a reasonable sum was due for hire.[214] Two decisions in 1735 raised the availability of *quantum meruit* more starkly in terms of the existence of a contract. In *Miller* v. *Duell*,[215] on a *quantum meruit* for the occupation of a house and in the face of evidence of a lease to pay a certain sum, it was explained that, 'The action is improper, *quantum meruit* will lie where there is no agreement, or where an agreement is executed and afterwards an express promise to pay; where a contract is executed an indebitatus assumpsit will lie'.[216] In *Clark* v. *Smith*[217] the defendant held over after the term of a lease had expired. The plaintiff asked for half a year's rent and the defendant promised to pay at next Candlemas. This was said to be sufficient evidence of a lease. Baron Carter rejected a *quantum meruit* on the grounds that it was only appropriate where 'there was no promise'.

None of these decisions squarely deals with the situation where a contract has failed or become unenforceable and the plaintiff uses

[209] Baker, *ibid.*, pp. 39–41. [210] (1795) 6 TR 320.

[211] Some of these cases are discussed from a different perspective by John Barton, who also makes some use of manuscript reports: J.L. Barton, 'Contract and Quantum Meruit: The Antecedents of Cutter v. Powell' (1987) 8 *Journal of Legal History* 48.

[212] (1726) 1 Str 648, LI MS Hill 12 (1) f. 6.

[213] LI MS Hill 12 (1) f. 6. The report in Strange omits the last ten words. Given that Raymond C.J. was talking about goods rather than services, he presumably meant *quantum valebant* rather than *quantum meruit*. For the purposes of the discussion the distinction is not significant.

[214] Barton, 'Contract and Quantum Meruit', p. 54. [215] (1735) HLS MS 4062 f. 90.

[216] *Ibid.* [217] (1735) LI MS Misc. 37 f. 98.

quantum meruit in order to recover the value of his labour. A contract may be unenforceable because the plaintiff himself has mis-performed. Barton has suggested *Salisbury* v. *Yates*[218] is a strong example. The defendant ordered a 'gout bespoke chaise' from the plaintiff. The chaise constructed was not identical to, but 'very little different' from, the defendant's directions. In carrying the defendant's motion for a new trial, Pratt C.J. held that the 'plaintiff says he made it as near his directions as possible, that is no answer; why did he undertake to do what he knew could not be done? If it had been made as convenient for him as if it had been according to his directions he ought indeed to have accepted, but this was not.'[219] The report is unclear, but the record of the case shows that the decision concerned a mis-performing plaintiff failing to recover on the contract rather than a mis-performing plaintiff failing to recover on a *quantum meruit.*[220]

All that has survived of a second possible candidate, *Mr Keck's Case*, is contained in Francis Buller's *An Introduction to the Law Relative to Trials at Nisi Prius.*[221] It follows a statement that reads, 'if he prove a special agreement and the work done, but not pursuant to such an agreement, he shall recover on the *quantum meruit* otherwise he shall not be able to recover at all'.[222] The account of the decision itself suggests that the existence of an agreement was insufficient to prevent a mis-performing plaintiff from recovering on a *quantum meruit.*

Whilst it would be unwise to put too much weight on an unreported case at nisi prius, *Mr Keck's Case* does suggest that some of the earlier restrictions on the use of non-contractual *quantum meruit* were beginning to be relaxed. Plaintiffs were pushing the boundaries of non-contractual *quantum meruit* elsewhere too. *Hayes* v. *Warren*[223] hinted that the receipt of a sufficient benefit may be enough to support a *quantum meruit* without alleging the work was done at the defendant's request.[224] In the absence of a request, there is no question that the claim is non-contractual. Two of the judges even gave an example of a father who would be liable for the burial of his child even in the absence of a request, as this was something he must himself have

[218] (1724) LI MS Hill 8 f. 208, Barton, 'Contract and Quantum Meruit', p. 58.
[219] *Ibid.* [220] PRO KB 122/109 f. 500.
[221] (London, 1767), p. 129. The decision is dated 1744. [222] *Ibid.*
[223] (1733) W Kelynge 117; 2 Stra 933; 2 Barn KB 55, 71, 140; LI MS Hill 39 f. 92; HLS MS 4055 f. 6.
[224] HLS MS 4055 f. 6, Raymond C.J., Probyn J., Page J. (perhaps more obliquely).

done.[225] A few years later there was an opportunity to test the limits of this sort of reasoning. In *Barton* v. *Hodgkinson*[226] the plaintiff brought a *quantum meruit* for the cost of maintaining a child. The defendant had abandoned his pregnant wife and gone to live six miles away. When the child was three and a half, the defendant's wife went to live with the plaintiff, with whom she left the child. The majority held that no action could be supported. Lee C.J. seemed to accept in principle that the receipt of a benefit could support an action in the absence of a request, but thought that on the facts there was no benefit to the father. The other members of the majority preferred even narrower approaches. Probyn J. conceded that the father was bound to maintain his child but thought that the father was the only person entitled to decide about the proper way of doing it and, hence, he was not liable when another brought up the child according to his own principles. Chapple J. held as a matter of principle that the obligation to maintain the child only lay between the father and the child and not a third party. Only Page J. was willing to uphold the action in the absence of a request on the basis of a precedent duty owed by a father to maintain his child.

The count for money laid out or paid alleged that the defendant was indebted to the plaintiff for money laid out at the defendant's request. Like the *quantum meruit*, it began to outgrow its contractual core once a request was no longer necessary. The seventeenth century authorities are largely inconclusive when it comes to determining when this particular change occurred.[227] *Morrice* v. *Redwyn*,[228] heard before Lord Raymond at Norwich Assize in 1731, is more definite. The plaintiff had provided security in order to prevent execution against the defendant, the principal debtor. The creditor in the former action then commenced another action on the security. The plaintiff paid, not because the defendant requested him to do so, but because of the creditor's action. It was held that he had a valid action against the principal to recover the value of his security in assumpsit for money laid out. *Morrice* v. *Redwyn* seems to have been largely forgotten.[229] For some time afterwards the principle may not have

[225] HLS MS 4055 f. 6, Lee J.; LI MS Hill 39 f. 92, Raymond C.J. Something similar was later adopted in the same context on an action for money laid out. The report in 2 Barn KB 140, 141 gives two further examples of giving bail and curing a child. These remarks were not attributed to a particular judge.

[226] (1739) LI MS Misc. 133 f. 33; LI MS Hill 25 f. 1; LI MS Hill 29 f. 225.

[227] Baker, 'Use of Assumpsit', pp. 41–5. [228] (1731) 2 Barn KB 26.

[229] It was not cited in any subsequent authority up until 1855. In Charles Cooper's note to his reports written in 1841 at vol. I, p. 666, it was described as a case 'which seems to have escaped our text writers'.

been free from doubt.[230] A decision unequivocally in favour of this sort of claim settled matters after 1750, by which time the action was growing in importance.

A steady stream of authorities dealing with the count for money had and received appeared from the early seventeenth century.[231] For classification purposes, money had and received was grouped alongside the other indebitatus assumpsits.[232] It was also designated a contractual action under the rules of joinder.[233] Yet unlike the other common counts, it was without a contractual core. The declaration alleged that the defendant was indebted 'for [so much money] had and received by the defendant to the use of the plaintiff'. As a result it could be used for non-contractual claims without resorting to fictions.

Judges were wrestling with the issue of the proper scope of money had and received long before the much commented on *Moses* v. *Macferlan*.[234] In 1725 an unnamed nisi prius judge confidently asserted that actions for money had and received 'are grounded on a supposed contract'.[235] The real problem lay less in how the claim was characterised, than in its potential to undermine well-established legal rules. In its earliest manifestation, money had and received 'enabled a third party beneficiary to enforce something like a trust of money, independently of contract and without recourse to the action of account'.[236] Payment made as a result of mistake or fraud were standard uses of money had and received.[237] Some remarks of Holt C.J. from the 1690s showed how far money had and received had come. In *Martin* v. *Sitwell*, an action to recover insurance premiums paid on a void policy, Holt C.J. allowed a claim on the grounds that 'money was received without any reason, occasion or consideration'.[238] The underlying nature of the remedy

230 *Woffington* v. *Sparks* (1754) 2 Ves Sen 569, 571.

231 Baker, 'Use of Assumpsit', pp. 47–53.

232 For example, in the abridgments: Charles Viner, *A General Abridgement of Law and Equity*, 20 vols. (Aldershot, 1746), vol. I, Actions Assumpsit (N2); Matthew Bacon, *A New Abridgment of the Law*, 5 vols. (London, 1736), vol. I, Assumpsit (A).

233 Tariq Baloch, *Unjust Enrichment and Contract* (Oxford: Hart, 2009), p. 12.

234 (1760) 2 Burr 1005; 1 Wm Bla 219; Baloch, *ibid.*, pp. 20–9.

235 *Harris* v. *Collins* (1725) LI MS Hill 6 f. 218.

236 Baker, 'Use of Assumpsit', p. 49.

237 Baker, 'Use of Assumpsit', pp. 49–52; *Tomkyns* v. *Barnet* (1693) Skin 411, Salk 22 (as *Tomkins* v. *Bernet*); *Astley* v. *Reynolds* (1731) 2 Stra 915, 2 Barn KB 40; *Attorney General* v. *Perry* (1735) 2 Com 481, 491.

238 (1691) 1 Show KB 156, 157. The same phrase was repeated in *Attorney General* v. *Perry* (1735) 2 Com 481, 491 discussed by Baloch, *Unjust Enrichment*, p. 26.

was explored in more detail in *Astley* v. *Reynolds*.[239] The plaintiff had paid a sum greater than allowable legal interest in order to redeem some plate from a pawn broker, which he sought to recover using money had and received. In a decision at nisi prius nearly forty years earlier, Treby C.J. had appeared to rule out claims of this sort:

> Where a man pays money on a mistake in an account, or where one pays money under or by a mere deceit, it is reasonable that he should have his money again; but where one knowingly pays money upon an illegal consideration . . . the party that pays it is particeps criminis, and there is no reason that he should have his money again; for he parted with it freely and volenti non fit injuria.[240]

In light of the unsatisfactory state of the usury laws, the fact that money had and received was sanctioned in this context is less surprising than the way in which the claim was justified in *Astley* v. *Reynolds*, and captured most fully in a manuscript report.[241] Raymond C.J. said that 'The question in this case will be whether the payment was free and voluntary for if it was without any compulsion it is not to be recovered again'.[242] The plaintiff recovered on the basis that the payment was compulsory. Page J. agreed, holding that the tender of the money 'was to be looked upon as a payment by duress'.[243] Probyn J. emphasised that in claiming more than lawful interest the defendant was committing a fraud.[244] Lee J. was notably less enthusiastic than his colleagues, repeating the maxim *volenti non fit inuria*.[245] Whilst the plaintiff was given judgment, concerns were raised that 'if this action could be maintained it would be a much more easy remedy than an action of trover'.[246]

From the late seventeenth century there were a number of instances of plaintiffs seeking to take advantage of the relative ease of pleading money had and received to the detriment of existing remedies. In 1697, Holt C.J. warned that, 'An indebitatus assumpsit hath been carried too far'.[247] He

239 The decision is reported in (1731) 2 Stra 915 and more fully at 2 Barn KB 40.
240 *Tomkins* v. *Bernet* (1693) Salk 22.
241 Several manuscript reports have been located: HLS MS 4055 f. 41; HLS MS 1110 f. 120; LI MS Misc. 98 f. 194; LI MS Hill 65 f. 41.
242 HLS MS 4055 f. 41.
243 HLS MS 4055 f. 41. In another report Page J. said that the 'payment is not voluntary, but the taking it is a wrong done to him', HLS MS 1110 f. 120.
244 HLS MS 4055 f. 41.
245 HLS MS 4055 f. 41, 2 Barn KB 40, 42.
246 (1731) 2 Barn KB 40, 42. The issue of trover was also raised in argument.
247 *Anon* (1697) Comb 446. In *Hussey* v. *Fiddall* (1699) 12 Mod 324, Holt C.J. said 'But my consent it shall go as far as it has gone, but not a step farther.'

made much the same point two years before when dismissing a claim with the words 'away with your indebitatus 'tis but a bargain'.[248] Tensions were greatest when money had and received began to be used to try questions of property.

Despite the scepticism of 'great counsel',[249] money had and received began to be used to litigate the title to offices[250] and to raise issues of title to land.[251] In *Shuttleworth* v. *Garnet*,[252] Holt C.J. found himself in a minority on the question of whether money had and received could be used to recover a customary fine on copyhold tenure. In rejecting the action, Holt C.J. took up the argument of counsel that the action does not lie because it 'is entirely in the realty', or as he put it, 'here both custom and tenure, appear, and it is of a higher nature, so as the action will not lie'.[253] The relationship between contract and money had and received, which would cause difficulties later on, hardly caused a ripple. In *Dutch* v. *Warren*,[254] the plaintiff had paid £262 to the defendant who agreed to transfer him five shares in the Welsh Copper Company on a later date.[255] The shares were not transferred, and on the date due for transfer they had fallen in value.[256] Rather than allow the plaintiff to

248 *Anon* (1695) Comb 341. The correct form of action was a special assumpsit on the contract.

249 *Lamine* v. *Dorrell* (1705) 2 Ld Raym 1216.

250 Baker, 'Use of Assumpsit', pp. 52–3; *Woodward* v. *Aston* (1676) 1 Mod 95, 1 Vent 296, 1 Freem 429; *Arris* v. *Stukely* (1677) 2 Mod 260, *Baker and Milsom*, pp. 503–4; *Howard* v. *Wood* (1680) 2 Show KB 21, 2 Lev 245, T Jones 126, 1 Freem 473, 478, *Baker and Milsom*, pp. 504–7.

251 This evidence is pretty thin but includes *Hasser* v. *Wallis* (1708) 1 Salk 28, and some remarks of counsel in *Hussey* v. *Finddall* (1699) 12 Mod 324.

252 (1689) 3 Mod 239, 3 Lev 261, Comb 151, Carth 90, 1 Show KB 35; *Baker and Milsom*, pp. 516–18.

253 (1689) 1 Show KB 35, 36. The way in which Holt C.J. distinguished *City of London* v. *Goree* (1676) 3 Keb 677, *Baker and Milsom*, pp. 515–16, in Carth 90, 92 also points to this interpretation, 'the cases are not parallel, for the duty of scavage doth arise out of things in the personalty; but the duty in the principal case issued out of realty'.

254 (1720) 1 Str 406. It is reported more fully in *Moses* v. *Macferlan* (1760) 2 Burr 1005, 1010–11. For comment, see A.W.B. Simpson, 'The Horwitz Thesis and the History of Contracts' (1978–1979) 46 *University of Chicago Law Review* 533, 553–5; Morton Horwitz, *The Transformation of American Law 1870–1960* (Oxford: Oxford University Press, 1992), p. 163.

255 This was an example of the sort of contract which had been criticised in the aftermath of the South Sea Bubble.

256 The Welsh Copper Company had risen in value throughout 1720 but by the date due for transfer, 22 August, the shares were falling in value, see John Carswell, *The South Sea Bubble* (London: Cresset Press, 1960), pp. 171–2, 174.

recover all of the sum paid, a jury awarded the value of the shares on the day agreed for transfer.[257] The manuscript report explains why the action was upheld and comments on the relationship between money had and received and contract:

> These actions have of late years been much extended beyond the role of the ancient law and the extending of them depends on the notion of fraud. If a man takes my money to do a thing and refuseth to do it is a fraud, and it is at the election of the party injured either to affirm the agreement by bringing the action for the non-performance of it, or to disaffirm the agreement *ab initio* by reason of the fraud and bring an action for the money paid in as so much money received to his use.[258]

The early eighteenth century saw the first wave of development in the non-contractual assumpsits. There was as yet no clear theoretical explanation. Different concepts like fraud, compulsion, and even the receipt of a benefit, were all used at various times to justify the imposition of liability. Despite the unease of Holt C.J., these claims were not sufficiently numerous to pose a threat to contract and property. This would all change as the century progressed. At the same time, a clearer rationale would emerge. It was not the only area in which greater clarity would become apparent by the end of the century. The relationship between law and mercantile practice was another.

[257] No explanation is recorded. It might be expected that the plaintiff could recover the amount of the money that he paid. The sum awarded reflects the expectation measure which formed the basis of damages for breach of contract. There is no clear evidence that juries did award expectation measures in all contract cases at this time. It is possible that the jury took the view that as a speculator the risk of a market fall was on the plaintiff.

[258] HLS MS 113 f. 221.

4

Lawyers and merchants II

The way in which bills of exchange and promissory notes came to be recognised within the Common law was probably the most significant event in the law of contract in the first half of the eighteenth century. The episode provides a good illustration of the frictions that could arise when well-established Common law rules ran up against a desire for legal change. The needs of commerce were one persistent and potent source of pressure. Something of the dilemma facing judges is captured in some remarks of Burnet J. in 1749 in *Ryall* v. *Rowles*,[1] who began his judgment with the words, 'This case is of so extensive a consequence to trade in general, it may be attended with such inconvenience either way, and in most respects is so wholly new, and no judicial determination, that I shall endeavour to lay my thoughts in as clear light as possible'.[2]

Many of these 'wholly new' questions continued to come before the courts. One consequence was that the period after 1750 continued to be dominated by a debate about the extent to which the Common law ought to adapt in the face of the demands placed upon it by commercial parties. These developments are also bound up with the mythology of one man, Lord Mansfield, Chief Justice of the King's Bench for a long period in the mid-eighteenth century.[3] Although much of this material is well-trodden ground,[4] some long held assumptions are open to question.

[1] (1749) 1 Ves Sen 348. [2] *Ibid*., p. 357.

[3] He was Chief Justice between 1756 and 1788. Ill-health prevented his attendance in the few years before he formally retired.

[4] For modern contributions to the literature, see C.H.S. Fifoot, *Lord Mansfield* (Oxford: Oxford University Press, 1938); Edmund Heward, *Lord Mansfield* (London: Barry Rose, 1979); James Oldham, *The Mansfield Manuscripts and the Growth of English Law in the Eighteenth Century*, 2 vols. (Chapel Hill: University of North Carolina Press, 2004). The commentaries on the substantive law are reproduced in James Oldham, *English Common Law in the Age of Mansfield* (Chapel Hill: University of North Carolina Press, 2004). References are to the *Mansfield Manuscripts*. Lord Mansfield features prominently in more general accounts of the period: W.S. Holdsworth, *A History of English Law*, 17 vols.

Lord Mansfield attracted unstinting praise from some of his fellow judges. Francis Buller described his mentor as 'the founder of the commercial law of this country'.[5] Lord Chancellor Thurlow is reported to have said 'Lord Mansfield was a surprising man; ninety-nine times out of a hundred he was right in his opinions and decisions. And when he was wrong, ninety-nine men out of a hundred could not discover it.'[6] Even the notoriously fickle Lord Campbell was impressed.[7] Lord Mansfield was a truly public figure. A hagiography was produced within a few years of his death.[8] Poetry was composed in his honour.[9] A ship was even named after him. He was also a popular subject in satirical prints.[10]

Alongside the plaudits there were what Campbell described as 'a few narrow-minded and envious people'[11] who were more critical. These cannot be dismissed easily. Some were significant figures in their own right including, if Campbell is to be believed, Lord Mansfield's successor

(London: Sweet & Maxwell, 1938), vol. XII, pp. 493–560; W.R. Cornish and G. de N. Clark, *Law and Society in England 1750–1950* (London: Sweet & Maxwell, 1989), pp. 36–7, 198–9, 207; J.H. Baker, *An Introduction to English Legal History* (London: Butterworths, 2002), pp. 351–2. For a useful overview of the life and work of Lord Mansfield, see James Oldham, 'Murray, William', *Oxford Dictionary of National Biography*.

5 *Lickbarrow* v. *Mason* (1787) 2 TR 63, 73. Buller was a friend as well as colleague of Lord Mansfield who left him a legacy of £2,000, see Heward, *Mansfield*, p. 167. For similar sentiments, see Richard Wooddeson, *Elements of Jurisprudence* (London, 1783), p. 92.

6 Croake James, *Curiosities of Law and Lawyers* (London: Sampson Low, 1882), p. 35.

7 John Campbell, *The Lives of the Chief Justices of England*, 3 vols. (London: John Murray, 1849), vol. II, pp. 395, 397.

8 John Holliday, *A Life of William Late Earl of Mansfield* (London, 1797); Campbell, *Lives*, vol. II, p. 307 described Holliday's book as 'the worst specimen of biography to be found in any language', which is somewhat ironic given his own shortcoming as a biographer.

9 For a particularly florid example, see Lady Sophie Burrell, *Poems Dedicated to the Right Honourable The Earl of Mansfield* (London, 1793), p. i:

> Him Virtue tutor'd, Genius sir'd,
> His words by Hermes were inspir'd,
> His work the Muses lov'd;
> Deep Learning shew'd him all her stores,
> Fancy illum'd his leisure hours,
> And Pope his thoughts appro'd.'

Whilst this type of poetry looks odd to modern eyes, it was not unusual to find poetry in praise of public figures particularly in a patriotic context, see Dustin Griffin, *Patriotism and Poetry in Eighteenth Century Britain* (Cambridge: Cambridge University Press, 2002), p. 36.

10 There are numerous examples, see Oldham, *Mansfield Manuscripts*, vol. I, pp. 31, 45, 126.

11 Campbell, *Lives*, vol. II, p. 397.

as Chief Justice, Lord Kenyon, and future Lord Chancellor, Lord Eldon.[12] The fact that a judge as prominent as Lord Mansfield should attract opprobrium is less interesting than the content of the criticism. Much was made of the fact that Lord Mansfield introduced uncertainty into the law, whether through his willingness to consider the needs of merchants or in his apparent enthusiasm for 'equity'.

George Meredith, the Victorian novelist, coined the aphorism 'caricature is rough truth',[13] and there is a good deal of rough truth in the way that Lord Mansfield is often characterised. At the same time, his reforming zeal is sometimes overstated. Many of his achievements built on existing well-established principles in both Common law and Equity. The role of Equity is considered in the next chapter. Like most judges he was not always consistent. Particularly towards the later end of his tenure as Chief Justice, Lord Mansfield was often unwilling to re-open matters recently settled. He would sometimes exhibit a conservative streak.

The merchants of London, negotiable instruments and insurance

James Park dedicated the first edition of his work on insurance to Lord Mansfield with the words, 'your extensive knowledge, joined to an unwearied application to every part of commercial jurisprudence ... has endeared your Lordships name to the Merchants of London.'[14] Reading some histories of the period it would be easy to assume that judges before Lord Mansfield paid little heed to the needs of merchants. This interpretation, which is at least as old as Lord Campbell's *Lives of the Chief Justices*,[15] has attracted some scholarly support.[16] As the previous chapter demonstrates, it is not borne out by the evidence. Lord Mansfield's approach was a continuation of what had gone before. If anything changed, it was less the existence of mercantile influence, but

[12] *Ibid.*, pp. 394–5. In Lord Eldon's case there are good grounds to believe that Campbell's view was not without foundation.

[13] George Meredith, *The Egoist: A Comedy in Narrative* (London: Constable, 1915).

[14] *System of the Law of Marine Insurance*, 2nd edn (London, 1790), p. iii.

[15] Campbell, *Lives*, vol. II, pp. 402–3.

[16] For example, from Morton Horwitz, see Morton Horwitz, *The Transformation of American Law 1780–1860* (Cambridge, Mass.: Harvard University Press, 1977), p. 167. Brian Simpson criticised Horwitz on this point but mainly concentrated on other aspects of the transformation thesis, A.W.B. Simpson, 'The Horwitz Thesis and the History of Contracts' (1979) 46 *University of Chicago Law Review* 533, 538–40.

its extent. Lord Mansfield was even more prepared than some other judges to listen to the views of merchants and to receive mercantile opinion in evidence. Special juries made up of merchants became more and more significant as a channel for the mercantile point of view.[17] A case like *Lewis* v. *Rucker*[18] illustrates the potential value of mercantile jurors. Lord Mansfield explained that, 'They understood the question very well, and knew more of the subject than anybody else present; and formed their judgement from their own notions and experience.'[19]

Individual merchants were also capable of wielding considerable influence that went beyond membership of a jury.[20] Nevertheless, the fact that Lord Mansfield was well informed about mercantile opinion did not necessarily mean that legal certainty was sacrificed on the altar of mercantile convenience. He was just as likely to ignore merchants as to follow them. This position sometimes led him into conflict with mercantile jurors as the decisions on horse sales show.

Although criticised for introducing uncertainty into the law, Lord Mansfield explicitly highlighted the dangers of uncertainty in matters of mercantile law on several occasions. As early as 1774 he stated that, 'in all mercantile transactions the great object should be certainty'.[21] A few years later he reiterated the point, 'I desire nothing so much, as that all questions of mercantile law should be fully settled and ascertained'.[22] In the 1780s he would warn that, 'Nothing is more mischievous than uncertainty in mercantile law'[23] and as a result 'in all mercantile cases there are two objects, convenience and certainty'.[24] Particularly where

[17] Oldham, *Mansfield Manuscripts*, vol. I, pp. 82–99; James Oldham, 'The Origins of the Special Jury' (1983) 50 *University of Chicago Law Review* 137, 173–5. Lord Mansfield was not the only judge to favour the use of special juries, see James Oldham, *The Varied Life of the Self-Informing Jury* (London: Selden Society, 2005), pp. 24–31. The term 'special jury' and 'mercantile jury' were not synonymous. Special juries need not be comprised of merchants. Others with particular insights to bring to the litigation were also deployed. Oldham, *Mansfield Manuscripts*, vol. I, p. 96 gives the example of a jury of gentlemen in cases of criminal conversation.

[18] (1761) 1 Burr 1167. [19] *Ibid.*, p. 1168.

[20] Oldham, *Mansfield Manuscript*, vol. I, p. 94 where he gives the examples of Edward Vaux and Thomas Gorman. For an example of Gorman in a trial making a distinction between 'convoy' and 'convoy for voyage', see *Lilly* v. *Ewer* (1778), Oldham, *Mansfield Manuscripts*, vol. I, p. 551.

[21] *Vallejo* v. *Wheeler* (1774) 1 Cowp 143, 153.

[22] *Buller* v. *Harrison* (1777) 2 Cowp 565, 567.

[23] *Medcalf* v. *Hall* (1782) 3 Doug 113, 115.

[24] *Medcalf* v. *Hall* (1782) 3 Doug 113. Lord Mansfield made these remarks in a direction to a jury.

the law was well settled, Lord Mansfield was anxious that established rules should not be undermined by evidence of contrary mercantile usage.[25] The way in which a balance was struck between 'convenience and certainty' can be illustrated by examining the growing body of law on negotiable instruments and insurance.

Despite the legislation there was still a good deal to be settled in relation to negotiable instruments. The appearance of a large body of literature[26] gives some indication of the importance that negotiable instruments had come to play in commercial life by the mid-eighteenth century. Writing in 1760, Timothy Cunningham described the bill of exchange as 'the principal medium of foreign and inland commerce'.[27] A few years later George Crooke observed that, 'There is scarce any person either gentleman, tradesman, or farmer, but what must, at some times, have occasion for bills of exchange'.[28] Lord Mansfield himself admitted that bills of exchange were, 'of great consequence to trade and commerce; especially, in this country, and at this time'.[29]

The process by which negotiable instruments were absorbed into the Common law in the late seventeenth and early eighteenth centuries left deep scars.[30] Important differences between the rules relating to foreign and inland bills of exchange remained. Promissory notes were still not fully integrated. According to Lord Mansfield 'The essence of a bill of exchange is, that it is negotiable, or payable to order, and that it is payable generally, not out of a particular fund'.[31] For negotiability to be truly achieved it was important to minimise the obstacles in the way of a holder of a bill of exchange from enforcing it.

25 *Edie* v. *East India Company* (1761) 2 Burr 1216, 1222. Mercantile custom was still relevant if the law remained to be settled, see *Carvick* v. *Vickery* (1783) 2 Doug 653.

26 William Forbes, *A Methodical Treatise Concerning Bills Of Exchange* (Edinburgh, 1703); Anon, *Obscurities and Defects of the Mercantile Law Considered, in an Essay on Bills of Exchange* (London, 1769). Later works include: John Bayley, *A Short Treatise on the Laws of Bills of Exchange, Cash Bills and Promissory Notes* (London, 1789); Stewart Kyd, *A Treatise on the Law of Bills of Exchange and Promissory Notes* (London, 1790); Joseph Chitty, *A Treatise on the Law of Bills of Exchange, Checks on Bankers, Promissory Notes, Bankers' Cash Notes and Banknotes* (London, 1799).

27 Timothy Cunningham, *The Law of Bills of Exchange, Promissory Notes, Bank-Notes, and Insurances* (London, 1760).

28 George Crooke, *The Merchant, Tradesman and Farmer's Director* (Lincoln, 1778), p. iii.

29 *Blesard* v. *Hirst* (1770) 5 Burr 2670, 2671; *Grant* v. *Vaughan* (1764) 1 Wm Bla 485, 487.

30 J. Milnes Holden, *The History of Negotiable Instruments in English Law* (London: Athlone Press, 1955), pp. 99–144; James Rogers, *The Early History of the Law of Bills and Notes* (Cambridge: Cambridge University Press, 1995), pp. 210–22.

31 *White* v. *Ledwick* (1785) 4 Doug 247, 249.

It was easy enough to blame earlier generations of law reporters for mixing up their terminology,[32] but actually unifying the rules relating to negotiable instruments in practice was a more formidable task. In *Heylyn* v. *Adamson*,[33] A drew an inland bill of exchange on B to C or his order. B accepted. C then indorsed the bill of exchange to D. The question before the King's Bench was whether D could sue C. Lord Mansfield held that D's immediate action was against B. If B refused or was unable to pay, then provided D could show due diligence in enforcing his claim, he had a remedy against C. Crucially this meant that it was unnecessary for a holder to bring an action against the original drawer before proceeding against an indorser. The decision brought inland bills into line with foreign bills.[34] From a holder's point of view this was an attractive development given that he was no longer thrown back on a more distant drawer who might be more difficult to trace, especially if the bill had passed through many hands.[35] Lord Mansfield was also keen that identical rules should apply to promissory notes and explained that, 'the same law must be applied to the same reason' he said, because promissory notes and bills of exchange were 'on the same footing'.[36]

By the same token, where the rules applying to promissory notes provided a convenient solution, Lord Mansfield was prepared to import them into bills of exchange. *Grant* v. *Vaughan*[37] raised the question of whether a bill made out to bearer gave a *bona fide* holder of the bill, who had provided consideration, a right of action against the drawer. The King's Bench held that he had.[38] Lord Mansfield disposed of the objection that a finder might bring an action by stressing that the bearer must have provided valuable consideration.[39] *Hodges* v. *Steward*,[40] which had distinguished bearer bills from bills made to order, also had to be overcome. Lord Mansfield, having referred to the statute of Anne, said that it 'puts promissory notes upon the same foot, throughout, with inland bills

[32] *Heylyn* v. *Adamson* (1758) 2 Burr 669, 678; *Grant* v. *Vaughan* (1764) 3 Burr 1516, 1525.

[33] (1758) 2 Burr 669. Holden, *Negotiable Instruments*, p. 128; Rogers, *Bills and Notes*, pp. 216–18.

[34] For the rule in foreign bills, see *Bomley* v. *Frazier* (1721) 1 Str 441.

[35] (1758) 2 Burr 669, 676. In the context of foreign bills it was earlier observed that such a restriction 'will deter everybody from taking them'.

[36] (1758) 2 Burr 669, 677. Rogers, *Bills and Notes*, p. 218 argues that the rule in promissory notes was not 'fully settled'. For the contradictory case law, see Rogers, *Bills and Notes*, p. 216, fn. 75.

[37] (1764) 3 Burr 1516, 1 Wm Bla 486. Holden, *Negotiable Instruments*, pp. 116–17.

[38] For an application of the rule, see *Peacock* v. *Rhodes* (1781) 2 Doug 633.

[39] (1764) 3 Burr 1516, 1523. [40] (1692) 1 Salk 125.

of exchange. And therefore whatever is the rule as to inland bills of exchange must be so likewise as to notes payable to bearer.'[41]

This passage is rather ambiguous on the proper classification of the instrument. Another report is clearer. Lord Mansfield described the instrument as a bill and stated that 'the statute expressly provides for notes payable to bearer; and therefore it may reasonably be construed to suppose, that such was the law for bills also'.[42] Wilmot J. said it is 'a negotiable instrument, which, I think, participates more of the nature of a promissory note, than of a bill of exchange'.[43] But he also said that the same result followed if the instrument was a bill of exchange. Lord Mansfield pointed out when discussing the turn of the century authorities that 'it is difficult to discover . . . when the question arises upon a bill and when upon a note: for the reporters do not express themselves, with sufficient precision, but use the words note and bill promiscuously'.[44] The sense of ambiguity strengthened the argument that the same rules should apply to bills of exchange as were laid down under the statute for promissory notes. At the same time, there were also good practical reasons for proceeding in this manner. According to Wilmot J., there was an 'infinite inconvenience'[45] if a *bona fide* holder was not allowed to recover.

The impact of *Grant* v. *Vaughan* went beyond the operation of bearer bills. From this point onwards there was, Lord Mansfield said, 'no distinction' between a bill of exchange and a bank note.[46] As well as tidying things up, this approach also emphasised that bills and notes formed a special class within the Common law. It was no longer necessary to explain away assignment because 'the holder of a bill of exchange, or promissory note, is not to be considered in the light of an assignee of the payee'.[47] Once again, there were sound commercial reasons for this point of view. In *Peacock* v. *Rhodes*, Lord Mansfield stated, 'An assignee must take the thing assigned, subject to all the equity to which the original party was subject. If this rule applied to bills and promissory notes, it would stop their currency.'[48] As a result of these decisions,

[41] (1764) 3 Burr 1516, 1524. [42] (1764) 1 Wm Bla 486, 488.

[43] (1764) 3 Burr 1516, 1528. [44] *Ibid.*, p. 1525. [45] *Ibid.*, p. 1528.

[46] *Ibid.*, p. 1524. Lord Mansfield referred to his earlier decision in *Miller* v. *Race* (1758) 1 Burr 452. In *Miller* v. *Race* he had held that trover could be used to recover a stolen bank note in the hands of a *bona fide* possessor for valuable consideration. Were it otherwise, he said at 457, the 'consequences to trade and commerce' would 'be much incommoded'.

[47] *Peacock* v. *Rhodes* (1781) 2 Doug 633, 636. [48] *Ibid.*

although they were drawn and pleaded differently, there was little to distinguish bills of exchange, promissory notes and bank-notes.[49]

If William Braund, a London merchant of the period, is anything like representative, by the 1740s, merchants were resorting to the law in insurance disputes on a regular basis.[50] Writing in 1752 in his *Lex mercatoria rediviva*, Wyndham Beawes remarked that:

> Policies having been filled up, in such various terms, and such unexampled expressions inserted, according to the different conceptions, fancies, or exigencies of the insured, it has naturally occasioned many disputes, and consequently brought on lately the most famous trials that ever employed our courts on this subject.[51]

The trade in insurance was carried out by corporations and private underwriters. Beawes describes a vibrant insurance market not just in London[52] but in the other major ports at Bristol, Exeter, Liverpool, Newcastle, Hull and Glasgow.[53] Fire and marine insurance were well established by 1750.[54] Life insurance lagged behind and was just beginning to become popular.[55]

When Lord Mansfield stressed the need for clear guidance he particularly singled out insurance contracts: 'All questions upon mercantile transactions, but more particularly upon policies of insurance, are extremely important and ought to be settled.'[56] There was a good deal

[49] Writing in the 1780s Bayley endorsed this view, *Bills of Exchange*, p. iii.

[50] Lucy Sutherland, *A London Merchant 1695–1774* (London: Frank Cass, 1962), p. 47. There are eight references to lawyers' costs in insurance disputes in Braund's cash book between 1742 and 1751.

[51] (London, 1752), p. 264.

[52] Associated with Lloyd's Coffee-house, though at this stage this was no more than an informal gathering of underwriters, see Frederick Martin, *The History of Lloyd's and of Marine Insurance in Great Britain* (London: Macmillan, 1876), pp. 65–85.

[53] For a discussion of Hull, see Gordon Jackson, *Hull in the Eighteenth Century: A Study in Economic and Social History* (Oxford: Oxford University Press, 1972), pp. 148–56.

[54] For some snapshots of the sometimes erratic growth in the insurance industry, see Barry Supple, *The Royal Exchange Insurance* (Cambridge: Cambridge University Press, 1970), pp. 61–2. With a large increase in imports, exports and re-exports between 1700 and 1800, the conditions for marine insurance were particularly favourable, see B.R. Mitchell, *Abstract of British Historical Statistics* (Cambridge: Cambridge University Press, 1962), pp. 279–81.

[55] P.G.M. Dickson, *The Sun Insurance Office* (Oxford: Oxford University Press, 1960), p. 101; Geoffrey Clark, *Betting on Lives: The Culture of Life Insurance in England, 1695–1775* (Manchester: Manchester University Press, 1999), pp. 71–113.

[56] *Nutt* v. *Bourdieu* (1786) 1 TR 323, 330, see also *Milles* v. *Fletcher* (1779) 1 Doug 231, 232; *Simond* v. *Boydell* (1779) 1 Doug 268, 270–1.

to be settled. Beawes was not the only writer to comment on the increase in insurance litigation. James Park made much the same point.[57] John Wesket noted that insurance 'is of all the transactions among mankind the most abundant source of disputes and perplexities'.[58]

Park, in his description of the law before 1750, outlined the main challenge facing Lord Mansfield and his fellow judges: 'there have been but few positive regulations upon insurance, the principles, on which they were founded, could never have been widely diffused, nor very generally known.'[59] A House of Commons Committee had proposed reforming marine insurance in the mid-1740s, but these recommendations were never implemented.[60] Despite a handful of authorities on insurance from the turn of the century, the comparative paucity of case law and statutory guidance was such that even Lord Mansfield occasionally felt exasperated.[61]

Mercantile practice may have had some influence when it came to developing negotiable instruments after 1750, but because, in relative terms, there were even fewer existing authorities on the subject of insurance, mercantile practice was even more crucial, just as in earlier attempts to deal with bills of exchange.[62] Special juries of merchants also had a particularly important role.[63] Those involved in insurance and shipping were called as expert witnesses.[64]

57 James Park, *A System of the Law of Marine Insurances*, 1st edn (London, 1786), preface. The preface is reproduced in the second edition of 1790. References are to the second edition.

58 John Wesket, *A Complete Digest of the Theory, Laws, and Practice of Insurance* (London, 1781), p. i.

59 Park, *Marine Insurance*, p. xliv. For similar remarks, see John Millar, *Elements of the Law of Insurance* (Edinburgh, 1787), pp. v–vi. Park and Millar had a point but were still guilty of exaggerating the absence of earlier authorities, see W.S. Holdsworth, 'The Early History of the Contract of Insurance' (1917) 17 *Columbia Law Review* 85.

60 A summary of the proposals is reported in (1747) House of Commons Journal 597–9. One of the recommendations on losses that could be recovered was in any event judicially introduced in *Lewis* v. *Rucker* (1761) 2 Burr 1167.

61 *Hamilton* v. *Mendes* (1761) 2 Burr 1198, 1214.

62 On the importance of mercantile practice, see *Gardiner* v. *Croasdale* (1760) 2 Burr 904, 907.

63 *Lewis* v. *Rucker* (1761) 2 Burr 1167, 1168.

64 Deidre Dwyer, 'Expert Evidence in the English Civil Courts 1550–1800' (2007) 28 *Journal of Legal History* 93, 100 for examples of expert witnesses mentioned in the printed reports at this time across a range of litigation. The evidence of expert witnesses could have an extremely important bearing on the outcome. For example, in *Harrington* v. *Halked* (1778), Oldham, *Mansfield Manuscripts*, vol. I, pp. 549–50, Park, *Marine*

Underwriters[65] and others with knowledge of particular types of insurance[66] were also consulted informally. John Wesket may even have had Lord Mansfield in mind when he complained that a judge may be 'as often misled as assisted, by these extrajudicial and *ex parte* conversations'.[67]

Lord Mansfield's claim that the law of insurance 'is the same all over the world',[68] if not strictly true, meant that he was prepared to utilise a cosmopolitan range of sources. Insurance contracts were not unique in this respect. Lord Mansfield referred to Roman law[69] and Civilian writers in other contexts.[70] The fact that ships were not confined by jurisdictional boundaries, combined with the international nature of marine insurance, meant that the law of insurance was particularly well suited to this sort of treatment.[71] In *Goss* v. *Withers*,[72] having sought the advice of Sir George Lee[73] on Admiralty practice, Lord Mansfield went on to refer to Grotius,[74] Cornelius van Bynkershoek[75] – who he had praised in the course of argument[76] – Johannes Voet[77] and the Roman law on prize.[78]

Insurances, pp. 302–3 sea captains were called to comment on a ship's course on a question of deviation.

65 *Glover* v. *Black* (1763) 3 Burr 1394; *Camden* v. *Cowley* (1763) 1 W Bla 417, Oldham, *Mansfield Manuscripts*, vol. I, pp. 500–1, fn. 6; *Wilson* v. *Smith* (1764) 3 Burr 1550, 1556.

66 *Salvador* v. *Hopkins* (1765) 3 Burr 1707, 1714.

67 Wesket, *Digest*, p. xviii.

68 *Pelly* v. *Royal Exchange Assurance Co.* (1757) 1 Burr 341, 347. Wesket, *Digest*, p. ii was a firm supporter of this type of approach.

69 Lord Mansfield made use of Roman law in many different contexts besides the law of contract: *Windham* v. *Chetwynd* (1757) 1 Burr 414, 425–6; *Hamilton* v. *Mendes* (1761) 2 Burr 1198, 1214; *Frogmorton, ex dimiss' Bramstone* v. *Holyday et al.* (1765) 2 Burr 1618, 1624; *Hogan* v. *Jackson* (1775) 1 Cowp 299, 305. On Lord Mansfield's admiration for Roman law, see Campbell, *Lives*, vol. II, p. 327.

70 On the influence of Civilian writers on Lord Mansfield, see Daniel Coquillette, 'Legal Ideology and Incorporation IV: The Nature of Civilian Influence on Modern Anglo-American Commercial Law' (1987) 67 *Boston University Law Review* 877, 949–62.

71 *Mayne* v. *Walter* (1782) 3 Doug 79.

72 (1758) 2 Burr 683.

73 Lee was the brother of Sir William Lee, Chief Justice of the King's Bench between 1737–1754. George Lee was a noted authority on Ecclesiastical and Admiralty matters, see W.P. Courtney, rev. Matthew Kilburn, 'Lee, Sir George', *Oxford Dictionary of National Biography*.

74 (1758) 2 Burr 683, 694. For other references to Grotius and Pufendorf, see *Jones* v. *Randall* (1774) Lofft 383, 386; *Robinson* v. *Bland* (1760) 1 Wm Bla 234, 239.

75 Lord Mansfield spoke of his admiration for Bynkershoek during the course of argument. His *De Domino Maris* was published in 1702.

76 (1758) 2 Burr 683, 692.

77 The relevant passage is found in Percival Gane (ed.), Joannes Voet, *The Selective Voet Being the Commentary on the Pandects* (Durban: Butterworth, 1957), book 49, title 15.

78 (1758) 2 Burr 683, 693. On prize more generally, see Oldham, *Mansfield Manuscripts*, vol. I, pp. 656–71.

The law of insurance provides a particularly striking example of a more general trend which saw Common lawyers becoming more receptive to Civilian and Natural law ideas.[79] Many of these works were readily accessible in England[80] and began to appear more freely in the argument of counsel.[81] Buller J. would later recall that 'Most of us have heard these principles stated, reasoned upon, enlarged, and explained, till we have been lost in admiration at the strength and stretch of human understanding'.[82] It is more difficult to be certain about the precise patterns of influence. In 1802, Lawrence J. would state that the law of insurance was largely derived from foreign writers,[83] but the context of his remarks was significant. He made the claim, in an attempt to discredit the old Common law position, that it was impossible to insure a profit.[84] On some occasions Civilian sources may simply be used to add lustre to arguments that were essentially taken from the Common law or mercantile practice. There may be more than a grain of truth in the remarks of the defence counsel in *Goss* v. *Withers*, whose withering response to an

[79] See Coquillette, 'Legal Ideology'; C.P. Rogers, 'Continental Literature and the Development of the Common Law by the King's Bench: c.1750–1800', in Vito Piergiovanni (ed.), *Courts and the Development of Commercial Law* (Berlin: Duncker & Humblot, 1987), pp. 161–93; P.G. Stein, *The Character and Influence of the Roman Civil Law* (London: Hambledon, 1988), pp. 209–29; D. Ibbetson, 'Natural Law and Common Law' (2001) 5 *Edinburgh Law Review* 4.

[80] Holdsworth, *History of English Law*, vol. XII, pp. 605–46. For a more pessimistic view, see Wesket, *Digest*, p. ii: 'Several of the books in foreign languages, mentioned in the annexed list are in great esteem and use among intelligent and prudent merchants abroad, as well as among lawyers; and contain divers very interesting matters expressly on the subject of Insurance; although they are but little known and some of them not met with, in England.'

[81] For examples across a range of subjects, see *Pelly* v. *Royal Exchange Assurance Co.* (1757) 1 Burr 341, 343; *Goss* v. *Withers* (1758) 2 Burr 683, 685–7, 688; *Luke* v. *Lyde* (1759) 2 Burr 882, 886; *Robinson* v. *Bland* (1760) 1 Wm Bla 234, 238–9; *Hamilton* v. *Mendes* (1761) 2 Burr 1198, 1201; *Ross* v. *Walker* (1765) 2 Wil KB 264; *Ricord* v. *Bettenham* (1765) 1 Wm Bla 563, 567; *London Warf's Case* (1766) 1 Wm Bla 581, 584; *Blesard* v. *Hirst* (1770) 5 Burr 2670, 2671; *Earl of March* v. *Pigot* (1771) 5 Burr 2802, 2804; *Vallejo* v. *Wheeler* (1774) 1 Cowp 143, 145, 147; *Rich* v. *Coe* (1777) 2 Cowp 636, 637–8; *Salomons* v. *Stavely* (1783) 3 Doug 298, 299; *Yates* v. *Hall* (1785) 1 TR 73, 74; *Nutt* v. *Bourdieu* (1786) 1 TR 323, 326; *Lickbarrow* v. *Mason* (1787) 2 TR 63, 65.

[82] *Lickbarrow* v. *Mason* (1787) 2 TR 63, 73.

[83] *Barclay* v. *Cousins* (1802) 2 East 544, 548.

[84] Michael Lobban, 'Commercial Law', in William Cornish, Stuart Anderson, Raymond Cocks, Michael Lobban, Patrick Polden and Keith Smith, *The Oxford History of the Laws of England, Vol. XII 1820–1914: Private Law* (Oxford: Oxford University Press, 2010), p. 686.

opponent who had reeled off a list of Civilian writers was: 'as to Molloy and Malines – almost anything may be proved by citations from them'.[85]

A series of decisions began to shed some light on the nature of the contract of insurance. In the 1760s Lord Mansfield had asserted that 'policies of insurance are more governed by principles of equity, than anything else'.[86] One of the ways in which the parties were required to act equitably was in the matter of disclosure. In *Carter* v. *Boehm*, Lord Mansfield explained that:

> Insurance is a contract based on speculation. The special facts, upon which the contingent chance is to be computed, lie most commonly in the knowledge of the insured only: the under-writer trusts to his representation, and proceeds upon confidence that he does not keep back any circumstances in his knowledge, to mislead the under-writer into a belief that the circumstance does not exist, and to induce him to estimate the risque, as if it did not exist.[87]

The provenance of the duty of disclosure was not discussed. In *Da Costa* v. *Scandret*,[88] forty years before, relief was granted in Equity after an attempt to claim on an insurance policy where the insured had failed to disclose at the time that the policy was entered into that the ship was in great danger. This was justified on the basis of fraud, a broad notion in Equity at the time. Lord Mansfield had borrowed from Equity on other occasions.[89] Yates J. would attribute the duty of disclosure to Natural law.[90] In fact, there was no need to seek justification in either Equity or Natural law. A clear line of authority existed at Common law. At the end of the seventeenth century, Holt C.J. held that where goods were insured on the basis that they were the goods of a German, and in fact belonged to a Frenchman, at a time when England was at war with France,[91] a fraud was committed and a claim on the contract barred.[92] In *Seaman* v. *Fonereau*, Lee C.J. went further when he said 'as these are contracts on chance, each party ought to know all the circumstances'.[93] The following year the same judge added, 'These contracts are made upon mutual faith

85 (1758) 2 Burr 683, 690.

86 *Stevenson* v. *Snow* (1761) 1 Wm Bla 315, 316. These remarks do not appear in Burrow's report of the case.

87 (1766) 3 Burr 1905, 1909. 88 (1723) 2 P Wms 170.

89 For example, in the liberalisation of money had and received in *Moses* v. *Macferlan* (1760) 2 Burr 1005; 1 Wm Bla 219.

90 *Hodgson* v. *Richardson* (1764) 1 Wm Bla 463, 465.

91 As a result of the Nine Years War which took place between 1688 and 1697.

92 *Anon* (1693) Skin 327. 93 (1742) 2 Stra 1183.

and credit, and that to conceal such circumstances which may make any difference in the adventure is fraudulent'.[94]

The requirement of disclosure reflected the way in which the insurance industry worked. Brokers were at the centre. Reputation and trust were important, along with a degree of self-regulation.[95] These factors affected the way in which the principle of disclosure was applied in practice. In *Da Costa* v. *Alcock*, Lord Mansfield gave details of an exception which proved the rule:

> In insuring merchant ships, all possible information ought to be given to the insurers; but the case of privateers was an exception from this rule. The insured are not to give them any information of their destination or where they are to cruise.[96]

The application of disclosure involved allocating the risk between underwriter and insured. When an underwriter knew or *ought to have known* material facts about which the insured remained silent then, as in *Carter* v. *Boehm*, the risk fell on him.[97] Where both parties contracted in ignorance of some material fact, the risk also fell on the underwriter.[98] Trade usage was important in determining where the risk should fall: 'Every underwriter is presumed to be acquainted with the practice of the trade that he insures . . . if he does not know it, he ought to inform himself.'[99]

Sometimes the burden was on the insured to disclose the information.[100] At other times the underwriter was under a duty to find out the information for themselves.[101] In the way that the decision sought to clarify the grounds for avoiding an insurance contract, *Carter* v. *Boehm* was also about showing 'how, and why, there had to be limits to an

94 *Rooke* v. *Thurmond* (1743) reproduced in Nicholas Magens, *An Essay on Insurances*, 2 vols. (London, 1755), vol. I, p. 85.

95 These themes are explored in Christopher Kingston, 'Marine Insurance in Britain and America 1720–1844: A Comparative Institutional Analysis' (2007) 67 *Journal of Economic History* 379, 385–7.

96 From the *London Chronicle* 28 July 1781 reproduced in Oldham, *Mansfield Manuscripts*, vol. I, p. 565. Privateering was the practice whereby the Government hired private ships to attack enemy vessels, see David Starkey, *British Privateering Enterprise in the Eighteenth Century* (Exeter: University of Exeter Press, 1990).

97 (1766) 3 Burr 1905, 1910. See also *Planché* v. *Fletcher* (1779) 1 Doug 251.

98 *Mayne* v. *Walter* (1782) 3 Doug 79.

99 *Noble* v. *Kennoway* (1780) 2 Doug 510, 513.

100 *Hodgson* v. *Richardson* (1764) 1 Wm Bla 463, 465.

101 *Noble* v. *Kennoway* (1780) 2 Doug 510, 513.

insurer's entitlement to avoid liability'.[102] Where the burden was on the insured to disclose a material fact,[103] and he fraudulently[104] or actively concealed that information, then the contract was void.[105]

By the 1770s insurance contracts were increasingly sophisticated in the way that they were drafted.[106] In order to give himself a firm basis for withholding payment, a cautious underwriter was well advised to include as many express warranties as possible.[107] The content of warranties and other terms were determined by reference to trade practice.[108] In this respect, Lord Mansfield was also following a well-trodden path.[109] As early as 1743 in *Tierney* v. *Etherington* at Guildhall, Lee C.J. held that 'policies ought to be construed largely, and for the benefit of the insured; and according to the course of trade and methods usual at the place'.[110] Marine insurance[111] was an early example of standard form contracting which became widespread in the nineteenth century.[112]

Writing in the 1760s, Blackstone was full of praise for recent developments:

102 Stephen Watterson, 'Carter v. Boehm (1766)', in Charles Mitchell and Paul Mitchell (eds.), *Landmark Cases in the Law of Contract* (Oxford: Hart, 2008), pp. 59–118.

103 *Hodgson* v. *Richardson* (1764) 1 Wm Bla 463, 465.

104 *Tyler* v. *Horne* (1783) Park, *Marine Insurances*, p. 218, Oldham, *Mansfield Manuscripts*, vol. I, p. 589; *Pawson* v. *Watson* (1778) 2 Cowp 785, 788.

105 *Hodgson* v. *Richardson* (1764) 1 Wm Bla 463; *Fernandes* v. *da Costa* (1764) Park, *Marine Insurances*, pp. 177–8, Oldham, *Mansfield Manuscripts*, vol. I, p. 502; *Fillis* v. *Brutton* (1782) Park, *Marine Insurances*, p. 182, Oldham, *Mansfield Manuscripts*, vol. I, p. 571. A concealment need not be active: where it arose through a mistake, the contract could also be void, see *Carter* v. *Boehm* (1766) 3 Burr 1905, 1910.

106 *Vallejo* v. *Wheeler* (1774) 1 Cowp 143, 145.

107 *Woolmer* v. *Muilman* (1763) 1 Wm Bla 427, 3 Burr 1419; *Bean* v. *Stupart* (1778) 1 Doug 11; *De Hahn* v. *Hartley* (1786) 1 TR 343. Park, *Marine Insurances*, p. 325 identified warranty as to the time of sailing, warranty as to convoy and warranty of neutrality as three common types. Warranties could also be implied, but implied warranties were confined to fundamental matters like seaworthiness: *Eden* v. *Parkison* (1781) 2 Doug 732, 735; *Schoolbred* v. *Nutt* (1782) Oldham, *Mansfield Manuscripts*, vol. I, p. 586.

108 *Pelly* v. *Royal Exchange Insurance* (1757) 1 Burr 341, 347–8.

109 *Bond* v. *Gonsales* (1704) 2 Salk 445, Holt 469.

110 The case is unreported but appears in the course of argument in *Pelly* v. *Royal Exchange Insurance* (1757) 1 Burr 341, 343–4.

111 For examples, see Wesket, *Digest*, pp. 338–9.

112 Steve Hedley, 'From Individualism to Communitarianism? The Case of Standard Forms', in Thomas Watkin (ed.), *Legal Record and Historical Reality* (London: Hambledon Press, 1989), p. 234; Ross Cranston, 'The Rise and Rise of Standard Form Contracts: International Commodity Sales 1800–1970', in Ross Cranston, Jan Ramberg and Jacob Zeigler (eds.), *Commercial Law Challenges in the Twenty First Century* (Stockholm: Iustus Forlag, 2007), p. 11.

> The learning relating to marine insurance hath of late years been greatly improved by a series of decisions, which have now established the law in such variety of cases, that (if well and judiciously collected) they would form a very complete title in a code of commercial jurisprudence.[113]

Thomas Parker, in the preface to his work on shipping and insurance, contended that Lord Mansfield had rendered the law so 'plain and clear' that 'those who consult the judgments ... may frequently find it unnecessary to bring new questions to trial'.[114] John Wesket was rather less sanguine:

> What, in any country, could be more preposterous and intolerably grievous; or more reproachful to a great commercial Nation, in particular; than the Administration of private Justice, in the Affairs of MERCHANTS should be solely in the Hands of Inconclusiveness![115]

Wesket may have been unduly pessimistic, but the law of insurance was certainly still not free from difficulties. Warranties, deviation and the nature of indemnity in particular generated plenty of litigation.[116] One of the most intractable problems was the way that insurance was used as a vehicle for wagers, leading Lord Mansfield to complain that insurance was 'perverted by its being turned into a wager'.[117] The problem had evidently become sufficiently serious that it was damaging confidence in the insurance market:

> They render insurance suspected, foreigners apprehensive, the security of commerce precarious, contaminate probity, create ill will, as amongst other gamblers, produce lame ducks, and may in time introduce at Lloyds as well as Jonathan's such apposite and polite appellations as Bull and Bear.[118]

Certain types of wager were prohibited by statute.[119] These came to include wager by marine insurance[120] and life insurance or any other event where the 'person ... shall have no interest whatsoever'.[121] An

[113] William Blackstone, *Commentaries on the Laws of England*, 4 vols. (Oxford, 1766), vol. II, p. 461.

[114] Thomas Parker, *The laws of shipping and insurance* (London, 1775), p. v.

[115] Wesket, *Digest*, p. xvi.

[116] Oldham, *Mansfield Manuscripts*, vol. I, pp. 459–69.

[117] *Kent* v. *Bird* (1777) 2 Cowp 583, 585.

[118] Wesket, *Digest*, p. lvi.

[119] Wagers on the War of Spanish Succession were an early casualty of statutory regulation: (1708) 7 Ann c. 16.

[120] (1746) 19 Geo II c. 37. On the application of the statute, see *Kent* v. *Bird* (1777) 2 Cowp 583; *Grant* v. *Parkinson* (1781) 3 Doug 16.

[121] (1774) 14 Geo III c. 48.

unreported decision, *Mary Spencer's Case*,[122] illustrates some of the potential problems. Underwriters refused to pay £5,000 on a policy taken out by a widow on her husband's life. The underwriters argued that no interest was proved on the basis that her husband had arranged for an annuity of £500 to be paid to his wife on his death. Lord Mansfield allowed the widow to recover but the decision demonstrates that the statute may sometimes have been difficult to apply, even when on the face of it the facts appear to be a long way from a wager. On another occasion Lord Mansfield made the distinction on the grounds that:

> There are two sorts of policies of insurance; mercantile and gaming policies. The first sort are contracts of indemnity, and of indemnity only . . . The second sort may be in the same in form; but in them there is no contract of indemnity, because there is no interest upon which a loss can accrue.[123]

The plaintiff's absence of an interest was a well-established way of ruling out a legitimate insurance contract which long predated the use of that form of words in the statute.[124] But the real difficulty for those judges who were uneasy with wagers, was that unless prohibited by statute, wagers were valid unless contrary to morality or public policy.[125] If Wesket was correct, then 'a very slight matter takes the policy out of the statute'.[126] Mercantile practice proved to be particularly potent in shaping insurance contracts were there was a relative dearth of earlier authority. It also had a part to play outside more obviously mercantile contracts, such as negotiable instruments and insurance, where it was capable of influencing mainstream contract doctrine more indirectly.

The doctrine of consideration and contractual interpretation

In *Pillans* v. *Van Mierop*[127] the King's Bench held that an agreement to accept a bill of exchange was equivalent to actually accepting it.[128] Yates J. found consideration for the agreement using a traditional analysis based on reciprocity.[129] Lord Mansfield on the other hand used the

[122] (1777) a note appears in Wesket, *Digest*, pp. 336–8.
[123] *Lowry* v. *Bourdieu* (1780) 2 Doug 468, 470, see also *Kent* v. *Bird* (1777) 2 Cowp 583, 585.
[124] *Wittingham* v. *Thornborough* (1690) Pre Cha 20; *Sadlers' Co.* v. *Badcock* (1743) 2 Atk 554.
[125] *Da Costa* v. *Jones* (1778) 2 Cowp 729.
[126] Wesket, *Digest*, p. 340. Wesket specifically mentioned the statute of 1774.
[127] (1765) 3 Burr 1663. [128] (1765) 3 Burr 1663, 1669, 1672–3, 1674.
[129] (1765) 3 Burr 1663, 1673–4.

opportunity to suggest that, 'in commercial cases amongst merchants, the want of consideration is not an objection'.[130] Consideration remained central to the Common law mind-set. It still had to be alleged in a declaration on a bill of exchange until the early nineteenth century,[131] albeit the fact that consideration was presumed left the doctrine somewhat diminished in status.[132] Negotiable instruments could be explained away as a special case. To go further and argue that a commercial contract between merchants, when reduced into writing, removed the need for consideration, was more radical still. Although he drew no explicit parallels, it is quite possible that Lord Mansfield was influenced by the practice of bills of exchange and wanted to extend it into other types of written contracts between merchants. The expectations of commercial parties were strongly emphasised when the case was first argued.[133] He may also have had his native Scots law in mind.[134] Whilst Scots law preferred formality over consideration,[135] the very transactions where formality was relaxed were identical to those ones where Lord Mansfield was proposing to abandon consideration.[136] It was difficult to justify this position with reference to the mainstream

[130] (1765) 3 Burr 1663, 1669.

[131] Edward Lawes, *A Practical Treatise on Pleading in Assumpsit* (London: W. Reed, 1810), pp. 49, 302; Joseph Chitty, *A Treatise on the Parties to Actions, the Forms of Action and on Pleading*, 2 vols. (London: J. Butterworth & W. Clark, 1809), vol. I, p. 295.

[132] If the defendant could show duress or fraud, the plaintiff was required to prove consideration, see Rogers, *Bills and Notes*, p. 241; Holden, *Negotiable Instruments*, pp. 102–3; Joseph Chitty, *A Practical Treatise on Bills of Exchange, Checks on Bankers, Promissory Notes, Bankers' Cash Notes and Bank Notes*, 3rd edn (London: W. Clark, 1809), pp. 9, 31; John Byles, *A Practical Treatise on the Law of Bills of Exchange, Promissory Notes, Bank-Notes, Bankers' Cash-Notes and Checks*, 2nd edn (London: S. Sweet, 1834), pp. 60–1; *Bishop* v. *Young* (1800) 2 B & P 78, 81; *Holliday* v. *Atkinson* (1826) 5 B & C 501; *Guichard* v. *Roberts* (1763) 1 Wm Bla 445.

[133] (1765) 3 Burr 1663, 1666. For other references to the commercial nature of the transaction, see (1765) 3 Burr 1663, 1669 (Lord Mansfield), 1672 (Wilmot J.), 1675 (Aston J.). On this aspect of the decision, see N. Benke, '"No Inefficacy Arises Merely from the Naked Promise" Bermerkungen zu Consideration und Versprechen in Pillans v. Van Mierop (1765)' (1987) 14 *Ius Commune* 1.

[134] Frederick Pollock somewhat unexpectedly noticed the same parallel: Frederick Pollock, *Principles of Contract at Law and in Equity* (Oxford: Oxford University Press, 1876), p. 153.

[135] Gerhard Lubbe, 'Formation of Contract', in Kenneth Reid and Reinhard Zimmermann (eds.), *A History of Private Law in Scotland*, 2 vols. (Oxford: Oxford University Press, 2000), vol. II, p. 24.

[136] D.M. Walker (ed.), Viscount Stair, *The Institution of the Law of Scotland* (Edinburgh: University of Edinburgh and Glasgow Press, 1981), 1.10.3; Lord Bankton, *An Institute of the Laws of Scotland 1751* (Edinburgh: Stair Society, 1993), 1.11.31.

Common law. All of the examples used to illustrate the point were concerned with deeds rather than written contracts.[137] Lord Mansfield also referred to the Statute of Frauds, which placed a requirement of writing on certain types of agreements before they could be enforced. But this analogy was also flawed given that under the Statute, writing was an additional rather than alternative requirement to consideration.[138]

Wilmot J. was just as alive to the needs of commerce as Lord Mansfield,[139] but in *Pillans* v. *Van Mierop* he put forward a different argument for reforming consideration. Described by his son as 'well versed in the Civil law', which he considered to be 'the best introduction to the knowledge of Law in general, as well as a leading feature in the Laws of most nations of Europe',[140] Wilmot J. began his judgment with a discussion of the Roman contract by *stipulatio*, noting that the binding force of such agreements came from formalities rather than consideration.[141] Such formalities were designed, he said, 'to put people upon attention and reflection, and to prevent obscurity and uncertainty'.[142] Writing performed the same function as a 'guard against rash inconsiderate declarations'.[143] Wilmot J. then moved on to Natural Law, implying that writing was good evidence of deliberate purpose.[144] His analysis appears to involve a threefold division of contract between written contracts, formal contracts and contracts that are neither formal nor in writing. Elegant though this approach appears at first glance, it jarred very badly with English law which only recognised two categories of contract: those that were made by deed and those that were not.

137 (1765) 3 Burr 1663, 1669.

138 (1677) 29 Car II c. 3. This point was made by Perryn B., Eyre B. and Blackstone J. in *Rann* v. *Hughes* (1770) in the Exchequer Chamber, LI MS Misc. 130 f. 134.

139 *Grant* v. *Vaughan* (1764) 3 Burr 1516, 1528.

140 John Wilmot, *Memories of the Life of The Right Honourable Sir John Eardley Wilmot Knt. Late Lord Chief Justice of the Court of Common Pleas*, 2nd edn (London: J. Nicholls, 1811), p. 210.

141 (1765) 3 Burr 1663, 1670.

142 (1765) 3 Burr 1663, 1670. On stipulation, see Peter Stein (ed.), W.W. Buckland, *A Textbook of Roman Law from Augustus to Justinian*, 3rd edn (Cambridge: Cambridge University Press, 1963), pp. 433–9; Reinhard Zimmermann, *The Law of Obligations: Roman Foundations of the Civilian Tradition* (Oxford: Oxford University Press,1996), pp. 69–70.

143 (1765) 3 Burr 1663, 1670.

144 (1765) 3 Burr 1663, 1670. Wilmot J. referred to Grotius and Pufendorf: F. Kelsey (trans.), Hugo Grotius, *The Rights of War and Peace (1646 edn)* (Oxford: Oxford University Press, 1925), 2.11.5; Charles and William Oldfather (trans.), Samuel Pufendorf, *Of the Law of Nature and Nations (1688 edn)* (Oxford: Oxford University Press, 1934), 3.5.11.

Contracts in the first category were always enforceable in the absence of a valid defence.[145] Those in the second were unenforceable without good consideration.

A decade later Lord Mansfield appears to have come round to Wilmot J.'s position. In *Williamson* v. *Losh*, an unreported decision,[146] he was prepared to accept that a non-commercial agreement that was written down and witnessed was binding in the absence of consideration. He went on to explain that:

> the doctrine as to *nuda pacta* was borrowed from the civil law, intended only to guard against rash promises and such as were given inconsistently or made in consequence of surprize . . . and he could not find one case in which it had been determined that a gift or a promise to give, in writing attested by witnesses had been set aside as a *nudum pactum*.

Within a quarter of a century the traditional approach would be re-asserted. This particular attempt to reform consideration was very emphatically stamped on by both the Exchequer Chamber and House of Lords in *Rann* v. *Hughes*. In the Exchequer Chamber, any suggestion that consideration was no longer required was said to be contrary to all authority.[147] It was pointed out that to allow such agreements to be enforced would create a new third category of obligations in addition to simple contracts and specialty.[148] The House of Lords agreed.[149] Baron Skynner made the point:

> All contracts are by the laws of England distinguished into agreements by specialty, and agreements by parol; nor is there any such third class as some of the counsel have endeavoured to maintain, as contracts in writing. If they be merely written and not specialties, they are parol, and a consideration must be proved.[150]

145 Defences to a deed included *non est factum* and duress: A.W. Brian Simpson, *A History of the Common Law of Contract: The Rise of the Action of Assumpsit*, pbk edn (Oxford: Oxford University Press, 1987), pp. 98–9.

146 Part of a manuscript report of the case is reproduced in Oldham, *Age of Mansfield*, pp. 85–6. A note on the case can also be found in Joseph Chitty, *A Practical Treatise on Bills of Exchange, Checks on Bankers, Promissory Notes, Bankers' Cash Notes and Bank Notes*, 5th edn (London: S. Brooke, 1818), pp. 93–4.

147 (1776) LI MS Misc. 130 f. 134. Eyre B. and Hotham B. pointed out that *Sharington* v. *Sharington* (1565) 1 Plow 298 was not in point because the case concerned a deed rather than a written agreement.

148 (1776) LI MS Misc. 130 f. 134, Eyre B. and Hotham B.

149 (1778) 4 Bro PC 27, 7 TR 350 note, LI MS Misc. 130 f. 74.

150 7 TR 350 note. For similar statements post *Rann* v. *Hughes*, see *Randall* v. *Morgan* (1806) 12 Ves Jun 67, 73; *Barrell* v. *Trussell* (1811) 4 Taunt 117, 121.

Consideration was too strongly entrenched to be overthrown in such a direct manner. If there was any attempt to argue that Lord Mansfield's more limited commercial exception was good law, it has left no trace. As John Austin noted somewhat sadly, many years later 'the doctrine of Lord Mansfield and Wilmot is the just one. The contrary opinion, however, is consistent with the actual law.'[151]

Then, as now, many disputes turned on contractual interpretation. The most contentious question of contractual interpretation of the eighteenth century was whether or not the performance by one party was dependent on the performance of the other.[152] The traditional default rule was that performance by each party was independent from the other.[153] In *Thomas* v. *Cadwallader*, Willes C.J. complained that there were too many old cases to be overruled, but that he disliked the outcome on the grounds that that result was to 'make two actions instead of one, and to a circuity of action and multiplying actions, both which the law so much abhors'.[154] Independency was still only a presumption. The parties remained at liberty to make their promises dependent. In the end it all came down to the way that the contract was interpreted. *Pordage* v. *Cole*[155] saw a relaxation of the older literal approach to interpretation,[156] but the process was still dependent on rules of interpretation, and so remained highly mechanical.[157]

By the late eighteenth century two different methods of interpreting conditions, both of which probably drew on earlier practice,[158] were

[151] He made these remarks in notes of a lecture that were never actually delivered. These are contained in Robert Campbell (ed.), John Austin, *Lectures on Jurisprudence or the Philosophy of Positive Law*, 2 vols. (London: John Murray, 1869), vol. II, p. 941.

[152] S.J. Stoljar, *A History of Contract at Common Law* (Canberra: Australian National University Press, 1975), pp. 148–63; S. Stoljar, 'Dependent and Independent Promises' (1956–1958) 2 *Sydney Law Review* 217.

[153] For a discussion of these issues, see Tariq Baloch, *Unjust Enrichment and Contract* (Oxford: Hart, 2009), pp. 98–100.

[154] (1744) Willes 496, 500. For a discussion of *Oddin* v. *Duffield* (1716) LI MS Hill 80 f. 45, a decision preserved in manuscript which went the other way, see James Oldham, 'Underreported and Underrated: The Court of Common Pleas in the Eighteenth Century', in Hendrik Hartog *et al.* (eds.), *Law as Culture and Culture as Law* (Madison, Wis.: Madison House, 2000), pp. 131–2.

[155] (1669) 1 Wms Saund 319, 1 Lev 274, T Raym 183, 2 Keb 542, 2 Keb 533, 1 Sid 423.

[156] Stoljar, *History*, pp. 151–8.

[157] *Thorpe* v. *Thorpe* (1702) 1 Ld Raym 662, 12 Mod 455; *Blackwell* v. *Nash* (1722) 1 Stra 535, 8 Mod 105; *Dawson* v. *Myer* (1726) 1 Stra 712.

[158] For the historical antecedents with reference to some manuscript sources, see Baloch, *Unjust Enrichment*, pp. 102, 104.

coming to the fore. In *Kingston* v. *Preston*[159] Lord Mansfield, having accepted the existence of concurrent conditions,[160] emphasised that conditions should be interpreted according to the intentions of the parties.[161] Ashhurst J. and Aston J. agreed,[162] and this quickly became the standard view. Lord Kenyon's later remarks were typical:

> It has frequently been said, and common sense seems to justify it, that conditions are to be construed to be either precedent or subsequent, according to the fair intention of the parties to be collected from the instrument, and that technical words (if there be any to encounter such intention, and there are none in this case,) should give way to that intention.[163]

Conditions were also defined as terms which went to the whole of the consideration. This line of reasoning may have originated in Chancery,[164] but it was given firm focus in *Boone* v. *Eyre*,[165] where the plaintiff conveyed the equity of redemption of a plantation in the West Indies and the slaves upon it for £500 and an annuity of £160 per annum for life. The conveyance also contained a covenant that the plaintiff had good title to the plantation and was lawfully possessed of the slaves. In an action of covenant, the plaintiff assigned non-payment of the annuity and the defendant pleaded that at the time of making the deed the plaintiff was not in lawful possession of the slaves. Lord Mansfield held that:

> The distinction is very clear, where mutual covenants go to the whole of the consideration on both sides, they are mutual conditions, the one precedent to the other. But where they go only to a part, where a breach may be paid for in damages, there the defendant has a remedy on his covenant, and shall not plead it as a condition precedent.

[159] (1773) Lofft 194 also cited in argument in *Jones* v. *Barkley* (1781) 2 Doug 684, 689–91. For a discussion of *Kingston* v. *Preston*, see James Oldham, 'Detecting Non-Fiction: Sleuthing among Manuscript Case Reports for What Was Really Said', in Chantal Stebbings (ed.), *Law Reporting in Britain* (London: Hambledon Press, 1995), pp. 140–4.

[160] Stoljar, *History*, pp. 157–9; *Glazebrook* v. *Woodrow* (1799) 8 TR 366, 371, 374.

[161] He was probably not the first judge to think in this way about conditions. There are earlier hints but nothing so concrete in *Thorpe* v. *Thorpe* (1702) 12 Mod 455, 460; *Russen* v. *Coleby* (1733) 7 Mod 236.

[162] (1773) Lofft 194, 198.

[163] *Porter* v. *Shephard* (1796) 6 TR 665, 668. For similar statements see: *Glazebrook* v. *Woodrow* (1799) 8 TR 366; *Campbell* v. *Jones* (1796) 6 TR 570; *Havelock* v. *Geddes* (1809) 10 East 555; *Storer* v. *Gordon* (1814) 3 M & S 308.

[164] This is suggested by Baloch, *Unjust Enrichment*, p. 105.

[165] (1777) 1 H Bla 273 (note); Stoljar, *History*, pp. 159–61.

Both of these approaches would continue to cast a shadow in the nineteenth century. These decisions reflected judicial attempts to create workable definitions. Juries also had an important role to play in determining whether those terms had been breached.

Contract law and the limits of the jury

The jury continued to remain critical to the smooth operation of the law of contract. The relationship between judge and jury was not always harmonious. Something of its flavour can be gleaned by using litigation on breach of warranty in horse sales as a case study. The period after 1750 was something of a golden age of horse sale litigation, as a combination of judicial and jury activism, and a growth in legal and non-legal literature thrust these transactions, which featured in at least one popular novel of the time,[166] to prominence. The form of the claim also evolved. The traditional way of trying a breach of warranty lay in tort rather than contract using trespass on the case for deceit. In *Stuart* v. *Wilkins*,[167] Ashhurst J. held that, 'Whatever may have been the old form, I believe it has been long settled that this form of action is right; and having been long established, I am of opinion that it ought to be supported.'[168] Buller J. agreed that assumpsit for breach of warranty had existed 'ever since I have known anything of practice'.[169] There is an example in Dudley Ryder's notebooks from the 1750s[170] and an even earlier one in a leading abridgment in which this method of pleading was described as 'settled'.[171] Changes in the way that breach of warranty was framed provide no indication about the definition and operation of a warranty.

The purchase of a horse remained fraught with difficulty.[172] Veterinary medicine was still fairly primitive[173] and the inexperienced

[166] Arthur Friedman (ed.), Oliver Goldsmith, *The Vicar of Wakefield* (Oxford: Oxford University Press, 2006), p. 60. The novel was originally published in 1766.

[167] (1778) 1 Doug 18. [168] *Ibid.*, p. 21.

[169] *Ibid.*, p. 21. Buller began in practice as a Special Pleader in 1765.

[170] *Ross* v. *Edgar* (1754) LI Harrowby MS Doc. 13 f. 62 cited by Michael Lobban, 'Contractual Fraud in Law and Equity' (1997) 17 *Oxford Journal of Legal Studies* 441, 460, fn. 116.

[171] Matthew Bacon, *A New Abridgment of the Law*, 5 vols. (London, 1736), vol. I, p. 52.

[172] ER Gent, *The Experienc'd Farrier or Farring Completed*, 4th edn (London, 1720), p. 63.

[173] The late eighteenth century nevertheless witnessed the origins of a distinct veterinary profession, see L.P. Pugh, *From Farriery to Veterinary Medicine 1785–1795* (Cambridge: Heffer, 1962).

buyer was particularly at risk of being hoodwinked.[174] Henry Bracken warned that, 'in the art of horsemanship, the most difficult part is that of giving proper directions for the purchasing of a horse free from fault and blemish'.[175] The dice was not inevitably loaded in favour of the seller, however. In *Hollingsworth* v. *Tattersall*, an action for the breach of warranty of a horse,[176] one witness, Thomas Hull, described in Lord Mansfield's trial notes as a stable keeper and in a press report as a 'great-dealer in horses',[177] caused 'great laughter' from the assembled company when he:

> told Lord Mansfield that it was now the mode among all the horse-dealers in the kingdom, though they knew the horse sound when sold, and sound when returned, yet rather than come before his Lordship, they always took the horse and returned the money, as they were of opinion his Lordship was, right or wrong, in favour of purchasers, and against the dealers.[178]

These events were sufficiently notorious to be included in Lord Eldon's *Anecdote Book* a quarter of a century later.[179] The suggestion that Lord Mansfield was unsympathetic to horse dealers was somewhat ironic in the circumstances. The jury in the very same case found for the plaintiff contrary to the Chief Justice's own directions, leaving him 'much dissatisfied with the verdict' and shaking his head at the 'extraordinary conduct of the jury'.[180] James Oldham has concluded, on the evidence of Lord Mansfield's notebooks, that after Mr Hull's intervention a verdict in the seller's favour was more likely than before.[181] Juries remained unpredictable. Despite Lord Mansfield's well-deserved reputation for his skilful use of mercantile juries, as in *Hollingsworth* v. *Tattersall*, jurors were capable of acts of defiance.[182] Given their poor reputation

174 William Taplin, *The gentleman's stable directory: or, modern system of farriery* (London, 1788), p. 13.

175 Henry Bracken, *Ten Minutes Advice to Every Purchaser of a Horse out of a Dealer, jockey or groom's stable* (London, 1774), p. 1.

176 (1778). The case is overlooked by the nominate reports. As a decision at Guildhall rather than in banc, the omission is not surprising. Lord Mansfield's note of the trial survives: Oldham, *Mansfield Manuscripts*, vol. I, pp. 332–3. Two different newspaper reports have also been located: *London Chronicle*, 30 May 1778; *Morning Post*, 1 June 1778.

177 *London Chronicle*, 30 May 1778.

178 *Ibid.*

179 Anthony Lincoln and Robert McEwen (eds.), *Lord Eldon's Anecdote Book* (London: Stevens & Sons, 1960), [236].

180 *Morning Post*, 1 June 1778.

181 Oldham, *Mansfield Manuscripts*, vol. I, p. 232.

182 *Capstack* v. *Williams* (1782), Oldham, *Mansfield Manuscripts*, vol. I, p. 367.

for probity, horse dealers were perhaps not a class of defendant likely to engender the sympathy of their fellow merchants. It was difficult to get such a verdict overturned provided the jury had addressed the correct matters.[183]

The existence of a warranty was a question for the jury, and jurors were sometimes prepared to discover one of the slimmest pretext. On one occasion, a jury found for a buyer who refused to pay even though he knew all about the defect and an express warranty was absent.[184] By the 1760s, implied warranties had begun to be imposed in horse sales. John Lawrence in *A Philosophical and Practical Treatise on Horses* explained that where a horse was sold for more than £10, the law required the animal to be sound irrespective of whether the vendor gave an express warranty. He complained that it had the result of 'manifestly affording the purchaser an undue advantage'.[185] Lawrence was describing a version of the sound price doctrine, whereby a horse that was sold for a sound or fair price carried an implied warranty of soundness. This sort of warranty attracted the attention of legal writers. John Joseph Powell, in his *Essay Upon the Law of Contracts and Agreements*, argued that a purchaser will be taken not to have assented to contract 'if a man sell a horse for a price, which it could not be worth unless it were sound, the contract will be void'.[186] The existence of such a far reaching rule should be viewed with a degree of scepticism. Powell's work, reflecting his interest in first principles[187] and Natural law theory,[188] is not always a very reliable guide of existing legal doctrine.[189] A different version of the sound price doctrine is found in Wooddeson's *Systematical View*, a work based on his Vinerian lectures of the 1770s, and which contrasted the earlier dominance of *caveat emptor* with 'a more reasonable principle . . . that a fair price implies a warranty'.[190]

Twenty years before Wooddeson, Blackstone, in his *Commentaries on the Laws of England*, made no mention of implying a warranty on

183 It was possible to argue that the jury reached a decision against the evidence on a motion for new trial but judges were reluctant to support such an argument, see John Morgan, *Essays Upon the Law of Evidence, New Trials, Special Verdicts, Trials at Bar and Repleaders*, 3 vols. (London, 1789), vol. II, pp. 52–3.

184 *Taylor* v. *Broderick* (1782), Oldham, *Mansfield Manuscripts*, vol. I, p. 372.

185 2 vols. (London, 1796–1798), vol. II, p. 143.

186 2 vols. (London, 1790), vol. I, p. 150.

187 *Ibid.*, vol. I, p. vi.

188 *Ibid.*, vol. I, p. xliii.

189 Most of the authorities cited by Powell pre-date 1750, Tariq Baloch, 'Law Booksellers and Printers as Agents of Unchange' (2007) 66 *Cambridge Law Journal* 389, 416.

190 *A Systematical View of the Laws of England*, 3 vols. (London, 1792–3), vol. II, p. 415.

payment of a fair price and merely reinforced the idea that a warranty of quality needed to be express.[191] This may just be because a good deal of contract law was omitted, but his silence suggests that the idea may have gained currency after the mid-1760s. In 1778 in *Stuart* v. *Wilkins*,[192] Lord Mansfield explained that, 'A warranty extends to all faults known and unknown to the seller. Selling for a sound price without warranty may be a ground for an assumpsit, but, in such a case, it ought to be laid that the defendant knew of the unsoundness.'[193] A manuscript report of the same judgment states that:

> The difference between an express warranty and where there is no warranty but the full price given as if sound, is, that in the case of an express warranty the law implies an assumpsit in all events, whether the unsoundness was in the knowledge of the defendant or not. But in the other case the law only implies the assumpsit if the defendant knew of it.[194]

A quarter of a century on, Grose J. denied that Lord Mansfield had supported a sound price doctrine.[195] *Stuart* v. *Wilkins* was, strictly speaking, concerned with the appropriate form of action.[196] But in conjunction with other authorities, it can be read as supporting the sound price doctrine.

Lord Mansfield's version of the sound price doctrine was never as far reaching as Wooddeson's.[197] A sound price was not in itself enough to imply a warranty. A warranty would only be implied where there was a sound price and the seller knew of the defect. A genuine latent defect would not be covered. More than a decade before *Stuart* v. *Wilkins* at Hertford Assize,[198] the *London Chronicle* reported that Lord Mansfield made clear to those present, who included some jockeys, that 'if at any time they took a sound price for a horse they knew not to be sound, or concealed any defect, the not warranting him should not avail them at all.'[199]

191 *Commentaries on the Laws of England*, 4 vols. (Oxford, 1766), vol. II, p. 452.
192 (1778) 1 Doug 18. 193 *Ibid.*, p. 20. 194 LI MS Hill 13 f. 258.
195 *Parkinson* v. *Lee* (1802) 2 East 314, 322.
196 Simpson, 'Horwitz Thesis', pp. 581–3. Simpson argued that the sound price doctrine was no more than an expression used by some judges in directing juries and not a doctrine at all.
197 Horwitz accepts Wooddeson's definition at face value, Morton Horwitz, 'The Historical Foundations of Modern Contract Law' (1973–4) 87 *Harvard Law Review* 917, 926–7.
198 The decision survives in Mansfield's notebook, *Worth* v. *Pank* (1764), Oldham, *Mansfield Manuscripts*, vol. I, p. 266.
199 *London Chronicle*, 14 August 1764.

Having established the existence of a warranty, there were three further considerations, as Lord Mansfield explained to a jury in *Hopkins* v. *Hopkins*: 'whether the beast was sound according to the engagement; whether she was returned in due time, according to the conditions; and, whether she was returned in reasonable time, according to the law'.[200] The horse in question had been sold with an express warranty of soundness. The jury heard witnesses on both sides as to the soundness of the horse and came to the conclusion that the horse was both unsound and returned as required by the conditions of sale.[201] Horse sales actually fell into three main categories. Horses were either sold with an express warranty as 'sound, free from vice or blemish, and quiet to ride or draw', 'sold without warranty to be taken with all faults'[202] or sold as sound with the exception of those faults which were highlighted.[203]

When horses were sold conditions were often attached. In sales by auction at horse repositories the conditions were posted up for any buyer to read,[204] thereby giving sufficient notice to incorporate the conditions into the sale.[205] One key term at the well-known auction house Tattersalls stated that:

> The purchaser of any lot warranted in any way, and not answering the warranty given, must return the same on or before the evening of the second day from the sale, otherwise the purchaser shall be obliged to keep the lot with all faults.[206]

When a condition of this sort was used, the warranty was only valid for a very short period.[207] There is some evidence that judges and juries were

200 As reported in the *Daily Advertiser*, 27 February 1778. For Lord Mansfield's trial note, see Oldham, *Mansfield Manuscripts*, vol. I, pp. 327–8. For similar instructions, see *Cook* v. *Tattersall*, *Morning Chronicle*, 24 May 1777, cited by Oldham, *Mansfield Manuscripts*, vol. I, p. 233.

201 The witnesses might prove unhelpful to the side that called them, for example in *Neate* v. *Davis* (1764), Oldham, *Mansfield Manuscripts*, vol. I, pp. 274–5 the witnesses for the defendant all gave evidence that the horse was unsound.

202 Lawrence, *Horses*, vol. II, p. 142.

203 *Ibid.*, vol. II, pp. 144–5; *Redfern* v. *Tattersall* (1781), Oldham, *Mansfield Manuscripts*, vol. I, p. 235.

204 *Hopkins* v. *Hopkins* (1778), Oldham, *Mansfield Manuscripts*, vol. I, p. 328. One of the witnesses, a clerk at the repository, said in evidence that 'the conditions of sale, all dealers know them. Plaintiff frequently buys and sells.'

205 *Mesnard* v. *Aldridge* (1801) 3 Esp 271.

206 Paul Mitchell, 'The Development of Quality Obligations in Sale of Goods' (2001) 117 *Law Quarterly Review* 645, 649, citing George Oliphant, *The Law Concerning Horses, Racing, Wager and Gambling* (London: S. Sweet, 1847), p. 29.

207 *Fielder* v. *Starkin* (1788) 1 H Bla 17.

willing to ameliorate the effects of the type of term used by Tattersalls. In *Hopkins* v. *Hopkins*, the standard term required the horse to be returned by the evening of the day following the sale. The horse was kept for five days. Lord Mansfield rewrote the condition, directing the jury that the buyer was allowed to retain the horse for a reasonable period on the grounds that it was impossible to make a full discovery of latent defects in such a short period.[208] In *Buchanan* v. *Parnshaw*,[209] a horse was sold warranted sound and six years old. A condition was attached that the horse be returned within two days if unsound. Lord Kenyon recognised the value of such a condition in public sales because of the risk of accident to the horse between the sale and the time when the horse may be returned. At the same time, he held that whilst a condition was appropriate for unsoundness, it did not apply when after ten days the horse was discovered to be twelve years old.

By the end of the eighteenth century, judges were making a conscious effort to place tighter controls on jury discretion, and by the mid-nineteenth century the power of the jury had been largely eroded. This shift would have implications for disputes about horse sales. These were not the only example of a power struggle between judge and jury. Towards the end of the eighteenth century, new, less cumbersome, methods for controlling juries were coming into common usage. These procedural changes began to have a noticeable impact. The process by which discretion came to be removed from juries in the award of damages provides a particularly stark illustration.

Before the eighteenth century, the assessment of damages had, on the face of it, been rather an unprincipled exercise.[210] Juries were unable to award more than the sum claimed as part of the allegation of breach,[211] but below this maximum figure the level of damages was a matter within the jury's discretion either at trial or on a writ of inquiry.[212] Even where the trial judge directed a jury to award a particular sum, it was difficult to

208 These remarks were contained in the press report in the *London Chronicle*, 27 February 1778.

209 (1788) 2 TR 745.

210 George Washington, 'Damages in Contract at Common Law' (1931) 47 *Law Quarterly Review* 345, (1932) 48 *Law Quarterly Review* 90.

211 Lawes, *Assumpsit*, p. 283.

212 On the writ of inquiry, see B.J. Sellon, *The Practice of the Courts of King's Bench and Common Pleas*, 2 vols. (London, 1792), vol. II, pp. 15–28. This device was used when the trial jury failed to assess the damages at trial or judgment was given upon default, confession or demurrer.

mount a challenge when a jury ignored the direction. Once it was easier to challenge jury decisions, legal rules for the assessment of damages developed in turn.[213] To some extent these rules may represent the formalisation of existing practices.

The law of contract was split between entitlement-based debt and damage-based assumpsit.[214] Debt was a claim for a fixed sum, but plaintiffs were able to recover damages as well as the debt itself.[215] Damages were awarded for the defendant's detention of the plaintiff's money and were sometimes substantial.[216] In the 1760s, Francis Buller described the newer practice of awarding only nominal damages[217] with damages for detention replaced by interest.[218] In the general run of cases, interest represented a lower sum than damages.[219] Nineteenth century juries retained discretion over whether or not interest should be awarded,[220] but the interest rates came to be regulated by statute.[221]

The precise method of calculating loss in special assumpsit is unknown. The natural method for assessing damages for non-performance is perhaps to look at the position if the contract had been performed. Evidence from the late sixteenth century suggests that in virtually every case, juries assessed damages on the basis of lost expectations.[222] Juries in assumpsit still enjoyed the freedom to calculate damages in any other way they thought fit without risk of interference from a judge.

Indebitatus assumpsit occupied a more ambiguous position. As an assumpsit, it was an action for damages. At the same time, the indebitatus count closely resembled the entitlement-based debt.[223] Lord Mansfield explained that, if a plaintiff in indebitatus assumpsit recovered

[213] *Huckle* v. *Money* (1763) 2 Wils KB 205.

[214] David Ibbetson, *A Historical Introduction to the Law of Obligations* (Oxford: Oxford University Press, 1999), pp. 147–8.

[215] Frederick Pollock and Frederic Maitland, *The History of English Law Before the Time of Edward I*, 2nd edn, 2 vols. (Cambridge: Cambridge University Press, 1968), vol. II, pp. 215–16.

[216] *Skinner* v. *Andrews* (1669) 1 Wms Saund 163; *Hodsden* v. *Harridge* (1671) 2 Wms Saund 61.

[217] *An Introduction to the Law Relative to Trials at Nisi Prius* (London, 1767), p. 165.

[218] *Anon* (1694) Comb 243; *Lapiere* v. *Duke of St Albans* (1702) 2 Ld Raym 773; *Osbourne* v. *Hosier* (1705) 6 Mod 167; *Holroi* v. *Ebizson* (1714) 10 Mod 274.

[219] Washington, 'Damages', p. 368. [220] *Attwood* v. *Taylor* (1840) 1 M & G 279.

[221] (1833) 3 & 4 Will IV c. 42 s. 28.

[222] David Ibbetson, 'The Assessment of Contractual Damages at Common Law in the Late Sixteenth Century', in Matthew Dyson and David Ibbetson (eds.), *Law and the Legal Process* (Cambridge: Cambridge University Press, 2013), pp. 137–46.

[223] Ibbetson, *Historical Introduction*, p. 149.

the sum itself, damages would be nominal.[224] His analysis was already becoming dated. The fact that the plaintiff was unable to prove the fixed sum in his declaration was due no longer ensured that he went away empty handed. A reasonable sum assessed on a *quantum meruit* basis could also be recovered.[225] The fixed sum set an upper limit. The same rule was soon adopted in debt, where Lord Loughborough confidently asserted that, 'the opinion indeed which was erroneously entertained that in an action for debt on a simple contract the whole sum must be proved has been some time since corrected'.[226]

These changes blurred the boundary between damages and entitlement, which was never entirely rigid in the first place. Juries in indebitatus assumpsit had always been able to depart from the entitlement measure. In *James* v. *Morgan*,[227] the defendant had bought a horse promising to pay a barleycorn per nail and then doubling for every nail. There were thirty-two nails in every shoe. Although the plaintiff proved, on the basis of the calculation, that the defendant owed 500 quarters of barley, the jury awarded a lower sum of £8 to compensate for the value of the horse. The facts here suggest not merely that the price was inflated, but that the plaintiff used a confidence trick on the defendant.[228] In the *Owl's Case*,[229] the owner of a pet owl offered £1,000 for its return. The finder brought an action for £1,000 but a lesser sum was awarded. The evidence is too thin to come to any firm conclusions, but in both instances the jurors were following the direction of the trial judge. This, to put it no more strongly, suggest that the default position in indebitatus assumpsit was to assess damages on the basis of the sum owed. The facts of these cases are very unusual. In *James* v. *Morgan* the

[224] *Robinson* v. *Bland* (1761) 1 Wm Bla 256, 263; *Lowe* v. *Peers* (1768) 4 Burr 2225.

[225] David Ibbetson, 'Implied Contracts and Restitution: History in the High Court of Australia' (1988) 8 *Oxford Journal of Legal Studies* 312, 315–16; *Gardiner* v. *Crosedale* (1760) 1 Wm Bla 198; *Thompson* v. *Spencer* (1768) noted in Joseph Sayer, *The Law of Damages* (London, 1770), p. 44; William Blackstone, *Commentaries on the Laws of England*, 4 vols. (Oxford, 1768), vol. III, pp. 154–5.

[226] *Rudder* v. *Price* (1791) 1 H Bla 547, 550. This was not the law of the 1760s in debt according to Blackstone, *Commentaries*, vol. III, pp. 154–5.

[227] (1663) 1 Lev 111.

[228] Sayer, *Damages*, p. 46 and Powell, *Contracts*, vol. II, p. 159 both treat *James* v. *Morgan* as a case of dishonest conduct rather than a grossly inflated price. The facts of *Thornborough* v. *Whitacre* (1704) 6 Mod 305, 3 Salk 97, 2 Ld Raym 1164 were similar but it was treated as an example of impossibility.

[229] Bacon, *Abridgment*, vol. II, Damages D (1) (undated), see Ibbetson, *Historical Introduction*, p. 211.

behaviour of the plaintiff was close to fraudulent. In the *Owl's Case* the sum in question was hugely disproportionate when set against the value of the owl. Neither decision proves whether juries always, often, or rarely awarded a lower sum when the price was unfair.[230]

To begin with, the motion for new trial was only used in claims for a fixed sum.[231] Liquidated damages, and therefore special assumpsit, were excluded.[232] Judicial reluctance to interfere with an assessment of damages generally might be overcome if the jury had acted wrongfully in some way. So for example, in *Woodford* v. *Eades*,[233] the jury were mistaken on a point of law; in *Parr* v. *Purbeck*,[234] damages were wrongly mitigated on account of legally irrelevant matters and on evidence not before the court; in *Pinock* v. *Willett*,[235] the jury wrongly gave interest (which was a mistake of law); and in *Markham* v. *Middleton*,[236] a sheriff failed to adjourn on a writ of inquiry when he should have done so.

In his *Essays Upon the Law of Evidence*, Morgan claimed that a motion for new trial would be granted for excessive or for insufficient damages.[237] Even into the nineteenth century, other observers were more cautious.[238] In the absence of obvious jury wrongdoing, there is some evidence that an award of excessive damages might furnish good grounds for a motion for new trial,[239] but the issue usually arose in tort rather than contract actions where it remained controversial.[240] There is only the weakest indirect evidence of a motion for new trial for excessive damages in contract actions.[241] Where the jury awarded too little, judges were even more reluctant to grant a motion.[242] Sayer

[230] Simpson, 'The Horwitz Thesis', pp. 551–6.

[231] *Parr* v. *Purbeck* (1723) 8 Mod 196; *Woodford* v. *Green* (1721) 11 Mod 349.

[232] *Parr* v. *Purbeck* (1723) 8 Mod 196, 197–8.

[233] (1721) 1 Stra 425, 11 Mod 349 (indebitatus assumpsit).

[234] (1723) 8 Mod 196 (covenant).

[235] (1734) Barnes 228 (indebitatus assumpsit).

[236] (1746) 2 Stra 1259 (indebitatus assumpsit). See the description of this case in the note to *Mauricet* v. *Brecknock* (1780) 2 Doug 509, 510, fn. 2.

[237] 3 vols. (London, 1789), vol. II, p. 1.

[238] *Eyre* v. *Bank of England* (1819) 1 Bligh PC 582, 596; Joseph Chitty, *A Practical Treatise on the Law of Contracts Not Under Seal* (London: S. Sweet, 1826), p. 344.

[239] *Anon* (1701) 12 Mod 439, excessive damages were said to be one of the causes of new trial. The practice of granting new trials for excessive damages was said to have begun around 1652: *R* v. *Corporation of Helston* (1714) 10 Mod 202, 203.

[240] *Jones* v. *Sparrow* (1793) 5 TR 257; *Pleydel* v. *The Earl of Dorchester* (1798) 7 TR 529.

[241] *Sharpe* v. *Brice* (1773) 2 Wm Bla 942, 943.

[242] *Hayward* v. *Newton* (1733) 2 Stra 940; *Barker* v. *Dixie* (1736) 2 Stra 1051.

claimed that it never happened,[243] and as late as the 1820s, such an event was still unusual.[244]

With jury autonomy still highly valued, the motion for new trial was never a very successful method, in the absence of wrongdoing, for overturning an assessment of damages. It had much greater significance when used in connection with the trial judge's direction to the jury. Rather than the assessment, it focused on the direction itself. Motions for new trials were used to overturn damage awards when juries had ignored the judge's direction as to how damages should be calculated,[245] and even when the jury had followed what turned out to be a misdirection.[246] By the nineteenth century, motions for new trials of this sort were widespread.[247]

By the late eighteenth century, the expectation measure had become a rule of law enforceable through the motion for new trial. The unreported case of *Smee* v. *Huddlestone*[248] is an early example. A plaintiff broker contracted with the defendant on the 1st of October in order to buy a quantity of tea to be paid for on the 1st of December. When the 1st of December arrived, the defendant refused to take delivery of the tea and it was sold at public auction for £200 less than the contract price. The trial judge directed the jury to award £200 in damages. On a motion for new trial, the plaintiff contended that he should be awarded the whole contract price. Wilmot C.J. held that there was 'no reason that the plaintiff should recover damages to a greater amount than the loss he sustained

243 Sayer, *Damages*, p. 201. Jacob Giles, *Every Man his own Lawyer or, a Summary of the Laws of England in a New Instructive Method*, 7th edn (London, 1772), p. 161 made a similar comment.

244 Chitty, *Contracts*, p. 345.

245 *Wood* v. *Gunston* (1655) Style 462, 466 (in the context of defamation); Sayer, *Damages*, p. 211, 'one Reason for the granting of a new trial . . . was, that the Jury had not in finding the Verdict paid a proper Attention to the Direction of the Judge'. Examples may not be very numerous, see J.L. Barton, 'Contractual Damages and the Rise of Industry' (1987) 7 *Oxford Journal of Legal Studies* 40, 46–7.

246 *Anon* (1702) 2 Salk 649; *Anon* (1704) 6 Mod 242; *Foxcraft* v. *Devonshire* (1760) 2 Burr 931, 1 Wm Bla 193; *Grant* v. *Vaughan* (1764) 1 Wm Bla 486, 487. For an unusually contrite Lord Mansfield as judge in banc overturning his own direction at nisi prius, see *How* v. *Strode* (1765) 2 Wils KB 269.

247 *Butler* v. *Dorant* (1810) 3 Taunt 229; *Chamberlain* v. *Williamson* (1814) 2 M & S 408; *Colley* v. *Streeton* (1823) 2 B & C 273; *Startup* v. *Cortazzi* (1835) 2 C, M & R 165. The two famous damages cases *Robinson* v. *Harman* (1848) 1 Ex 850 and *Hadley* v. *Baxendale* (1854) 9 Ex 341 were both motions for new trial on the grounds of misdirection.

248 (1768) Sayer, *Damages*, pp. 49–52. Rather surprisingly this authority subsequently falls from view without a single instance where it was cited in the reports.

by the non-performance of the contract, which is certainly no more than the difference between what the defendant had contracted to pay for the tea and what it was afterwards sold for'.

Judges who departed from the expectation measure felt compelled to justify their actions. In *Flureau* v. *Thornhill*,[249] in the context of a contract for the sale of land, the court found an implied condition that if the vendor was unable to make good title, the buyer was entitled to a return of his deposit.[250] By ensuring that the case turned on the return of a deposit, the integrity of the damages rule remained intact. If the expectation measure had not become a rule of law by this time, none of this would have been necessary. Although the process of calculating loss on the basis of expectation had become an established legal rule in other respects, contractual damages in the late eighteenth century did not resemble the finished article. This came later. But none of it would have been possible without these changes to the operation of jury trial.

[249] (1776) 2 Wm Bla 1078. The plaintiff could only recover his deposit plus interests and costs. Blackstone J. said this was a result of an express or implied condition. Also, see *Hopkins* v. *Grazebrook* (1826) 6 B & C 31; *Walker* v. *Moore* (1829) 10 B & C 416.

[250] 2 Wm Bla 1078–9.

5

Equity and the Common law

Writing in the 1770s, 'Junius', the pseudonymous political commentator, complained that:

> Instead of those certain, positive rules, by which the judgment of a court of law should invariably be determined, you have fondly introduced your own unsettled notions of equity and substantial justice . . . In the mean time the practice gains ground; the court of King's Bench becomes a court of equity, and the judge, instead of consulting strictly the law of the land, refers only to the wisdom of the court, and to the purity of his own conscience.[1]

Junius was a persistent critic of Lord Mansfield,[2] but his complaints also resonated with others. When Lord Eldon recalled a remark that Lord Mansfield is supposed to have made to De Grey C.J., that 'he never liked law as well as when it was like equity', he did not intend the anecdote as a compliment.[3] Lord Eldon also regarded Lord Mansfield as a malign influence on his friend Buller J., claiming that when he was appointed he was 'utterly unacquainted' with Equity[4] but was encouraged to follow in his mentor's footsteps. In a letter to Baron Lyndhurst, Eldon grumbled that Buller 'in some measure in Chancery made a mixture of Law and Equity, which spoiled both – as in the King's Bench he made a mixture of Equity with Law, which likewise spoiled both'.[5] His exaggerated view of Buller was not universally shared. In Rede's opinion, Buller was a 'too staunch and too systematic a lawyer to suffer the stubborn and general principles of law to give way in any instance to the wilder inferences of

[1] John Cannon (ed.), *The Letters of Junius* (Oxford: Oxford University Press, 1978), pp. 209–10.

[2] A debate about Junius's true identity continues into modern times, see Francesco Cordasco, 'Junius', *Oxford Dictionary of National Biography*; Alvar Ellegård, *Who Was Junius?* (Stockholm: Almquist & Wiksell, 1962).

[3] *Dursley* v. *Fitzharedinge* (1801) 6 Ves 251, 260; Anthony Lincoln and Robert McEwen (eds.), *Lord Eldon's Anecdote Book* (London: Stevens & Sons, London, 1960), § 238.

[4] Lincoln and McEwen, *Lord Eldon*, § 238.

[5] Cited by James Oldham, 'Buller, Sir Francis', *Oxford Dictionary of National Biography*.

equity'.[6] The strong association between Lord Mansfield and Equity was carried into the nineteenth century by critics[7] and admirers alike.[8] The debate, about the proper place of Equity in the Common law, still has contemporary resonances.[9]

Particularly during the earlier part of his tenure as Chief Justice, Lord Mansfield made free use of not just the term 'equity' but also 'natural justice'[10] and 'conscience',[11] and in *Anderson* v. *Temple* he explained that, 'The most desirable object in all judicial determinations, especially in mercantile ones, (which ought to be determined upon natural justice, and not upon the niceties of law,) is, to do substantial justice'.[12] These words may suggest that the critics had a point. But they also need to be put into some sort of context.

Lord Mansfield's remarks on this and other occasions should be judged against the more fluid notions of precedent then in existence, as opposed to the more rigid system of adherence to past authorities which emerged in the nineteenth century.[13] The slightly haphazard nature of law reporting also allowed a greater degree of flexibility when it came to the interpretation of earlier judgments than was possible later on.[14] Even

6 Leman Rede, *Strictures on the Lives and Characters of the Most Eminent Lawyers of the Present Day* (London, 1790), p. 109.

7 Archer Polson, *Law and Lawyers: A Sketch Book of Legal Biography, Gossip, and Anecdote* (London: Routledge, 1858), p. 149; *Strannon* v. *Bradstreet* (1803) 1 Sched. & Lef 52, 66.

8 Rede, *Strictures*, p. 38; John Campbell, *The Lives of the Chief Justices of England*, 3 vols. (London: John Murray, 1849), vol. II, pp. 440–3.

9 Lord Denning, who in some respects was Lord Mansfield's spiritual heir, was unsurprisingly an admirer for this very reason, see Lord Denning, *Borrowing from Scotland* (Glasgow: Jackson, 1963), p. 8.

10 *Vintner's Co.* v. *Passey* (1757) 1 Keny 500, 503; *Windham* v. *Chetwyn* (1757) 1 Burr 414, 430; *Rose* v. *Green* (1758) 2 Kenyon 173, 178; *Godin* v. *London Exchange Assurance* (1758) 2 Keny 254, 256; *Burton* v. *Thompson* (1758) 2 Keny 375, 376; *Hawkes* v. *Crofton* (1758) 2 Keny 389, 390; *Foxcraft* v. *Devonshire* (1760) 1 Wm Bla 193, 195; *Robinson* v. *Bland* (1761) 1 Wm Bla 256, 263; *Baskerville* v. *Brown* (1761) 1 Wm Bla 293, 294; *Ingle* v. *Wordsworth* (1762) 3 Burr 1284, 1286; *Plumer* v. *Marchant* (1762) 3 Burr 1380, 1384; *Goodright d. Carter* v. *Staphan* (1774) 1 Cowp 201, 203; *Holman* v. *Johnson* (1775) 1 Cowp 341, 343.

11 *Anderson* v. *George* (1757) 1 Burr 352, 353; *Bird* v. *Randall* (1762) 3 Burr 1345, 1353.

12 (1767) 4 Burr 2235, 2239 in the context of an action of trover.

13 On the role of precedent in the eighteenth century, see David Lieberman, *The Province of Legislation Determined: Legal Theory in Eighteenth Century Britain* (Cambridge: Cambridge University Press, 1989), pp. 85–7. For an overview of the historical development of precedent, see Neil Duxbury, *The Nature and Authority of Precedent* (Cambridge: Cambridge University Press, 2008), pp. 31–57.

14 James Oldham, *The Mansfield Manuscripts and the Growth of English Law in the Eighteenth Century*, 2 vols. (Chapel Hill: University of North Carolina Press, 1992),

a writer as conservative as William Blackstone, whilst stressing the value of precedents, felt no embarrassment about admitting that a 'flatly absurd or unjust' decision need not be followed.[15] Lord Mansfield's position was more sophisticated. He stressed the importance of principles. At the same time, he recognised the value of precedents, not through unthinking adherence, but in helping to promote certainty:

> The law would be a strange science if it rested solely upon cases; and if after so large an increase of commerce, arts and circumstances accruing, we must go to the time of Richard I to find a case, and see what is law. Precedent indeed may serve to fix principles, which for certainty's sake are not suffered to be shaken, whatever might be the weight of the principle, independent of precedent. But precedent, though it be evidence of law, is not law in itself; much less the whole law.[16]

On other occasions Lord Mansfield was quite prepared to stress the value of certainty and rest his decision on earlier precedents, especially, but not exclusively, in a mercantile context.[17]

One of the difficulties in examining the exact role that equity played at this time is that the term was such a slippery one. It was sometimes just a shorthand way of saying that the law ought to be fair or just.[18] Whether these remarks signify anything meaningful in terms of doctrine is difficult to assess. Lord Mansfield was certainly not the only judge to deploy 'equity' in this manner.[19] It has echoes in the comment of Blackstone that 'equity is synonymous with justice'.[20] This use of equity, where it

vol. I, p. 102 makes this important point. The King's Bench was better served by the law reporters than either the Common Pleas or Chancery. For a recent overview, see P.W. Young and A.A. Gomez, 'The Status of Law Reports Produced in England Prior to 1865' (2013) 87 *Australian Law Journal* 844.

15 William Blackstone, *Commentaries on the Laws of England*, 4 vols. (Oxford, 1765), vol. I, p. 70.

16 *Jones* v. *Randall* (1774) Lofft 383, 385. This important passage only appears in full in this version of the report and not the one in Cowper.

17 For other examples, see *Doe* v. *Davy* (1774) 1 Cowp 158, 160; *R* v. *Roupell* (1776) 2 Cowp 458.

18 *Robinson* v. *Bland* (1760) 2 Burr 1077, 1078, 1086, 1088; *Grant* v. *Vaughan* (1764) 3 Burr 1516, 1522; *Lowe* v. *Peers* (1768) 4 Burr 2225, 2228; *Martyn* v. *Podger* (1770) 5 Burr 2631, 2633.

19 *Goodtitle* v. *Stokes* (1753) 1 Wil KB 341, 342; *Goslin* v. *Wilcock* (1766) 2 Wil KB 302, 306; *Hewit* v. *Mantell* (1768) 2 Wil KB 372, 374.

20 William Blackstone, *Commentaries on the Laws of England*, 4 vols. (Oxford, 1760), vol. III, p. 429. On Blackstone and equity, see W. Holdsworth, 'Blackstone's Treatment of Equity' (1929–1930) 43 *Harvard Law Review* 1. On the parallel between Blackstone and Mansfield, see W.S. Holdsworth, *A History of English Law*, 17 vols. (London: Methuen, 1938), vol. XII, p. 593.

was equated with good faith or fairness, has a long history. Baldus the medieval jurist distinguished generic equity, which meant reaching a just result, and specific equity, which meant departing from the law where circumstances require.[21]

Equity had a more specific usage. In England it denoted the Court of Chancery. When 'equity' was used in the context of the Common law it also had a more precise meaning than fairness. It was the term used to describe doctrines imported from Chancery and in this sense it may have had more significance for Lord Mansfield and his colleagues. When used in this way, Equity need not be associated with uncertainty or an absence of rules. The defining feature of Equity was the notion of conscience. But the Court of Chancery had started to become more rule bound a century earlier under the Chancellorship of Lord Nottingham. This was less because Lord Nottingham had developed a coherent theory of conscience but rather because he 'more fully established the kinds of particular situations to which that conscience would extend – and to which it would be limited'.[22] The process of regularising Equity continued under the eighteenth century Chancellors.[23] Lord Mansfield would have been familiar with Equitable doctrine having built up a successful Chancery practice before he was appointed to the Bench.[24] He turned down the opportunity to become Lord Chancellor and Master of the Rolls several times.[25] Although Lord Eldon acidly remarked that 'Lord M. had not retained a very accurate Memory of Cases in Equity',[26] in fact, along with other contemporaries, Lord Mansfield showed himself to be very adept at spotting parallels in Equity by integrating those solutions into the Common law. His attitude was perfectly summed up by a brief remark in *Bird* v. *Randall* that, 'This

[21] James Gordley, 'Good Faith in Contract Law in the Medieval Ius Commune', in Reinhard Zimmermann and Simon Whittaker (eds.), *Good Faith in European Contract Law* (Cambridge: Cambridge University Press, 2000), p. 108.

[22] Dennis Klinck, *Conscience, Equity and the Court of Chancery in Early Modern England* (Farnham: Ashgate Publishing, 2010), p. 261.

[23] D.E.C. Yale, *Lord Nottingham's Chancery Cases* (London: Selden Society, 1954), pp. xxxvii–cxxxiv. Lord Nottingham was Lord Chancellor from 1673 to 1682. On the role of precedent in Chancery, see Clyde Croft, 'Lord Hardwick's Use of Precedent in Equity', in Thomas Watkin (ed.), *Legal Record and Historical Reality* (London: Hambledon, 1989), pp. 121–55; Lieberman, *Province of Legislation*, pp. 81–3.

[24] He was for example counsel in the famous Equity case of *Earl of Chesterfield* v. *Janssen* (1750) 2 Ves Sen 125.

[25] Campbell, *Lives*, vol. II, pp. 382, 446, 450. Lord Mansfield sat for the Lord Chancellor as Speaker in the House of Lords on several occasions.

[26] Eldon, *Anecdote Book*, § 238.

is an action upon the case, which I have often observed is almost equivalent to a bill in equity'.[27]

Equity and the doctrine of consideration

Atkins v. *Hill*[28] and *Hawkes* v. *Saunders*[29] are two of Lord Mansfield's best known decisions. The orthodox interpretation of these authorities by legal historians, from Holdsworth and Fifoot onwards, is that Lord Mansfield was trying to reform consideration so that moral obligations could be treated as giving rise to valuable consideration.[30] More recently Oldham has suggested that Lord Mansfield's judgments simply illustrate his desire to find consideration where both parties intended a contract.[31] Sheehan has argued that Lord Mansfield was attempting to impose what in Roman law were known as natural obligations.[32] All three approaches are difficult to square with traditional notions of reciprocal consideration based on an exchange, and all arguably fail to pay sufficient attention to the specific context of the decisions.

In the simple case of an executor who promised to pay the debts of the deceased, there was no difficulty in allowing a claim against them in either their capacity as executor or personally.[33] The fact that *Atkins* v. *Hill* and *Hawkes* v. *Saunders* were both concerned with legacies rather than an outstanding debt is of crucial importance. In *Atkins* v. *Hill*, Lord Mansfield described how, when there were sufficient assets to discharge the estate, the executor was bound to pay the bequests.[34] If he failed to pay the bequests the executor's obligations could be enforced in the Ecclesiastical Courts[35] or Chancery.[36] In contrast, Lord Mansfield

[27] (1762) 1 Wm Bla 387, 388. [28] (1775) 1 Cowp 284. [29] (1782) 1 Cowp 289.

[30] W.S. Holdsworth, *A History of English Law*, 17 vols. (London: Methuen, 1925), vol. VIII, pp. 26–9, 31; Fifoot, *Mansfield*, pp. 135–41; C.H.S. Fifoot, *History and Sources of the Common Law* (London: Stevens & Sons, 1949), pp. 409–10.

[31] Oldham, *Mansfield Manuscripts*, vol. I, pp. 224–5.

[32] Duncan Sheehan, 'Natural Obligations in English Law' [2004] *Lloyds Maritime and Commercial Law Quarterly* 171.

[33] A.W. Brian Simpson, *A History of the Common Law of Contract: The Rise of the Action of Assumpsit*, pbk edn (Oxford: Oxford University Press, 1987), p. 442 citing *Pinchon's Case* (1612) 9 Co Rep 86b, 2 Brownl 137, Cro Jac 293. There is a good example in Lord Mansfield's notebooks where an executor promises to pay a medical bill, see *Bromfield* v. *Wilson* (1772), Oldham, *Mansfield Manuscripts*, vol. I, pp. 304–5.

[34] (1775) 1 Cowp 284, 288.

[35] (1775) 1 Cowp 284, 289; *Clarke* v. *Douce* (1816) 2 Phil Ecc 335; *Grignion* v. *Grignion* (1828) 1 Hagg Ecc 535.

[36] Joseph Story, *Commentaries on Equity Jurisprudence as Administered in England and America*, 2nd edn, 2 vols. (Boston: Little & Brown, 1839), vol. I, pp. 477–8; Henry White

admitted that 'there is scarce an instance of a legatee attempting to sue at law'.[37]

In this context, it seems more likely that Lord Mansfield was trying to bring legacies into the Common law, rather than to raise more fundamental questions about the proper scope of the doctrine of consideration. The fact that he sought to reform consideration in other ways may be no more than a coincidence. The importance of these decisions lies in the fact that a claim was allowed at Common law provided it was framed in the action of assumpsit. Rather than liability resting on the legacy itself, liability in assumpsit was founded on a promise by the executor to pay the legatee. The consideration for this promise was not founded on a moral obligation or an intention to be bound, but on the fact that the executor was liable in Equity. As Lord Mansfield explained in his judgment:

> In this case the promise is grounded upon a reasonable and conscientious consideration; namely, that the defendant had assets to discharge the legacy.[38] If so, he was compellable in a Court of Equity, or in the Ecclesiastical Court, to pay it.[39]

He laboured the point further when he said: 'the legacy became a demand which in law and conscience he was liable to pay'.[40] There were several very good reasons why a potential recipient of a legacy may have framed his claim in this novel way. A bill in Equity was subject to equitable accounting which involved sharing out the estate between all of the potential legatees.[41] If the assumpsit claim was successful then the plaintiff could recover the amount that he was promised. This later figure was potentially higher and may explain why the practice of declaring in assumpsit would eventually fall into disrepute.[42] Assumpsit had other advantages for a legatee. Whereas in *Atkins* v. *Hill* the executor was sued in their capacity as executor (*de bonis testoris*), they were only bound to pay the amount promised if there were sufficient assets in the estate.[43] In contrast the action of assumpsit in *Hawkes* v. *Saunders* was brought

(ed.), R. Roper, *A Treatise on the Law of Legacies*, 3rd edn, 2 vols. (London: Butterworth, 1828), vol. II, pp. 692–6.

37 (1775) 1 Cowp 284, 288.

38 This was admitted because the defendant challenged the plaintiff's action using a demurrer.

39 (1775) 1 Cowp 284, 289.

40 *Ibid*., p. 288.

41 Story, *Commentaries*, vol. I, pp. 353–432.

42 *Deeks* v. *Strutt* (1794) 5 TR 690, 692.

43 In such a situation the executor could plead *plene administravit*: Edward Williams, *A Treatise on the Law of Executors and Administrators*, 3rd edn, 2 vols. (London: Saunders & Benning, 1841), vol. II, pp. 1532–59.

against an executrix in her personal capacity (*de bonis propriis*). By counting in this way, she was liable for the amount promised even if there were insufficient assets in the estate to cover the claim. In finding 'the strongest consideration',[44] Lord Mansfield used the same reasoning that he had deployed in *Atkins* v. *Hill*:

> But an executor who has received assets, is under every kind of obligation to pay a legacy. He receives the money by virtue of an office which he swears to execute duly. He receives the money as a trust or deposit to the use of the legatee. He ought to assent if he has assets. He has no discretion or election. He retains what belongs to the legatee, and therefore, owes him to the amount.[45]

Neither decision sits very easily with the remarks of Chief Baron Skynner in *Rann* v. *Hughes*, that 'if I promise generally to pay upon request what I was liable to pay upon request in another right, I derive no advantage or convenience from this promise, and therefore there is not sufficient consideration for it'.[46] In both cases, the executor was clearly liable 'in another right', meaning a right not derived from the Common law. They were liable in Equity.

Despite the strong link with Equitable liability, in several passages Lord Mansfield also seemed to go further. He suggests that even where there was no liability in Law or Equity, a promise to pay could be enforced if it was based on obligations which would otherwise only bind a man's conscience. Contracts rendered unenforceable through the Statute of Limitations, infancy or bankruptcy are used as examples.[47] Lord Mansfield had used similar language five years earlier in a case concerned with a bankrupt's promise to pay.[48] These situations are certainly much closer to the type of moral obligation envisaged by Holdsworth and Fifoot. Yet even this development is not as novel as commonly supposed. It owes more to form than substance. There was no significant extension of liability. As the law already stood, many of these promises were binding without the need to resort to moral consideration. Moral consideration was simply a new way of expressing the old formula that subsequent promises revived an existing debt.[49]

44 (1782) 1 Cowp 289, 291. 45 *Ibid.*, p. 290. 46 (1778) 7 TR 350 (note).

47 *Atkins* v. *Hill* (1775) 1 Cowp 284, 288–9; *Hawkes* v. *Saunders* (1782) 1 Cowp 289, 290.

48 *Trueman* v. *Fenton* (1777) 2 Cowp 544.

49 Kevin Teeven, *Promises on Prior Obligations at Common Law* (Westport: Greenwood Press, 1998), pp. 75–6. On a subsequent promise to pay for an action barred by the Statute of Limitations (1623) 21 Jac I c. 16 s. 3, see *Heyling* v. *Hastings* (1698) 1 Ld Raym 389, 1 Ld Raym 421; *Dean* v. *Crane* (1704) 6 Mod 309; *Yea* v. *Fouraker* (1760) 2 Burr 1099. On a promise by an infant on reaching his majority, see *Southerton* v. *Whitlock* (1726) 2 Stra 690.

Although there was no adverse comment at the time, a fact which in itself may be significant, the new formula still had the potential to stretch the doctrine of consideration almost to breaking point. One way of smoothing over these difficulties was to slot the formula into the existing description of consideration. Several years before *Atkins* v. *Hill*, William Blackstone had argued that consideration could be founded on a 'prior moral obligation'.[50] In common with Lord Mansfield, Blackstone uses an agreement barred by the Statute of Limitations as an example. Blackstone's analysis of consideration is far from convincing. He erroneously attributes the idea of reciprocity to the Civilians, 'the civilians hold, that in all contracts, either express or implied, there must be something given in exchange, something that is mutual or reciprocal'.[51] The fact that Blackstone goes through such contortions to support a reciprocal analysis of consideration shows just how central it remained to the law of contract in the mid-eighteenth century.[52] In reality, and irrespective of the mode of expression, agreements falling within the categories discussed by Lord Mansfield and Blackstone were difficult to square with a reciprocal model of consideration. But then the doctrine of consideration had always allowed some flexibility at the boundary. Since the doctrine was formed, the courts were in some circumstances willing to make a finding of good consideration where on the face of it there was no genuine reciprocity,[53] and all without undermining the central principle.

Money had and received and Equity

Moses v. *Macferlan*[54] arose out of a dispute about promissory notes. Jacob made out four notes in the name of Moses. Macferlan, wishing to recover in his own name against Jacob, asked Moses to indorse them. By indorsing the notes, Moses, as well as Jacob, was potentially liable to Macferlan. Macferlan entered into a written agreement with Moses not to sue on the indorsement. In spite of the agreement, Macferlan brought

[50] Blackstone, *Commentaries*, vol. II, p. 445.

[51] Blackstone, *Commentaries*, vol. II, p. 444. As later editors pointed out, and Blackstone must surely have known, Civil law did not recognise consideration, see Edward Christian (ed.), William Blackstone, *Commentaries on the Laws of England*, 13th edn, 4 vols. (London: A. Strahan, 1800), vol. II, p. 445, fn. 2.

[52] Blackstone, *Commentaries*, vol. II, p. 445.

[53] Simpson, *Contract*, pp. 485–6; David Ibbetson, 'Consideration and the Theory of Contract in the Sixteenth Century', in John Barton (ed.), *Towards a General Law of Contract* (Berlin: Dunker and Humblot, 1990), pp. 77–9.

[54] (1760) 2 Burr 1005; 1 Wm Bla 219.

an action in a Court of Conscience, which refused to receive the agreement in evidence and ordered Moses to pay. At nisi prius,[55] Lord Mansfield ruled that on the merits of the case Moses should be allowed to recover.[56] A verdict was given for the plaintiff, subject to the opinion of the court in banc as to whether money had and received was an appropriate form of action.

The defendant raised three objections. The first, that indebitatus assumpsit would not lie because there would be no action of debt on these facts, was easily disposed of.[57] The third objection, that the plaintiff was using money had and received in order to re-open a matter which had already been settled, was more serious.[58] Lord Mansfield's response was to stress that the plaintiff was not alleging that the Court of Conscience had ruled incorrectly, rather that there was no mechanism for him to raise the defendant's unjust retention of the money.[59]

Lord Mansfield's dismissal of counsel's remaining objection that 'no assumpsit lies, except upon an express or implied contract: but here it is impossible to presume any contract to refund money, which the defendant recovered by an adverse suit',[60] is the decision's most important legacy:[61]

> If the defendant be under an obligation, from the ties of natural justice to refund; the law implies a debt, and gives this action, founded in the equity of the plaintiff's case, as it were upon a contract ('quasi-ex contractu' as the Roman law expresses it.). This species of assumpsit ('for money had and received to the plaintiff's use') lies in numberless instances, for money the defendant has received from a third person; which he claims

55 For counsel's argument at nisi prius, see Oldham, *Mansfield Manuscripts*, vol. I, pp. 258–9.

56 (1760) 2 Burr 1005, 1006.

57 (1760) 2 Burr 1005, 1008. In a note at 2 Burr 1005, 1009, fn. (c), Sir James Burrow, the law reporter, was particularly dismissive of this argument. In *Hard's Case* (1702) 1 Salk 23 it was said that indebitatus assumpsit would lie only where an action of debt could be brought, but the two were not co-extensive, not least because indebitatus assumpsit would not lie on a specialty and could be brought for an instalment.

58 (1760) 2 Burr 1005, 1009.

59 Lord Mansfield's sleight of hand is even more apparent given that in *Silk* v. *Rennett* (1764) 3 Burr 1583 he explained that the 'Court of Conscience has a mixed jurisdiction, as well equitable as legal: they proceed *secundum æquum et bonum*'.

60 (1760) 2 Burr 1005, 1008.

61 Percy Winfield, *The Province of the Law of Tort* (Cambridge: Cambridge University Press, 1931), pp. 128–41; R.M. Jackson, *The History of Quasi-Contract in English Law* (Cambridge: Cambridge University Press, 1936), pp. 117–19, 121; Percy Winfield, *The Law of Quasi-Contract* (Cambridge: Cambridge University Press, 1952), pp. 9–23; H.G. Hanbury, 'The Recovery of Money' (1924) 40 *Law Quarterly Review* 31, 35–6.

> title to, in opposition to the plaintiff's right; and which he had, by law, authority to receive from such third person.[62]

In a later passage, Lord Mansfield expanded on the nature of money had and received:

> This kind of equitable action, to recover back money, which ought not in justice to be kept, is very beneficial, and therefore much encouraged. It lies only for money which, *ex æquo et bono*, the defendant ought to refund: it does not lie for money paid by the plaintiff, which is claimed of him as payable in point of honour and honesty, although it could not have been recovered from him by any course of law.[63]

The importance of these statements lies in the way that Lord Mansfield sought to find a coherent juridical basis for money had and received. The inspiration behind his remarks has been widely debated.[64] Birks argued that Lord Mansfield developed money had and received out of the *obligatio naturalis* (natural obligations) which prevented recovery of payment under a *condictio indebiti* in Roman law.[65] Sir William Evans, writing forty years later, agreed.[66] But this view of the rule's paternity is not totally convincing.[67] Lord Mansfield certainly deployed Roman terminology referring to 'quasi-ex-contractu' and 'ex æquo et bono',[68] but if he was influenced by the substance of Roman law as well, it is out of character for him not to be more explicit that he was drawing on Roman principles.[69]

MacQueen and Sellar have suggested that Lord Mansfield may have been influenced by Lord Kames's *Principles of Equity*.[70] Kames dedicated the

[62] (1760) 2 Burr 1005, 1008–9. [63] (1760) 2 Burr 1005, 1012.

[64] For the latest contribution, see Tariq Baloch, *Unjust Enrichment and Contract* (Oxford: Hart, 2009), pp. 33–7.

[65] Peter Birks, 'English and Roman Learning in Moses v. Macferlan' (1984) 37 *Current Legal Problems* 1, 16–18; Peter Stein (ed.), W.W. Buckland, *A Textbook of Roman Law from Augustus to Justinian*, 3rd edn (Cambridge: Cambridge University Press, 1963), pp. 552–4.

[66] William Evans (trans.), R. Pothier, *A Treatise on the Law of Obligations or Contracts*, 2 vols. (London: A. Strahan, 1806), vol. II, pp. 378–81. See also Peter Birks, 'Comparative Unjust Enrichment', in Peter Birks and Arienna Pretto (eds.), *Themes in Comparative Law* (Oxford: Oxford University Press, 2002), p. 139.

[67] John Dawson, *Unjust Enrichment: A Comparative Analysis* (Boston: Little, Brown & Co., 1951), p. 12.

[68] On the Roman roots of this terminology, see Carleton Kemp Allen, *Law in the Making*, 4th edn (Oxford: Oxford University Press, 1946), p. 316; W.W. Buckland, *Equity in Roman Law* (London: University of London Press, 1911), p. 11.

[69] Wilmot J.'s use of Roman law on this occasion may have been more significant, see David Ibbetson, *A Historical Introduction to the Law of Obligations* (Oxford: Oxford University Press, 1999), p. 272, fn. 50.

[70] (Edinburgh, 1760).

work to Lord Mansfield and it was published in the same year as *Moses* v. *Macferlan* was decided.[71] Lord Kames's friendship with Lord Mansfield also makes this an attractive hypothesis. Lord Kames's discussion of quasi-contract blended Roman law, Common law and Equity. Having likened Roman quasi-contract with the situation where 'some relief is given that would be given upon an express covenant',[72] he described a *negotiorum gestio* where 'Equity interposes and makes liable, as the Common law would do had I given a mandate or commission',[73] and *condictio indebiti* which had a 'good foundation in equity'.[74] But although Lord Kames used the language of equity, there was an important difference. His analysis was not intended to put forward the kind of generalised liability envisaged by Lord Mansfield.[75]

Given the tenor of his judgment, a third explanation may be more convincing. In general terms, the jurisdiction of Chancery may be said to rest on a principle of *ex æquo et bono*,[76] but there was also a more concrete link.[77] Three years before *Moses* v. *Macferlan*, in an action for money laid out against a surety, Lord Mansfield had said that:

> And as to the objection that the Court of Chancery is the proper court for a surety to be relieved in, there are many cases in which a court of equity may be necessary to come at the facts yet if a court of law is once possessed of facts I know of no case where it may not give relief by an action on the case.[78]

[71] Hector MacQueen and W. David Sellar, 'Unjust Enrichment in Scots Law', in Eltjo Schrage (ed.), *Unjust Enrichment. The Comparative Legal History of the Law of Restitution* (Berlin: Duncker & Humblot, 1995), pp. 314–16; Ibbetson, *Historical Introduction*, p. 272, fn. 50. Baloch suggests the similarities lay more in approach than outright borrowing, Baloch, *Unjust Enrichment*, pp. 35–6.

[72] Kames, *Equity*, p. 35. [73] *Ibid.*, p. 35. [74] *Ibid.*, p. 92.

[75] For the contrary view that Lord Kames was attempting to generate a general theory, see Michael Lobban, 'The Ambition of Lord Kames' Equity', in Andrew Lewis and Michael Lobban (eds.), *Law and History* (Oxford: Oxford University Press, 2003), pp. 112–15.

[76] Kames, *Equity*, p. 40 explained 'the extraordinary branch devolved on the court of chancery is termed Equity; the name being derived from the nature of the jurisdiction, directed less by precise rules, than *secundum æquum et bonum*, or according to what the judge in conscience thinks right'. For the wider questions about the meaning of conscience, see Mike McNair, 'Equity and Conscience' (2007) 27 *Oxford Journal of Legal Studies* 659; Klinck, *Conscience*.

[77] Other writers have stressed the close relationship between money had and received and Equity: Ben Kremer, 'The Action for Money Had and Received' (2001) 17 *Journal of Contract Law* 93; Graham Virgo, 'Restitution Through the Looking Glass: Restitution Within Equity and Equity Within Restitution', in Joshua Getzler (ed.), *Rationalizing Property, Equity and Trusts: Essays in Honour of Edward Burn* (London: Lexis/Nexis, 2003), pp. 87–8.

[78] *Decker* v. *Pope* (1757) LI MS Misc. 129 (unfol.). This decision provides a good example of Lord Mansfield seeking an informal consensus amongst the judges, see James Oldham, 'Law-Making at Nisi Prius in the Early 1800s' (2004) 25 *Journal of Legal History* 221, 235.

The action for money laid out had a direct equivalent in Equity in the form of a bill for contribution.[79] Money had and received was sometimes likened to a bill in Equity,[80] and although it was not an exact match, it covered some of the same ground.[81] Money had and received was described by Lord Mansfield as a 'liberal action'[82] and proved to be very popular. In the 1760s it had the potential to grow into a broad remedy protecting against the unconscionable receipt of another person's money.[83] By the late 1770s, 'great friend' of the action though he still professed to be,[84] even Lord Mansfield was becoming more cautious:

> Great benefit arises from a liberal extension of the action for, but it ought not to be carried too far, nor used by way of surprise. And therefore if thrown in as of course, and the plaintiff comes prepared to try another question, he shall not by surprise be let into evidence on this, though originally the action for money had and received might have been maintained.[85]

His remarks were echoed by Buller J., who also made an explicit reference to Bills in Equity:

> Of late years this court has very properly extended the action for money had and received; it is founded on the principles of justice, and I do not wish to restrain it in any respect. But it must be remembered that it was extended on the principle of its being considered like a bill in equity. And therefore, in order to recover money in this form of action, the party must shew that he has equity and conscience on his side, and that he could recover it in a Court of Equity.[86]

Despite striking a note of caution, Buller J. remained sufficiently enthusiastic about money had and received to contemplate using it as an

79 Gareth Jones, 'The Role of Equity in the English Law of Restitution', in Schrage (ed.), *Unjust Enrichment*, p. 165.
80 *Clarke* v. *Shee* (1774) 1 Cowp 197, 199; *Jestons* v. *Brooke* (1778) 2 Cowp 793, 795.
81 In particular, Chancery would order the repayment of money paid as a result of mistake or fraud: Ibbetson, *Historical Introduction*, pp. 273–4.
82 *Sadler* v. *Evans* (1766) 4 Burr 1984, 1986. He used similarly expansionist terminology to describe the action for money paid around this time, see *Decker* v. *Pope* (1757) LI MS Misc. 129 (unfol.). Lord Mansfield made the same comment about actions of the case generally in *Gardiner* v. *Crosedale* (1760) 1 Wm Bla 198, 199.
83 *Hoam* v. *Scott* (1767) LI MS Misc. 129 f. 107; *Dale* v. *Sollet* (1767) 4 Burr 2133, 2134; *Lindon* v. *Hooper* (1776) 1 Cowp 414, 419; *Buller* v. *Harrison* (1777) 2 Cowp 565, 568; *Jestons* v. *Brooke* (1778) 2 Cowp 793, 797; *Stevenson* v. *Mortimer* (1778) 2 Cowp 805, 806; *Bize* v. *Dickason* (1786) 1 TR 285, 286; *Straton* v. *Rastall* (1788) 2 TR 366, 370.
84 *Weston* v. *Downes* (1778) 1 Doug 23, 24; *Towers* v. *Barrett* (1786) 1 TR 133, 134.
85 *Longchamp* v. *Kenny* (1778) 1 Doug 137; LI MS Hill 13 f. 311.
86 *Straton* v. *Rastall* (1778) 2 TR 366, 370.

alternative rationale in *Hawkes* v. *Saunders*.[87] In a draft judgment which was never delivered he also emphasised once again that money had and received was founded upon Equity. Various explanations can be put forward for the new found caution. Money had and received, on the back of a broad notion of equity, could be seen as a threat to the stability of the Common law. Liberally applied, money had and received had the potential to upset commercial bargains.[88]

One of the great attractions of all types of non-contractual assumpsits, including money had and received, was the way in which they could be pleaded. By the mid-century, when counting on the contract, plaintiffs were also adding *quantum meruits* for the value of their labour or one of the other general indebitatus counts. The advantage of this mode of pleading was that it provided a safety net. If the claim on the contract was unsuccessful it was still possible to recover something. The traditional rules that prevented this mode of pleading[89] were relaxed in *Harris* v. *Oke*, where Lord Mansfield pointed out that it was often difficult to succeed in an action on the contract itself because the broad general issue in contract claims allowed the defendant to introduce a wide range of evidence to the jury, so that 'it was impossible even for the ablest counsel to know without prophecy what may be proved'.[90] Within twenty years this method of pleading had become standard practice.[91]

There were also very specific pleading advantages attached to money had and received. As Lord Mansfield explained, 'neither party is allowed to entrap the other in form'.[92] Small wonder that plaintiffs soon began to use the remedy as an indirect method for trying a breach of warranty. By counting in money had and received instead of special assumpsit, there was no need to set out the way in which a warranty was breached and thereby avoiding putting the defendant on notice of the evidence that the plaintiff intended to lead at the trial. The courts were quick to spot and disapprove of this ruse.[93] By the mid-1780s a rule against using money

87 James Oldham, 'Reinterpretations of Eighteenth Century English Contract Theory: A View From Lord Mansfield's Trial Notes' (1988) 76 *Georgetown Law Journal* 1949, 1989–90.

88 Baloch, *Unjust Enrichment*, p. 38 citing *Floyer* v. *Edwards* (1774) 1 Cowp 112.

89 This sort of pleading was allowed by Holt C.J. in *Francam* v. *Foster* (1693) Skinner 326, Holt 25, but he soon sought to restrict it: *Anon* (1695) Comb 341; *Anon* (1697) Comb 446.

90 (1759) LI MS Hill 6 f. 217.

91 *Payne* v. *Bacomb* (1781) 2 Doug 651. For what looks like an early attempt to use this type of pleading, see *Forrester* v. *Hodgson* (1778), Oldham, *Mansfield Manuscripts*, vol. I, pp. 326–7.

92 *Stevenson* v. *Mortimer* (1778) Cowp 805, 807.

93 *Weston* v. *Downes* (1778) 1 Doug 23; Warren Swain, 'Cutter v. Powell and the Pleading of Claims of Unjust Enrichment' [2003] *Restitution Law Review* 46, 51.

had and received to try warranties had broadened out into a rule against using money had and received where the contract remained open. In *Towers* v. *Barrett*, Buller J. explained the new restriction:

> The distinction between those cases where the contract is open, and where it is not, is this; if the contract be rescinded, either, as in this case, by the original terms of the contract, where no act remains to be done by the defendant himself, or by a subsequent assent by the defendant, the plaintiff is entitled to recover back his whole money; and then an action for money had and received will lie. But if the contract be open, the plaintiff's demand is not for the whole sum, but for damages arising out of that contract.[94]

In addition to warranties, other problems began to surface as pleaders began to push the boundaries of money had and received too far.[95] Once it was admitted that the action was analogous to a bill in Equity, it teetered on the edge of property. The plaintiff recovered because the money 'belonged' to the plaintiff and the defendant was acting contrary to justice in retaining it.[96] The courts were soon forced to make clear that money had and received could not be used to recover a specific thing as opposed to money.[97] To allow such claims would be to undermine the action of trover.[98] The attempts to reign in money had and received, which began when Lord Mansfield was still on the Bench, would pick up pace in the decades that followed. In *Moses* v. *Macferlan*, Lord Mansfield listed the situations where money had and received could be brought,[99] but it seems unlikely that this was intended to limit the action as opposed to providing examples that reflected existing practice.[100]

94 (1786) 1 TR 133, 136.

95 *Lindon* v. *Hooper* (1776) 1 Cowp 414, 419. It may also have posed a threat to the bankruptcy laws, see Baloch, *Unjust Enrichment*, pp. 38–9 citing *Brown* v. *Bullen* (1780) 1 Doug 407.

96 *Clarke* v. *Shee* (1774) 1 Cowp 197 the plaintiff is described as the 'true owner' of the money in the head-note.

97 *Nightingal* v. *Devisme* (1770) 5 Burr 2589.

98 *Longchamp* v. *Kenny* (1778) 1 Doug 137. Trover was an action in tort against someone for misappropriating goods, see J.H. Baker, *An Introduction to English Legal History*, 4th edn (London: Butterworths, 2002), pp. 397–9.

99 (1760) 2 Burr 1005, 1012.

100 The list may have been pretty standard. A similar one was used in the much earlier decision of *Attorney General* v. *Perry* (1735) 2 Com 481 and by counsel in *Mattos* v. *Parker* (1756) LI MS Harrowby 17 at 35, see Baloch, *Unjust Enrichment*, pp. 26–7.

Rationalising money had and received

Despite Lord Mansfield's attempt to generalise liability in money had and received, by the early nineteenth century the action was in retreat. The relationship with property and the problems of pleading warranties were not the only causes of concern. From early in the eighteenth century, reconciling money had and received and the other non-contractual assumpsits with the law of contract had proved troublesome. Not all the problems were practical. The non-contractual assumpsits proved to be difficult to classify. As a matter of form, assumpsit was an action in contract, yet as a matter of substance these claims were not based on a contract. Roman law solved the problem nearly 1,500 years ago. Justinian's *Institutes* declared that obligations 'arise ex contractu or quasi-ex contractu, ex maleficio or quasi-ex maleficio'.[101] Modern lawyers prefer to attach the label of unjust enrichment or restitution to this type of claim. The principle of unjust enrichment first appeared in Justinian's *Digest* in two texts attributed to Pomponius.[102] In Roman law unjust enrichment did not describe a distinct legal remedy.[103] The early glossator Martinus Gosia tried to turn it into one but his analysis did not catch on.[104] Instead by the sixteenth century the European Civilians were equating 'quasi-ex contractu' with implied contract.[105]

The Natural lawyers diverged from the Civilians in this respect. By drawing instead on the work of Thomas Aquinas, in his *Inleidinge*

101 Thomas Sandars (trans.), *The Institutes of Justinian* (London: Longman, 1948), 3.12.2.

102 A. Watson (trans.), *The Digest of Justinian* (Philadelphia: University of Pennsylvania Press, 1985), 12.6.14: 'For it is by nature fair, that nobody should enrich himself at the expense of another'; 50.17.206: 'By the law of nature it is fair that nobody become richer by the loss and injury of another'.

103 Fritz Schulz, *Classical Roman Law* (Oxford: Oxford University Press, 1951), p. 610 described the *Digest* texts as a general idea or principle, not a legal rule. Other scholars broadly agree: Ibbetson, *Historical Introduction*, p. 10; Robert Feenstra, 'Grotius' Doctrine of Unjust Enrichment as a Source of Obligation: Its Origin and Its Influence in Roman-Dutch Law', in Schrage (ed.), *Unjust Enrichment*, p. 198; Jan Hallebeek, *The Concept of Unjust Enrichment in Late Scholasticism* (Nijmegen: Gerard Noodt Instituut, 1996), p. 1. Reinhard Zimmermann, *The Law of Obligations: Roman Foundations of the Civilian Tradition* (Oxford: Oxford University Press, 1996), pp. 852, 873 puts greater weight on these passages.

104 Hallebeek, *Unjust Enrichment*, pp. 4, 41.

105 Peter Birks and Grant MacLeod, 'The Implied Contract Theory of Quasi-Contract: Civilian Opinion Current in the Century Before Blackstone' (1986) 6 *Oxford Journal of Legal Studies* 46, 68–77.

tot de Hollandsche rechtsgeleerdheid,[106] Hugo Grotius distinguished between contract and quasi-contract, which was said to be analogous to,[107] or 'as if' there were, a contract.[108] Grotius also made some progress in turning Pomponius's principle into a concrete remedy. But the impact of this potentially far reaching breakthrough was rather muted. In his later and better known work *De iure belli ac pacis*, Grotius described quasi-contract as 'ex lege', and unjust enrichment was only discussed in the context of the institution of property. His earlier and more radical analysis was also ignored by Samuel Pufendorf, whose *De iure naturae et gentium* offered little more than a reheated version of Roman law.[109]

English writers largely shied away from the subject until the early eighteenth century. Robert Eden, who was heavily influenced by Heineccius,[110] favoured the implied contract analysis used by the European Civilians. Thomas Wood, another English Civilian, in his *A New Institute of the Imperial or Civil Law*,[111] was more adventurous. In a chapter headed 'Of obligations from Improper or Quasi-Contracts created by Law without Agreement or Consent', he wrote:

> There are some Obligations which arise amongst Mankind without any previous Consent or Agreement; and they are call'd Improper or Quasi-Contracts; yet they have as firm a foundation in Justice as those which are made directly and by consent . . . An Improper or Quasi-Contract is as binding to those who are unwilling or ignorant of it, as strongly as those Contracts which are enter'd into by Agreement.[112]

Wood's description of quasi-contract was closer to Roman law than it was to the Civilian conception.[113] When in a later book he set out to describe the law in England rather than Rome, he was much less confident about the nature of the distinction between contract and quasi-contract, preferring to assert that some contracts were implied in law and omitting accident and fraud which had appeared as grounds for a claim in quasi-contract in the earlier work. The implied contract theory was not confined to Civilian writers. It was also used by Sir Jeffrey Gilbert in

106 R.W. Lee (trans.), Hugo Grotius, *Introduction to the Jurisprudence of Holland* (Oxford: Oxford University Press, 1926).
107 *Ibid.*, 3.26.2. 108 *Ibid.*, 3.26.3.
109 Charles and William Oldfather (trans.), Samuel Pufendorf, *Of the Law of Nature and Nations (1688 edn)* (Oxford: Oxford University Press, 1934), 4.13.5.
110 H.F. Jolowicz, 'Some English Civilians' (1949) 2 *Current Legal Problems* 139, 151.
111 2nd edn (London, 1712). 112 *Ibid.*, p. 255.
113 Wood's category was broader than Justinian's. He included accident at pp. 260–3 and fraud at pp. 262–3. These were the only examples of quasi-contract where Wood did not refer to the *Digest* or *Institutes*.

his unpublished treatise, where he observed that when an obligation arises quasi-ex contractu, then the law implies a contract.[114]

Lord Mansfield's attempt to fashion a remedy out of equity had little immediate impact on the way that legal writers rationalised the non-contractual assumpsits. In William Blackstone's lectures, delivered in the 1750s, money had and received appeared as a form of implied assumpsit alongside *quantum meruit*, *quantum valebant*, money paid, account stated, and liability of an office holder.[115] In a concession to *Moses* v. *Macferlan* in the published *Commentaries*, Blackstone cites Lord Mansfield's judgment verbatim without generalising liability in the way that the Chief Justice had done.[116] When it came to Blackstone's successors, Robert Chambers took a broad view of the implied contract, which he placed right at the heart of his treatment of obligations, seeing it as the primary vehicle for dealings between men.[117] He wrote that 'an implied contract is violated when either of the parties to the transaction refuses to act according to the known and natural relation of things as acknowledged by the customary commerce of life'.[118] Richard Wooddeson followed Blackstone more closely, stressing that in the action for money had and received the defendant 'is obliged by the ties of natural justice and equity to refund the money', but in the same paragraph declared that 'the law implies a promise'.[119]

Moving into the nineteenth century, the approaches of the various legal writers to the question of the juridical basis of these claims were more than a little schizophrenic. Henry Colebrooke wrote that in quasi-contract 'no consent intervenes' because such obligations were the product of law or 'natural equity'.[120] But he qualified his remarks by stating that quasi-contract is based on 'tacit or presumed consent'.[121] Writers on contract included the non-contractual assumpsits in their treatises as a matter of course. In the first edition of his treatise, Joseph Chitty

[114] BL MS Hargrave 265 f. 202. [115] All Souls MS 300 vol. XVIII (unfol.).

[116] Blackstone, *Commentaries*, vol. III, p. 162.

[117] Thomas Curley (ed.), Robert Chambers, *A Course of Lectures on English Law Delivered at the University of Oxford 1767–73*, 2 vols. (Oxford: Oxford University Press, 1986), vol. II, p. 224.

[118] *Ibid.*

[119] Richard Wooddeson, *A Systematical View of the Laws of England as Treated of in a Course of Vinerian Lectures*, 3 vols. (London, 1792–3), vol. III, p. 158.

[120] H.T. Colebrooke, *A Treatise on Obligations and Contracts* (London, 1818), pp. 15–16.

[121] *Ibid.*, p. 182.

prefaced a section on money had and received with Lord Mansfield's remarks in *Moses* v. *Macferlan*.[122] In the second edition he was even more explicit about the need to distinguish contract and quasi-contract, with the latter being formed 'without the intervention of any agreement'.[123] Most of the writers of this period, on the other hand, simply continued to equate the non-contractual assumpsits with implied contract.[124] The next generation of legal writers were less contented with the terminology of implied contract. William Fox supported the description of money had and received as 'equitable',[125] Henry Maine drew a firm distinction between contract and quasi-contract,[126] Leake argued that these obligations rested in justice and equity,[127] Pollock stressed that there was no true contract as opposed to something analogous to one,[128] and Anson suggested that the contract classification was a historical accident rather than the product of a well-reasoned theory.[129]

Little progress was made in developing a coherent theoretical rationale for money had and received. The exception was Sir William Evans. In the introduction to his translation of Pothier he argued that:

> Quasi-contracts, which with us would be treated by implication, as actual contracts. They differ from contracts, as not being founded upon actual consent; and also differ from injuries. Such are the cases of receiving money which ought to be refunded, the obligation of accounting for business done for another in his absence on one hand, and remunerating the expenses sustained in doing so on the other.[130]

122 Joseph Chitty, *A Practical Treatise on the Law of Contracts not under Seal* (London: S. Sweet, 1826), p. 182.

123 Joseph Chitty, *A Practical Treatise on the Law of Contracts not under Seal*, 2nd edn (London: S. Sweet, 1834), p. 22.

124 Samuel Comyn, *The Law of Contracts and Promises*, 2nd edn (London: A. Strahan, 1824), pp. 4–5; C.G. Addison, *A Treatise on Contracts and Liabilities Ex-Contractu* (London: W Benning, 1847), pp. 206–37.

125 William Fox, *A Treatise on Simple Contracts and the Action of Assumpsit* (London: Stevens, 1842), p. 122.

126 Henry Maine, *Ancient Law* (London: Dent, 1861), pp. 343–4, noted by Ibbetson, *Historical Introduction*, p. 284.

127 Stephen Leake, *The Elements of the Law of Contracts* (London: Stevens & Sons, 1867), pp. 38–75 esp. pp. 38–9.

128 Frederick Pollock, *Principles of Contract at Law and in Equity* (London: Stevens & Sons, 1876), pp. 28–9.

129 William Anson, *Principles of the English Law of Contract* (Oxford: Clarendon Press, 1879), pp. 7, 321–7.

130 William Evans (trans.), R. Pothier, *A Treatise on the Law of Obligations or Contracts*, 2 vols. (London: A. Strahan, 1806), vol. I, p. 85.

Whilst Evans begins by equating quasi-contract with contract, he also recognised that one rested on assent and the other did not. His discomfort with the implied contract analysis was evident later in the work when he came to explain that 'implied contract' was 'applicable rather to the evidence than to the nature or quality of the obligation', so that 'an implied promise is deemed to have taken place'.[131] In his *Essays: On the Action for Money Had and Received, on the Law of Insurances, and on the Law of Bills of Exchange and Promissory Notes*,[132] Evans went even further. Not only did he unequivocally support Lord Mansfield's generalisation of money had and received,[133] he closely identified money had and received with unjust enrichment.[134]

Evans's analysis would not attract much support in England before the twentieth century.[135] Some judges would continue to refer to equity, good conscience, or the maxim *ex æquo et bono*, in the context of money had and received.[136] Others were worried that the supposedly equitable foundation of money had and received was undermining the boundary between Common law and Equity:

> In the case of *Moses* v. *Macferlan* some principles were laid down, which are certainly too large, and which I do not mean to rely on, such as that, wherever one man has money which another ought to have, an action for money had and received may be maintained; or that wherever a man has an equitable claim he has also a legal action.[137]

Others preferred instead to tie such claims into the law of contract. When it was necessary to classify these claims for technical purposes they were seen as contractual.[138] Substantive principles also began to move across from contractual assumpsit, including the entire contracts

[131] *Ibid.*, vol. I, p. 69. [132] (Liverpool: Merritt & Wright, 1802). [133] *Ibid.*, p. 7.
[134] *Ibid.*, p. 8.
[135] American lawyers were in ahead of their English counterparts in this respect: William Keener, *Treatise on the Law of Quasi-Contracts* (New York: Baker Voorhis, 1893); Frederic Woodward, *The Law of Quasi-Contract* (Boston: Little, Brown & Co., 1913).
[136] *Master* v. *Miller* (1791) 4 TR 320, 342–3; *Harrison* v. *Walker* (1791) Peake 150, 151; *Cotton* v. *Thurland* (1793) 5 TR 405, 409; *Greville* v. *Da Costa* (1797) Peake Add 113, 114; *Wright* v. *Hunter* (1800) 1 East 20, 29; *Surtees* v. *Hubbard* (1802) 4 Esp 203, 204; *Simpson* v. *Swan* (1812) 3 Camp 291, 293; *Foster* v. *Stewart* (1814) 3 M & S 191, 200; *De Silvale* v. *Kendall* (1815) 4 M & S 37, 46.
[137] *Johnson* v. *Johnson* (1802) 3 B & P 162, 169. See also *Cooth* v. *Jackson* (1801) 6 Ves Jun 12, 39.
[138] Ibbetson, *Historical Introduction*, pp. 278–9.

rule[139] and an early form of privity of contract.[140] In 1849, Pollock C.B. articulated the new orthodoxy when he explained that money had and received 'is a perfectly legal action, and no good can result from calling it an equitable one'.[141]

Once money had and received lost its equitable foundations it took a long time to recover. The rest of the non-contractual assumpsits remained confined to specific factual situations. The absence of a convincing framework, of the sort that would be important in helping to reshape the law of contract, was also a contributory factor. Even those writers who were not persuaded by the implied contract analysis failed to produce a workable alternative. Rather than a potentially vigorous and flexible remedy, money had and received had become stifled. Even Evans, who favoured a broad rationale for money had and received, confined himself to Lord Mansfield's list of examples, with the addition of money paid under an illegal contract.[142] It was all a long way from the potentially broad equitable remedy initially envisaged by Lord Mansfield. Whilst the equitable underpinnings of money had and received may have fallen away, the debate on the relationship between Equity and Common law was not quite at an end. Nor was it the end of equitable influences on the Common law. Indeed, these would play a significant role in the development of contract doctrine in the nineteenth century.

139 *Sinclair* v. *Bowles* (1829) 9 B & C 92; *Roberts* v. *Havelock* (1832) 3 B & Ad 404; *Hughes* v. *Lenny* (1839) 5 M & W 183; *Appleby* v. *Myers* (1867) LR 2 CP 651.

140 Compare *Israel* v. *Douglas* (1789) 1 H Bla 239 with *Williams* v. *Everett* (1811) 14 East 582. See also *Baron* v. *Husband* (1833) 4 B & Ad 611; *Howell* v. *Batt* (1833) 5 B & Ad 504.

141 *Miller* v. *Atlee* (1849) 13 Jur 431.

142 Evans, *Essay*, pp. 37–80. For another attempt at listing the situations in which money had and received could be brought, see Charles Petersdorff, *A Practical and Elementary Abridgement of the Common Law*, 5 vols. (London: Stevens & Norton, 1843), vol. IV, pp. 666–79.

6

Lord Mansfield and his successors

The period during which Lord Mansfield was Chief Justice remains a popular subject for legal historians. In contrast, the thirty years which followed his retirement in 1788 have been comparatively neglected at best, or at worse have been used in order to make an unflattering contrast with the preceding few decades.[1] Lord Mansfield's successors are portrayed as conservative-minded individuals hostile to change. The reputation of Lord Kenyon, who himself described Lord Mansfield as a 'great judge',[2] has suffered when set against his illustrious predecessor. Some appraisals are damning. One contemporary argued that 'Lord Kenyon must, comparatively with the great Earl Mansfield, hold a very inferior station in the temple of fame'.[3] Other observers were slightly more generous: 'In dignity, urbanity and grace there was a sad falling off in the court, but in knowledge of law, application of principle, discrimination of character, infinite readiness, and honesty of purpose the new Chief Justice need not fear a comparison with his great predecessor.'[4] Some positively welcomed a change of style. In the opinion of James Boswell, Lord Kenyon was 'a good fuller's mill to thicken and consolidate the law, which was very necessary after the loose texture which Lord Mansfield had given it'.[5] On any assessment of Lord Kenyon's abilities, it seems more likely than not that the direction of the law of contract would

[1] P.S. Atiyah, *The Rise and Fall of Freedom of Contract* (Oxford: Oxford University Press, 1979), p. 362 wrote of Lords Eldon, Kenyon and Ellenborough that: 'It is well known that these three men opposed practically all legal reform for nearly thirty years.' In contrast, see W.S. Holdsworth, *A History of English Law*, 17 vols. (London: Sweet & Maxwell, 1938), vol. XII, p. 580, who described Kenyon 'as no blind conservative'.

[2] *Bent* v. *Baker* (1789) 3 TR 27, 32.

[3] Leman Rede, *Strictures on the Lives and Characters of the Most Eminent Lawyers of the Present Day* (London, 1790), p. 94.

[4] Edward Foss, *The Judges of England*, 9 vols. (London: John Murray, 1864), vol. VIII, p. 316.

[5] Irma Lustig and Frederick Pottle (eds.), James Boswell, *Boswell: The English Experiment, 1785–1789* (London: Heinemann, 1986), pp. 234–5.

have been different if, as many expected, Buller J. had succeeded Lord Mansfield as Chief Justice of the King's Bench in the late 1780s.[6]

Rede prefaced his study of Lord Kenyon with an epigram taken from *Othello*, 'Rude am I, of speech.'[7] His two immediate successors, Lord Ellenborough and Lord Tenterden, also had a reputation for irascibility.[8] Ballantine described Lord Tenterden as 'a sour old man'.[9] Bouts of bad temper are perhaps to be expected given the work load required of the Chief Justice of the King's Bench both in banc and also at nisi prius.[10] But there were also more positive similarities.[11] Before elevation to the bench, Lord Ellenborough and Lord Tenterden were both highly regarded for their expertise in commercial matters.[12] Tenterden had even published a book on maritime law in 1802.[13] During an era of rapid economic expansion in which plenty of commercial questions came before the courts, this sort of knowledge would prove to be particularly valuable.[14]

[6] Buller J. was certainly not short of admirers, see Rede, *Strictures*, p. 106, who described him as 'the Coke of the present age'; Anon, 'My contemporaries from the note book of a retired barrister' (1832) 6 *Fraser's Magazine* 220, 225. There was open disagreement between Buller J. and Lord Kenyon on more than one occasion: *Brown* v. *Davies* (1789) 3 TR 80; *Smart* v. *Wolff* (1789) 3 TR 323; *Leftley* v. *Mills* (1791) 4 TR 170.

[7] Rede, *Strictures*, p. 93. These remarks were uttered by Othello about himself, Kenneth Muir (ed.), William Shakespeare, *Othello* (London: Penguin, 1968), act 1, scene 3.

[8] James Grant, *The Bench and the Bar*, 2 vols. (London: Henry Colburn, 1837), vol. I, p. 69 (Lord Ellenborough), p. 83 (Lord Tenterden). Lord Eldon in contrast, Chief Justice of the Common Pleas between 1799 and 1801, and more famously Lord Chancellor between 1801 and 1806 and again between 1807 and 1827, has been described as 'mild and gentle', see Rose Melikan, *John Scott, Lord Eldon, 1751–1838: The Duty of Loyalty* (Cambridge: Cambridge University Press, 1999), p. 155.

[9] William Ballantine, *Some Experiences of a Barristers Life* (New York: Henry Holt, 1882), p. 359.

[10] For detail of the work load at nisi prius, see James Oldham, 'Law-Making at Nisi Prius in the Early 1800s' (2004) 25 *Journal of Legal History* 221, 226–9.

[11] Which is not to say that a short temper cannot, when combined with other virtues, be a positive benefit. Britain's greatest twentieth century peace-time Prime Minister, Margaret Thatcher, is testimony to this fact: Robin Harris, *Not For Turning: The Life of Margaret Thatcher* (London: Bantam Press, 2013), p. 161.

[12] On Ellenborough and commercial law, see *Thompson* v. *Williamson* (1831) 7 Bligh NS 432, 443–4; M. Lobban, 'Law, Edward', *Oxford Dictionary of National Biography*, stresses Lord Ellenborough's commercial expertise.

[13] Charles Abbott, *A Treatise of the Law Relative to Merchant Ships and Seaman* (London: E. Brooke, 1802). In the hands of a series of editors the treatise ran to fourteen editions, the last of which appeared in 1901. In *Wilson* v. *Dickson* (1818) 2 B & Ald 2, eight counsel cited the work even though Abbot J. was one of the judges in the case.

[14] Many commercial contract disputes were coming before the courts around this time: M.S. Hardcastle, *Life of John, Lord Campbell*, 2 vols. (London: John Murray, 1881), vol. I,

The perception that the emergence of the classical model of contract, a period around 1790 to 1820, witnessed a conservative-led retreat from an earlier golden age of legal innovation is not without foundation. Lord Kenyon himself stated that 'I confess that I do not think that the Courts ought to change the law so as to adapt it to the fashion of the times: if an alteration in the law be necessary, recourse must be had to the legislature for it.'[15] Yet the orthodox view amounts to a serious oversimplification on a number of levels. It ignores the extent to which some of the more radical reforms of contract doctrine, such as the attempt to side-line consideration for contracts in writing, had already come to grief. There were other instances of attempts to stifle innovation in the decades before 1790. Lord Mansfield's desire to place some limits on money had and received is the most obvious example. The negative perception of this era also ignores those occasions where the courts built on, rather than attempted to dismantle, what had gone before or even broke out into entirely new directions altogether. Some attempts at reform of contract doctrine were just as radical as anything proposed by Lord Mansfield and his contemporaries. The growth in law reporting also shed light on trials at nisi prius and helped to emphasise that law making was not confined to judges sitting in banc.[16] Nisi prius hearings would play a significant role in shaping the direction of contract doctrine. Legal literature also entered an important new stage. A considerable body of literature on contract law already existed, but legal writing entered a more fruitful and sophisticated phase.

Contract law and doctrinal innovation

Judges were candid about the nature of the judicial process. Lord Kenyon explained that 'The situation of judges is such that they are sometimes obliged to decide against their own feelings as men'.[17] At the same time, he warned that 'However technical rules are to be attended to, and in some cases cannot be dispensed with, yet in administering justice we must not lose sight of common sense'.[18] Lord Ellenborough also saw his

p. 214, Lord Campbell argued that the Napoleonic Wars, commodity price fluctuations, depreciation in value of paper money, and mass bankruptcy litigation all kept the courts busy, see Oldham, 'Law Making', p. 229. Oldham's figures on the type of cases to appear before Lord Ellenborough support this anecdotal observation, Oldham, 'Law Making', pp. 230–1 provides evidence of a large number of cases on contracts and negotiable instruments.

[15] *Ellah* v. *Leigh* (1794) 5 TR 679, 682. [16] Oldham, 'Law Making', pp. 229–39.

[17] *Geyer* v. *Aguilar* (1798) 7 TR 681, 695. [18] *Rawson* v. *Johnson* (1801) 1 East 203, 208.

role to 'act upon the law as it stands. Whether it be right or wrong, I cannot take upon me to change it.'[19] He also professed not to like judicial discretion.[20] Certainty was also highly valued. Lord Kenyon declared in *Rotch* v. *Edie* that 'it is proper that great commercial questions should be so satisfactorily determined so as to leave no room for doubt in after-ages'.[21] In *Williams* v. *Smith*, a case which was concerned with bills of exchange, Abbot C.J. stated 'It is of the greatest importance to commerce, that some plain and precise rule should be laid down'.[22]

Once it is recognised that Lord Mansfield was a more complex figure than the radical reformer of popular perception, then it becomes easier to concede that, at least in terms of contract law, there was more of a change of tone than a tectonic shift. There was perhaps not a great deal in these remarks out of step with what Lord Mansfield, especially in later years, was advocating.

In *Brough* v. *Whitmore* Lord Kenyon said that:

> But then I thought, and still continue to think, that the rule of law is to be given (not by merchants) but by the Court; though, when a question arises on the construction of the words of an instrument, which are in themselves ambiguous, it is a matter fairly within the province of those who alone act upon such instruments to declare the meaning of them.[23]

Buller J.'s judgment struck a rather different note: 'It is sufficient to say that a policy of assurance has at all times been considered in Courts of Law as an absurd and incoherent instrument: but it is founded on usage, and must be governed and construed by usage.'[24] Although on this occasion Lord Kenyon appeared cautious about the proper role of mercantile usage, the influence of merchants on the Common law did not disappear with Lord Mansfield's retirement.[25] Although important in matters of contract construction,[26] mercantile usage had wider applications. Judges continued to take mercantile opinion seriously. In *Senat* v. *Porter* Lord Kenyon recognised that 'great complaints have been made in the commercial world, and not without reason, of the

19 *Kingston* v. *M'Intosh* (1808) 1 Camp 517, 519.

20 *De Havilland* v. *Bowerbank* (1807) 1 Camp 50, 51.

21 (1795) 6 TR 413. On the importance of certainty in other contexts, see *Jones* v. *Roe* (1789) 3 TR 88.

22 (1819) 2 B & Ald 496, 500. 23 (1791) 4 TR 206, 208. 24 (1791) 4 TR 206, 210.

25 Lord Kenyon was quite prepared on other occasions to recognise the need to keep the law of contract in line with commercial expectations: *Cutter* v. *Powell* (1795) 6 TR 320, 324.

26 For the role of merchants in construction, see *Burnet* v. *Kensington* (1795) 1 Esp 416.

enormous expense attending the trial of insurance'.[27] Judges were prepared to consider the impact of a particular ruling, for good or ill, on commercial parties.[28]

Merchants continued to be called as expert witnesses[29] and the value of mercantile juries was widely recognised.[30] Lord Kenyon even suggested that juries of merchants in Westminster were superior to ordinary juries in the country.[31] Oldham has argued that the role of mercantile juries was changing with what he terms a more 'active model' emerging.[32] Mercantile juries had sufficient influence in matters of mercantile usage that they were quite capable of prompting a judicial change of heart.[33] The opinions of individual jurors also carried considerable weight as illustrated by *Brough* v. *Whitmore*, where the trial was halted until some investigation could be made of a case raised by a juryman.[34] The degree of familiarity between the Bench and individual jurors was such that they were sometimes referred to by name.[35] Between 1790 and 1820 mercantile literature made the occasional appearance in the law reports.[36]

Identifying the precise needs of the mercantile community was sometimes fraught with difficulty. The position of the *bona fide* holder of a negotiable instrument for value was one of the principal problems facing the courts in this period.[37] In *Lawson* v. *Warren*[38] a bill of exchange

27 (1797) 7 TR 158.

28 *Brown* v. *Harraden* (1791) 4 TR 148, 151; *Boehm* v. *Sterling* (1797) 2 Esp 575, 577; *Idle* v. *Thornton* (1812) 3 Camp 274, 276; *Sargent* v. *Morris* (1819) 3 B & Ald 277, 279.

29 *Thornton* v. *Royal Exchequer Assurance Company* (1790) Peake 37 (evidence of shipbuilder on seaworthiness); *Chaurand* v. *Angerstein* (1791) Peake 61 (evidence of underwriters on insurance); *Middlewood* v. *Blakes* (1797) 7 TR 162 (evidence of sailors on sea route).

30 For explicit statements on the value of the jury, see James Oldham, *The Varied Life of the Self-Informing Jury* (London: Selden Society, 2005), p. 28; *Driscol* v. *Passmore* (1798) 1 B & P 200, 203; *Langhorne* v. *Allnutt* (1812) 4 Taunt 511, 518–19; *Levy* v. *Buck* (1812) 4 Taunt 387.

31 *Allesbrook* v. *Roach* (1795) Peake Add Cas 27, 28.

32 Oldham, *Self-Informing Jury*, p. 26 which he characterises as 'a jury of experts who were permitted, perhaps encouraged to participate in the trial and to articulate, where relevant, mercantile practices'.

33 *Amery* v. *Rogers* (1794) 1 Esp 208. For an example of a jury and mercantile usage, see *Cohen* v. *Paget* (1814) 4 Camp 96.

34 (1791) 4 TR 206, 207. 35 *Wright* v. *Shiffner* (1809) 2 Camp 247, 249.

36 *Power* v. *Whitmore* (1815) 4 M & S 141, 149 (Beawes cited by Lord Ellenborough); *Busk* v. *Royal Exchange Assurance Company* (1818) 2 B & Ald 73, 80 (Mayles cited by Bayley J.).

37 J. Milnes Holden, *The History of Negotiable Instruments in English Law* (London: Athlone Press, 1955), p. 177.

38 (1801) 4 Esp 56.

which had been lost or stolen was brought to the plaintiff bank where it was discounted[39] for the holder who indorsed the bill to the defendant. The defendant then refused to pay. It was argued that the bank ought not to have discounted a bill to an unknown person without using due diligence in inquiring into the person and the bill. The bank argued that this was normal practice amongst bankers. Lord Kenyon was not prepared to consider evidence of banking practice on the grounds that it might differ between banks acting with 'equal integrity'. At the same time, he accepted that imposing a duty to make inquiries would 'paralyse the circulation of all the paper in the country, and with it all its commerce'.[40] Just twenty years later, in *Gill* v. *Cubitt*,[41] on very similar facts, Abbott C.J. came to a totally different conclusion about the needs of commercial parties and the correct rule of law. Where the bill was discounted in circumstances which ought to have excited the suspicion of a prudent and careful man, then the defendant who had accepted the bill was not liable. Abbot C.J. justified this change on the grounds that the earlier decision had encouraged the robbing of stage coaches for negotiable instruments.[42] It was, he said, not in the interests of commerce that 'any individual should be enabled to dispose of bills or notes without being subject to enquiry'.[43] Best C.J. would subsequently point out that the test of due diligence would be easy enough for a mercantile jury to apply.[44] References to the interests of commerce in cases on bills of exchange seemed to fall away. By 1800 they had become rather vague. Specific inquiries into business practice were resisted. By the time Lord Denman substituted 'gross negligence' for 'due diligence',[45] and then adopted '*mala fides*',[46] any mention of commerce had completely disappeared. These situations were some of the last where a basic principle of bills remained to be established. For the most part the law relating to negotiable instruments was largely settled by the mid-eighteenth century. In these circumstances, it might be expected that certainty would not be sacrificed on the altar of commercial convenience, though of

[39] The process of discounting involved converting a bill for cash. The holder then sought to recover on the bill. His profit came from the difference between the value of the bill and the amount of cash advanced. On discounting, see James Rogers, *The Early History of the Law of Bills and Notes* (Cambridge: Cambridge University Press, 1995), pp. 121–2.

[40] (1801) 4 Esp 56, 57. [41] (1824) 3 B & C 466. [42] *Ibid.*, p. 471. [43] *Ibid.*, p. 472.

[44] *Snow* v. *Peacock* (1826) 3 Bing 406, 412. See also *Beckwith* v. *Corral* (1826) 3 Bing 444.

[45] *Crook* v. *Jadis* (1834) 5 B & Ad 909; *Backhouse* v. *Harrison* (1834) 5 B & Ad 1098.

[46] *Goodman* v. *Harvey* (1836) 4 Ad & E 870.

course it remains possible that, even if not articulated, it was a factor that retained its hold over judges.

The precise influence of merchants on the development of contract doctrine is difficult to assess. This is all the more true of the Civilian writers, who were a familiar feature of Lord Mansfield's court, particularly, but not solely, in the field of marine insurance law. Wilmot J.'s judgment in *Pillans* v. *Van Mierop* clearly showed that in the hands of a skilful judge, knowledge of legal literature could be used in order to advance the cause of doctrinal reform. Between 1790 and 1820 Civilian writers continued to feature in the law reports.[47] In *Wolff* v. *Oxholm*,[48] Lord Ellenborough referred to Bynkershoek, Vattel, Grotius, and Pufendorf alongside Hale. But he was also acutely aware of the limitations of Civilian literature. Having praised Emerigon, the French writer, for his 'great ability, diligence and learning', he cautioned that 'his opinion, like the opinion of any other learned man, is fallible; and, in the present instance, it is founded on a great many ordinances which do not govern our decisions'.[49] From the 1790s onwards one Civilian writer, John Joseph Pothier, began to stand out. Pothier was a major figure and his writings a significant influence on the development of contract law in England in the nineteenth century. The precise nature of this process is complex. It can be traced in the case law and literature after 1820.

There was much less continuity when it came to a third feature of the decades before 1790: the willingness of Common law judges to borrow from Equity. Richard Wooddeson observed that 'Our courts of Equity at present differ from those of law more in exterior matters of practice than in principle, and more in mode of relief than in determining the essential merits of the cause, as to the naked question of who shall prevail in litigation'.[50] That Wooddeson should be willing to countenance a degree of substantive overlap is not all that surprising given the timing of his remarks. Although not published until the 1790s, the lectures were first delivered in the late 1770s around the time that the boundary between the two jurisdictions was at its most fluid. The nature of that relationship was changing. The mood of the 1790s was more accurately captured by John Fonblanque in his notes to Ballow's *Treatise on Equity*, 'The

[47] *Brotherston* v. *Barber* (1816) 5 M & S 418, 425 (Emerigon cited by Abbot J.).

[48] (1817) 6 M & S 92. [49] *Powell* v. *Gudgeon* (1816) 5 M & S 431, 436.

[50] Richard Wooddeson, *A Systematical View of the Laws of England as Treated of in a Course of Vinerian Lectures*, 3 vols. (London, 1792–3), vol. I, p. 203.

jurisdiction exercised by courts of equity may be considered in some cases to be assistant to, in some concurrent with, and in others exclusive of, the jurisdiction of courts of common law'.[51] John Joseph Powell in his treatise on contract went further, proclaiming that a 'blending of legal and equitable rights' was 'subversive of first principles'.[52]

Lord Kenyon, who had served as Master of the Rolls,[53] and could be expected to be familiar with both jurisdictions, expressed a similar sentiment, 'A Court of Equity can mould interests differently from a Court of Law; and can give relief in cases where a Court of Law cannot'.[54] Treating the two bodies of law as distinct is bound up with the idea that Chancery was a better forum than the Common law for some sorts of claim. One question of 'infinite importance to the public'[55] which starkly raised this issue was whether or not an action lay to recover a legacy at Common law. Lord Mansfield had allowed Common law claims on a legacy indirectly through the medium of the action of assumpsit. In *Deeks* v. *Strutt*,[56] the King's Bench firmly set its face against these sorts of approach whilst not actually overruling *Atkins* v. *Hill*[57] and *Hawkes* v. *Saundars*.[58] Lord Kenyon made the point that because there was no equitable accounting at Common law, some beneficiaries of the settlement were able to recover unfairly at the expense of others. This was no doubt why they were so keen to pursue a claim at Common law in the first place.

Although debate about the relationship between Law and Equity may have largely quietened, it had not gone away entirely. In *Tooke* v. *Hollingworth*, Lord Kenyon accepted that because he was dealing with a bankruptcy, the same rules should prevail in Law as in Equity.[59] Perhaps not surprisingly given his well-established enthusiasm for drawing parallels with Equity, Buller J. went further:

> During the fifteen years that I have sat on this Bench I have never known any case which established a distinction between Courts of Equity and Law on subjects of this kind. I have always thought it highly injurious to

[51] John Fonblanque (ed.), Henry Ballow, *A Treatise of Equity*, 2 vols. (London, 1793), vol. I, p. 10, fn. (f).

[52] John Joseph Powell, *Essay Upon the Law of Contracts*, 2 vols. (London, 1790). vol. I, pp. vii–viii.

[53] Kenyon held the office between 1784 and 1788.

[54] *Clayton* v. *Adams* (1796) 6 TR 604, 605. For a similar analysis, see *Bauerman* v. *Radenius* (1798) 7 TR 663, 667.

[55] *Deeks* v. *Strutt* (1794) 5 TR 690, 693. The phrase was Ashhurst J's.

[56] *Ibid.*

[57] (1775) 1 Cowp 284.

[58] (1782) 1 Cowp 289.

[59] (1793) 5 TR 215, 225.

> the public that different rules should prevail in the different Courts on the same mercantile case . . . The mercantile law of this country is founded on principles of equity.[60]

The link between Common law and Equity forged by Lord Mansfield in *Moses* v. *Macferlan* remained superficially strong during this period, but most judges were no longer explicitly drawing on Equity as a way of developing the Common law of contract. Away from the discussion of its juristic foundations, the non-contractual assumpsits also provide a good example of one of the main themes of the 1790s – the process of working out the limits of the earlier reforms.

Working out the limits of doctrinal development

By the 1780s judges were becoming increasingly hostile towards attempts to bring money had and received rather than a special count on the contract when the contract remained open. By the 1790s the debate had broadened into one about the propriety of using any form of non-contractual assumpsit when the contract remained open and contractual remedies were not yet exhausted. Lord Kenyon was one of the early cheerleaders[61] for what modern lawyers term the doctrine of subsidiarity.[62] He first alluded to the principle at nisi prius in *Pepper* v. *Burland*[63] when he noted that, 'so far as it [the contract] can be traced to have been followed', the sum that the plaintiff could recover was governed by the contract. It was only when the work sufficiently deviated from the contract so that 'it is impossible to trace the contract', that the plaintiff might recover on a *quantum meruit* for the value of his labour.

60 (1793) 5 TR 215, 229.

61 Tariq Baloch, *Unjust Enrichment and Contract* (Oxford: Hart, 2009), p. 132 argues that the subsidiarity of *quantum meruit* to a claim on the contract was older and is found in a passage in *An Introduction to the Law Relative to Trials at Nisi Prius* (London, 1767), pp. 129–30. As Baloch admits, the passage is ambiguous.

62 The idea remains controversial in the modern law: Ross Grantham and Charles Rickett, 'On the Subsidiarity of Unjust Enrichment' (2001) 117 *Law Quarterly Review* 273; Jack Beatson, 'Restitution and Contract: Non-Cumul?' (2001) 1 *Theoretical Inquiries in Law* 83, 88; Andrew Tettenborn, 'Subsisting Contract and Failure of Consideration – A Little Scepticism' [2002] *Restitution Law Review* 1; Ralph Cunnington, 'Failure of Basis' [2004] *Lloyds Maritime and Commercial Law Quarterly* 234, 248–51.

63 (1791) Peake 139.

The full implications only became apparent in the much commented upon *Cutter* v. *Powell*.[64]

The facts of *Cutter* v. *Powell* were commonplace enough.[65] Whilst in Jamaica, a sailor took a promissory note from the defendant, who agreed to pay thirty guineas provided he 'proceeds, continues and does his duty as second mate . . . from hence to the port of Liverpool'. Having died part way through the voyage his widow sued on a *quantum meruit* for the work and labour performed prior to his death.[66] There were several very good grounds for rejecting the claim within the existing authorities. The *quantum meruit* breached the rule in *Martin* v. *Webb*,[67] namely, that where the evidence showed that the parties had agreed a fixed sum then the plaintiff could not recover a reasonable sum. Because the contract was not so much brought to an end as stalled part way through performance,[68] it was also possible to apply Buller J.'s *dicta* in *Weston* v. *Downes* to the effect that when a contract was still open, the plaintiff had no choice but to sue on the agreement.

Notwithstanding the state of the authorities, the King's Bench recast their objections in a much more doctrinal form, stating that the non-contractual action was subsidiary to the action in contract.[69] Lord Kenyon explained 'that where the parties have come to an express contract none can be implied has prevailed so long as to be reduced to an axiom in the law'.[70] Ashhurst J. said 'but she has no right to desert the agreement; for wherever there is an express contract the parties must be

[64] (1795) 6 TR 320. For some commentary, see Samuel Stoljar, 'The Great Case of Cutter v. Powell' (1956) 34 *Canadian Bar Review* 288; Martin Dockray, 'Cutter v. Powell: A Trip Outside the Text' (2001) 117 *Law Quarterly Review* 664; Warren Swain, 'Cutter v. Powell and the Pleading of Claims of Unjust Enrichment' [2003] *Restitution Law Review* 46.

[65] For a discussion of the factual background, see Dockray, 'Cutter v. Powell'.

[66] *Ibid.*, p. 673 shows that the original declaration was for straight indebitatus assumpsit. Only at a later stage was *quantum meruit* added. Cutter's ship, *The Governor Parry*, was a slave vessel. Mortality for seaman on these types of vessels was particularly high, see Peter Earle, *Sailors: English Merchant Seamen 1650–1775* (London: Methuen, 2007), p. 130.

[67] (1763) LI MS Misc. 129 f. 71.

[68] The term 'stalled' is taken from David Ibbetson, *An Historical Introduction to the Law of Obligations* (Oxford: Oxford University Press, 1999), p. 279.

[69] It is certainly true, as both Dockray, 'Cutter v. Powell', pp. 677–8 and J.L. Barton, 'Contract and Quantum Meruit: The Antecedents of Cutter v. Powell' (1987) 8 *Journal of Legal History* 48, 61–2 note, the outcome in the case broke no new ground but this particular doctrinal approach was both new and significant.

[70] (1795) 6 TR 320, 324. In this context, 'implied contract' was used to mean non-contractual assumpsits.

guided by it; and one party cannot relinquish or abide by it as it may suit his advantage.'[71]

The decision was probably not motivated by legal doctrine alone.[72] The high level of sailors' wages, particularly on sailings from the West Indies, had attracted some adverse comment around this time.[73] It was assumed in *Cutter* v. *Powell* that the Admiralty courts[74] would have reached the same result. This assumption may be misplaced.[75] The result was certainly difficult to reconcile with earlier King's Bench authorities in which a sailor impressed into the Royal Navy could recover for those wages he had earned prior to being impressed, even though he had failed to complete his existing contract.[76]

The outcome in *Cutter* v. *Powell* was ultimately dependent on the way in which the agreement was interpreted. The plaintiff was unable to recover on the express contract because it was a condition precedent of the contract that the whole of the voyage be completed.[77] A different interpretation and different result was reached three years earlier in *Chandler* v. *Grieves*.[78] On this occasion the Common Pleas held that, where the plaintiff sailor was injured part way through a voyage and thereafter unable to work, he was able to recover wages for the entire

[71] (1795) 6 TR 320, 325.

[72] Dockray, 'Cutter v. Powell', pp. 671–3 shows that given that Cutter was also a shipwright as well as a sailor, his rate of pay was reasonable for the period.

[73] (1796) 37 Geo III c. 73 s. 3. This may have been due to a shortage of sailors in the market which was a problem around this time, see *The Times*, 7 January 1794.

[74] F.L. Wiswall, *The Development of Admiralty Jurisdiction and Practice Since 1800* (Cambridge: Cambridge University Press, 1970), p. 10; Francis Holt, *A System of the Shipping and Navigation Laws*, 2nd edn (London: Butterworth, 1824), pp 288–94. On the scope of Admiralty jurisdiction, see *Howe* v. *Nappier* (1766) 4 Burr 1944.

[75] (1795) 6 TR 320, 326 where Lawrence J. conceded that mercantile practice could lead to exceptions. Under the European Ordinances the sailor would have recovered. This point was mentioned by Grose J., (1795) 6 TR 320, 325. See also: Charles Abbott, *A Treatise of the Law Relative to Merchant Ships and Seamen*, 5th edn (London: Butterworth, 1827), p. 445. On *Cutter* v. *Powell* and mercantile practice, see Peter Luther, 'Campbell, Espinasse and the Sailors: Text and Context in the Common Law' (1999) 19 *Legal Studies* 526, 543–5.

[76] *Wiggins* v. *Ingleton* (1705) 2 Ld Raym 1211; *Paul* v. *Eden* (1785) 4 Doug 280; *Clements* v. *Mayborn* (1784); Abbott, *Merchant Ships and Seamen*, p. 444.

[77] (1795) 6 TR 320, 324 (Lord Kenyon), 324–5 (Ashhurst J.), 325–6 (Grose J.), 326 (Lawrence J.).

[78] (1792) 2 H Bla 606 (note). In *Cutter* v. *Powell* (1795) 6 TR 320, 325 Grose J. was the only judge to mention *Chandler* v. *Grieves*, admitting that, 'I do not know the precise grounds on which the Court proceeded'.

voyage when he sued on the express contract. Several other decisions around this period went the same way as *Cutter* v. *Powell*.[79]

In the immediate aftermath of *Cutter* v. *Powell*, judges continued to favour the older formula as expressed by way of the objection that the contract remains open. This rule was sometimes easier to state than to apply. The easiest case occurred when a contract was brought to an end by one of its own terms.[80] In *Giles* v. *Edwards*,[81] Lord Kenyon held that the plaintiff had a right to rescind and so bring the contract to an end if the defendant's default left him unable to perform. The right to rescind came to be hemmed in by restrictions. In *Hulle* v. *Heightman*,[82] the plaintiff sailor was hired for a voyage from Altona to London and back again. On reaching London he left the ship and did not return, claiming ill-treatment. The contract only allowed him to recover on completion of the entire trip. At nisi prius, Le Blanc J. held that the contract was not rescinded and warned that there would be 'dangerous consequences from allowing sailors, upon any disagreement with the captain, to leave the ship' if the action was allowed to succeed.[83] In the King's Bench it was argued that the wrongful behaviour of the defendant was sufficient to rescind the contract.[84] There was no specific mention of this issue in a judgment that runs to a handful of lines in the report. But the fact that the contract was said to remain open suggests, at the very least, that judges were not prepared to take a relaxed view of rescission at this point in time; a view which is given further support by *Hunt* v. *Silk*,[85] which restricted rescission to those circumstances where the parties could be restored to the position in which they were before the defendant's default.

Changes in the rules of pleading also placed obstacles in the way of non-contractual assumpsit claims. Plaintiffs were required to count on the contract rather than on a *quantum meruit* for work and labour when the defendant had failed to fully perform his side of the agreement.[86]

79 *Hernaman* v. *Bawden* (1766) 3 Burr 1844; *Appleby* v. *Dods* (1807) 8 East 300.

80 *Towers* v. *Barrett* (1786) 1 TR 133. 81 (1797) 7 TR 181.

82 (1802) 2 East 145. See Ibbetson, *Historical Introduction*, pp. 318–19.

83 (1801) 4 Esp 75, 78.

84 The difficulty of reconciling these cases was noted in the 1824 edition of Douglas's Reports, vol. I, p. 24, fn. 2.

85 (1804) 5 East 449.

86 This rule was based on a misunderstanding of *Mulloy* v. *Backer* (1804) 5 East 316, 322 per Lord Ellenborough; Edward Lawes, *A Practical Treatise on Pleading in Assumpsit* (London: W. Reed, 1810), p. 8; 1 Wms Saund 269 (b); Ibbetson, *Historical Introduction*, pp. 312, 318.

Lord Mansfield's relaxation of the rules of pleading in *Payne* v. *Bacomb*[87] was reversed in part in *Cooke* v. *Munstone*.[88] Where a plaintiff's special count on the contract had failed for variance,[89] he was prevented from falling back on a count in money had and received. The other general indebitatus counts were not affected.

After a period of growth in the 1760s, followed by retrenchment in the 1770s and 1780s, by the 1790s there was a sense of decay surrounding the non-contractual assumpsits. When Lord Kenyon said that he thought that *Moses* v. *Macferlan* had 'gone far enough',[90] his complaint centred on the way that money had and received had been used to re-open a matter that had already been settled in the court of conscience. But it captured the spirit of the time. There was plenty of continued support for Lord Mansfield's conscience-based analysis of money had and received, but this merely masked the fundamental point that the action had begun to calcify both in the books and in practice. Even relatively minor incremental extensions of the action were resisted. Whilst Evans advocated using money had and received in order to recover money paid under a mistake of law as well as fact,[91] this view was not without support,[92] yet was decisively rejected in the year his *Essay* was published.[93] It was much the same story in relation to the action for money paid. Having added an additional category in *Exall* v. *Partridge*, in which the court upheld an action to recover money paid to secure the release of property distrained as payment of another's debt,[94] there were to be no further innovations.

The reasons why the courts failed to build upon the rapid developments in the non-contractual assumpsits of the previous few decades are complex. Lord Mansfield's rationalisation of money had and received

[87] (1781) 2 Doug 651. [88] (1805) 1 B & P (NR) 351.

[89] Variance occurred where the evidence presented in proof contradicted the allegation in the declaration, see Henry Stephen, *A Treatise on Pleading in Civil Actions*, 1st edn (London: Butterworth, 1824), pp. 107–8.

[90] *Marriot* v. *Hampton* (1797) 2 Esp 546, 548.

[91] William Evans, *Essays: On the Action for Money Had and Received, on the Law of Insurances, and on the Law of Bills of Exchange and Promissory Notes* (Liverpool: Merritt & Wright, 1802), pp. 21–2.

[92] *Chatfield* v. *Paxton* (1798), James Oldham (ed.), *Case Notes of Sir Soulden Lawrence* (London: Selden Society, 2013), pp. 192–4.

[93] *Bilbie* v. *Lumley* (1802) 2 East 469. Evans continued to press the case for not making a distinction between mistakes of fact and law, see William Evans (trans.), R. Pothier, *A Treatise on the Law of Obligations or Contracts by M. Pothier*, 2 vols. (London: A. Strahan, 1806), vol. II, pp. 391–5. The division between mistake of law and fact would remain intact until recent times: *Kleinwort Benson Ltd* v. *Lincoln CC* [1999] 2 AC 349.

[94] (1799) 8 TR 308.

continued to be used, but it was rapidly on its way towards becoming a set formula rather than a genuine inquiry. Attitudes towards borrowing from Equity had also begun to harden, which cannot have helped. Around this time judges also began to articulate concerns, which may have been present in the background long before, about the way in which the non-contractual assumpsits had the potential to undermine bargained-for agreements. If these actions could always be resorted to, they would be an attractive option where the value of the labour exceeded the contract price. This sort of outcome made Ashhurst J. uneasy in *Cutter* v. *Powell*.[95] Problems also arose where a contract was performed badly. Despite earlier authorities which had allowed the cost of labour to be recovered, in *Ellis* v. *Hamlen* Mansfield C.J. signalled a change in attitudes when he made clear that having entered into a contract the plaintiff could not 'be permitted to turn round and say, I will be paid by a measure-and-value price'.[96]

The development of contract doctrine: the case of consideration

It would be surprising if there was much of a change in the character of contractual litigation after 1790, and so it proved. Marine insurance and negotiable instruments continued to make frequent appearances in the law reports.[97] Fire and life insurance were also becoming more commonplace,[98] such that Lord Kenyon said of the former, 'this kind of insurance is as much to be favoured as marine insurances'.[99] Sailors bringing actions to recover wages had traditionally favoured the Admiralty Court, attracted by its rapid procedure and the fact that it was easy to bring a group action.[100] Some sailors continued to bring claims in Admiralty,[101] but *Cutter* v. *Powell* was one of a number of authorities to deal with the issue of sailors' wages at Common law. By the 1820s there were around twenty thousand ships in Britain, and perhaps it is to be expected that

95 (1795) 6 TR 320, 325. 96 (1810) 3 Taunt 52, 53.

97 For example, *Brown* v. *Davies* (1789) 3 TR 80.

98 By the 1790s, the Sun Fire Office was the market leader in fire insurance with gross premium income of more than £100,000 per annum, see P.G.M. Dickson, *The Sun Insurance Office* (Oxford: Oxford University Press, 1960), p. 73.

99 *Tarleton* v. *Staniforth* (1794) 5 TR 695, 699.

100 George Steckley, 'Litigious Mariners: Wage Cases in the Seventeenth-Century Admiralty Court' (1999) 42 *The Historical Journal* 315.

101 Wiswall, *Admiralty Jurisdiction*, pp. 24–5; Steckley, 'Litigious Mariners', p. 322.

such a common transaction as a contract for sailors' wages would end up before the courts.[102] In *Cutter* v. *Powell* itself, and later in *Hulle* v. *Heightman*, considerations of public policy were just beneath the surface. Parliament had intervened some years before, ensuring that sailors' contracts of service were regulated by statute from 1729.[103] One consequence of the statute was that sailors were entitled to their wages as agreed in the ship's articles. These regulations were also to the benefit of a ship's master because sailors were prevented from claiming a sum greater than that already agreed. The statute specifically highlights the threat posed by sailors who part way through the voyage refused to proceed without an increase in their wages.[104] The legislation was applied strictly and irrespective of custom and status.[105] The Common law came to much the same conclusion. In *Harris* v. *Watson*,[106] Lord Kenyon dismissed an attempt by a sailor to recover on an agreement to pay extra wages offered for carrying out additional duties when a ship was in danger. His justification was:

> This rule was founded upon a principle of policy, for if sailors were in all events to have their wages, and in times of danger entitled to insist on an extra charge on such a promise as this, they would in many cases suffer a ship to sink, unless the captain would pay an extravagant demand they might think proper to make.[107]

The brief report made no mention of the ship's articles and so it is difficult to speculate whether or not the statute might also have applied. A few decades later, in the factually similar but more famous *Stilk* v. *Myrick*,[108] the sailor was described as having entered into articles. The remarks of counsel, that 'any engagement by the master for a larger sum than was stipulated for by the articles was void', may be an allusion to the statute, but nothing more was said on the matter.[109] Lord

[102] B.R. Mitchell, *European Historical Statistics 1750–1975*, 2nd edn (London: Macmillan, 1981), p. 641.

[103] (1729) 2 Geo II c. 36. The statute was later made perpetual: (1761) 2 Geo III c. 37. For details of the legislation, see Luther, 'Campbell, Espinasse and the Sailors', pp. 542–3.

[104] (1729) 2 Geo II c. 36 s. 1.

[105] *White* v. *Wilson* (1800) 2 B & P 116; *Elsworth* v. *Woolmore* (1803) 5 Esp 84, cited by Luther, 'Campbell, Espinasse and the Sailors', p. 542.

[106] (1791) Peake 102. [107] (1791) Peake 102, 103.

[108] (1809) 2 Camp 317, 6 Esp 129.

[109] For some suggestions as to why there was no discussion of this point, see Luther, 'Campbell, Espinasse and the Sailors', p. 543.

Ellenborough decided that the sailor was unable to enforce an agreement to pay an increased wage after two sailors deserted part way through the voyage, and the master agreed to share their wages between the remaining crew. The two reports of the case provide differing accounts of his reasoning. In Espinasse's version, Lord Ellenborough in rejecting the claim is said to have applied *Harris* v. *Watson*, which was 'founded on just and proper policy'.[110] In Campbell's version, Lord Ellenborough declared that the contract was 'void for want of consideration'.[111] Whilst *Harris* v. *Watson* was 'rightly decided', Lord Ellenborough is said to have doubted whether 'the ground of public policy ... be the true principle on which the decision is to be supported'.[112]

Eighteenth and early nineteenth century judges were less shy about utilising public policy than has sometimes been the case since. Because Campbell is usually, if perhaps unfairly, seen as a more reliable reporter than Espinasse,[113] the influence of public policy on the decision has tended to be downplayed. In fact, it is crucial. Both *Harris* v. *Watson* and *Stilk* v. *Myrick* consisted of situations close to the concerns of the statute. There is no evidence that in either case the sailors attempted to coerce the masters or even refused to proceed without an increase in pay. A favourable position came their way and they exploited it. But as Lord Kenyon pointed out in *Harris* v. *Watson*, there was the potential for abuse which overlapped with a wider fear that was hinted at in the opening line of his judgment: 'If this action was to be supported, it would materially affect the navigation of the kingdom.'[114] A newspaper report of the decision makes this concern even more explicit: 'Every sailor was bound to exert himself in perilous situations, otherwise they might neglect the ship, and if such actions as this were allowed, it would be subversive of all navigation.'[115]

The stress here was on a sailor's primary duty to the safety of the vessel. Any other solution was potentially a threat both to the ship and to good order. From a modern perspective this outcome either seems harsh on the sailors or needs to be explained away by the doctrine of economic duress.[116] Around 1800 it was unlikely to have been

110 (1809) 6 Esp 129, 130. 111 (1809) 2 Camp 317, 319. 112 *Ibid.*, p. 319.

113 This may have more to do with legal politics than reliability, see Luther, 'Campbell, Espinasse and the Sailors', pp. 531–7.

114 (1792) Peake 102, 103. 115 *Star*, 16 July 1791.

116 *Williams* v. *Roffey* [1991] 1 QB 1, 19 (Russell L.J.), 23 (Purchas L.J.).

controversial.[117] Taken together there was a good case for such contracts to be regulated on the grounds of public policy. There is insufficient evidence to conclude that Lord Ellenborough was particularly unsympathetic towards sailors, although it is worth noting that in one unreported decision he went counter to both earlier authority and the statutory regulations by ruling that a sailor was unable to recover *pro rata* for work done prior to being impressed.[118]

The reasons behind Lord Ellenborough's decision to abandon public policy in favour of the absence of consideration in Campbell's report, is left unexplained.[119] One possibility suggests itself. In *Harris* v. *Watson* the ship was in danger when the promise to pay extra wages was made. In *Stilk* v. *Myrick* the ship was safely in port. An argument can still be put on the grounds of public policy in *Stilk* v. *Myrick* based either on the statute or on the potential to 'materially affect the navigation of the kingdom' if the agreement was upheld. But such arguments probably carry less weight than they did in *Harris* v. *Watson*. Subsequent generations of lawyers have taken the case as authority for the proposition that there is no consideration for an agreement to do what one is already bound to do. *Stilk* v. *Myrick* is not a typical case where a party is seeking to recover on a subsequent more favourable contract to do the same thing that they were required to do under the original contract. The sailors were 'bound by the terms of their original contract to exert themselves to the upmost to bring the ship home', but there were additional reasons for the sailors to 'exert themselves'. The sailors were under a duty to the ship by virtue of the fact that they were a member of the ship's crew.[120] The original contract did not determine the limits of their obligations. By a small irony, when the reasoning of *Harris* v. *Watson* came to be reconsidered

[117] This is not to say that in certain circumstances judges were not extremely sympathetic towards sailors, see Luther, 'Campbell, Espinasse and the Sailors', p. 541. In *Turtle* v. *Hartwell* (1795) 6 TR 246, 427, Lord Kenyon described sailors as the 'most useful and deserving bodies of men'.

[118] *Anon* (1806) noted at 2 Camp 317, 320–1.

[119] Grant Gilmore's suggestion that want of consideration 'is a phrase that would have come more readily to the mind of an English judge in 1809 than in 1791' is not convincing, see Grant Gilmore, *The Death of Contract* (Columbus: Ohio State University Press, 1974), p. 27. Consideration remained in the foreground of legal thinking in the late eighteenth century, as evidenced by cases like *Rann* v. *Hughes* (1778) 4 Bro PC 27, 7 TR 350 note, LI MS Misc. 130 f. 74.

[120] For a discussion in the Admiralty Court of the sort of duties expected of members of the ship's crew, see *Robinett* v. '*The Exeter*' (1799) 2 C Rob 261.

by Lord Campbell in the 1850s, he questioned Lord Ellenborough's decision to disregard public policy in *Stilk* v. *Myrick*.[121]

Given the context of *Stilk* v. *Myrick*, Lord Ellenborough's ruling that there was no consideration for the subsequent agreement is easy enough to understand. From a purely doctrinal viewpoint the outcome is less convincing. No analysis is provided beyond the bald statement that the contract was 'void for want of consideration'. Had the sailor gone beyond their normal duties, as in *Yates* v. *Hall*,[122] there was good consideration. Even where the agreement was simply to do what he was already bound to do, the earlier authorities did not all point in one direction. For example, a promise to pay an existing debt was still a valid contract. In an era before formalistic legal reasoning had taken hold, the doctrine of consideration retained a degree of flexibility in application and scope. *Stilk* v. *Myrick* may be no more than an example of this phenomenon. The brief rise of the moral consideration doctrine was another.[123]

Atkins v. *Hill*[124] and *Hawkes* v. *Saunders*[125] can be fitted into an older tradition, with a concept of consideration that was slightly blurred at the edges, but which essentially preserved the principle of exchange. The language used in both cases was sometimes much broader, particularly a passage in *Hawkes* v. *Saunders* where Buller J. said that 'the true rule is, that wherever a defendant is under a moral obligation, or liable in conscience and equity to pay, that is a sufficient consideration'.[126] In the early nineteenth century, these decisions began to be used to create a wider principle in which moral obligations were treated as good consideration.

The law reporters Bosanquet and Puller wrote in 1814 that 'an idea has prevailed of late years that an express promise, founded simply on an antecedent moral obligation, is sufficient to support an assumpsit'.[127] *Barnes* v. *Hedley*[128] is an early example. The plaintiff sued on a subsequent

[121] *Harris* v. *Carter* (1854) 3 El & Bl 559, 562. The precise public policy identified by Lord Campbell was different, namely, that it would be 'mischievous to commerce' if captains were able to bind ship owners by a promise to pay more than was agreed.

[122] (1785) 1 TR 73.

[123] For a discussion of this subject, see W.S. Holdsworth, *A History of English Law*, 17 vols. (London: Methuen, 1925), vol. VIII, pp. 31–2, 36–8; C.H.S. Fifoot, *History and Sources of the Common Law* (London: Stevens & Sons, 1949), pp. 410–11; Kevin Teeven, *Promises on Prior Obligations at Common Law* (Westport: Greenwood Press, 1998), pp. 81–96; Warren Swain, 'The Changing Nature of the Doctrine of Consideration 1750–1850' (2005) 26 *Journal of Legal History* 55, 67–9.

[124] (1775) 1 Cowp 284. [125] (1782) 1 Cowp 289. [126] *Ibid.*, p. 294.

[127] (1802) 3 B & P 249. [128] (1809) 2 Taunt 184.

promise after the original security was void for usury. It was argued that, by giving up the deeds to be cancelled, there was a detriment to the defendant because it might have prejudiced his chances of proving the bond was usurious. The plaintiff's main argument rested on the altogether more unorthodox position that post *Atkins* v. *Hill* and *Hawkes* v. *Saunders* it was enough to prove that the defendant had an obligation in conscience to support a finding of good consideration.[129]

In *Barnes* v. *Hedley* the reporter was silent on the reasons behind the success of the action. *Lee* v. *Muggeridge*[130] was more clearly an instance of consideration founded upon a moral obligation. Mary Hiller had an estate settled to her separate use. The plaintiff advanced money to her son-in-law and a bond was drawn up with Mary Hiller and John Muggeridge (her new husband) as security for the loan. The son-in-law failed to repay the loan. On John Muggeridge's death, Mary promised that her executors would repay the loan. Mary then died. Unable to recover on the bond, Mary, being a feme covert at the time, recovered on the subsequent promise to pay. The language of the judgment supported a general doctrine of moral consideration rather than specific exceptions: 'The only question, therefore, is whether upon this declaration there appears a good moral obligation? Now I cannot conceive that there can be a stronger moral obligation, than is stated upon this record';[131] 'The notion that a promise may be supported by a moral obligation is not modern; in Charles the Second's time it was said, if there be an iota of equity, it is enough consideration for the promise';[132] 'There cannot be a stronger or clearer case of a moral obligation than this';[133] and finally, 'It cannot, I think, be disputed now, that wherever there is a moral obligation to pay a debt, or perform a duty, a promise to perform that duty, or pay that debt, will be supported by the previous moral obligation'.[134]

The way was now clear for plaintiffs to argue that *any* moral obligation was sufficient consideration.[135] In the first edition of his contract treatise

[129] *Ibid.*, pp. 188–9.

[130] (1813) 5 Taunt 36. Teevan, *Promises*, p. 83 emphasises the importance of this authority.

[131] (1813) 5 Taunt 36, 46 (Mansfield C.J.).

[132] *Ibid.*, p. 46 (Heath J.). No evidence was provided that this was truly the position in the time of Charles II.

[133] *Ibid.*, p. 47 (Chambre J.). [134] *Ibid.*, p. 47 (Gibbs J.).

[135] For examples, see *Holliday* v. *Atkinson* (1826) 5 B & C 501, 502; *Littlefield* v. *Shee* (1831) 2 B & Ad 811, 812; *Meyer* v. *Haworth* (1838) 8 Ad & E 467, 469; *Eastwood* v. *Kenyon* (1840) 11 Ad & E 438, 443.

of 1826, Joseph Chitty asserted with some confidence that 'it appears to be now settled, that a mere moral obligation will be a sufficient consideration to support an express promise, although no legal responsibility ever existed'.[136] Best C.J. was a particularly enthusiastic supporter of the doctrine of moral consideration, and in *Wells* v. *Horton* he stated that 'there was a moral obligation to pay, and I hope that the judges in Westminster Hall will always hold, that a moral obligation to pay is a sufficient consideration for a promise to pay'.[137] Others never accepted the idea. In a note to *Wennall* v. *Adney*, Bosanquet and Puller adopted a narrow reading of the eighteenth century authorities, arguing that they went no further than allowing the courts to find consideration where an existing duty was 'barred by any legal maxim or statute provision'.[138] The lifespan of the moral consideration doctrine would prove to be quite short. Defendants began to put forward the views of Bosanquet and Puller in argument[139] and, from the 1830s, opinion began to turn against moral consideration. In *Littlefield* v. *Shee*, Lord Tenterden held that 'I must also observe, that the doctrine that a moral consideration is a sufficient consideration for a subsequent promise, is one which should be received with some limitation'.[140] Moral consideration was not decisively rejected until the 1840s, when, in *Eastwood* v. *Kenyon*,[141] the law was returned to the position it had occupied before *Lee* v. *Muggeridge*, with a range of specific exceptions rather than a general moral obligations doctrine.[142]

[136] Joseph Chitty, *A Practical Treatise on the Law of Contracts Not Under Seal* (London: S. Sweet, 1826), p. 11.

[137] (1826) 1 C & P 383, 386 (at nisi prius), in the context of a promise by a testator that on his death his executor would pay his debt to the plaintiff. When the case reached the Common Pleas it was treated as one of forbearance and turned on whether the promise was within the Statute of Frauds: (1826) 4 Bing 40.

[138] 3 B & P 252 (note).

[139] *Paynter* v. *Williams* (1833) 1 Cr & M 810, 816; *Haigh* v. *Brooks* (1839) 10 Ad & E 309, 315–16.

[140] (1831) 2 B & Ad 811, 813. The actual reason for the decision was that the declaration was unsupported by the proof. On which, see the argument of counsel in *Haigh* v. *Brooks* (1839) 10 Ad & E 309, 315. See also *Meyer* v. *Haworth* (1838) 8 Ad & E 467 which held that there was no liability because the moral obligation was not stated in the declaration.

[141] (1840) 11 Ad & E 438, 3 P & D 276.

[142] *Beaumont* v. *Reeve* (1846) 8 QB 483, 487. C.G. Addison, *A Treatise on Contracts and Liabilities Ex-Contractu* (London: W Benning, 1847), p. 31; Stephen Leake, *The Elements of the Law of Contracts*, 1st edn (London: Stevens & Sons, 1867), pp. 317–18. Promises by bankrupts ceased to be actionable as a result of statute: (1849) 12 & 13 Vict c.106 s. 204.

The contract treatise in a period of transition

Legal writers had begun to think in terms of a unified law of contract with clear theoretical foundations before 1790. But the pace of these developments quickened in the decades around 1800. John Joseph Powell's *Essay Upon the Law of Contracts and Agreements*, published in 1790,[143] is often described as the first treatise on the whole of contract law.[144] Powell explained in his introduction:

> All reasoning must be founded on first principles. The science of the Law derives its principles either from that artificial system which was incidental to the introduction of feuds, or from the science of morals. And, without a knowledge of these principles, we can no more establish a conclusion in law than we can see with our eyes shut, measure without a standard, or count without arithmetic.[145]

This was hardly a novel insight. Sir William Jones had expressed similar sentiments nine years earlier.[146] The same sort of agenda was also implicit in the earlier works by Gilbert and Ballow. Powell's statement nevertheless helps to emphasise that the momentum was moving away from dependence on the forms of action as an organising concept. There was a growing belief that legal writing should reflect scientific principles. Frederick Ritso even called his treatise of 1815 *An Introduction to the Science of Law*.[147] He explained in the preface that 'The law is not a mere series of unconnected decrees and ordinances but in the strictest sense of the word a science founded on principle, and claiming an exalted rank in the empire of reason'.

In his attempts to develop a more scientific approach, Powell turned to Natural law.[148] It was reflected in his definition of contracts, which were binding because 'there is a mutual consent of the minds of the parties concerned in them'.[149] As a result, 'it is of the essence of every contract or agreement, that the parties to be bound thereby should consent to whatever is stipulated'.[150] Much of the first volume was concerned with factors which negative assent. At the same time, like earlier writers, Powell was forced to concede that assent was not sufficient. A deed must

143 2 vols. (London, 1790).

144 For example, A.W.B. Simpson, 'Innovation in Nineteenth Century Contract Law' (1975) 91 *Law Quarterly Review* 247, 253.

145 Powell, *Essay*, vol. I, p. vi.

146 David Ibbetson (ed.), William Jones, *An Essay on the Law of Bailments* (Bangor: Welsh Legal History Society, 2004), p. 202.

147 (London: 1815). 148 Powell, *Essay*, vol. I, p. xliii. 149 *Ibid.*, p. vii. 150 *Ibid.*, p. 9.

be used or consideration be present.[151] Powell's *Essay* was a significant work but not a comprehensive one. Some recent authorities like *Pillans* v. *Van Mierop*[152] were mentioned, but Powell largely concentrated on decisions which pre-dated the 1750s.[153] Most of the authorities were taken from the Equity reports. The second volume is almost entirely concerned with Equitable remedies. These features of Powell's work meant that he had more in common with someone like Ballow than the nineteenth century textbook writers.

In the early nineteenth century legal writing about the law of contract was not yet set on a particular course. There were almost as many different approaches as there were authors. Much of the literature remained quite conservative. John Newland's *Treatise on Contracts within the Jurisdiction of Courts of Equity*, published in 1806, was,[154] as the title suggests and in common with some eighteenth century writers, largely concerned with the court of Chancery. Newland's definition of contract, which came straight out of Blackstone, offered nothing new: 'A contract is an agreement, upon a sufficient consideration to do or not to do a particular thing.'[155] Samuel Comyn's *A Treatise of the Law Relative to Contracts and Agreements not under seal*,[156] published the following year, was far more comprehensive than any of the earlier works. The authorities were up to date and Equity less prominent. In other ways Comyn's book was also quite old fashioned. He had none of the theoretical pretensions of writers like Gilbert and Ballow or even Powell. He set out the law as it stood, largely without comment. Each element of a contract claim followed in turn, as might be expected for a work aimed at legal practitioners.

The contrast between Comyn's *Treatise* and Henry Colebrooke's *Treatise on Obligations and Contracts*[157] of 1818 could hardly be greater. A biography of Colebrooke, written by his son, suggests that his father intended to write an introduction on contract for the Indian Service, but that his work attracted little attention and was 'perhaps too succinct, and

[151] *Ibid.*, pp. 330–3.
[152] (1765) 3 Burr 1663. Discussed by Powell, *Essay*, vol. I, pp. 333–4.
[153] For these figures, see Tariq Baloch, 'Law Booksellers and Printers as Agents of Unchange' (2007) 66 *Cambridge Law Journal* 389, 416: out of 507 cases only 63 post-date 1750 and 192 were from the seventeenth century or before.
[154] (London: Butterworth, 1806).
[155] *Ibid.*, p. 1. The passage is taken from William Blackstone, *Commentaries on the Laws of England*, 4 vols. (Oxford, 1766), vol. II, p. 442.
[156] 2 vols. (London: A. Strahan, 1807). [157] (London, 1818).

it is wanting in practical examples and illustrations'.[158] Colebrooke may have intended to remedy this defect in the second volume which was never finished.[159] As it stood it was of little value for lawyers bringing a claim in contract. But as the most theoretical work then in existence, it was an impressive achievement. His marginal notes contain references to a large range of sources from Common law writers like Blackstone and Comyn, through Erskine, the Natural lawyers, Justinian and the Code Civil. One name stands out from the rest. It is that of the Frenchman Robert Joseph Pothier. Pothier is mentioned nearly thirty times in the first ten pages alone. Colebrooke's biographer credits Pothier along with Roman law as the main inspiration behind his *Treatise*.[160] But this approach also left Colebrooke facing a tricky blending process. When he defined an agreement as 'an aggregation of minds; where two or more minds are united in a thing done or to be done, or where a mutual assent is given to do or not to do a particular act',[161] he cited Pothier. But significantly he also felt it necessary to refer to a similar sixteenth century English definition.[162] These tensions were also evident when it came to the doctrine of consideration. Colebrooke conceded, as others had before, that a contract was 'an agreement upon sufficient consideration'.[163] At the same time, his definition of consideration hints at a subtle shift:

> A consideration is the material cause of a contract. It is the motive of the act which becomes the cause of the obligation . . . The will of a party to engage, his assent to become bound, is the essence of a voluntary engagement. The consideration is required only as evidence of his will.[164]

This differs from the traditional position, where the contract was generated by an exchange, to one where the contract is generated by agreement and consideration is evidence of that agreement. In this form consideration was closer to the Continental idea of *causa*.[165]

Colebrooke was not the first English writer to recognise the value of Pothier. Sir William Jones had urged his readers to consult Pothier

[158] Thomas Colebrooke, *The Life of H.T. Colebrooke* (London: Trüber, 1873), p. 297.
[159] *Ibid.*, p. 345. [160] *Ibid.*, p. 279. [161] Colebrooke, *Treatise*, p. 2.
[162] The authority referred to was *Reniger* v. *Fogossa* (1550) Plo 1, 17.
[163] Colebrooke, *Treatise*, p. 2. [164] *Ibid.*, p. 38.
[165] Rather than reciprocity, *causa* reflected the idea that contracts should be an agreement that was seriously intended. For an overview of the history of *causa*, see Reinhard Zimmermann, *The Law of Obligations* (Oxford: Oxford University Press, 1996), pp. 549–56.

nearly forty years earlier.[166] Pothier cropped up several times in legal writing in the late 1790s.[167] By the turn of the century there was even the odd reference to Pothier in the law reports.[168] He was evidently of sufficient renown to feature in John Aikin's work on 'eminent persons', where he was described as 'an estimable French writer on legal subjects'.[169] He was described by Lord Ellenborough as 'a most learned and eminent writer upon every subject connected with the law of contracts, and intimately acquainted with the law merchant in particular'.[170] Pothier was probably not more widely known in England until a translation by Sir William Evans appeared in 1806.[171] Evans acknowledged that some attempts had already been made towards a more scientific exposition of English law – he recognised the contribution of writers like Blackstone and Wooddeson.[172] At the same time, he had a more

166 Jones, *Bailment*, p. 29. As a letter to Viscount Althorp in late 1780 reveals, Jones was anxious to make Pothier better known in England: Garland Cannon (ed.), *The Letters of Sir William Jones* (Oxford: Oxford University Press, 1970), vol. 1, [251].

167 The editor of Ballow's treatise was an early champion of Pothier, J. Fonblanque (ed.), *A Treatise of Equity*, 2 vols. (London, 1793), vol. I, pp. 3, 28, 115, 121, 341, 380, vol. II, p. 420. For another early reference to Pothier, see Joseph Chitty, *A Treatise on the Law of Bills of Exchange* (London, 1799), p. 10. The author was the father of Joseph Chitty of contract fame.

168 For examples in argument, see *Duke of Melan* v. *Fitzjames* (1797) 1 B & P 138, 140; *Cooth* v. *Jackson* (1801) 6 Ves Jun 12, 23; *Beale* v. *Thompson* (1803) 3 B & P 405, 413–14; *M'Carthy* v. *Abel* (1804) 5 East 388, 392; *Richie* v. *Atkinson* (1808) 10 East 295, 304, 305; *Christie* v. *Row* (1808) 1 Taunt 300, 308; *Bell* v. *Carstairs* (1811) 14 East 374, 386; *Green* v. *Royal Exchange Assurance* (1815) 6 Taunt 68, 69; *M'Iver* v. *Henderson* (1816) 4 M & S 576, 581; *Young* v. *Rowe* (1816) 5 M & S 291, 293; *Taylor* v. *Curtis* (1816) 6 Taunt 608, 614; *Busk* v. *Royal Exchange Assurance* (1818) 2 B & Ald 73, 77. For examples in judgments, see *Raper* v. *Birkbeck* (1811) 15 East 17, 20 (Lord Ellenborough); *Birley* v. *Gladstone* (1814) 3 M & S 205, 216 (Lord Ellenborough); *Butler* v. *Wildman* (1820) 3 B & Ald 398, 402 (Abbot C.J.), 406 (Best J.).

169 John Aikin, *General Biography: or Lives, Critical and Historical of the most eminent persons of all ages, countries, conditions, and professions*, 10 vols. (London: John Stockdale, 1813), vol. VIII, p. 318.

170 *Hoare* v. *Cazenove* (1812) 16 East 391.

171 Pothier, *Treatise*. An even earlier English translation was published in America in 1802 by Francois-Xavier Martin as *A Treatise on Obligations Considered in a Moral and Legal View* (Newbern: Martin & Ogden, 1802). Pothier's best known work apart from his *Traité des Obligations* (Paris, 1761) was probably his *Traité du Contrat de Vente* (Paris, 1762). The later work was also translated into English, L.S. Cushing (trans.), R.J. Pothier, *Treatise on the Contract of Sale* (Boston: Little & Brown, 1839).

172 Pothier, *Treatise*, p. 75, where Blackstone's *Commentaries* were described as 'a more beautiful specimen of elegant literature than has in any other instance been applied to a professional subject'.

ambitious agenda, he wrote that English law 'has been too generally estimated as a mere collection of positive rules, the knowledge of which was no otherwise desirable than as it might be conducive to immediate interest or security, or technical forms, the instruments of professional employment'.[173] Whilst Evans recognised the value of the Common law,[174] he argued that legal writers were under-employed in England[175] and criticised English lawyers for being too insular.[176]

One of the attractions of Pothier's *Treatise*, then and later, was that it was appealingly simple. Nowhere is this better demonstrated than in Pothier's definition of a contract: 'A contract is a kind of agreement ... An agreement or a pact ... is the assent of two or more persons, to form an engagement between them, or to dissolve or modify one already formed.'[177] Pothier jettisoned the moral underpinning of Natural law promissory theories. It was presented as self-evidently true that a contract was binding because of a meeting of minds, without resorting to making a connection between truth telling and keeping a promise. Pothier's theory was attractive in other ways too. It was in tune with philosophical fashion. In his *The Metaphysics of Morals*, first published in Germany in 1797, Kant described a contract as 'an act of the united choice of two persons by which anything at all that belongs to one passes to another'.[178] Hegel also utilised the idea of will in his definition of a contract:[179]

> Since the two contracting parties relate to each other as immediate self-sufficient persons, it follows that (α) the contract is the product of the arbitrary will; (β) the identical will which comes into existence through the contract is only a will posited by the contracting parties, hence only a common will, not a will which is universal in and for itself; (γ) the object of the contract is an individual external thing, for only things of this kind are subject to the purely arbitrary will of the contracting parties.[180]

Whether philosophical fashion mattered to most lawyers or whether there is any discernible link between the use of will by philosophers

[173] Pothier, *Treatise*, p. 35. [174] *Ibid.*, pp. 58, 65. [175] *Ibid.*, p. 76.
[176] *Ibid.*, pp. 76–7. [177] *Ibid*, 1.1.1 § 1.
[178] Mary Gregor (ed.), Immanuel Kant, *The Metaphysics of Morals* (Cambridge: Cambridge University Press, 1996), p. 57.
[179] Dudley Knowles, *Routledge Philosophy Guidebook to Hegel and the Philosophy of Right* (London: Routledge, 2002), pp. 136–8.
[180] Allen Wood (ed.), Georg Hegel, *Elements of the Philosophy of Right* (Cambridge: Cambridge University Press, 1991), § 75.

and the rise of Pothier is perhaps doubtful.[181] Certainly if there was any connection it has left no trace.

One reviewer of Evans's translation claimed that Pothier's works 'are in the hands of every scientific jurist on the continent, and are frequently referred to even in this country'.[182] Especially in this early period his influence should not be exaggerated. Colebrooke was exceptional in this regard. Even after 1820 it was still perfectly possible to produce a coherent treatment of contract and ignore Pothier altogether. Tracing the precise influence of Pothier, and through him the writers of legal treatises, is not a straightforward exercise. It raises important questions about the nature of legal development in the nineteenth century more generally.

181 James Gordley, 'Contract, Property, and Will – The Civil Law and Common Law Tradition', in Harry Scheiber (ed.), *The State and Freedom of Contract* (Stanford, Calif.: Stanford University Press, 1998), p. 80.

182 Anon, 'Treatise on the Law of Obligation or Contracts by M. Pothier' (1807) 3 *Law Journal* 297, 301.

7

Equity and the regulation of unfairness in contracting: the usury laws as a case study

Legal doctrine derived from the Court of Chancery made an important contribution to the Common law of contract. The Court of Chancery was also significant on its own terms. Not only were some contracts, largely relating to land, enforced in Equity, but the court also sought to provide relief against unfairness and exploitation in contracting. There are a number of specific examples. One of the most important was the way in which from the sixteenth century, injunctions prevented a creditor enforcing a judgment for a sum in excess of his actual loss.[1] Because Equitable relief was not confined to specific situations and was built on the notion of conscience, judges possessed a degree of discretion. By Lord Nottingham's time precedent was becoming more pronounced,[2] but even by the seventeenth century the shifting sands of conscience had not completely been replaced by the firm foundations of Equity.[3] The process begun by Lord Nottingham was continued by Lord Hardwicke between 1737 and 1756.[4] The extent to which, even by this stage, the court's jurisdiction was firmly mapped out should not be exaggerated. Equity's strength throughout the eighteenth century was the way in which a significant degree of flexibility was retained. It allowed the court to adapt to meet changing circumstances and different factual situations. This was particularly helpful when dealing with

[1] Edith Henderson, 'Relief from Bonds in the English Chancery: Mid-sixteenth Century' (1974) 18 *American Journal of Legal History* 298.

[2] D.E.C. Yale (ed.), *Lord Nottingham's Chancery Cases Vol. I* (London: Selden Society, 1954), pp. xxxvii–cxxiv. Lord Nottingham served as Lord Chancellor from 1673 to 1681.

[3] The continued importance of conscience has traditionally been overlooked by legal historians. For a recent corrective, see Dennis Klinck, *Conscience, Equity and the Court of Chancery in Early Modern England* (Farnham: Ashgate, 2010), pp. 219–61.

[4] Clyde Croft, 'Lord Hardwick's Use of Precedent in Equity', in Thomas Watkin (ed.), *Legal Record and Historical Reality* (London: Hambledon, 1989), pp. 121–55; David Lieberman, *The Province of Legislation Determined: Legal Theory in Eighteenth Century Britain* (Cambridge: Cambridge University Press, 1989), pp. 81–3.

unfairness in contracting. By the early nineteenth century Chancery was a by-word for procrastination and delay.[5] Its component parts began to be more fully mapped out. The old energy was lost but not entirely dissipated. The inner workings of Chancery in the eighteenth century and its relationship with statute and the Common law can be illustrated by reference to the prohibition on usury.

The usury laws: the changing face of statutory regulation

John Baxton described usury as 'lending for gaine',[6] the 'gaine' meaning the additional sum paid to the lender above the amount of the loan.[7] His definition pre-dated the seventeenth century. It was derived from the Canon law[8] as applied by the Ecclesiastical courts, which had largely policed these transactions in the Middle Ages.[9] In Canon law, usury, any usury, was totally prohibited.[10] Money lending continued unabated, but those who wanted to avoid the risk of religious sanction were required to go to the trouble of disguising the true nature of the transaction.[11]

By the late sixteenth century the old consensus was starting to collapse. In Thomas Wilson's *A Discourse Upon Usury*, published in 1572, a preacher, a lawyer, a merchant, and a doctor of Civil law debate the merits of usury. In the eyes of the preacher, usurers were little better than common criminals: 'I will wyshe some penall lawe of death be made

[5] Michael Lobban, 'Preparing for Fusion: Reforming the Nineteenth Century Court of Chancery' (2004) 22 *Law and History Review* 389.

[6] *The English vsurer; or Vsury condemned, by the most learned and famous diuines of the Church of England* (London, 1634), p. 1.

[7] *Ibid.*, p. 2.

[8] The Canon law on this point was derived from the mid-twelfth century text Gratian's *Decretum*, see Peter Landau, 'The Development of Law', in David Luscombe and Jonathan Riley-Smith (eds.), *The New Cambridge Medieval History IV*, 7 vols. (Cambridge: Cambridge University Press, 2004), vol. IV, pp. 128–9. On the Ecclesiastical jurisdiction, see R.H. Helmholz, *The Oxford History of the Laws of England vol. I The Canon Law and Ecclesiastical Jurisdiction from 597 to the 1640s* (Oxford: Oxford University Press, 2004), pp. 378–82; R.H. Helmholz, 'Usury and the Medieval English Church Courts' (1986) 61 *Speculum* 364.

[9] The role of the Common law increased over time but it was not unimportant even in the Middle Ages: Gwen Seabourne, *Royal Regulation of Loans and Sales in Medieval England* (Woodbridge: The Boydell Press, 2003), pp. 25–69.

[10] For the intellectual background to the Medieval debate on usury, see Diana Wood, *Medieval Economic Thought* (Cambridge: Cambridge University Press, 2002), pp. 159–80.

[11] For examples of the Ecclesiastical Courts attempting to tackle evasion, see Helmholz, 'Usury', p. 371.

against those usurers, as well as agaynste theeves or murtherers, because their offence hurtheth more universallye and toucheth a greater number.'[12] By the end of the discussion, the more pragmatic lawyer and merchant are convinced by the force of the preacher's argument. The reality was rather different.

First of all the Ecclesiastical courts were emasculated,[13] and then a statute of 1571 was widely interpreted as removing the prohibition on usury at Common law.[14] Loans with a rate of interest below 10 per cent were treated as perfectly legal, whether falling within the traditional definition of usury or not.[15] Two hundred years later, the new distinction between 'moderate' and 'exorbitant profit' was captured by William Blackstone.[16] The former was lawful interest, the latter was usury.

There was some resistance, particularly amongst religious writers, to the new order.[17] But even staunch advocates of prohibition were prepared to concede that it was difficult to enforce.[18] There was a growing, if sometimes grudging, acceptance that money lending was a fact of life essential to economic progress.[19] John Benbrigge made the point that 'To speak of abolishing usury is idle; All states have ever had it, in one kind, or rule, or other, so as that opinion must be sent to Utopia'.[20] Francis Bacon, who had himself suffered at the hands of money lenders, accepted that 'Since there must be borrowing and lending, and men are so hard of

[12] R.H. Tawney (ed.), Thomas Wilson, *A Discourse Upon Usury 1572* (London: Bell & Sons, 1925), p. 232.

[13] J.H. Baker, *An Introduction to English Legal History*, 4th edn (London: Butterworths, 2002), pp. 130–2.

[14] For a wealth of detail on the statute, see Norman Jones, *God and the Moneylenders* (Oxford: Basil Blackwell, 1989).

[15] The earliest authorities were not all one way: A.W. Brian Simpson, *A History of the Common Law of Contract: The Rise of the Action of Assumpsit*, pbk edn (Oxford: Oxford University Press, 1987), pp. 514–15.

[16] William Blackstone, *Commentaries on the Laws of England*, 4 vols. (Oxford, 1766), vol. II, pp. 456–7.

[17] Anon, *A Brief Survey of the Growth of Usury in England* (London, 1671), p. 2; Anon, *The death of usury* (Cambridge, 1594); T.P., *The case of usury further debated* (London, 1684).

[18] William Burton, *A Sermon Preached in the Cathedral Church of Norwich the XX1 Day of December 1589 Sig. Hi-ii*, cited by Jones, *God and the Moneylenders*, p. 168.

[19] Joyce Appleby, *Economic Thought and Ideology in Seventeenth Century England* (Princeton: Princeton University Press, 1978), pp. 63–72, 87–93. On the expanding economy of the sixteenth and seventeenth centuries, see C.G.A. Clay, *Economic Expansion and Social Change: England 1500–1700, Industry, Trade and Government* (Cambridge: Cambridge University Press, 1984), vol. II, pp. 1–102.

[20] John Benbrigge, *Usura Accommodata* (London, 1646), p. 1.

heart as they will not lend freely, usury must be permitted'.[21] At the same time, the whole character of money lending was changing. Professional money lenders became increasingly common[22] and lending more sophisticated, all underpinned by a growing body of literature on the mathematics of interest rates.[23]

With the prohibition removed, attention shifted to the appropriate level of lawful interest, which by 1713 had fallen to 5 per cent.[24] Some money lenders, no doubt, kept within the new law.[25] Others reacted as they had done to the prohibition, by attempting to disguise the real nature of their loans. Mark Ord, writing in the early nineteenth century, grumbled that:

> After a long contest between the usurer and the legislature, the ingenuity of the former hath prevailed over the authority of the latter; for the legislature have never yet been able to extirpate the practices of usurers, to get extravagant interest.[26]

Methods of statutory avoidance were both varied and extensive.[27] In the early nineteenth century, Robert Comyn listed fifteen types of loan transactions which fell outside the statutes.[28]

The difficulty for the courts was, as the political theorist Robert Filmer observed, that there was often little in substance to separate loans that fell

21 For a similar view, see Roger Fenton, *A Treatise of Usurie* (London, 1611); Miles Mosse, *The Arraignment and Conviction of Usurie* (London, 1595).

22 There were some professional lenders prior to the late sixteenth century but much of the lending was more of a small scale activity between friends and neighbours. For details, see Craig Muldrew, *The Economy of Obligation* (Basingstoke: MacMillan, 1998), pp. 199–271; Marjorie McIntosh, 'Money Lending on the Periphery of London' (1988) 20 *Albion* 557.

23 C.G. Lewin, *Pensions and Insurance Before 1800: A Social History* (East Linton: Tuckwell Press, 2003), pp. 137–74.

24 Lawful interest fell in stages: (1623) 21 Jac I c. 17 (8 per cent); (1660) 12 Car II c. 13 (6 per cent); (1713) 12 Ann st. 2 c. 16 (5 per cent). A number of writers advocated reducing interest rates as a way of encouraging the economy: Thomas Culpeper, *A tract against the high rate of usury* (London, 1668); Josiah Child, *Brief Observations Concerning Trade and Interest of Money* (London, 1668). These views were not shared by everyone, as was evident in Thomas Culpeper's reply to his critics: Thomas Culpeper, *A Short Appendix to the Late Treatise Concerning the Abatement of Usury* (London, 1668).

25 Peter Temin and Hans-Joachim Voth, 'Banking as an Emerging Technology: Hoare's Bank, 1702–1742' (2006) 13 *Financial History Review* 149, 176 provides evidence that Hoare's Bank reduced their rate of interest to 5 per cent after 1713.

26 Mark Ord, *Essay on the Law of Usury*, 2nd edn (London: W. Clark, 1804), pp. 82–3 cited by Sybil Campbell, 'The Economic and Social Effect of the Usury Laws in the Eighteenth Century' (1933) 16 *Transactions of the Royal Historical Society 4th Series* 197, 205.

27 Anon, *A Common Law Treatise of Usury* (London, 1710).

28 Robert Comyn, *A Treatise on the Law of Usury* (London: R. Pheney, 1817), pp. 29–161.

within the statutes and those that did not.[29] In these circumstances, it is perhaps unsurprising that attempts to counter evasion produced mixed results. *Richards* v. *Brown*[30] provides a good snapshot of the kind of tensions which could arise. The parties had entered into an annuity agreement. In his evidence the borrower quoted the lender's statement that 'he never lends money but by way of annuity'. Lord Mansfield underlined the passage in his notebook.[31] In the face of this apparently strong evidence, and the very evident pecuniary desperation of the borrower, the first instinct of a streetwise jury at Guildhall, possibly themselves merchants, was to hold that the loan fell outside the statute. Only when the matter was put to the jurors a second time, and pressure applied by Lord Mansfield, did they find the transaction usurious.[32]

The problem went much deeper than persuading mercantile juries that a given transaction was usurious. Both Lord Hardwicke and Lord Mansfield pronounced on the wrongfulness of statutory evasion,[33] but the traditional way in which usurious transactions were identified proved to be a major obstacle to achieving their objectives. In *Murray* v. *Harding*, Blackstone J. explained, 'I do not know an instance where the principal is *bona fide* hazarded, that the contract has been held to be usurious'.[34] Provided the transaction involved a hazard, so that there was no guaranteed return of the principal, and no mention of a loan, and sometimes even if there was,[35] it was difficult to show that the usury laws had been compromised.[36] One possible escape route, which had proved popular with the Ecclesiastical courts but which brought no guarantee of success, was to look beneath the surface of the transaction to the intent of the parties. Lord Mansfield was particularly taken with the rhetoric of

29 Robert Filmer, *Quæstio quod liberica* (London, 1653), Preface.

30 (1778) 2 Cowp 770.

31 Lord Mansfield's note is reproduced in James Oldham, *The Mansfield Manuscripts and the Growth of English Law in the Eighteenth Century*, 2 vols. (Chapel Hill: University of North Carolina Press, 2004), vol. I, p. 649.

32 Oldham, *Mansfield Manuscripts*, vol. I, p. 651.

33 Lord Hardwicke: *Lawley* v. *Hooper* (1745) 3 Atk 278, 279; *Searle* v. *Carpenter* (1754) Amb 243. Lord Mansfield: *Floyer* v. *Edwards* (1774) 1 Cowp 112, 114–5; *Richards* v. *Brown* (1778) 2 Cowp 770, 776–7; *Jestons* v. *Brooke* (1778) 2 Cowp 793, 796; *Lowe* v. *Waller* (1781) 2 Doug 736, 740.

34 (1773) 2 Wm Bla 859, 865. De Grey C.J. made a similar point at 863.

35 (1773) 2 Wm Bla 859, 864 (De Grey C.J.): 'Communication concerning a loan has sometimes infected the cases and turned a contract into usury. But then the communication must be mutual. Application for a loan is not such a case, provided the party applied to refuses a loan but treats for an annuity.'

36 Mark Ord, *Essay on the Law of Usury* (London, 1797), pp. 68–9.

intention. On one occasion he noted that, 'The question is, what was the substance of the transaction, and the true intent and meaning of the parties? For they alone are to govern, and not the words used.'[37] A couple of years later he said, 'It is impossible to wink so hard, as not to see, that there was no idea between the parties of any thing but a loan of money'.[38]

It is doubtful whether this technique was an effective way of shoring up statutory regulation.[39] The fact that the parties were not competent witnesses in the Common law until the mid-nineteenth century must have been a significant obstacle. One of Lord Mansfield's contemporaries was not convinced by the effectiveness of the regulations, complaining that the 'laws in force against usury have been notoriously eluded'.[40] By the eighteenth century, one device, perhaps more than any other, came to encapsulate the problem.

Annuities for the life of the seller: a study in statutory avoidance

The annuity for the life of the seller[41] was labelled a 'public nuisance' by a Parliamentary Committee,[42] but it was relatively simple to draw up and proved to be enormously popular.[43] A lender (the buyer) offered a borrower (the seller) a capital sum (the principal). In return the borrower undertook to pay a sum of money each year (the annuity) for the

37 *Richards* v. *Brown* (1779) 2 Cowp 770, 776.

38 *Lowe* v. *Waller* (1781) 2 Doug 736, 740.

39 It may even be questioned how far intention was relevant. Certainly if an agreement had the characteristics of a usurious one it fell under the statute even if that was not what the parties intended but arose out of a mistake of the clerk drawing up the contract, see *Moffat* v. *Hargraves* (1795), James Oldham, *Case Notes of Sir Soulden Lawrence* (London: Selden Society, 2013), pp. 88–9.

40 Anon, *Reflections on Usury* (London, 1783), p. 13.

41 An invaluable guide is provided by Sybil Campbell, 'Usury and Annuities of the Eighteenth Century' (1928) 44 *Law Quarterly Review* 473. These devices seem to have been around from at least the early eighteenth century. William Bohun, *The Practising Attorney: or Lawyer's Office* (London, 1724), p. 386 contains an example. For an example of one of the common newspaper advertisements for this sort of transaction, see Anon, *Reflections*, p. 5. Annuities for the life of the buyer on the other hand were attended 'with little mischief' and for the benefit of both parties, see Thomas Erskine, *Reflections on gaming, annuities, and usurious contracts* (London, 1776), p. 24.

42 *Report From The Committee Appointed To Take Into Consideration The Laws now in being against Usury, And The present Practice of purchasing Annuities for the Life of the Grantor* (London, 1777). Anon, *Reflections*, p. 10 'where one annuity is bought at seven or eight years purchase, ten are bought at six'.

43 Campbell, 'Usury and Annuities', provides evidence from the Close Rolls of the popularity of annuities.

rest of his life. The period taken to repay the principal (the years' purchase) was usually set at six years.[44] The number of years' purchase represented the price. To take a simple example, A sells an annuity of £1,000 a year for his own life to B at six years' purchase. In return, B pays £6,000 to A. The lender's profit (or interest) came from the annual payments beyond six years which he hoped to receive. The hallmark of an annuity for the life of a seller was that a typical borrower could only offer fairly poor security such as a bond, personal property, or a life estate, and was unable to repay the whole sum in one go.[45]

One future and one current Lord Chancellor were both scathing about this type of annuity. Thomas Erskine wrote that:

> There is no honest trade so lucrative as to allow a profit on money borrowed by annuity at 6 years' purchase, and therefore there can seldom be one of that sort sold but upon some sudden emergency, or some very pungent distress, which this scandalous contract palliates for a moment, to rivet it closer and to confirm it for ever; like the medicines of a quack, or the bottle of a drunkard, which rock the senses for an hour to awake an idiot or a cripple.[46]

Lord Hardwicke complained that 'I really believe in my conscience, that ninety-nine in a hundred of these bargains are nothing but loans turned into this shape to avoid the statutes of usury'.[47] From the lender's point of view, the beauty of an annuity for the life of the seller was that, provided that it was carefully drafted, it had all the advantages of a loan without any of the drawbacks.[48] The interest charged was above the legal maximum, but on the face of it there was no risk so the transaction was not usurious.[49] The seller agreed to make an annual payment rather than simply to repay the principal. As a result, if the seller died before any payment was made, the buyer recovered nothing.[50] In truth there was rarely much of a hazard. The ready availability of life insurance by the eighteenth century

[44] *Report From The Committee*, p. 4. Some were even shorter where the security was less good or the borrower was in poor health, *ibid.*, p. 5.

[45] Robert Withy, *A Practical Treatise Upon The Law of Annuities* (London: Butterworth, 1800), p. 2.

[46] Erskine, *Reflections*, p. 27. [47] *Lawley* v. *Hooper* (1745) 3 Atk 278, 279.

[48] Attorneys were important not just in drafting these agreements but as brokers. This may be one reason why this legally watertight way of avoiding usury was so popular: C.W. Brooks, *Pettyfoggers and Vipers of the Commonwealth: The 'Lower Branch' of the Legal Profession in Early Modern England* (Cambridge: Cambridge University Press, 2004), pp. 196–7.

[49] For an example, see Campbell, 'Usury and Annuities', p. 479.

[50] *Roberts* v. *Tremayne* (1616) Cro Jac 507 (though not in the context of an annuity).

saw to that.[51] By insuring the life of the seller, buyers were usually protected in the event of an early death.[52] Lord Hardwicke observed that 'everybody knows, that this casualty of losing the Principal is secured, by insuring the life, upon which the annuity depends'.[53]

The courts were largely untroubled by this practice. Francis Plowden stated that 'So many Annuities however have been established by the courts, in which such insurances have been known to subsist, that we must conclude, that this circumstance does not of itself render the transaction usurious'.[54] Rather feeble attempts at statutory intervention failed to regulate annuities for the life of the seller.[55] In the end it was, perhaps, this device more than any other which contributed to the death of the statutory restrictions on usury in the nineteenth century. In the meantime, and in the absence of a very effective scheme of statutory regulation, Equity had an important role to play in regulating financial transactions.

Why Equity intervened and early attempts at relief

The subject of loan transactions continued to generate strong views beyond the confines of legal London. One early eighteenth century polemicist carped that 'The scandalous practice of usury, ought to be an abomination to every honest person, and common interest of money may sometimes be a grievance'.[56]

Loans also left a mark on the mercantile literature of the seventeenth and eighteenth centuries.[57] Hogarth's rake would have felt at home in

[51] On the growth of life insurance, see Lewin, *Pensions*, pp. 325–31; Oldham, *Mansfield Manuscripts*, vol. I, pp. 474–8. For some minor practical problems, see Withy, *Annuities*, p. 17.

[52] There was a small risk that the life insurance would be invalidated, or if the borrower left the jurisdiction it became difficult to realise the security, see Campbell, 'Usury and Annuities', pp. 478–80.

[53] *Lawley* v. *Hopper* (1745) 3 Atk 278, 280.

[54] Francis Plowden, *A Treatise Upon the Law of Usury and Annuities* (London, 1797), p. 274.

[55] Campbell, 'Usury and Annuities', pp. 484–5; Anon, *Reflections*, pp. ii–iii, 9–10. Robert Hannay, *Defence of the Usury Laws* (Edinburgh: William Blackwood, 1823), p. 45 described this legislation as 'useless'.

[56] Anon, *Law quibbles. Or, a treatise of the evasions, tricks, turns and quibbles, commonly used in the profession of the law, to the prejudice of clients, and others* (London, 1724), p. 28.

[57] Daniel Defoe, *The Complete English Tradesman in Familiar Letters* (London, 1726), p. xiv: 'the tragic stories of tradesmen undone by usury are so many, and the variety so great'. For examples, see Anon, *A Gentleman's Assistant*, 2nd edn (London, 1709); Sylvanus Howard, *Every tradesman his own lawyer* (London, 1794).

some of the authorities.[58] High levels of borrowing amongst the aristocracy were not uncommon.[59] The trappings of status needed to secure social position and influence at the dawn of a consumer society[60] did not come cheaply. It was easy to lose large sums of money at the gaming table. Agricultural depressions which blighted the eighteenth century would have depleted income.[61] In these circumstances, it was easy to see how the fears of Thomas Lodge, that usurers 'inriche themselves mightelye by others misfortunes, but also eate our English Gentrie out of house and home',[62] might be realised. But it was not just the spendthrift who found it difficult to borrow at low rates of interest. A series of financial crises combined with high government borrowing threatened the private credit market throughout the eighteenth century.[63] The relatively low level of lawful interest may have made the problem worse. As some lenders became more circumspect,[64] borrowers were pushed into the arms of more unscrupulous lenders charging punitive rates of interest.[65]

58 Hogarth painted 'A Rake's Progress' in 1734. Ironically the main protagonist, Tom Rakewell, who loses his fortune, inherited his great wealth from his money lender father. For details on the painting, see Mark Hallett and Christine Riding, *Hogarth* (London: Tate, 2006), pp. 86–93.

59 Lawrence Stone, *The Crisis of the Aristocracy 1558–1641* (Oxford: Oxford University Press, 1965), pp. 505–46.

60 On the rise of consumer society amongst the upper reaches of society, see Maxine Berg, *Luxury and Pleasure in Eighteenth Century Britain* (Oxford: Oxford University Press, 2005). For an account of the elite, see Hannah Greig, *The Beau Monde* (Oxford: Oxford University Press, 2013).

61 G.E. Mingay, 'The Agricultural Depression 1730–1750' (1956) 8 *Economic History Review (NS)* 323. Though at the same time improvements in agricultural methods increased profitability, see John Rule, *The Vital Century* (London: Longman, 1995), pp. 47–55.

62 *An alarum against vsurers* (London, 1584).

63 T.S. Ashton, *An Economic History of England: The 18th Century* (London: Methuen, 1959), p. 29; Julian Hoppit, 'Financial Crises in Eighteenth-Century England' (1986) 39 *Economic History Review (NS)* 39.The biggest crisis of course was a result of the South Sea Bubble, see Julian Hoppit, *A Land of Liberty? England 1689–1727* (Oxford: Oxford University Press, 2002), pp. 334–5. Government debt was enormous. By 1820 it was twice national income: Gregory Clark, 'Debt, Deficits, and Crowding Out: England, 1727–1840' (2001) 5 *European Review of Economic History* 403. The Government paid higher rates of interest than permitted under the usury statutes, which, combined with better security, ensured that it was a desirable borrower: Wydham Beawes, *Lex Mercatoria Rediviva or the Merchant's Directory* (London, 1792), p. 411.

64 Peter Temin and Hans-Joachim Voth, 'Interest Rate Restrictions in a Natural Experiment: Loan Allocation and the Change in the Usury Laws in 1714' (2008) 118 *The Economic Journal* 743.

65 Jeremy Bentham made this very point in his famous *Defence of Usury; Shewing the Impolicy of the Present Legal Restraints on the terms of Pecuniary Bargains* (London, 1787), p. 29.

In the event that a debtor was sued for failure to repay his loan, it was open to him to plead usury.[66] If successful, then the contract was rendered void.[67] If the contract fell outside the usury laws, he was in a vulnerable position at Common law. In the absence of other grounds to avoid the contract, such as illegality or fraud, the agreement stood. A debtor who stopped paying was likely to be liable for the full value of the loan. There is no compelling evidence to suggest that juries were prepared to mitigate the damages awarded where the price paid was out of proportion to the value received, for example in the typical transaction where hidden interest was payable.[68]

The Court of Chancery was less forgiving when it came to financial transactions which fell outside the wording, but not the spirit, of the usury laws. The nineteenth century writer Hugh Bellot summarised the position before 1750:

> The reports of cases . . . are very meagre, and it is difficult to ascertain whether they proceeded on any uniform principle; but it may be assumed that the policy of the Court of Chancery was to relieve against what were called catching bargains, which were transactions looked upon as evasions of the usury laws then in force and which transactions were very narrowly watched.[69]

Equitable relief consisted of little more than a series of common situations loosely bound together by some shared themes. Most of the authorities are concerned with attempts to evade the usury laws, many involved heirs, and some raised the issue of inadequacy of value. There is no consistent terminology. The word 'unconscionable' does not always appear, but all of the authorities are concerned with some sort of unfairness.

Where the transaction fell within the statutes of usury, there was no difficulty in Chancery granting relief.[70] Those transactions which had a whiff of usury but fell outside the statutes were more troublesome. The early cases typically involve a sale of goods, which was a popular way of evading the usury laws before annuities became

[66] William Tidd, *The Practice of the Court of King's Bench in Personal Actions*, 2 vols. (London, 1794), vol. I, p. 374.

[67] *Loyd* v. *Williams* (1771) 3 Wils KB 250.

[68] J.L. Barton, 'The Enforcement of Hard Bargains' (1987) 103 *Law Quarterly Review* 118.

[69] Hugh Bellot and R. James Willis, *The Law Relating to Unconscionable Bargains with Money Lenders* (London: Stevens & Hayes, 1897), p. 35.

[70] *Lawley* v. *Hooper* (1745) 3 Atk 278, 279–81; *Earl of Chesterfield* v. *Janssen* (1750) 2 Ves Sen 125, 142–4, 147–8, 150–1, 153–5; *Spurrier* v. *Mayoss* (1792) 4 Bro CC 28, 30.

fashionable.[71] A borrower approached a lender or intermediary. The lender then agreed to sell the borrower goods at a grossly extravagant price on credit using a bond. The borrower sold the goods and generally received a fraction of what he paid. The lender's profit, provided he could recover on the bond, amounted to the difference between the price paid by the borrower and what he could have got for the goods if he sold them himself.

In *Fairfax* v. *Trigg*, Lord Nottingham poured opprobrium on these arrangements: 'This court ought to discountenance and relieve against all corrupt traffic between the shopkeepers and young gentleman who are usually drawn in and entangled with such kind of bargains.'[72] The usual measure of relief, he explained, was to reduce the sum owing to the 'true and real' value of the goods sold. The party seeking relief on this occasion was simply described as a student in Lincoln's Inn. In the early reported authorities, most are described as heirs.[73] Sheridan treats these authorities as the origin of Equitable jurisdiction over young heirs.[74] The judgments provide few clues about why relief was granted. Chancery judges may have been motivated by a desire to prevent evasion of the usury laws, dislike of sales at an exorbitant price, a desire to protect young heirs, or a mixture of all three. It is not difficult to imagine why so many of these cases involve young heirs as well as naiveté. The borrowers in these transactions lacked ready cash. Their only valuable asset was their future inheritance. It was only on inheriting that they would be able to pay the money back. This sort of scenario was sometimes obvious on the face of the agreement. In *Bill* v. *Price*, for example, several young heirs bound themselves to pay severally and jointly upon the death of their fathers.[75]

Loans disguised as sales were not the only method of avoiding usury which caught the attention of Chancery judges in the 1680s. The post-obit bond usually provided the borrower with an immediate payment. In return he promised that on the death of his father or other relative he would repay a much larger sum. The risk of death before inheritance

[71] For details on this method of evasion, see A Barrister, *Legal Recreations or Popular Amusements*, 2 vols. (London, 1792), vol. I, p. 410.

[72] (1676) [581], D.E.C. Yale (ed.), *Lord Nottingham's Chancery Cases Vol. II* (London: Selden Society, 1961), p. 448.

[73] *Bill* v. *Price* (1686) 1 Vern 467; *Lamplugh* v. *Smith* (1688) 2 Vern 77; *Witley* v. *Price* (1688) 2 Vern 78; *Wiseman* v. *Beake* (1690) 2 Vern 121.

[74] L.A. Sheridan, *Fraud in Equity: A Study in English and Irish Law* (London: Pitman, 1957), p. 143.

[75] (1686) 1 Vern 467.

ensured that the post-obit bond fell outside the ambit of the usury laws. Lord Nottingham, on giving relief on a post-obit bond, warned that 'no family can be safe if this be suffered'.[76] The case before him was a strong one. In addition to a post-obit bond, the agreement involved a sale at an exorbitant price, in which the plaintiff had agreed to purchase various items which he planned to sell and clear his debts.

In Lord Nottingham's opinion, 'this infamous kind of trade and circumvention ought by all means to be suppressed'.[77] Lord Keeper North, who heard the next stage of the litigation, was less paternalistic. He recognised that it was a 'hazardous bargain', but in the absence of 'proof of any fraud' the claim was dismissed.[78] When the case came on a third time, Lord Chancellor Jeffreys sought to discharge Lord Nottingham's decree, with the observation that the bargain was unconscionable.[79] As this litigation demonstrates, there were plainly differences of opinion between Chancery judges about the appropriateness of intervention. Lord Keeper North seems to have been particularly averse to granting relief. In *Batty* v. *Lloyd*, he said that:

> One that is necessitous must sell cheaper than those who are not. If I had a mind to buy of a rich man a piece of ground that lay near mine, for my convenience, he would ask me almost twice the value: so where people are constrained to sell, they must not look to have the fullest price.[80]

In a statement that resonates even today, he makes the point that those whose finances are in a poor state of repair should not be able to expect to negotiate a favourable arrangement with a lender and to expect the law to bail them out when everything comes unstuck. *Wiseman* v. *Beake*, a few years later, represents the opposing position. The plaintiff was a long way from being a young heir. He was a forty year old proctor in Doctors' Commons.[81] He was still granted relief. Although the agreement was described as a 'contrivance'[82] and 'fraud',[83] there is nothing to suggest that this was anything other than a perfectly standard post-obit bond. The tensions generated by these two extreme positions would bubble to the surface in the eighteenth century, particularly in cases of financial transactions at an under value.[84]

[76] *Anon* (1680) [1089], Yale, *Nottingham Vol. II*, p. 868. [77] *Ibid.*

[78] *Barny* v. *Beak* (1682) 2 Chan Cas 136. [79] *Berney* v. *Pitt* (1686) 2 Vern 14.

[80] (1682) 1 Vern 141.

[81] Doctors' Commons was a court practising Civil law dealing in Admiralty and matrimonial matters. A proctor was equivalent to an attorney in the Common law.

[82] (1698) 2 Vern 121, 122; (1698) 2 Freeman 111. [83] (1698) 2 Freeman 111.

[84] Even within the same hearing: *Keen* v. *Stuckely* (1721) Gilb Rep 155.

Irrespective of the precise format, what all these transactions had in common was that one party, in urgent need of ready cash, was prepared to enter into a highly disadvantageous agreement.[85] *Nott* v. *Hill* is a good early example. The plaintiff, who was entitled to the estate tail, sold his expectancy at a considerable under value.[86] Lord Nottingham, in setting the agreement aside, expressed himself in quite broad terms:

> Put the case Hill had given him £30 to have five times so much on the father's death, should not the court relieve in such a case? Here you have five times the value in land . . . He said, by the Civil Law a bargain of double the value shall be avoided, and wish'd it were so in England.[87]

As in *Batty* v. *Lloyd*, Lord Keeper North once again refused to set the agreement aside.[88] But when the executor of the original defendant tried to get specific performance of the agreement, he was not sympathetic: 'A contract which carries an equity to have it decreed in specie, ought to be without all objection . . . and the practice of purchasing from heirs was grown too common, and therefore he would not in any sort countenance it.'[89] A refusal to grant specific performance had less drastic consequences than setting the contract aside because the plaintiff was still left with a remedy at Law.[90]

It is dangerous to draw many firm conclusions about under value from the earliest cases. Part of the difficulty in making sense of these authorities is that many different factors may have influenced the outcome. In the seventeenth century in particular, the reasoning is not fully set out. There are examples of agreements that appear to be set aside for inadequacy of value, but they are not strong authorities,[91] and others where Equity came to the opposite conclusion.[92] When inadequacy was combined with some other factor, the courts were more responsive. Evidence of fraud was particularly helpful.[93] In the absence of fraud, an

85 On hard bargains more generally, see Barton, 'Hard Bargains'.

86 The estate tail was a very typical form of dynastic land holding, see A.W.B. Simpson, *A History of the Land Law*, 2nd edn (Oxford: Oxford University Press, 1986), pp. 90–1.

87 (1682) 2 Chan Cas 120. 88 (1683) 1 Vern 141.

89 *Johnson* v. *Nott* (1684) 1 Vern 271.

90 At Common law they could bring an action for debt or damages. In *Nott* v. *Johnson* (1687) 2 Vern 27, Lord Chancellor Jeffreys held that the agreement should be set aside, thereby restoring Lord Nottingham's original position.

91 In *Fawcet* v. *Bowers* (1693) 2 Vern 287 no explicit reasoning was provided. In *Francis Pawlett* v. *Pleydell* (1679) [935], Yale, *Nottingham Vol. II*, p. 739, Lord Nottingham said that he saw no reason for Chancery to interpose but the parties agreed a compromise.

92 *Hobert* v. *Hobert* (1683) 2 Chan Cas 159.

93 *Ardglasse* v. *Muschamp* (1684) 1 Vern 237.

'unreasonable advantage made of a necessitous man' could be enough to tip the balance.[94] As demonstrated by *Nott* v. *Hill* itself, an heir dealing with his expectancy who sold at an under value was also likely to receive a favourable hearing.

Earl of Chesterfield v. Janssen: structuring relief in Equity

By the middle of the eighteenth century a clearer picture was beginning to emerge. This came about, in part, as a result of *Earl of Chesterfield* v. *Janssen*.[95] In their commentary, White and Tudor, the authors of *A Selection of Leading Cases in Equity*, wrote that:

> *Chesterfield* v. *Janssen*, is a case of very frequent reference, celebrated . . . above all for the learned judgment of Lord Hardwicke himself, in which he has so admirably classified the different species of fraud against which equity will give relief.[96]

Relief was rationalised on the basis that it was the job of Chancery to protect against fraud. That Lord Hardwicke should single out fraud is not very surprising. Fraud was one of the three traditional heads of Chancery jurisdiction.[97] Lord Hardwicke set down five heads of fraud. Three are particularly relevant in this context:

> [Fraud] apparent from the intrinsic nature and subject of the bargain itself; such as no man in his senses and not under delusion would make on the one hand and no honest and fair man would accept on the other; [Fraud] presumed from the circumstances and condition of the parties contracting . . . it is wisely established in this court to prevent taking surreptitious advantage of the weakness or necessity of another: which knowingly to do is equally against conscience as to take advantage of his ignorance; the last head of fraud, on which there has been relief, is that which infects catching bargains with heirs, reversioners, or expectants in the life of the father.[98]

A few years later, in a letter to his friend Lord Kames, Lord Hardwicke would claim that 'fraud is infinite' and that 'no invariable rules can be

[94] *Cole* v. *Gibbons* (1734) 3 P Wms 290, 294. [95] (1750) 2 Ves Sen 125, 1 Atk 301.

[96] Frederick White and Owen Tudor, *A Selection of Leading Cases in Equity*, 2 vols. (London: W. Maxwell, 1849), vol. I, p. 410.

[97] Henry Rolle, *Un Abridgement des plusieurs cases et resolutions del Common Ley* (London, 1668), p. 374; Edward Coke, *Institutes of the Laws of England*, 4 vols. (London, 1644), vol. IV, p. 84; D.E.C. Yale (ed.), *Lord Nottingham's Manual of Chancery Practice and Prolegomena of Chancery and Equity* (Cambridge: Cambridge University Press, 1965), p. 191.

[98] (1750) 2 Ves Sen 125, 155–7.

established'.[99] Whether fraud by this time, even in Equity, was as broad as Lord Hardwicke's remarks suggest, is perhaps doubtful.[100] Ironically his classification would contribute to the growth of 'invariable rules', which by the nineteenth century would change the face of Equitable relief.[101] A flavour of what was going on can be gleaned from two late eighteenth century statements, one from a legal writer and one from a judge. In an editorial note to his 1793 edition of Ballow's *A Treatise of Equity*, John Fonblanque explained:

> Even in cases of fraud, which from their nature must be almost infinitely various in their circumstances, courts of equity constantly proceed upon some clear and established principle sufficiently comprehensive to meet the circumstances of the particular case to which it is applied, and not upon a vague, arbitrary, and indefinite power.[102]

Lord Thurlow made a very similar point when he said that 'The Court will not correct a contract, merely because a man of nice honour would not have entered into it; it must fall within some definition of fraud; the rule must be drawn so as not to affect the general transactions of mankind.'[103]

The desire to come up with clear definitions reflected the intellectual climate of the time and the growing influence of the doctrine of precedent. As the categories of relief became fixed, the prospect of an overarching doctrine of unconscionability was probably killed off for good. But in the meantime there was still a good deal that remained to be settled. Lord Hardwicke's first category[104] would prove particularly problematic.[105] The pre-1740 cases were largely one way. Inadequacy

[99] Phillip Yorke, *The Life and Correspondence of Philip Yorke, Earl of Hardwicke*, 3 vols. (Cambridge. Cambridge University Press, 1913), vol. II, pp. 550–5.

[100] Michael Lobban, 'Contractual Fraud in Law and Equity, c1750-c1850' (1997) 17 *Oxford Journal of Legal Studies* 441, 448–50.

[101] John Newland, *A Treatise on Contract Within the Jurisdiction of Courts of Equity* (London: Butterworth, 1806); George Jeremy, *A Treatise on the Equitable Jurisdiction of the High Court of Chancery* (London: Clarke, 1828).

[102] 2 vols. (London, 1793), vol. I, book 1, ch. 1, § 3 (k).

[103] *Fox* v. *Mackreth* (1788) 2 Bro CC 400, 420.

[104] The first category mentioned above. It is the second category in Lord Hardwicke's original scheme after actual fraud.

[105] Morton Horwitz, 'The Historical Foundations of Modern Contract Law' (1974) 87 *Harvard Law Review* 917; Morton Horwitz, *The Transformation of American Law 1780–1860* (Cambridge, Mass.: Harvard University Press, 1977), pp. 160–210; A.W. B. Simpson, 'The Horwitz Thesis and the History of Contracts' (1979) 46 *University of Chicago Law Review* 533; P.S. Atiyah, *The Rise and Fall of Freedom of Contract* (Oxford: Oxford University Press, 1979), pp. 169–77; James Gordley, *The Philosophical Origins of Modern Contract Doctrine* (Oxford: Oxford University Press, 1991), pp. 147–58.

of price was not enough to achieve relief, either by setting the contract aside or refusal of specific performance.[106] In the early 1740s, some remarks by Lord Hardwicke seem to suggest that the position had changed, but significantly these comments were made in the context of claims which involved more than just inadequate price.[107] Matters reached a head in 1749 when Lord Hardwicke announced that specific performance might be refused solely on the basis of an inadequate price.[108] These developments had obvious significance for loan transactions, but the cases were still not all one way. In what were both apparently straightforward annuity cases, specific performance was refused in one case and granted in the other.[109]

In the seventeenth century, fraud was usually understood to be something distinct from inadequacy of price. It was just one of a number of factors that the courts took into account, like being an heir or taking advantage of weakness, albeit a particularly strong one. By the middle of the eighteenth century, fraud had come more to the fore. In *Lawley* v. *Hooper*, Lord Hardwicke explained that 'wherever they have found the least tincture of fraud in any of these oppressive bargains, relief hath always been given'.[110] This did not mean that Lord Hardwicke was any more likely to set aside contracts than his predecessors.[111] From around 1780 something extraordinary began to happen. In *Gwynne* v. *Heaton*,[112] Lord Thurlow held that whilst mere 'inadequate consideration' was not alone sufficient to merit setting a contract aside, where there was an 'inequality so strong, so gross, and manifest, that it must be impossible to state it to a man of common sense, without producing an exclamation at the inequality of it',[113] then the situation was different. *Gwynne* v. *Heaton* can be explained on the basis that the plaintiff was an heir.[114]

[106] Barton, 'Hard Bargains', pp. 124–6.

[107] *Barnardiston* v. *Lingood* (1740) 2 Atk 133 (expectant heir); *Buxton* v. *Lister* (1746) 3 Atk 383 (misrepresentation).

[108] *Underwood* v. *Hitchcox* (1749) 1 Ves Sen 279.

[109] Refused: *Vaughan* v. *Thomas* (1783) 1 Bro CC 556. Granted: *Lord Carbery* v. *Weston* (1757) 1 Bro PC 429. One reason for the different outcome may arise from the fact that the annuity in the former was sold at five years' purchase and in the latter at seven years' purchase. Six years' purchase was generally accepted to be the market price. The annuity in *Vaughan* v. *Thomas* was therefore below the normal market price.

[110] (1745) 3 Atk 278, 279.

[111] *Lawley* v. *Hooper* (1745) 3 Atk 278; *Nichols* v. *Gould* (1752) 2 Ves Sen 422.

[112] (1778) 1 Bro CC 1. [113] *Ibid*., p. 9.

[114] The plaintiff, who had entered into an annuity because he was destitute having been 'turned out of doors' by his father for marrying a servant, could count himself lucky to come before the judge who heard his case. Lord Thurlow, who had co-habited with a

Heathcote v. *Paignon*[115] went one stage further. The plaintiff was not an heir and Lord Thurlow expressly found 'no evidence of distress'. The annuity was still set aside on the basis that 'There is such inadequacy as to shew that the person did not understand the bargain he made, or was so oppressed that he was glad to make it, knowing its inadequacy, it will shew a command over him which may amount to fraud'.[116]

The line between inadequacy of value as a ground to set an agreement aside, and inadequacy of value as evidence of oppression sufficient for an agreement to be set aside, is a fine one. Particularly where, as here, it was the only evidence before the court.[117] Because fraud must still be present,[118] there were two great advantages. Superficially, at least, it allowed an escape from Lord Thurlow's fear that 'if the court should take such a ground as to rest the case upon the market price, every transaction of this kind would come into the court of equity'.[119] There is probably a good deal of truth in the remarks of one Irish Lord Chancellor who said that 'Inadequacy of price is not of itself sufficient, but the Court has got at it by indirect means – it has been astute, as it is said to infer fraud from inadequacy, so as to raise it indirectly into a ground for relief'.[120]

At the same time, this approach retained a degree of flexibility, given that each particular instance turned on whether or not there was a fraud. The way in which specific performance operated told a similar story. In *Day* v. *Newman*, Arden M.R. had refused specific performance on the grounds of inadequacy of price whilst admitting that there was 'no pressure of circumstances whatever'.[121] Later judges clarified his position. It was made clear that inadequacy of price was only relevant as evidence of fraud.[122]

For a while, heirs continued to be treated as a special group particularly worthy of protection.[123] This paternalistic attitude was as much

bar-maid who gave birth to three daughters, might be expected to have some sympathy for the plaintiff's plight.

115 (1787) 2 Bro CC 167. 116 *Ibid.*, p. 175.

117 In most situations there was additional evidence.

118 *Speed* v. *Philips* (1796) 3 Anstr 732, 734; *Moth* v. *Atwood* (1801) 5 Ves Jun 845.

119 *Heathcote* v. *Paignon* (1787) 2 Bro CC 167, 175. For similar statements, see *Nichols* v. *Gould* (1752) 2 Ves Sen 422, 423; *Griffith* v. *Spratlay* (1787) 1 Cox 383, 388.

120 *Drought* v. *Eustace* (1828) 1 Mol 328, 335 cited by Sheridan, *Fraud in Equity*, p. 130.

121 (1788) 2 Cox 77, 82.

122 *Collier* v. *Brown* (1788) 1 Cox 428; *White* v. *Damon* (1802) 7 Ves Jun 30; *Coles* v. *Trecothick* (1804) 9 Ves Jun 234, 246, Lord Eldon: 'Unless the inadequacy of price is such as shocks the conscience, and amounts in itself to conclusive and decisive evidence of fraud in the transaction, it is not itself a sufficient ground for refusing a specific performance.'

123 *Barker* v. *Vansommer* (1782) 1 Bro CC 149 (sale); *Darley* v. *Singleton* (1810) Wight 25 (post-obit bond).

about protecting family property as individual heirs,[124] and is particularly evident in sales of reversions.[125] Sailors dealing with prize money were also seen as a special case.[126] After *Gowland* v. *De Faria*,[127] which involved a sale of an annuity using a reversion as security, this strict position was relaxed. Provided the purchaser could show that they had given a fair price, the transaction stood.[128] This was a significant shift in those cases where the heir was relying on his status alone.[129] The special protection for heirs was further eroded by legislation in 1867 which stated that, in the absence of fraud or unlawful dealing, *bona fide* sales of reversions were to be upheld, even if at an undervalue.[130] This meant that after more than a century, the most serious threat to the landed interest, the sale of reversions, was put on the same footing as all other transactions. Reforms of the usury laws in any event meant that such drastic measures were no longer necessary.

The end of the usury laws

A Select Committee Report of 1818 painted a gloomy picture:

> That it is the opinion of this Committee, that the Laws regulating or restraining the rate of Interest have been extensively evaded, and have failed of the effect of imposing a maximum on such rate; and that of late years, from the constant excess of the market rate of interest above the rate limited by law, they have added to the expense incurred by borrowers on real security, and that such borrowers have been compelled to resort to the mode of granting annuities on lives, a mode which has been made a cover for obtaining higher interest than the rate limited by law, and has

124 Newland, *Contract*, p. 436. These concerns were sometimes openly expressed: *Twisleton* v. *Griffith* (1716) 1 P Wms 312, 313; *Cole* v. *Gibbons* (1734) 3 P Wms 290, 293; *Walmesley* v. *Booth* (1741) 2 Atk 27, 28; *Baugh* v. *Price* (1752) 1 Wils KB 320, 322; *Davis* v. *Duke of Marlborough* (1819) 2 Swan 108, 140.

125 *Coles* v. *Trecothick* (1804) 9 Ves Jun 234, 246.

126 *Baldwin* v. *Rochford* (1748) 1 Wils KB 229; *Taylour* v. *Rochford* (1751) 2 Ves Sen 281; *How* v. *Weldon* (1754) 2 Ves Sen 516. Prize money consisted of the proceeds from cargo captured from enemy ships: Edward Roscoe, *A History of the English Prize Court* (London: Lloyds, 1924), p. 52.

127 (1810) 17 Ves Jun 20.

128 The process of establishing a fair value caused a split between those who favoured using actuarial and market values: *Headen* v. *Rosher* (1824) M'Cle & Yo 89.

129 *Hincksman* v. *Smith* (1827) 3 Russ 433; *Earl of Portmore* v. *Taylor* (1831) 4 Sim 182; *Newton* v. *Hunt* (1833) 5 Sim 511.

130 (1867) 31 Vict c. 4.

> further subjected the borrowers to enormous charges, or forced them to make very disadvantageous sales of their estates.[131]

Little more than a quarter of a century later, the usury laws would be repealed.[132] Imperfect though judicial regulation undoubtedly was, there is little doubt that without the intervention of Chancery in the seventeenth and eighteenth centuries, the situation for borrowers would have been very much worse.

131 *Select Committee on Usury Laws* (1818) [376] PP vol. VI, 137.
132 Usury Laws Repeal Act (1854) 17 & 18 Vict c. 90.

8

The classical model of contract: the product of a revolution in legal thought?

Morton Horwitz has argued that modern contract law is 'fundamentally a creature of the nineteenth century'.[1] He characterised these events as a transformation of contract law under the influence of economic, political and social forces, from an essentially equitable body of law into the classical model of contract more familiar today.[2] Most English legal historians have approached the subject differently, preferring instead to portray changes in the law of contract as emerging from within the legal system itself on the back of an outbreak of theorising[3] and the growth of legal treatises.[4] Although potentially just different perspectives on the same subject, these writers hold strongly opposing views on the nature of legal change and proper interpretation of the evidence.[5] On one

[1] Morton Horwitz, *The Transformation of American Law 1780–1860* (Cambridge, Mass.: Harvard University Press, 1977), p. 160.

[2] In addition to Horwitz, *ibid*., see Morton Horwitz, 'The Historical Foundation of Modern Contract Law' (1974) 87 *Harvard Law Review* 917. From a more English-focused perspective, see P.S. Atiyah, *The Rise and Fall of Freedom of Contract* (Oxford: Oxford University Press, 1979).

[3] A.W.B. Simpson, 'Innovation in Nineteenth Century Contract Law' (1975) 91 *Law Quarterly Review* 247; D.J. Ibbetson, *A Historical Introduction to the Law of Obligations* (Oxford: Oxford University Press, 1999), pp. 220–44; J.H. Baker, *An Introduction to English Legal History*, 4th edn (London: Butterworths, 2003), pp. 352–3. James Gordley, an American, also belongs in this group: James Gordley, *The Philosophical Origins of Modern Contract Doctrine* (Oxford: Oxford University Press, 1991). For a slightly different approach, see W.R. Cornish and G. de N. Clark, *Law and Society in England* 1750–1950 (London: Sweet & Maxwell, 1989), pp. 200–20. For a note of caution, see Michael Lobban, 'Introduction', in William Cornish, Stuart Anderson, Raymond Cocks, Michael Lobban, Patrick Polden and Keith Smith, *The Oxford History of the Laws of England, Vol. XII 1820–1914: Private Law* (Oxford: Oxford University Press, 2010), p. 302; Warren Swain, 'The Classical Model of Contract: The Product of a Revolution in Legal Thought' (2010) 30 *Legal Studies* 513.

[4] A.W.B. Simpson, 'The Rise and Fall of the Legal Treatise: Legal Principles and the Forms of Legal Literature' (1983) 48 *University of Chicago Law Review* 632.

[5] For a detailed critique of Horwitz's approach, see A.W.B. Simpson, 'The Horwitz Thesis and the History of Contracts' (1979) 46 *University of Chicago Law Review* 533. For a further critical examination of Horwitz's views, see Peter Karsten, *Heart versus Head:*

fundamental point there is, nevertheless, common ground, namely, that the law of contract underwent a significant revolution in the decades around 1800. This consensus has succeeded in obscuring the fact that an equally good case can be made for treating the classical model of contract as the end product of a long process of change rather than the beginning of a new one.

Aspects of the new

Writing in the preface to his new book on contract in 1826, Joseph Chitty remarked that 'Perhaps no branch of the jurisprudence of the country has of late years been more subject of judicial inquiry and decision than the Law of Contracts'.[6] If not an impartial observer, then, Chitty was an astute one. The period between around 1820 and 1850 saw a series of landmark contract cases, many of which remain on the contract law syllabus. Several factors came together serendipitously. Two of the most important are frequently overlooked.[7] Without changes in the operation of the jury and pleading, it is unlikely that new contract doctrine would have been able to develop in the way that it did.

The civil jury was still at the heart of litigation in the central Common law courts in 1820. Writing in 1845, George Stephen observed 'of all the component parts of a court of justice, the juryman is, beyond doubt the most important'.[8] The civil jury in contract actions had over a century of useful life left.[9] But the civil jury of 1820 was a very different institution from that of a century before. The distinction between law and fact was thrown into sharper relief than in the past.[10] As one writer of the 1840s

Judge-Made Law in Nineteenth-Century America (Chapel Hill: University of North Carolina Press, 1997), pp. 47–78.

6 *A Practical Treatise on the Law of Contracts, Not Under Seal* (London: S. Sweet, 1826), p. iii.

7 Though not entirely. As long ago as 1980, John Baker, in his review of Patrick Atiyah's *Rise and Fall of Freedom of Contract* in (1980) 43 *Modern Law Review* 467, 469, noted that 'In truth there was very little law of contract at all before the last century, because there was no machinery for producing it and most of the questions were left to juries as questions of fact'. More recently more attention has been paid to this aspect: Catharine MacMillan, *Mistakes in Contract Law* (Oxford: Hart, 2009), pp. 69–95.

8 George Stephen, *The Juryman's Guide* (London: Charles Knight, 1845), p. 18.

9 With the exception of defamation, the civil jury was abolished in the 1930s: Administration of Justice Act (1933) 23 & 24 Geo IV c. 36 s. 6; R.M. Jackson, 'The Incidence of Jury Trial During the Past Century' (1937–8) 1 *Modern Law Review* 132.

10 William Forsyth, *History of Trial by Jury* (London: John Parker, 1852), p. 282: 'The distinction between the province of the judge and that of the jury is, in the English law, clearly defined, and observed with jealous accuracy.'

explained, 'the administration of the law consists in annexing defined legal consequences to defined facts'.[11] In contract actions this meant that the task of the trial judge was to define the characteristics of a contract in line with doctrine laid down by the court in banc. The task of the jury was limited to following the judge's direction in order to determine, as a matter of fact, whether those characteristics were present.[12]

Pleading reform was a favourite topic in Benthamite circles.[13] Bentham himself proposed a characteristically radical solution which would have seen the current 'technical' procedure replaced by what he regarded as a much simpler 'natural procedure'.[14] Even those who thought that Bentham's procedural reforms went too far were prepared to concede that he had a point so far as pleading was concerned.[15] Reform of pleading was also put firmly on the political agenda by Henry Brougham,[16] who in a speech to Parliament in 1828[17] provided 'more a detailed critique of the law than a programme of reform'.[18] The precise details of reform were left to others.

The broad general issue in assumpsit was one of the defects in English law singled out by Brougham.[19] A Parliamentary Commission also

[11] Anon, 'Of the distinction between Law and Fact' (1844) 1 *Law Review* 37, 38.

[12] Anon, 'Of the function of the judge as distinguished from those of the jury' (1845) 2 *Law Review* 27, 28.

[13] On the influence of Bentham on nineteenth century reform more generally, see S.E. Finer, 'The Transmission of Benthamite Ideas 1820–50', in Gillian Sutherland (ed.), *Studies in the Growth of Nineteenth Century Government* (London: Routledge & Kegan Paul, 1972), p. 11; J. Hostettler, 'Jeremy Bentham – Reformer Extraordinary' (1992) 156 *Justice of the Peace and Local Government Law* 668. For more sceptical views on Bentham's influence, see David Roberts, 'Jeremy Bentham and the Victorian Administrative State', in Bhikhu Parekh (ed.), *Jeremy Bentham: Ten Critical Essays* (London: Cass, 1974), pp. 187–204; J.R. Dinwiddy, 'Early Nineteenth Century Reactions to Benthamism' (1984) 34 *Transactions of the Royal Historical Society 5th Series* 47.

[14] His full scheme was set out in his five-volume *Rationale of Judicial Evidence*, 5 vols. (London: Hunt & Clark, 1827) on which, see A.D.E. Lewis, 'The Background to Bentham on Evidence' (1990) 2 *Utilitas* 195.

[15] For example, the reviewer of Bentham's *Rationale of Judicial Evidence* in (1828) *The Edinburgh Review* 457–520.

[16] On the relationship between Bentham and Brougham, see Michael Lobban, 'Henry Brougham and Law Reform' (2000) 115 *The English Historical Review* 1184, 1188–9.

[17] (1828) 18 HC Deb 127. For some discussion of the speech which lasted over six hours, and during which Brougham is said to have consumed a hatful of oranges, see Robert Stewart, *H Brougham 1778–1868: His Public Career* (London: The Bodley Head, 1985), pp. 234–8.

[18] Lobban, 'Henry Brougham', p. 1189.

[19] (1828) 18 HC Deb 127, 201. The expert on pleading in assumpsit, Edward Lawes, writing a few years earlier, pointed out that, 'almost every sort of defence might be given in

recommended reform.[20] Once implemented, much that was hidden behind the blank general issue was revealed for the first time. Fraud is a good example.[21] Having been overlooked in this context up until now, after the reforms it was included in works on pleading.[22] Within a few years fraud was being presented as a general underlying principle which was a ground for vitiating a contract.[23] The Hilary Rules[24] were not an unqualified success.[25] One of the key changes saw the plea of 'non-assumpsit' reduced to a denial that there had been a promise. All other matters had to be pleaded specially.[26] Juries were no longer presented with a blank general issue. The elements of a claim were left fully exposed. When put alongside the fact that it was becoming easier to raise questions in banc, jury discretion was squeezed.[27] Needing to fill

evidence' under the general issue in assumpsit: Edward Lawes, *A Practical Treatise on Pleading in Assumpsit* (London: W. Reed, 1810), p. 520.

[20] *2nd Report of His Majesty's Commissioners Appointed to Inquire into the Practice and Procedure of the Superior Courts of Common Law* (1830) [123] PP vol. XI, 547.

[21] As part of the reforms fraud had to be pleaded specially which meant that it had to be specifically identified. In his evidence to the commission which preceded these reforms, Chitty explained that fraud was currently pleaded under the general issue: *2nd Report*, App B No. 4 § 56.

[22] The point can be illustrated with reference to the leading work on pleading by Joseph Chitty. Before the reforms fraud was omitted, Joseph Chitty, *A Treatise on the Parties to Actions, the Forms of Actions and on Pleading*, 2 vols. (London: W. Clarke, 1809), vol. I, pp. 476–81. After the Hilary Reforms it began to be included, Joseph Chitty, *A Treatise on the Parties to Actions, the Forms of Actions and on Pleading*, 6th edn, 2 vols. (London: W. Clarke, 1836), vol. I, p. 515.

[23] By C.E. Dodds in his lectures to the Law Society, (1836) 11 *Legal Observer* 505. The first full-length treatment of the subject in a treatise was still some way off, Stephen Leake, *The Elements of the Law of Contracts*, 1st edn (London: Stevens & Sons, 1867), pp. 181–205.

[24] Reg Gen HT 4 Will IV. The rules are reproduced in (1834) LJ Repts KB 5 and John Jervis, *All the New Rules in Relation to Pleading and Practice* (London: S. Sweet, 1839), pp. 113–40.

[25] W. Holdsworth, 'New Rules of Pleading of the Hilary Term 1834' (1923) 1 *Cambridge Law Journal* 261. The rise to prominence of special pleading had the undesirable side-effect that it increased the likelihood of a challenge on a technicality. This tactic was noted in the *1st Report of Her Majesty's Commissioners for Inquiring into the Process, Practice and System of Pleading in the Superior Courts of the Common Law* (1851) [1389] PP vol. XXII, 567 and satirised in *Crogate's Case: A Dialogue in Ye Shades on Special Pleading Reform* which is reproduced in W.S. Holdsworth, *A History of English Law*, 17 vols. (London: Methuen, 1944), vol. IX, pp. 417–31.

[26] For a discussion in the context of an assumpsit on a bill of exchange, see *Easton* v. *Pratchett* (1835) 1 C M & R 798, 806–7.

[27] Joshua Getzler, 'The Fate of the Civil Jury in Late Victorian England: Malicious Prosecution as a Test Case', in John Cairns and Grant McLeod (eds.), *The Dearest Birth Right of the People of England* (Oxford: Hart, 2002), pp. 218–37.

the gap caused by the demise of the jury, judges began to articulate general principles of contractual liability.

Although Pothier wrote for a very different audience in a foreign country, his books proved unexpectedly useful in assisting English judges to fill the void left by the winnowing out of the general issue. His work was scientific and principled but also full of examples for lawyers and judges looking for quick solutions to practical problems. It was easy to follow[28] and available in an English translation. Pothier's ideas had already been taken up by the more cosmopolitan legal authors like Henry Colebrooke and William Jones, but by the 1820s he began to attract attention from more mainstream legal opinion.[29] A comparison of the fate of Jean Domat's, *Les loix civiles dans leur ordre naturel*, translated by William Strahan, and published in 1722,[30] is instructive. It suggests that the Common law had become more ready to embrace Pothier's sort of approach by the early nineteenth century than a century before. Contract law was a major feature of Domat's treatise.[31] Whilst Domat influenced Pothier, he left almost no trace in England.[32] Pothier, on the other hand, was cited in court on more than 400 occasions in the nineteenth century.[33] That a Frenchman who lived in the previous century should prove so popular in England is, at first sight, surprising. Yet Evans's translation came along at the right time. Fashion no doubt

[28] Anon, 'The Law of Contracts' (1846) 5 *Law Magazine or Quarterly Review of Jurisprudence* 256, 258: 'To us there is no law book so pleasing as that of Mons. Pothier, by reason of the extremely clear manner in which various rules applicable to the law of contracts are expounded.'

[29] Pothier also attracted attention in Scotland, Kenneth Reid, 'From Text-Book to Book of Authority: The *Principles* of George Joseph Bell' (2011) 15 *Edinburgh Law Review* 6, 24–5.

[30] As *The Civil Law in its Natural Order* (London, 1722). A section of Domat's treatise had appeared in a translation by Wood some years earlier: *A Treatise of the First Principles of Laws in General* (London, 1705). For a discussion of Wood's and Strahan's translations, see Daniel Coquillette, *The Civilian Writers of Doctors' Commons, London* (Berlin: Duncker & Humblot, 1988), pp. 200, 203–9.

[31] Strahan specifically drew attention to Domat's treatment of contract and commercial issues, *ibid.*, pp. iii–iv.

[32] Examples in argument include: *Harvy* v. *Aston* (1740) 2 Com 726, 757; *Holdfast* v. *Dowsen* (1747) 1 Wm Bla 8, 11; *Robinson* v. *Bland* (1760) 1 Wm Bla 234, 235, 238; *Eyre* v. *Lovell* (1782) 3 Doug 66, 68. References to Domat in judgments are even rarer: *Ryall* v. *Rowles* (1749) Ves Sen 348, 370; *Miller* v. *Race* (1758) 2 Kenyon 189, 199; *Doe on the Demise Lancashire* v. *Lancashire* (1792) 5 TR 49, 64.

[33] B. Rudden, 'Pothier et la common law', in J. Monéger (ed.), *Robert-Joseph Pothier, d'hier à aujourd'hui* (Paris: Economica, 2001), p. 97.

played a part, to the extent that Pothier's treatise was even becoming recommended reading for students in the Inns of Court.[34]

What occurred was not a simple case of indiscriminate and wholesale borrowing. The correlation between the emerging contract doctrine and the legal writers was just as complex as the earlier, much more limited, borrowing from Civilian and Natural law literature. For every occasion on which legal literature may have influenced the direction of doctrine, there were others when it was used to add weight to principles already in existence, or where it was no discernible influence at all. The role played by Pothier, whilst significant in helping to shape contract doctrine in a period of flux, should not be overstated. Even without considering the role played by social and economic factors, the formation of the classical model of contract cannot be explained by legal literature alone, which was undoubtedly moving in new directions.

Legal literature: the past and the future

The paucity of legal literature on the law of contract prior to the nineteenth century has been exaggerated, but after 1800 it undeniably increased in scope, size and sophistication. Most treatises on contract before the 1870s were written by, and intended for, the use of legal practitioners. Joseph Chitty's *A Practical Treatise on the Law of Contracts* was typical. Chitty was born into a legal family.[35] His father, Joseph Chitty the elder, and his brothers, were lawyers and legal writers. The first edition of his treatise was published in 1826.[36] A contract treatise bearing his name still exists today.[37] In style and content the work fell mid-way between the existing well-established body of contract literature and the great late nineteenth century treatises. In some ways it looked backwards. There was nothing novel in his definition of contract as 'a mutual assent of two or more persons, competent to contract, founded on a sufficient consideration, to perform some legal act, or

[34] Samuel Warren, *A Popular and Practical Introduction to Law Studies*, 2nd edn (London: Maxwell, 1845), p. 757.

[35] For a discussion of the family, see Gilchrist Alexander, *The Temple of the Nineties* (London: William Hodge, 1938), pp. 98–9.

[36] Chitty only lived to see two editions into press. A second edition appeared in 1834. A third edition, edited by his brother Tompson Chitty, was published in 1841, after which the book passed out of the family.

[37] Hugh Beale (ed.), *Chitty on Contracts*, 31st edn (London: Sweet & Maxwell, 2012). The current work runs to two volumes and more than 4,000 pages. In contrast the first edition was a mere 397 pages. It had already grown to 792 pages by the second edition.

omit to do anything, the performance whereof is not enjoyed by law'.[38] Powell,[39] Comyn,[40] Colebrooke,[41] and even Blackstone,[42] had all said something similar. References to Pothier did not appear until the second edition, published eight years later. In other ways the treatise marked a break with the past and pointed towards a new sort of legal writing. Chitty aimed to provide practical guidance for lawyers litigating contract claims at nisi prius. His stated aim was to 'treat exclusively of those matters connected with simple contracts, which are of common occurrence in business, and are consequently of the highest practical utility'.[43] Chitty thought that this could be best achieved by extracting principles from the authorities rather than attempting to set down individual decisions at any length.[44] This marked a departure from Powell and Newland, both of whom had given individual cases far greater prominence. Because Chitty was less at the mercy of the case law, it was easier for him to impose a strong external framework on the material. In this respect, his *Treatise* more closely resembled the late nineteenth century contract textbooks than its predecessors. The basic structure of the work would also have strong echoes later on. Having defined a contract in Chapter One, he went on to discuss parties to a contract and incapacity, the subject-matter of a contract, the Statute of Frauds, illegality, defences, and damages.[45]

In his preface to his new treatise on contract, Charles Addison expressed the hope that the work would prove to be useful to suitors, lawyers and judges in the new County Courts.[46] But he also harboured wider ambitions. Having contrasted the state of the English literature unfavourably with the 'elaborate and elegant' work of Pothier and the 'varied and profound researches of Continental jurists',[47] Addison

[38] Chitty, *Contracts*, p. 3.
[39] John Joseph Powell, *Essay Upon the Law of Contracts*, 2 vols. (London, 1790), vol. I, p. vii.
[40] Samuel Comyn, *A Treatise of the Law Relative to Contracts and Agreements not under seal*, 2 vols. (London: A. Strahan, 1807), vol. I, p. 2.
[41] *Treatise on Obligations and Contracts* (London, 1818), p. 2.
[42] William Blackstone, *Commentaries on the Laws of England*, 4 vols. (Oxford, 1766), vol. II, p. 442.
[43] Chitty, *Contracts*, p. iv. [44] *Ibid.*, pp. iv–v.
[45] This framework was clearly important to Chitty who went to the trouble of setting it out in the preface.
[46] C.G. Addison, *A Treatise on the Law of Contracts and Rights and Liabilities Ex-Contractu* (London: W. Benning, 1847), p. iii, vii. The new County Courts had come into existence the previous year. For the early history of this institution, see Patrick Polden, *A History of the County Court, 1846–1971* (Cambridge: Cambridge University Press, 1999), pp. 38–73.
[47] Addison, *Contracts*, p. vii.

advanced the view that, 'The law of contracts may justly indeed be said to be a universal law adapted to all times and races, and all places and circumstances, being founded upon those great and fundamental principles of right and wrong which are immutable and eternal'.[48] If he intended to expose the 'broad and general principles of universal law',[49] which he supposed underpinned the law of contract, then the way he went about the task only lessened his chances of accomplishing it. His treatise was divided up according to types of contract, letting and hiring, partnership, marriage contracts, etc., rather than looking for general principles which might underpin all kinds of contract. The gap between Addison's rhetoric and the reality of his treatise was noted by a reviewer of the time who complained that:

> A careful examination of the entire work has not thrown additional light upon our mind with regard to the reasons which may have induced its author to decide in favour of the particular plan which he has adopted, and altogether failed in convincing us that it is all comparable to that so admirably conceived and executed by Pothier in his celebrated treatise.[50]

It would be another generation before legal writers would enjoy more success in this regard. A few more minor works on contract also appeared at this time. The advertisement at the front of William Fox's *A Treatise on Simple Contracts and the Action of Assumpsit*,[51] described the work as containing the 'leading principles . . . and those points of practical importance'. It was very much in the same mould as Chitty's treatise, albeit rather shorter. It provides a short summary of the types of simple problems likely to face a legal practitioner and the content largely consisted of the various types of contracting party and factors which invalidate a contract. Fox's profession as a special pleader was in evidence in the outline of the various counts in assumpsit and the discussion of when they could be used.

John William Smith is best known for his work on leading cases, but he also enjoyed a successful career as a writer for law students.[52] By the 1840s he was lecturing at the Law Institute, a body set up by the Law

48 *Ibid.*, p. v. 49 *Ibid.*, p. iv.

50 Anon, 'Addison's Treatise on Contracts' (1847) 6 *Law Magazine or Quarterly Review of Jurisprudence* 210, 212.

51 (London: Stevens, 1842).

52 He was author of the popular, *An Elementary View of the Proceedings in an Action at Law* (London: Saunders & Benning, 1835).

Society with the aim of providing training for solicitors.[53] His lectures on contract were published posthumously as *The Law of Contracts*[54] in the 1840s. The content reflected the interests of his audience and hence a large part of the work was devoted to the formalities of contracting under the Statute of Frauds.

As in the past, a steady stream of works on aspects of contract law continued to appear. As well as new editions of older works, these include the elder Joseph Chitty's *A Treatise on the Laws of Commerce and Manufacturers and the Contracts Relating Thereto*,[55] Colin Blackburn's *A Treatise on the Effect of the Contract of Sale on the Legal Rights of Property and Possession in Goods, Wares and Merchandise*,[56] and John William Smith's *A Selection of Leading Cases on Various Branches of the Law*[57] which was a new type of work entirely.[58] In addition to law books, the period after 1820 saw the rise of legal periodicals.[59] Law journals were not entirely new, but increased in both number and duration from the second decade of the nineteenth century. Within the pages of journals such as the *Law Magazine* and *Legal Observer*, it is possible to find discussion of practical questions of contract law.[60]

Moving towards doctrinal coherence

The fact that the classical model of contract endured for so long is not an accident. It was built on solid foundations. At its heart was a marriage of old and new. The old is represented by existing doctrine; the new by the work of Pothier and his English admirers. Contract law was not devoid of substantive principles or doctrine before 1820. Indeed, one of the reasons for the success of the classical model of contract was that many of the key

53 Christopher Brooks, *Lawyers, Litigation and English Society since 1450* (London: Hambledon Press, 1998), p. 169.

54 (London: William Benning, 1847).

55 2 vols. (London: J. Butterworth, 1824).

56 (London: William Benning, 1846).

57 2 vols. (London: A. Maxwell, 1837–40).

58 For its importance, see Simpson, 'Rise and Fall', p. 662.

59 The subject of nineteenth century legal periodicals, ignored for so long, has recently begun to attract the attention of scholars: David Ibbetson, 'Legal Periodicals in England 1820–1870' (2006) 28 *Zeitschrift für Neuere Rechtsgeschichte* 175 and Stefan Vogenauer, 'Law Journals in Nineteenth-Century England' (2008) 12 *Edinburgh Law Review* 26.

60 C.E. Dodd's lectures to the Law Society (formed just a few years earlier) on contract were published in the *Legal Observer* over a number of issues between 1835 and 1837, see (1835–6) 11 *Legal Observer* 233, 329, 331, 409, 501; (1836) 12 *Legal Observer* 161, 341, 345, 347, 425; (1836–1837) 13 *Legal Observer* 161, 241, 339. Other examples include: Anon, 'Sale and Warranty of Horses' (1828–1829) 1 *Law Magazine* 318.

elements of an apparently new version of contract law were already present. Some of these principles had long histories.

References to assent in contract can be found in the Middle Ages. In the Eyre of London in 1321, Herle J. stated that 'covenant is none other than the assent of parties that lies in specialty'.[61] A similar definition, this time in the context of assumpsit, was provided by Serjeant Pollard in *Reniger* v. *Fogossa*:

> *Aggreamentum* is a word compounded of two words, viz of aggregatio and mentium, so that *aggreamentum est aggregatio mentium in re aliqua facta vel facienda*. And so by the contraction of two words, and by the short pronunciation of them they are made one word, viz *aggreamentum*, which is no other than a union, collection, copulation, and conjunction of two or more minds in anything done or to be done.[62]

Around the same time as Serjeant Pollard's remarks, St German's *Doctor and Student* also highlighted the need for assent.[63] Such statements are a long way from the nineteenth century position in which assent is a central component of contract doctrine, but do demonstrate at least a degree of continuity.[64] Nineteenth century lawyers were not starting from scratch. The process is reflected in miniature in Chitty's *Treatise*. In the first edition he supports the proposition that contracts are a product of mutual assent with a reference to a recent judgment by Lord Ellenborough which referred to *Reniger* v. *Fogossa*.[65] These examples were retained when Chitty came to describe the need for an agreement in his second edition.[66] When he moved on to consider mutual assent, on the other hand, he supported his argument with a reference to Pothier instead.[67] References to mutual assent in the Common law of contract are not that difficult to find. But it was not usually necessary to allude to mutual assent in such clear doctrinal terms. Rather, it was

61 (1321), in Helen Cam (ed.), *Year Books of Edward II* (London: Selden Society, 1969), p. 286.

62 (1550) Plo 1, 17. Ibbetson, *Historical Introduction*, p. 146, cf. Gordley, *Philosophical Origins*, p. 136: 'One could scarcely imagine more wretched authority for the proposition that a contract at common law is a mutual agreement.'

63 T.F.T. Plucknett and J.L. Barton (eds.), *St German's Doctor and Student* (London: Selden Society, 1974), p. 228.

64 For a more radical take on this thesis, see Phillip Hamburger, 'The Development of Nineteenth-Century Consensus Theory of Contract' (1989) 7 *Law and History Review* 241.

65 *Wain* v. *Warlters* (1804) 5 East 10, 16.

66 Joseph Chitty, *A Practical Treatise on the Law of Contracts not Under Seal*, 2nd edn (London: S. Sweet, 1834), p. 1.

67 Chitty, *Contracts*, 2nd edn, p. 8.

something that fell within the remit of the jury. After 1820, something that had been quietly there all along took centre stage. Once mutual assent was the central organising concept at the heart of contract doctrine, it became necessary to develop rules for determining whether or not there was a meeting of wills between the parties.

Contract formation and the doctrine of offer and acceptance

According to Pothier, 'a contract includes a concurrence of intention in two parties' which occurred when the promisor made an offer which was accepted by the promisee.[68] This was a perfectly standard Civilian analysis. It had its origins in Scholastic theology that was later embraced by the Natural lawyers,[69] including Grotius[70] and Pufendorf.[71] Henry Ballow, the first English writer to discuss offer and acceptance, was transparently inspired by Pufendorf.[72] The doctrine of offer and acceptance was a natural corollary of the idea that a contract was formed by assent. As John Joseph Powell explained, a promise did not bind until it was accepted, in which case it became a contract, 'for, then, there was the assent of two persons to the thing promised'.[73]

Eighteenth century writers like Ballow and Powell had begun to recognise the value of rules relating to offer and acceptance, but in doing so they were ahead of the courts. In the typical contract action, whether or not an agreement had been reached was just a question for the jury under the general issue. There was no specific doctrine of offer and acceptance with general application in the Common law. At the same time, nor was the idea of an offer and acceptance creating a binding agreement an obscure one. The principle was well established in Scotland;[74] in England it was applied as a means of demonstrating

[68] William Evans (trans.), R. Pothier, *A Treatise on the Law of Obligations or Contracts*, 2 vols. (London: A. Strahan, 1806), vol. I, 1.1.1 §§ 1–2.

[69] Gordley, *Philosophical Origins*, pp. 81–2, 175–80.

[70] F. Kelsey (trans.), Hugo Grotius, *The Rights of War and Peace (1646 edn)* (Oxford: Oxford University Press, 1925), 3.11.14.

[71] Charles and William Oldfather (trans.), Samuel Pufendorf, *Of the Law of Nature and Nations (1688 edn)* (Oxford: Oxford University Press, 1934), 3.6.15.

[72] *A Treatise of Equity* (London, 1737), 1.3 § 12; Ibbetson, *Historical Introduction*, p. 218.

[73] Powell, *Essay*, vol. I, p. 334.

[74] Gerhard Lubbe, 'Formation of Contract', in Kenneth Reid and Reinhard Zimmermann (eds.), *A History of Private Law in Scotland*, 2 vols. (Oxford: Oxford University Press, 2000), vol. II, p. 44.

consent in marriage contracts,[75] and perhaps, most importantly of all, recognised in Chancery.[76]

It was still just about possible to give an account of the law of contract in the 1820s without mentioning offer and acceptance. The subject was completely ignored by Comyn and missing from the first edition of Chitty's treatise. Offer and acceptance analysis was already gaining ground. The notes accompanying *Ford* v. *Compton*[77] illustrate the point. The decision was concerned with an action in Chancery for specific performance of an agreement for a lease conducted by letter. The question arose whether the original letter could be presented in evidence. The existence of an offer and acceptance was raised in the pleadings,[78] but a comment explaining the exchange of letters in these terms did not appear until the fifth edition of Brown's Reports in 1820.[79] From the second edition of Chitty onwards, the doctrine of offer and acceptance was a standard feature of contract treatises.

In a series of decisions on written contracts in the early nineteenth century, judges emphasised the need for agreement rather than looking for a precise point in time at which a contract came into existence.[80] The fact that an offer had been accepted and the acceptance mirrored the offer determined that an agreement had been reached.[81] There was no special difficulty where the parties contracted by post. Lord Eldon explained the position in Chancery:

> If a person communicates his acceptance of an offer within a reasonable time after the offer being made, and if, within a reasonable time of the acceptance being communicated, no variation has been made by either party in the terms of the offer so made and accepted, the acceptance will be taken as simultaneous with the offer, and both constituting such an agreement as the Court will execute.[82]

These remarks suggest that, generally speaking, judges were prepared to take a fairly relaxed position on the precise point at which a contract was

[75] T. Salmon, *A Critical Essay Concerning Marriage* (London, 1794), pp. 180–213. On the similarities, see Ibbetson, *Historical Introduction*, p. 222.

[76] Powell refers to several such authorities in the context of the Statute of Frauds: Powell, *Essay*, vol. I, pp. 286–99. Examples include: *Moor* v. *Hart* (1683) 1 Vern 201; *Wanchford* v. *Fatherley* (1694) 2 Freem 201; *Seagood* v. *Meale* (1721) Pre Ch 560; *Ayliffe* v. *Tracy* (1722) 2 P Wms 65. See also Michael Lobban, 'Contract', in William Cornish *et al.*, *Oxford History XII*, p. 330.

[77] (1786) 2 Bro CC 32.

[78] D. Ibbetson, 'Natural Law and Common Law' (2001) 5 *Edinburgh Law Review* 4, 15.

[79] This edition was edited by Robert Belt.

[80] Lobban, 'Contract', pp. 334–5.

[81] *Gaunt* v. *Hill* (1815) 1 Stark 10; *Holland* v. *Eyre* (1825) 2 Sim & St 194.

[82] *Kennedy* v. *Lee* (1817) 3 Mer 441, 454–5.

concluded. In a few circumstances this issue merited more careful attention. In auction sales, where the bid was not accepted until the bringing down of the gavel,[83] auctioneers began to include a condition of sale preventing a buyer from retracting once the bid was made,[84] though, as one writer observed, the legal consequences of such a clause remained unclear.[85] In cases where acceptance was sent by post, the law was neutral on the question of the precise moment at which acceptance occurred – at the time of postage or at the time of receipt. *Kennedy* v. *Lee* left the issue open.[86] The following year, the King's Bench in *Adams* v. *Lindsell*[87] held that acceptance occurred at the time of postage. This was a convenient and practical solution.[88] It was said that if the alternative solution were adopted then:

> no contract could ever be completed by the post. For if the defendants were not bound by their offer when accepted by the plaintiffs till the answer was received, then the plaintiffs ought not to be bound till after they had received the notification that the defendants received their answer and assented to it. And so it might go on *ad infinitum*.[89]

Pothier was only mentioned in the context of the postal rule later on. Even then, the fact that Pothier's work on sale, quoted by Chitty and later Addison, was not entirely in accord with *Adams* v. *Lindsell*, seems not to have troubled anyone.[90] The precise origins of the rule are less significant than the fact that legal writers were prepared to draw on Pothier as a way of fixing both the doctrine of offer and acceptance and one of its most important applications securely in place. Nor were legal writers above manipulating the older English authorities in order to fit with the new orthodoxy. Most[91] traced the origins of offer and acceptance to *Cooke* v.

[83] *Simon* v. *Metivier* (1766) 1 W Bla 599, 601; *Payne* v. *Cave* (1789) 3 TR 148.

[84] Richard Babington, *A Treatise on the Law of Auctions* (London: Henry Butterworth, 1826), p. 30; J. Bateman, *A Practical Treatise on the Law of Auctions* (London: A. Maxwell, 1838), p. 23.

[85] Bateman, *Auctions*, p. 23. [86] (1817) 3 Mer 441. [87] (1818) 1 B & Ald 681.

[88] Simon Gardner, 'Trashing with Trollope: A Deconstruction of the Postal Rules in Contract' (1992) 12 *Oxford Journal of Legal Studies* 170.

[89] (1818) 1 B & Ald 681, 683.

[90] Pothier mentioned contracting by letter but he focused on the circumstances when an offer could be withdrawn: L.S. Cushing (trans.), R.J. Pothier, *Treatise on the Contract of Sale* (Boston: Little & Brown, 1839), 1.2.3.1; Chitty, *Contracts*, p. 12; Addison, *Contracts*, p. 38. For a discussion of this issue, see Joseph Perillo, 'Robert J. Pothier's Influence on the Common Law of Contract' (2004–2005) 11 *Texas Wesleyan Law Review* 267, 278–80.

[91] Chitty, *Contracts*, p. 11; Addison, *Contracts*, pp. 37–8; Leake, *Contracts*, pp. 13, 20–1; Frederick Pollock, *Principles of Contract at Law and in Equity* (London: Stevens & Sons, 1876), p. 8; William Anson, *Principles of the English Law of Contract* (Oxford: Oxford University Press, 1879), p. 18.

Oxley[92] and *Payne* v. *Cave*.[93] Judges did the same.[94] Yet neither authority provides unequivocal support. *Cooke* v. *Oxley* turned on the absence of good consideration rather than offer and acceptance.[95] *Payne* v. *Cave*, at best, shows that judges were familiar with the terminology of offer and acceptance, but does not prove that an offer and acceptance were a universal requirement for every valid contract.[96]

In *Dunlop* v. *Higgins*,[97] Lord Cottenham confirmed that *Adams* v. *Lindsell* governed contracts conducted by post. He explained that:

> If there is a usage of trade to accept such an offer, and to return an answer to such an offer, and to forward it by means of the post, and if the party accepting the offer puts his letter into the post on the correct day, has he not done everything he was bound to do?[98]

Adams v. *Lindsell* suggests that once an acceptance was posted the contract was concluded. There was no need for the acceptance to actually reach the offeror. Although this might have been a 'common sense' solution,[99] it is difficult to square with the fundamental tenet of Will Theory that contracts were formed by a meeting of wills. Even if it was possible to view contracts concluded by post as a special category,[100] then there are other examples in which the need for a mutual assent or meeting of wills is difficult to fit with the facts of the contract. Information given in ignorance of the offer was held to amount to an acceptance.[101] A further puzzle arises because, if a meeting of wills really was so important, why was it that the issue of communication of the acceptance received so little attention?[102] Whilst Will Theory was used to justify the rules of offer and acceptance, the new rules were never taken

[92] (1790) 3 TR 653. [93] (1789) 3 TR 148.

[94] For example, Best C.J. in *Routledge* v. *Grant* (1828) 4 Bing 653, 660–1.

[95] Comyn noted this at the time in the second edition of his work on contract, but he was in a minority and made no mention of offer and acceptance: Samuel Comyn, *The Law of Contracts and Promises*, 2nd edn (London: A. Strahan, 1824), pp. 79–80, 108.

[96] A question also arose in the context of auction sales about the application of the Statutes of Frauds, see Lobban, 'Contract', p. 333.

[97] (1848) 1 HLC 381. [98] *Ibid*., p. 398. [99] *Ibid*., p. 400.

[100] *Routledge* v. *Grant* (1828) 4 Bing 653, 661.

[101] *Neville* v. *Kelly* (1862) 12 CB NS 740; *Bent* v. *Wakefield Barnsley Union Bank* (1878) 4 CPD 1; *Gibbons* v. *Proctor* (1891) 64 LT 594, see Lobban, 'Contract', pp. 350–1. *Williams* v. *Carwardine* (1833) 4 B & Ad 621 is sometimes explained on this basis but the decision dealt less with whether the offeree knew of the offer than their motive for accepting it, Paul Mitchell and John Phillips, 'The Contractual Nexus: Is Reliance Essential?' (2002) 22 *Oxford Journal of Legal Studies* 115, 117–20.

[102] Lobban, 'Contract', p. 338.

to their logical conclusions. What mattered was that a practical solution could be justified and superficially looked coherent. The rise of the Will Theory had some part to play in the development of the rules of offer and acceptance. With some fudging around the edges it could be fitted with existing case law. Matters were not always so straightforward. Newer ideas sometimes ran into conflict with well-established ones. Not all developments can reasonably be attributed to Pothier and his English followers.

The doctrine of consideration: an inconvenient survivor

The doctrine of consideration was the Common law's great survivor.[103] Attempts by Lord Mansfield and others to side-line it where contracts were reduced to writing had failed. By the 1820s the moral consideration doctrine was still in full swing, but its demise was just around the corner. A far more serious threat to the continued existence of a reciprocal notion of consideration was posed by the growing interest in Will Theory. If a contract was formed by the meeting of wills then consideration seems to be otiose. Sir William Evans added some comments on consideration to his translation of Pothier's treatise, but this was more to do with fidelity to the Common law than a reflection of anything that Pothier actually wrote. Consideration left Pothier's English admirers with something of a dilemma. Henry Colebrooke tackled the problem head on with a radical attempt to argue that consideration was only evidence of will. Most writers before Pollock were more cautious. They sought to reconcile the need for consideration and assent. Consideration was described in terms of an exchange, but its edges were also blurred as it became bound up with showing an intention or motive to enter into legally binding relations. There are several examples in the contract literature. Addison argued that 'As contracts of this nature are lightly made, and frequently entered into without thought or deliberation, courts of law have wisely declined to give effect to them, unless there be some consideration, good cause, or sufficient motive in law for their compulsory fulfilment'.[104] Comyn noted 'This thing which is the price or motive of the contract, we call the consideration, and it must be a thing lawful in itself or the contract is void',[105] and Chitty claimed that 'A valid and sufficient consideration or recompense for making, or motive or

[103] For a discussion of some of these issues, see Lobban, 'Contract', pp. 358–76.
[104] Addison, *Contracts*, p. 17. [105] Comyn, *Contracts*, vol. I, p. 8.

inducement to make the promise upon which a party is charged, is of the very essence of a contract not under seal'.[106]

Rather than the type of head-on assault tried in the eighteenth century, judges began to engage in a more subtle attempts to modify consideration. At the beginning of the nineteenth century, Lord Ellenborough described the requirements of the doctrine of consideration in the traditional formula: 'It is a known rule of law that to make a promise obligatory there must be some benefit to the party making it, or some detriment to the party to whom it is made otherwise it is considered as *nudum pactum* and cannot be enforced.'[107] Although the outward appearance of consideration remained the same, the element of exchange began to be worn away. Judges started to find or 'invent' consideration[108] even in the absence of a genuine benefit or detriment.[109] The nature of this process was evident in those cases where the plaintiff alleged a forbearance to sue, which had long been recognised as a valid consideration.[110] To be consistent with the reciprocal analysis, the right given up had to be genuine. Where a claim was known to be invalid there was no benefit or detriment and no consideration.[111] By the 1820s, the courts were willing to extend the basis of forbearance consideration in ways which were difficult to fit with the reciprocal analysis. Forbearing to sue on a questionable suit began to be treated as good consideration. This outcome was achieved by taking a much broader view of benefit and detriment, which focused much less on the act of forbearance. In *Longridge* v. *Dorville*,[112] Abbot C.J. found a detriment to the plaintiff in releasing the defendant's ship from bail.[113] Holroyd J. held that, in giving up a claim to expenses, he was suffering a detriment and conversely the defendant benefited from no further trouble or investigation.[114]

106 Chitty, *Contracts*, pp. 6–7. 107 *Jones* v. *Ashburnham* (1804) 4 East 455, 463.

108 The phrase is Professor Treitel's: G.H. Treitel, 'Consideration: A Critical Analysis of Professor Atiyah's Fundamental Restatement' (1976) 50 *Australian Law Journal* 439, 449.

109 Ibbetson, *Historical Introduction*, p. 238.

110 *Ibid.*, pp. 75–7; A.W. Brian Simpson, *A History of the Common Law of Contract: The Rise of the Action of Assumpsit*, pbk edn (Oxford: Oxford University Press, 1987), pp. 449–50; S.J. Stoljar, *A History of the Common Law of Contract* (Canberra: Australian National University Press, 1975), pp. 69–72; Samuel Stoljar, 'The Consideration of Forbearance' (1965–1967) 5 *Melbourne University Law Review* 34.

111 *Jones* v. *Ashburnham* (1804) 4 East 455.

112 (1821) 5 B & Ald 117. See also *Watters* v. *Smith* (1831) 2 B & Ad 889, 895.

113 (1821) 5 B & Ald 117, 121–2 (Bayley J.) adopted the same view.

114 (1821) 5 B & Ald 117, 122–3.

From around 1840 the abandonment of reciprocal consideration became even more pronounced. In *Haigh* v. *Brooks*,[115] a plaintiff drew bills which were accepted by one Lees for £3,466, £3,000 and £3,200. The defendant gave a guarantee on behalf of Lees of £10,000. The plaintiff held the guarantee. The parties then entered into an agreement where the plaintiff surrendered the guarantee to the defendant and the defendant promised to pay the bills accepted by Lees on their reaching maturity. The defendant argued that because the guarantee was void,[116] giving it up was not a valuable consideration. In giving judgment on behalf of the Queen's Bench, Lord Denman failed to confirm whether or not the guarantee was void, but suggested that the simple giving up of the guarantee, irrespective of its actual value, was a good consideration:

> Here whether or not the guarantee could have been available within the doctrine of *Wain* v. *Warlters* the plaintiffs were induced by the defendant's promise to part with something which they might have kept, and the defendant obtained what he desired by means of that promise. Both being free and able to judge for themselves how can the defendant be justified in breaking this promise, by discovering afterwards that the thing in consideration of which he gave it did not possess that value which he supposed to belong to it? It cannot be ascertained that that value was what he most regarded. He may have had objects and motives; and of their weight he was the only judge.[117]

In *Westlake* v. *Adams*,[118] a series of IOUs promising to pay in return for a void indenture of apprenticeship were held to be supported by a good consideration.[119] Byles J. justified his decision on the grounds that:

> But still, the indenture was the very indenture which the plaintiff agreed to give, and which the defendant agreed to take . . . It cannot even be said that the deed, though liable to be proved void, was valueless; for, it was a good deed on the face of it, and had the evidence of the additional consideration perished or not been forthcoming, the deed would have had its full operation in every way.[120]

Wightman J. described *Haigh* v. *Brooks* as a decision which showed that 'giving up something which is of no real value may be a good

[115] (1839) 10 Ad & E 309; Atiyah, *Rise and Fall*, p. 451.
[116] For failure to conform with the Statute of Frauds on the basis of *Wain* v. *Warlters* (1804) 5 East 10.
[117] (1839) 10 Ad & E 309, 320. [118] (1858) 5 CB NS 248.
[119] This would seem to conflict with the previous authority of *Jackson* v. *Warwick* (1797) 7 TR 121, see the dissent of Williams J., (1858) 5 CB NS 248, 262–4.
[120] (1858) 5 CB NS 248, 265.

consideration'. The decision was not a one off.[121] A century earlier these were the very kind of cases in which the courts refused to make a finding of good consideration.[122] By the mid-nineteenth century, consideration seems to have provided a fairly minimal threshold which could be crossed without too much difficulty, even in the absence of a genuine exchange. In *Bainbridge* v. *Firmstone*,[123] the plaintiff gave consent for the defendant to weigh his boilers which the defendant promised to return. Lord Denman held:

> It seems to me that the declaration is well enough the defendant had some reason for wishing to weigh the boilers; and he could do so only by obtaining permission from the plaintiff which he did obtain by promising to return them in good condition. We need not enquire what benefit he expected to derive. The plaintiff might have given or refused leave.[124]

At the same time, judges sought to retain some control over what could amount to valuable consideration by clearly distinguishing between consideration and motive. In *Thomas* v. *Thomas*,[125] Patteson J. insisted that, 'consideration means something of value in the eye of the law, moving from the plaintiff'. Even when it was seen in these terms, consideration was still not totally devoid of content. In *White* v. *Bluett*,[126] the plaintiff executor sued on a promissory note given by the testator to his son, the defendant. The defendant pleaded that he had just grounds for complaining about the way in which his father distributed his own property and, as a result of the defendant's complaints, an agreement was reached whereby the father would discharge him from liability on the note if he no longer complained. The Exchequer Chamber refused to allow the agreement to be raised in defence. In response to the defendant's argument that the agreement was supported by consideration, Pollock C.B. complained that 'by the argument a principle is pressed to an absurdity, as a bubble is blown until it bursts'.[127] There was no consideration because the son had no right to complain, and abstaining from something which he had no right to do could not amount to good consideration.[128] Alderson B. also

[121] In addition to the authorities discussed, see also: *Hart* v. *Miles* (1850) 4 CB NS 371; *Moss* v. *Hall* (1850) 5 Exch 46.

[122] *Loyd* v. *Lee* (1718) 1 Stra 94.

[123] (1838) 8 Ad & E 743, 1 P & D 2, 1 W, W & H 600, see also the passages above cited from *Haigh* v. *Brooks* and *Westlake* v. *Adams* which seem to reflect a similar approach.

[124] (1838) 8 Ad & E 743, 744.

[125] (1842) 2 QB 851, 859.

[126] (1853) 23 LJ Exch 36, 22 LT 123.

[127] *Ibid*., p. 37.

[128] *Ibid*., p. 37.

thought consideration was absent, but on the basis that agreeing was not in itself a sufficient consideration.[129]

The third judge, Parke B., simply asserted that the agreement was not binding.[130] The reluctance to enforce the agreement can be explained by the fact that it was an informal one between family members. The problem facing the Exchequer Chamber was that, although much of the content of consideration had been eroded, there was not yet an alternative mechanism which could be used as a control device to limit the scope of liability. When Pothier discussed a factually similar situation to *White* v. *Bluett*, the agreement was unenforceable in the absence of an intention to be legally bound.[131] There were the faintest hints of such a doctrine in England in legal textbooks from the middle of the century,[132] but it was not fully recognised until the first edition of Pollock in 1876.[133] In time some of the functions of consideration would be taken over by the doctrine of intention to be legally bound, but in the nineteenth century the courts were not yet expressly articulating such a principle. It was not until 1919 that they unequivocally did so.[134]

Good contract doctrine and the limits of the Will Theory

Although lawyers experienced some difficulties in reconciling the Will Theory with existing rules, it played a large part in crystallising substantive contractual doctrine during the nineteenth century. At the same time, there were limits to its influence. At some points the Will Theory had a much

[129] *Ibid.*, p. 38. It was well settled that mutual promises were good consideration: J.H. Baker, *The Oxford History of the Laws of England Vol. VI 1483–1558* (Oxford: Oxford University Press, 2003), p. 859; Ibbetson, *Historical Introduction*, pp. 67, 85–8; Horst Lücke, 'Slade's Case and the Origins of the Common Counts' (1965) 81 *Law Quarterly Review* 422. This is not to say that the question did not continue to generate controversy in the nineteenth century and beyond. In the first edition of his *Principles*, Pollock treated mutual promises as good consideration. By the fourth edition he had changed his mind, see Neil Duxbury, *Frederick Pollock and the English Juristic Tradition* (Oxford: Oxford University Press, 2004), pp. 210–11.

[130] (1853) 23 LJ Exch 36, 37. [131] Pothier, *Obligations*, 1.1.1 § 1.

[132] Fox, *Contracts*, pp. 62–3; Leake, *Contracts*, pp. 9–10.

[133] Pollock, *Contract*, pp. 2–4. He was followed shortly afterwards by Anson, *Contract*, p. 2. Pollock's treatment was itself derived from Savigny, see Duxbury, *Pollock*, p. 207.

[134] *Balfour* v. *Balfour* [1919] 2 KB 571. Stephen Hedley, 'Keeping Contract in its Place – Balfour v. Balfour and the Enforceability of Informal Agreements' (1985) 5 *Oxford Journal of Legal Studies* 391; Ibbetson, *Historical Introduction*, pp. 233–4; A.W. B. Simpson, 'Innovation in Nineteenth Century Contract Law' (1975) 91 *Law Quarterly Review* 247, 263–5.

more marginal role. Sometimes developments in contract doctrine had more to do with commercial realities than Will Theory. The rules that grew up about the interpretation of contractual terms and the limitations imposed on the recovery of contractual damages are two examples. Both of these developments were consistent with the Will Theory in the way in which the courts borrowed the language of intention, but in reality they probably had more to do with the imposition of workable black and white rules than a genuine concern about the will of the parties.

Judges of the 1770s had attempted to lay down rules about the interpretation of contracts. One strand in the case law stressed the importance of intention. This approach proved attractive to some legal writers. A few years after *Kingston* v. *Preston*,[135] Powell described intention as the touchstone for interpreting all forms of contract term.[136] It is easy to see the attraction of intention for supporters of the Will Theory. If contracts were formed out of a meeting of wills, then the will was a product of intention. Behind the rhetoric things were rather different. Technical rules of construction, which had always been important, continued to do much of the work. The precise role of intention in contract interpretation remains elusive, even in modern times.[137]

When he addressed the nature of the relationship between intention and rules of construction, Henry Colebrooke insisted that: 'The leading principle is, that the intentions of the parties, as expressed or implied, shall be the rule of construction. Particular maxims of interpretation are illustrations of that principle, rather than substantive and authoritative rules of law.'[138] All of the writers of the period paid a great deal of attention to the rules of construction.[139] Pothier laid down a comprehensive set of twelve rules.[140] Samuel Comyn, a rather traditional writer in many other respects, simply followed Pothier, describing his rules of construction as 'quite consonant to the principles of the English law, and to the practice of our courts'.[141] Joseph Chitty reduced this long list to four maxims:[142] the construction shall be reasonable; the construction shall be favourable; the

[135] (1773) Lofft 194. [136] Powell, *Essay*, vol. I, pp. 243–4.

[137] Catherine Mitchell, *Interpretation of Contracts* (Abingdon: Routledge-Cavendish, 2007), pp. 47–51.

[138] Colebrooke, *Contracts*, p. 73. Leake, *Contracts*, p. 349 expressed a similar view.

[139] Colebrooke, *Contracts*, pp. 65–6; Chitty, *Contracts*, pp. 19–22; Leake, *Contracts*, p. 349; Pollock, *Contract*, p. 409.

[140] Pothier, *Obligations*, 1.1.7. [141] Comyn, *Contracts*, 2nd edn, p. 24.

[142] Anson, *Contract*, p. 241 was more concise: 1. words were to be understood in their plain meaning; 2. subject to inference of intention from the whole document.

popular meaning of words are to be adopted; and the whole agreement is to be considered.[143] In his second edition he added a fifth: the construction shall be liberal.[144]

Serjeant Williams complained that 'almost all of the old cases, and many of the modern ones on this subject, are decided upon distinctions so nice and technical, that it is very difficult, if not impractical, to deduce from them any certain rule or principle.'[145] By the 1871 edition of Williams Saunders Reports, these rules were spread across five pages[146] and were heavily relied upon in judgment[147] and in argument[148] as well as appearing in the influential *Smith's Leading Cases.*[149] Conditions present an extreme example of the complexity of interpreting contract terms,[150] and demonstrate the way in which the search for intention could become buried under rules of interpretation. Most legal writers persevered with the myth, linking the rules of construction with the parties' intentions. In reality, intention was often more a justification for mechanical application of the rules than an inquiry into the minds of the parties. Colin Blackburn, writing in the 1840s, was one of the few writers to admit as much when he wrote that, 'the intention must be collected from the whole agreement, and the Courts have within the last fifty years adopted for this purpose some rules of construction which are, perhaps some of them a little artificial'.[151]

Judges continued to cling to the language of intention. Reaching a practical consensus was often trickier. The way in which penalty clauses were construed illustrates the point. In *Astley* v. *Weldon*,[152] Lord Eldon

143 Chitty, *Contracts*, pp. 19–22. Later editions under different editors adopted similar formats but greatly expanded, e.g. John Russell (ed.), Joseph Chitty, *A Treatise on the Law of Contracts*, 8th edn (London: H. Sweet, 1868), pp. 71–96.

144 Chitty, *Contracts*, 2nd edn, pp. 66–7.

145 1 Wms Saund 320, fn. 4. On his rules of construction, see Stoljar, *History*, pp. 161–3.

146 This edition was edited by Sir Edward Vaughan Williams.

147 *Glazebrook* v. *Woodrow* (1799) 8 TR 366; *Carpenter* v. *Cresswell* (1827) 4 Bing 409; *Mattock* v. *Kinglake* (1839) 10 Ad & E 50; *Dicker* v. *Jackson* (1848) 6 CB 103; *Thames Haven Dock & Railway Co.* v. *Byrmer* (1850) 5 Exch 696.

148 For example: *Ferry* v. *Williams* (1817) 8 Taunt 62; *Lloyd* v. *Lloyd* (1837) 2 My & Cr 192; *Lord Howden* v. *Simpson* (1839) 10 Ad & E 793; *Giles* v. *Giles* (1846) 9 QB 164.

149 Smith, *Leading Cases*, vol. II, p. 9. This section increased in length, see John Willes and Henry Keating (eds.), John Smith, *A Selection of Leading Cases on Various Branches of the Law*, 4th edn, 2 vols. (London: William Maxwell, 1856), vol. II, pp. 11–14.

150 J.P. Benjamin, *Treatise on the Law of Sale of Personal Property* (London: Henry Sweet, 1868), pp. 418–21.

151 *Contract of Sale*, p. 151. Ibbetson, *Historical Introduction*, p. 225 makes the same point.

152 (1801) 2 B & P 346, 350.

complained, 'I felt as I have often done before in considering various cases on this head, much embarrassed in ascertaining the principle upon which those cases were founded'. In his attempt to rectify this uncertainty, his starting point was that even a 'very enormous and excessive' sum might be classified as liquidated damages provided it was a genuine pre-estimate of loss.[153] There was no genuine pre-estimate of loss when the clause exceeded money due under the contract, or where there were several different conditions in the agreement and the sum in the clause was payable on breach of any of them.

Rooke J. was explicit about the role of intention: 'the determination of the court in construing this instrument must be guided by the intention of the parties.'[154] Initially some judges were prepared to overlook Lord Eldon's guidelines, stressing that where the parties labelled a clause for liquidated damages, then the label determined its character.[155] By the 1820s a new consensus had started to emerge. Any authorities inconsistent with *Astley* v. *Weldon* were treated as wrongly decided.[156] In *Kemble* v. *Farren*,[157] an agreement worded 'to be liquidated and ascertained damages, and not a penalty or penal sum'[158] was treated as a penalty because the clause applied to various breaches of differing severity. *Astley* v. *Weldon* subsequently became more entrenched, both in the courts[159] and in legal literature.[160] Lord Eldon's position continued to be bound up with intention.[161] But the rules of interpretation had less to do with intention than applying set rules, in this instance whether or not there was a genuine pre-estimate of loss. The way in which terms were interpreted shows a formalistic cast of mind amongst judges. The process was thrown into sharp relief in cases concerning the sale of horses. These decisions also emphasise the way in which the role of the jury was just beginning to dwindle.

153 *Ibid.*, p. 351. 154 *Ibid.*, p. 353. Chambre J. used similar language at 354.

155 *Barton* v. *Glover* (1815) Holt NP 43; *Reilly* v. *Jones* (1823) 1 Bing 302.

156 Chitty, *Contracts*, 2nd edn, p. 678 described *Barton* v. *Glover* and *Reilly* v. *Jones* as irreconcilable with *Astley* v. *Weldon*. Addison, *Contracts*, did not even mention *Reilly* v. *Jones*.

157 (1829) 6 Bing 141.

158 Such a clause looks like a standard form of drafting and may have been common practice.

159 Subsequently continued in *Boys* v. *Ancell* (1839) 5 Bing NC 390; *Horner* v. *Flintoff* (1842) 9 M & W 678; *Sainter* v. *Ferguson* (1849) 7 CB 716.

160 Anson, *Contract*, p. 244 described *Kemble* v. *Farren* as the leading case on the subject.

161 *Davis* v. *Penton* (1827) 6 B & C 216, 222; *Kemble* v. *Farren* (1829) 6 Bing 141, 148–9. Chitty, *Contracts*, 2nd edn, p. 678; Leake, *Contracts*, p. 578; Anson, *Contract*, p. 243.

In the introduction to his book *The Horseman's Manuel*,[162] Robert Surtees[163] grumbled that:

> Owing to the nature of their profession, the Judges have not those opportunities of acquiring information, or of ascertaining by experience the various peculiarities and qualifications of the horse ... But their ignorance of the economy of the horse is not the only disadvantage under which their Lordships labour ... The contradictory evidence, not to say perjury, and the stabularian and technical terms which are made use of, tend to heighten the embarrassment under which they are placed.[164]

Whether or not the agreement amounted to a warranty had become a question of law,[165] eliminating the possibility of a sympathetic jury conjuring up the existence of a warranty.[166] The precise ambit of the warranty had always been a matter for the jury. Gibbs C.J. described the scope of a warranty of soundness as 'a question peculiarly fit for the consideration of a jury'.[167] He also made clear that the court in banc would not overturn a verdict simply because the trial judge came to a different conclusion to his jury. This approach was already becoming dated. In *Broennenburg* v. *Haycock*,[168] Burroughs J. described unsoundness as 'compounded' of both fact and law. Whilst the issue of whether the horse was in fact unsound remained a matter for the jury, the definition of unsoundness was now a matter for the judge.

Defining soundness as a matter of law was far from easy. Henry Jeremy wrote in 1825 that 'it is to be regretted that the term [unsoundness] is not capable of more easy construction and definite meaning'.[169] Some judges did attempt a definition. Lord Ellenborough held that, 'Any infirmity which renders a horse less fit for present use and convenience, is an unsoundness'.[170] Best C.J. directed a jury that 'sound meant perfect'.[171] Nearly twenty years later in *Kiddell* v. *Burnard*, Parke B.

162 (London: A. Miller, 1831).

163 Surtees is best known for his novels on foxhunting featuring Mr Jorrocks but in his youth he had also been articled to several firms of solicitors: N. Gash, 'Surtees, Robert Smith', *Oxford Dictionary of National Biography*.

164 Surtees, *Horseman's*, pp. v–vi.

165 *Dunlop* v. *Waugh* (1792) Peake 167; *Wood* v. *Smith* (1829) M & M 539.

166 The firming up of the line between representation and warranty is a good example, see *Budd* v. *Fairmaner* (1831) 8 Bing 47; *Hopkins* v. *Tanqueray* (1854) 15 CB 130.

167 *Lewis* v. *Peake* (1816) 7 Taunt 153, 154.

168 (1817) Holt 630, 631.

169 Henry Jeremy, *The Laws Relating to Horses* (London: J. Clarke, 1825), p. 23.

170 *Elton* v. *Jordan* (1815) 1 Stark 127, 4 Camp 281.

171 *Best* v. *Osborne* (1825) Ry & Mood 290, 291.

listed a series of conditions which rendered a horse unsound.[172] Positive proof that the horse was unsound at the time of sale presented practical difficulties for the buyer. Mere suspicion was insufficient.[173] Where the value of the horse made the expense worthwhile, buyers were wise to follow Stephen's advice, that before returning the animal, it was prudent to have it examined by two experts in horse ailments.[174] Even with expert evidence a buyer may still have failed to convince a jury that the horse was unsound.[175] Because a warranty was a statement of existing fact, a dealer who was determinedly dishonest might simply lie about the condition of the horse at the time of sale with a view to establishing that the illness or injury occurred after the animal had left his hands.[176] Individual conditions came to be classified as a matter of law. Horses that were nerved,[177] suffered from bone stavin,[178] a cough,[179] or were short-sighted,[180] were unsound; those with buck eyes,[181] a propensity to crib-biting,[182] were sound. It might be expected that this approach might have led to greater certainty, but at various times roaring[183] and temporary injuries[184] fell within both categories.

Even where the horse was warranted sound and the condition fell within a definition or category of unsoundness, the seller could still escape liability. Conditions of sale were increasingly sophisticated.[185] One term popular with dealers required the horse to be returned in two days along with a veterinary certificate that the horse was unsound.[186]

172 (1842) 9 M & W 668, 669–70. 173 *Eaves* v. *Dixon* (1810) 2 Taunt 343.

174 George Stephen, *The Adventures of a Gentleman in Search of a Horse* (London: Longmans, 1835), p. 143.

175 *Eaves* v. *Dixon* (1810) 2 Taunt 343.

176 This was perhaps a bigger threat once parties were competent witnesses in their own suit: (1833) 3 & 4 Will IV c. 42 s. 26, (1843) 6 & 7 Vict c. 85, (1851) 14 & 15 Vict c. 99 s. 2.

177 *Best* v. *Osborne* (1825) Ry & Mood 290. Nerving involved cutting a nerve in a horse's leg, usually to relieve pain in a foot.

178 *Watson* v. *Denton* (1835) 7 Car & P 85.

179 *Coates* v. *Stephens* (1830) 2 M & R 157.

180 *Holliday* v. *Morgan* (1858) 1 Ell & Ell 1.

181 *Earle* v. *Patterson* (1830) reported from manuscript in Surtees, *Horseman's*, pp. 20–3.

182 *Broennenburg* v. *Haycock* (1817) Holt 630; *Coates* v. *Stephens* (1838) 2 M & Rob 157.

183 Roaring is a common respiratory disease of horses, see Surtees, *Horseman's*, pp. 36–8; *Bassett* v. *Collis* (1810) 2 Camp 523; *Onslow* v. *Eames* (1817) 2 Stark 81.

184 *Bolden* v. *Brogden* (1838) 2 M & Rob 113; *Coates* v. *Stephens* (1838) 2 M & Rob 157.

185 Surtees, *Horseman's*, pp. 78–94 and Stephen, *Adventures of a Gentleman*, pp. 311–25 provide a range of examples from different dealers.

186 This particular condition was used by Tattersall's and the Bazaar, see Stephen, *Adventures of Gentleman*, pp. 312, 314.

Even on the assumption that the fault emerged in time,[187] terms of this type must have placed a heavy burden on buyers. Lord Mansfield had been prepared to rewrite a condition to ensure that it was reasonable. The sympathies of his nineteenth century counterpart were equally obvious when, in *Bywater* v. *Richardson*,[188] Denman C.J. stated that 'He [the seller] had every right to give such a limited warranty, and the plaintiff only was to blame if he did not avail himself of the time given to discover and object to the unsoundness'.[189]

Eighteenth century buyers may have been able to draw some consolation from the sound price doctrine, but this too had fallen out of favour.[190] Horse sales provide a particularly vivid illustration of two important shifts in the law of contract. These transactions gave rise to some of the earliest examples of standard form contracting. It is also a very clear example of judicial encroachment into the domain of the jury, which saw the role of the jury gradually diminish. The same was true in the sphere of contract damages.

When, in the late eighteenth century, the judges began to settle on the expectation measure of contract damages in their directions to juries, the courts were probably just adopting existing practice. It also had some resonance with those writers like Paley, who were prepared to explain the whole substance of contractual liability on the basis of the generation of expectations:

> Men act from their expectations. These expectations are in most cases determined by the assurances and engagements we receive from others. If no dependence could be placed upon these assurances, it would be impossible to know what judgment to form of many future events or how to regulate our conduct with respect to them.[191]

Paley and Smith did not represent mainstream opinion, in as much as there was such a thing, about contractual liability. The expectation measure of damages long pre-dated the influence of Pothier and his followers as well. It was, however, consistent with his treatment of damages.[192] Pothier imposed

[187] Stephen, *Adventures of Gentleman*, p. 138. [188] (1834) 1 Ad & E 508.
[189] *Ibid.*, p. 513.
[190] *Jones* v. *Bowden* (1813) 4 Taunt 847, 851; *Gray* v. *Cox* (1824) 1 C & P 184, 185. Neither decision concerned a horse, and, in both, the remarks that the sound price doctrine was 'long since exploded' came in the argument of counsel. See Stephen, *Adventures of a Gentleman*, p. 230.
[191] William Paley, *The Principles of Moral and Political Philosophy* (London, 1786), p. 105.
[192] Pothier, *Obligations*, 1.2.3 §§ 159–72.

some limits on damages for lost expectations, illustrated by the example of an agreement to sell a horse which the seller failed to deliver. Because the buyer had an immediate need for a horse, he was forced to go to another seller. Unfortunately this second horse was more expensive because the market had risen. In Pothier's example, the buyer was able to recover the cost of the more expensive horse. Pothier contrasted this example with the case of a non-delivery of a horse to a clergyman, who was thereby prevented from collecting extra tithes. Damages for the loss of extra tithes could not be recovered because 'it is a damage which is foreign to what was the object of the contract, which was not foreseen at the time of the contract'.[193]

At the beginning of the nineteenth century, the position of English law with regard to consequential losses was still uncertain. There are clear examples of the courts allowing damages for loss of expectation even where they were consequential to the original contract.[194] By the 1830s judges were beginning to exclude certain types of expectation damages on the grounds that they were too remote,[195] but the continued ambiguous state of the law probably has a lot to do with a residual reluctance of judges to interfere with something that was still seen as a matter for the jury.[196]

Any remaining ambiguities about consequential losses were resolved by *Hadley* v. *Baxendale*.[197] Having decided that jury discretion could be constrained, the Court of Exchequer addressed the question whether a jury could include loss of profit in their assessment of damages. It was held that they could not. Alderson B. also laid down the correct form for

193 *Ibid.*, 1.2.3 § 161.

194 *Bridge* v. *Wain* (1816) 1 Stark 504; *Lewis* v. *Peake* (1816) 7 Taunt 153; *Ward* v. *Smith* (1822) 11 Price 198; Kevin Teeven, *A History of the Anglo-American Common Law of Contract* (New York: Greenwood Press, 1990), p. 194; Florian Faust, 'Hadley v. Baxendale: An Understandable Miscarriage of Justice' (1994) 15 *Journal of Legal History* 41, 55.

195 *Walton* v. *Fothergill* (1835) 7 C & P 392; *Hodges* v. *Earl of Litchfield* (1835) 1 Bing NC 492; *Clare* v. *Maynard* (1837) 7 C & P 741, 6 Ad & El 519.

196 *Black* v. *Baxendale* (1847) 1 Ex 410, 17 LJ Ex 50; *Waters* v. *Towers* (1853) 8 Ex 401, 22 LJ Ex 186. George Washington, 'Damages in Contract at Common Law' (1932) 48 *Law Quarterly Review* 90, 101–2.

197 (1854) 9 Ex 341; 2 CLR 517; 23 LJ Ex 179; 18 Jur 358; 2 WR 302; 23 LT 69. For a detailed discussion of this case, see Ibbetson, *Historical Introduction*, pp. 229–32; Richard Danzig, 'Hadley v. Baxendale: A Study in the Industrialization of the Law' (1975) 4 *Journal of Legal Studies* 249; David Pugsley, 'The Facts of Hadley v. Baxendale' [1976] *New Law Journal* 420; J.L. Barton, 'Contractual Damages and the Rise of Industry' (1987) 7 *Oxford Journal of Legal Studies* 40; Faust, 'Hadley v. Baxendale'.

a trial judge's direction, namely, that a jury must award damages for those consequences arising naturally from the breach of contract or those that 'may reasonably be supposed to have been in the contemplation of both parties, at the time they made the contract, as the probable result of the breach of it'.[198]

Hadley v. *Baxendale* is treated as a leading case on contract even though, as Faust points out, it is not a simple contract case.[199] Ibbetson has argued that it 'fell in the awkward hinterland of contract and tort'.[200] Although there was an agreement between the parties, the claim was not based on the special contract but on the fact that the defendant was a common carrier. A special set of rules applied to common carriers. Actions against common carriers belonged to the law of tort.[201] The context may be significant because a restriction based on foreseeable damage was just becoming established in negligence cases in the period immediately preceding the decision.[202]

There were numerous possible inspirations behind *Hadley* v. *Baxendale*.[203] A similar remoteness rule to the one adopted by the Exchequer Chamber is found in Pothier,[204] the French Code Civil,[205] the Louisiana Civil Code,[206] Kent's *Commentaries*,[207] and Sedgwick's *A Treatise on the Measure of Damages*.[208] Though all of these sources may have been influential, the Court of Exchequer still had the choice whether or not to adopt such a potentially far-reaching restriction, particularly in the light of the uncertainty in the English authorities. The decision to adopt a strict remoteness rule probably reflects the concerns expressed by both Martin B. and Alderson B. that without such a rule a trivial breach could result in unexpectedly large damages.[209]

198 (1854) 9 Ex 341, 354. 199 Faust, 'Hadley v. Baxendale', p. 48.

200 Ibbetson, *Historical Introduction*, p. 230.

201 Ibbetson, *Historical Introduction*, p. 230; Faust, 'Hadley v. Baxendale', p. 46. Danzig, 'Hadley v. Baxendale', p. 247 suggests that the case was underscored by problems caused by the underdeveloped law of agency.

202 Ibbetson, *Historical Introduction*, pp. 175–6, 231; *Rigby* v. *Hewitt* (1850) 5 Ex 240; *Greenland* v. *Chaplin* (1850) 5 Ex 243.

203 Simpson, 'Innovation', p. 276.

204 Pothier, *Obligations*, 1.1.2.3 § 161; *Traité du contrat de vente* (Paris, 1762), 2.1.5.

205 (1804) Art 1150, 1151. 206 (1825) Art 1928.

207 James Kent, *Commentaries on American Law*, 9th edn, 4 vols. (Boston: Little, Brown & Co., 1858), vol. II, p. 480.

208 Theodore Sedgwick, *A treatise on the measure of damages, or, An inquiry into the principles which govern the amount of compensation recovered in suits at law*, 2nd edn (New York: John Voorhies, 1852), p. 6.

209 (1854) 9 Ex 341, 347 (Martin B.), 356 (Alderson B.).

Their concerns fed easily into a broader desire amongst judges to promote entrepreneurial economic activity[210] and to insulate common carriers.[211]

The remoteness rule was not the only restriction on contractual damages to emerge in the nineteenth century. It was already well established in mercantile practice that the plaintiff was under a duty to mitigate his losses, but by the 1820s the duty had grown into a legal rule.[212] The courts also put in place rules about the date when damages were to be assessed. The date of breach came to be used[213] except in stock transactions, where the date for assessment was the date of the trial.[214]

Nineteenth century juries retained a role in the assessment of damages, but it was much more closely regulated than had once been the case. The first book on damages, written by Joseph Sayer, had appeared as long ago as 1770, but the changing nature of damages in contract actions was slow to be reflected in the contract textbooks. Chitty offers little by way of guidance, merely stating that, 'it is, in general, entirely within the province of the jury to assess the amount, with reference to all the circumstances of the case'.[215] Colebrooke, Comyn and Addison omit the subject altogether, as, more surprisingly, does Pollock.[216] Leake was the first to describe damages using the modern formula:

> In actions for breach of contract, the general damage is commonly described as the loss sustained by the plaintiff from the non-performance of the contract; the benefit of which the plaintiff would have received if the contract had been kept is the measure of damages if the contract is broken.[217]

Anson also discussed damages, albeit briefly.[218] Other legal writers continued to eschew an analysis of damages. In the first edition of

210 Danzig, 'Hadley v. Baxendale', especially pp. 245–54 regards this as the prime motivation for the decision. For a contrary view, see Barton, 'Contractual Damages', especially pp. 58–9.

211 Faust, 'Hadley v. Baxendale', pp. 62–3.

212 *Maclean* v. *Dunn* (1828) 4 Bing 722; *Powell* v. *Horton* (1836) 2 Bing NC 668. In *Maclean* v. *Dunn* (1828) 4 Bing 722, 729 Best C.J. drew attention to the origins of the duty to mitigate in mercantile practice.

213 *Boorman* v. *Nash* (1829) 9 B & C 145; *Leigh* v. *Paterson* (1818) 8 Taunt 540; *Gainsford* v. *Carroll* (1824) 2 B & C 624.

214 *Shepherd* v. *Johnson* (1802) 2 East 211; *M'Arthur* v. *Lord Seaforth* (1810) 2 Taunt 257; *Harrison* v. *Harrison* (1824) 1 C & P 412.

215 Chitty, *Contracts*, p. 343.

216 Leake, *Contracts*, was the first to discuss damages. Later they were included in Anson, *Contract*, pp. 301–4.

217 Leake, *Contracts*, p. 565.

218 Anson, *Contract*, pp. 301–4.

Chitty to appear after *Hadley* v. *Baxendale*, damages were mainly discussed in the context of the distinction between a penalty and liquidated damages.[219] The first proper treatment of the case did not appear until the 1890 edition.[220] Pollock and his editors were even slower to embrace contractual damages. The topic was not included in Pollock's treatise until 1946.[221]

The view that damages were something apart from legal doctrine hung on for a long time. It is telling that the most comprehensive contemporary analysis appeared not in a book on contract but in a treatise on evidence.[222] Given that the main function of the Will Theory in the nineteenth century was the way in which it shaped substantive doctrine the fact that it had a peripheral role in the development of rules about damages is less surprising. The courts were more interested in putting in place a series of black and white rules which limited the scope of liability in the interests of promoting entrepreneurial activity. At best the Will Theory was no more than a convenient device for fastening these changes into wider developments in contract law in the same period.

219 John Russell (ed.), Joseph Chitty, *A Treatise on the Law of Contracts*, 6th edn (London: H. Sweet, 1857), pp. 772–85.

220 J.M. Lely and Neville Geary (eds.), Joseph Chitty, *A Treatise on the Law of Contracts*, 12th edn (London: Sweet & Maxwell, 1890), p. 851.

221 P.H. Winfield (ed.), Frederick Pollock, *Pollock's Principles of Contract*, 12th edn (London: Stevens & Sons, 1946), pp. 528–39. Winfield drew attention to the addition of damages in the preface.

222 Edmund Powell, *The Principles and Practice of the Law of Evidence*, 2nd edn (London: John Crockford, 1859), pp. 241–56.

9

Classical contract law and its limits

By the middle of the nineteenth century, contract law looked more coherent than ever before, superficially at least. Reforms in legal procedure had seen the forms of action diminish in importance. Lawyers were no longer thinking in terms of a law of contracts (in the plural), but rather the law of contract familiar today. Legal writers played a much larger role after 1850 and the relationship between judges and jurists was arguably closer than before. In this sort of environment it is easy to see how developments in contract doctrine came to be presented as the logical outcomes of a systematic body of law. This was not an accident. It was the impression that legal writers strove to achieve. Despite differences in emphasis and detail, the fact that their approaches were essentially the same in this regard contributed to the impression of stability. They relied on and read each other's work. Anson freely acknowledged his debt to Leake and Pollock.[1] Pollock would later repay the compliment.[2]

Despite appearances, coherence and uniformity were often more apparent than real, even within the covers of contract treatises. The fact that changes in contract law in the nineteenth century were deeply rooted in the past and built on what had gone before, was one obvious cause. The so-called classical law of contract was developed using the Will Theory. But cracks in the edifice were already very apparent. Key aspects of contract law simply did not fit with the idea of will. Some of which, consideration being the most obvious, have already been discussed. Even those legal writers who advocated the idea were beginning to recognise that the Will Theory did not always provide a convincing justification. In the courts, practical and pragmatic considerations mattered as much as they ever had.

[1] William Anson, *Principles of the English Law of Contract* (Oxford: Clarendon Press, 1879), p. vii. Anson also praised Leake's work on contract, W. Anson, 'Stephen Martin Leake' (1894) 10 *Law Quarterly Review* 2, 3 as 'the most scientific treatise'.

[2] Frederick Pollock, *Principles of Contract at Law and in Equity*, 3rd edn (London: Stevens & Sons, 1881), p. xi.

Legal writers and the foundations of the classical law of contract

Writing in the preface to his *Principles of the Law of Contract*, William Anson explained that:

> The main object with which I have set out has been to delineate the general principles which govern the contractual relation from its beginning to its end. I have tried to show how a contract is made, what is needed to make it binding, what its effect is, how its terms are interpreted, and how it is discharged and comes to an end.[3]

The idea that the law of contract could be reduced to a set of basic principles was ubiquitous in the legal writing of the period.[4] There was of course nothing new about attempts to explain the law of contract systematically. Various writers since Gilbert had purported to apply some sort of organising principle. Henry Colebrooke in particular had produced a sophisticated treatment of contractual liability. Later accounts were nevertheless rather different in both scale[5] and purpose. For all its elaborate twists and turns, Colebrooke did not design his treatise with students or lawyers in mind. Anson's treatise in particular was written for the law student and this was an important shift.

Stephen Leake's *The Elements of the Law of Contracts*,[6] published in 1867, was a new sort of contract treatise. The author made his intentions clear in the preface:

> The present work professes to treat of the elementary rules and principles of the law of contracts exclusively of the detailed application of the law to specific matters; such applications of that law being referred to only occasionally, as subsidiary to the main object of the work for the purposes of proof, argument and illustration.[7]

[3] (Oxford: Clarendon Press, 1879), p. v.

[4] Stephen Waddams, 'What *Were* the Principles of Nineteenth-Century Contract Law?', in Andrew Lewis, Paul Brand and Paul Mitchell (eds.), *Law in the City: Proceedings of the Seventeenth British Legal History Conference, London, 2005* (Dublin: Four Courts Press, 2007), pp. 305–18.

[5] The first edition of Frederick Pollock, *Principles of Contract at Law and in Equity* (London: Stevens & Sons, 1876), ran to more than 600 pages and contained nearly 1,500 authorities. Unless otherwise stated, reference is made to the first edition. Leake's treatise was 700 pages long.

[6] (London: Stevens & Sons, 1867). For a helpful discussion, see Catharine MacMillan, 'Stephen Martin Leake: A Victorian's View of the Common Law' (2011) 32 *Journal of Legal History* 3, 17–24.

[7] *Ibid.*, p. v.

Leake was more successful than many of his predecessors in presenting the law of contract as a single body of doctrine rather than an accumulation of individual types of contract. Chitty and others had already made steps in this direction, but as the editor of the fifth edition admitted, 'especially in so far as it [the previous edition] treated of the *Principles* of the Law of Contracts, it would admit of considerable improvement'.[8] One reason for Leake's relative success was his interest in jurisprudence and legal ordering. He was not satisfied with producing a reference work for practitioners. His opening chapter[9] drew on Austin[10] and Maine,[11] and less predictably Warnkoenig[12] and Mackeldey.[13] In common with legal writers of the immediately preceding generation, Pothier was constantly referred to.[14] Leake's attempt to impose a coherent order was only a partial success. Because he borrowed from Roman law, he came up against the same problem encountered by Blackstone a century before. English law was structured around remedies rather than rights. Leake attempted to reconcile the two in his definition of contract. The term contract, he wrote, was 'wide enough to include the sources of all rights against the person which have been described as primary ... it is also used, and perhaps more accurately, to denote the legal rights themselves which spring from those sources'.[15] Leake argued that the binding force of a contract was created by the presence of an agreement. A contract without a deed derived its 'legal effect ... from the mere fact of agreement'.[16] This was a perfectly orthodox view in the 1860s. Leake's inclusion of mistake and his recognition of the equitable basis for money had and received were more novel.

Frederick Pollock went to a great deal of trouble in order to provide a definition of a contract. In the first couple of editions of his treatise the influence of the German jurist Fredrich Karl von Savigny was very

[8] J.A. Russell (ed.), Joseph Chitty, *A Practical Treatise on the Law of Contracts*, 5th edn (London: S. Sweet, 1853), p. iii.

[9] MacMillan, 'Stephen Martin Leake', pp. 5–11.

[10] John Austin, *The Province of Jurisprudence Determined*, 3 vols. (London: John Murray, 1861–1863).

[11] Henry Mainc, *Ancient Law* (London: Dent, 1861).

[12] L. Warnkoenig, *Commentarii Juris Romani Privati* (Leiden: Leodii, 1825–1829).

[13] Ferdinand Mackeldey, *Lehrbuch der Institutionen des heutigen Römischen Privatrechts* (Leipzig: Giessen, 1814).

[14] Examples include, Leake, *Contracts*, pp. 9, 11, 20, 39.

[15] Leake, *Contracts*, p. 5.

[16] *Ibid.*, p. 76.

apparent.[17] He was not unique in this respect. Common law jurists on both sides of the Atlantic were attracted by the scientific nature of German legal writing of the period.[18] Whilst Pollock would later concede that he was sometimes too slavish in this regard,[19] in one important respect he remained a disciple. In common with Pothier, von Savigny viewed a contract as something formed by will. As Pollock wrote on the first page of his treatise 'A contract is before all things a transaction in which two or more persons consent'.[20] But as he conceded, many legal transactions involve consent without being contracts. A contract was a special sort of agreement:

> That which distinguishes it [the contract] from the genus of agreement is that the expression of intention is not only constituted by a proposal and acceptance, but includes the particular kind of expression which is called a promise.[21]

Anson began his treatise in similar style with an attempt to define the scope of his subject, which in the end came down to a simple proposition that a contract was 'an agreement enforceable in law'.[22] The way the book was structured, following the contract from 'its beginning to its end', has changed remarkably little over more than a century.[23] There are two main differences. The current edition contains a separate section on remedies for breach. The original appendix on quasi-contract last appeared under that name in 1975[24] and was renamed 'restitution' in 1979,[25] before the recognition of unjust enrichment caused it to disappear altogether.[26]

[17] Pollock, *Contract*, p. 2. For a discussion, see Neil Duxbury, *Frederick Pollock and the English Juristic Tradition* (Oxford: Oxford University Press, 2004), pp. 191–201. Leake had also read von Savigny and cites him in his treatise, Leake, *Contracts*, p. 2.

[18] Mathias Reimann, 'Nineteenth Century German Legal Science' (1989–1990) 31 *Boston College Law Review* 837.

[19] Pollock, *Contract*, 3rd edn, p. v, where Pollock conceded that in earlier editions he had shown 'overmuch deference' to von Savigny in his treatment of persons affected by contract.

[20] Pollock, *Contract*, p. 1. [21] *Ibid*., p. 5. [22] Anson, *Contract*, p. 8.

[23] Writing about the 1979 edition of *Anson*, Brian Simpson described the work as 'a venerable archaeological site, whose surface rests upon layer and layer of material which has, in the course of time, become mere rubbish', see A.W.B. Simpson, 'Contract: The Twitching Corpse' (1981) 1 *Oxford Journal of Legal Studies* 265, 266. I am grateful to Professor Dave Campbell for drawing this description to my attention.

[24] A.G. Guest (ed.), William Anson, *Principles of the English Law of Contract*, 24th edn (Oxford: Oxford University Press, 1975).

[25] A.G. Guest (ed.), William Anson, *Principles of the English Law of Contract*, 25th edn (Oxford: Oxford University Press, 1979), p. v.

[26] J. Beatson, *Anson's Law of Contract*, 27th edn (Oxford: Oxford University Press, 1998), p. v.

Nineteenth century treatise writers were unanimous in their adherence to versions of the Will Theory. The theory was nevertheless difficult to square with aspects of English contract doctrine. It was not just problematic from the point of view of details. It was unsatisfactory in a more fundamental respect too. When the Natural lawyers came to justify the binding force of contracts, they did so on the ground that promises had moral force. The Will Theory was devoid of moral content. This weakness at its heart was never addressed. One consequence was that the role of promises is never adequately explained. If a contract is formed by a meeting of wills it is difficult to see what role if any promises should play. Leake treats a promise as no more than the 'signification of intention'.[27] Anson fudges the issue, describing a promise as an 'essential feature of a contract'.[28] In the third edition of Pollock's treatise he would concede that his first account of contractual obligations was in 'sundry respects inadequate'.[29] Whilst retaining the notion that contracts were consensual,[30] there was also a change of emphasis. Promises had greater prominence. He noted that, 'The most popular description of a contract that can be given is also the most exact one, namely that it is a promise or set of promises which the law will enforce'.[31]

This change of direction may simply reflect Pollock's desire to simplify his earlier treatment. Promise and agreement seem to be used interchangeably, 'every agreement and promise enforceable by law is a contract'.[32] But there may also be a more significant shift. In the introduction to the third edition of his treatise, Pollock tentatively began to equate promises with reliance.[33] He re-wrote the opening chapter again in 1889. The fifth edition began:

> The Law of Contract may be described as the endeavour of the State ... to establish a positive sanction for the expectation of good faith which has grown up in the mutual dealings of men of average right-mindedness.[34]

Pollock would also stress that a contract involved the 'creation of a right ... to another man's conduct in the future'.[35] Whilst Pollock

[27] Leake, *Contracts*, p. 9. [28] Anson, *Contract*, p. 4.
[29] Pollock, *Contract*, 3rd edn, p. vi. [30] *Ibid.*, p. 1.
[31] *Ibid.*, p. xx; Roy Kreitner, *Calculating Promises* (Stanford, Calif.: Stanford University Press, 2007), pp. 38–9.
[32] Pollock, *Contract*, 3rd edn, p. 1. [33] *Ibid.*, p. xxi.
[34] Frederick Pollock, *Principles of Contract at Law and in Equity*, 5th edn (London: Stevens & Sons, 1889), p. 1.
[35] *Ibid.*

seemed to be moving towards a different justification for contractual liability based on reliance or expectation, these ideas were never really developed. After the opening few pages he reverts to the same discussion of contracts as agreements which had appeared in previous editions.[36] As a letter to Oliver Wendell Holmes showed, Pollock was a long way from abandoning his commitment to the Will Theory.[37]

If there were problems with the Will Theory from the start, its great strength lay in the way that the idea that contracts were formed out of a meeting of wills could be used to re-interpret and re-organise the English case law. But even here the results were mixed. Contractual mistake and undue influence are both examples. In these terms the former can be regarded as a success; the latter less so.

Building contract doctrine from scratch

Contractual mistake can be dealt with quite briefly. The story is as complex as it is fascinating. It is covered in great detail by a recent study which comes to many of the same conclusions.[38] Before the mid-nineteenth century, one might be forgiven for thinking that mistake was unimportant. Certainly there was no discussion of a doctrine of mistake at Common law. A more highly developed doctrine of mistake existed in Equity.[39] There is a simple explanation. In the Common law, when parties made a mistake when contracting, it was a question for the jury under the general issue. Whether or not the parties had come to an agreement was a matter to be considered on the evidence. In combination, the emasculation of the jury and the reforms of pleading meant that by the mid-nineteenth century the subject could no longer be ignored.

Legal writers largely overlooked mistake until the mid-nineteenth century. One exception was Henry Colebrooke. His treatment of mistake was not derived from the Common law. It was inspired by Pothier[40] and a text from the Roman jurist Ulpian.[41] Colebrooke explained that:

[36] *Ibid.*, pp. 2–3.

[37] Mark De Wolfe Howe (ed.), *The Pollock–Holmes Letters*, 2 vols. (Cambridge: Cambridge University Press, 1942), vol. I, p. 70. The letter is dated 29 May 1896.

[38] Catharine MacMillan, *Mistakes in Contract Law* (Oxford: Hart, 2010).

[39] *Ibid.*, pp. 38–68.

[40] William Evans (trans.), R. Pothier, *A Treatise on the Law of Obligations or Contracts*, 2 vols. (London: A. Strahan, 1806), vol. I, 1.1.3.1.

[41] A. Watson (trans.), *The Digest of Justinian* (Philadelphia: University of Pennsylvania Press, 1985), D.50.17.166.2 (Ulpian).

> Error, as well as ignorance of rights, renders a contract or agreement invalid by invalidating the assent given to it by one of the contracting parties. For there is no consent, if the parties are in error, or if one of them is so, respecting the subject of their agreement; that is, concerning the essentials of it.[42]

As the passage makes clear, an error as to an essential term of an agreement meant there was no consent and no contract. Colebrooke was not the only person to be influenced by Pothier. In his *Outlines of the Law of Contracts as Administered in the Courts of British India*,[43] William Macpherson cribbed Pothier's treatment of error and relabelled it mistake.[44] A mistake, he wrote 'in the very substance of the thing which is the object of the agreement' invalidated consent.[45] Macpherson's views on mistake were influential in India. He was Secretary to the Indian Law Commission and a Pothier-inspired version of mistake was integrated into the Indian Contract Act 1872.[46]

Henry Leake was the first mainstream English writer to address contractual mistake in any detail. Mistake, alongside duress and fraud, was presented as one of the 'causes which may . . . qualify the legal effect of an apparently valid agreement'.[47] Leake took the underlying premise, if not the substance of his discussion, from Pothier.[48] Equity also played an important role. In 1854, Sir John Romilly commented that in Equity 'in matters of mistake, the court undoubtedly has jurisdiction . . . though this jurisdiction is to be exercised with great caution and care'.[49] The Common Law Procedure Act[50] became law in the same year. One consequence was that mistake and other Equitable defences could be pleaded at Common law. Leake referred to the legislation quite extensively[51] and it was probably one factor which forced the Common lawyers to confront the question of mistake for the first time. They were hampered in this task by the absence of a clear, unified and coherent doctrine of mistake in the case law. As the century progressed all of this changed. In the process veracity was sacrificed on the altar of doctrinal coherence.

42 Henry Colebrooke, *Treatise on Obligations and Contracts* (London, 1818), p. 46.
43 (London: R.C. Lepage, 1860).
44 MacMillan, *Mistakes*, p. 109, notes that by his relabeling Macpherson added a Common law flavour.
45 Macpherson, *Contracts*, p. 2.
46 In subsections 10, 13, 20–2.
47 Leake, *Contracts*, p. 168.
48 MacMillan, *Mistakes*, makes this important point in more detail, see pp. 122–3.
49 *Murray* v. *Parker* (1854) 19 Beav 305, 308.
50 (1854) 17 & 18 Vict c. 125 ss. 83–6.
51 Leake, *Contracts*, pp. 179–81.

In part the changes which occurred were less of substance than form. With the arrival of a single unified doctrine of mistake, a range of other devices for addressing mistakes in contracting were no longer necessary. In *Thornton* v. *Kempster*,[52] a broker acting for both parties delivered a sale note to the purchaser for 'Riga Rhine hemp' and to the vendor a sale note for 'Petersburg clean hemp'. The Common Pleas held that 'the parties, so far as appeared, had never agreed that the one should buy and the other accept the same thing; consequently there was no agreement subsisting between them'.[53] The trial jury had come to a different conclusion, finding an agreement between the parties. This decision not only highlights the role of the general issue,[54] but also illustrates the difficulties of refuting an agreement on the grounds of mistake. The parties were not competent witnesses in civil actions until 1851.[55] Parol evidence was inadmissible when used to contradict the terms of a written agreement unless there was a 'latent ambiguity'.[56]

When goods were sold, and there was a mistake so that the goods were not as the buyer believed them to be, then it was sometimes possible to raise mistake by alleging a breach of warranty.[57] Even within the class of sale of goods this was not easy to do because of the general unwillingness of the courts, by the early nineteenth century, to imply a warranty outside the context of manufactured goods.[58] The way in which the court interpreted a contract could also be crucial. In *Barr* v. *Gibson*,[59] unknown to both vendor and purchaser, a ship, which was the subject-matter of a contract of sale, had run aground at the time of the sale and consequently was useless. The court interpreted the agreement as a contract for the sale of a ship, not a contract for the sale of a seaworthy ship. Although judges were reluctant to imply a warranty of good quality in *Couturier* v. *Hastie*,[60] the court was willing to imply a condition that the subject-matter of the agreement existed. In February 1848, the

52 (1814) 5 Taunt 786, 1 Marsh 355. 53 5 Taunt 786, 788.

54 For other explicit examples, see *Lindsay* v. *Limbert* (1826) 2 C & P 526; *Raffles* v. *Wichelhaus* (1864) 2 H & C 906, 33 LJNS 160.

55 (1851) 14 & 15 Vict c. 99 s. 2. 56 *Smith* v. *Jeffryes* (1846) 15 M & W 561.

57 J.L. Barton, 'Redhibition, Error and Implied Warranty in English Law' (1994) 62 *Tijdschrift voor Rechtsgeschiedenis* 317; James Gordley, *The Philosophical Origins of Modern Contract Doctrine* (Oxford: Oxford University Press, 1992), pp. 144–5.

58 Paul Mitchell, 'The Development of Quality Obligations in Sale of Goods' (2001) 117 *Law Quarterly Review* 645, 650–6; *Jones* v. *Bright* (1829) 5 Bing 533, 544.

59 (1838) 3 M & W 390.

60 (1852) 8 Exch 40 (Court of the Exchequer); (1853) 9 Exch 102 (Exchequer Chamber); (1856) 5 HLC 673 (House of Lords).

plaintiff shipped a cargo of corn at Salonica for delivery in London. On 1 May the defendants were employed to sell the corn, which they succeeded in doing on 15 May. The corn was not delivered to the purchasers who refused to pay. Neither party knew that at the time of their agreement the corn had already been sold because it had started to overheat and ferment. At every level the case was said to turn on the correct interpretation of the agreement. In the House of Lords it was plainly stated that 'the whole question turns upon the construction of the contract' and the view was taken that, 'the contract plainly imports that there was something which was to be sold at the time of the contract, and something to be purchased'.[61]

In the hands of legal writers, a straightforward case on interpretation became a leading case on mistake.[62] The same fate befell a number of other authorities. *Raffles* v. *Wichelhaus*[63] came to stand for the proposition that where one party meant one thing and the other another, then there is a mistake and the contract was invalid. In short, there was no *consensus ad idem.*[64] In fact, no reasons were given by the Court of Exchequer. Comments by Pollock C.B. and Martin B. in the course of argument suggest that they reached their decision on traditional lines, that there was no agreement, rather than a doctrine of mistake. The expression *consensus ad idem* was uttered by counsel rather than one of the judges. A third decision, *Boulton* v. *Jones*,[65] was also reinvented as an authority on mistake.[66] The defendants had a running account with Brocklehurst, a pipe hose manufacturer. Having taken over the business, the plaintiff received an order from the defendants. When the defendants refused to pay, the plaintiff brought an action for the price. The principal

61 (1856) 5 HLC 673, 681.

62 Macpherson, *Contracts*, p. 3; Leake, *Contracts*, p. 176; J.P. Benjamin, *A Treatise of the Law of Sale of Personal Property* (London: Henry Sweet, 1868), pp. 57–8; Pollock, *Contract*, p. 398; Anson, *Contract*, p. 121.

63 (1864) 2 H & C 906, 33 LJNS 160. There is a wonderful discussion of the background to the decision in A.W. Brian Simpson, *Leading Cases in the Common Law* (Oxford: Oxford University Press, 1995), pp. 135–62 and A.W. Brian Simpson, 'Contracts for Cotton to Arrive: The Case of the Two Ships Peerless' (1989–1990) 11 *Cardozo Law Review* 287.

64 The first writer to emphasise the phrase 'consensus ad idem' was Benjamin, *Sale*, p. 37. Other writers stressed that it was a case of mistake: Leake, *Contracts*, p. 178; Pollock, *Contract*, p. 387; Anson, *Contract*, p. 122.

65 (1857) 2 H & N 564, 27 LJ Ex 117, 6 WR 107.

66 Pollock, *Contract*, p. 381; Anson, *Contract*, p. 119. Leake alone treats the decision as turning on the absence of an agreement, Leake, *Contracts*, p. 16. Benjamin, *Sale*, pp. 303–6 stressed the relevance of set-off. Pollock, *Contract*, p. 428 responded by asserting that the case was decided on general principles independent of set-off.

question was whether the plaintiff was the correct claimant. There might have been a contract with (or enforceable by) Brocklehurst, but the plaintiff had no rights under it. Pollock C.B. explained 'It is a rule of law, that if a person intends to contract with A, B. cannot give himself any right under it. Here the order in writing was given to Brocklehurst.'[67] Intention was being used to identify the contracting party. There is nothing to suggest that mistake is seen as having any vitiating effect. One report of the case suggests that the court was worried about the effect an action would have on the defendant's right of set-off. As Bramwell B. put it, 'if the plaintiff were at liberty to sue, it would be a prejudice to the defendant, because it would deprive him of a set-off, which he would have if the action had been brought by the party with whom he supposed he was dealing'.[68] In only one report is there the slightest hint that mistake might be relevant.[69]

In *Kennedy* v. *Panama, New Zealand and Australian Royal Mail Company*,[70] Blackburn J. stated:

> And, as we apprehend, the principle of our law is the same as the civil law; and the difficulty in every case is to determine whether the mistake or misapprehension is as to the substance of the whole consideration, going, as it were, to the root of the matter, or only to some point, even though a material point, an error as to which does not affect the substance of the whole consideration.[71]

The word mistake was unambiguously present. Reference was also made to some passages in Justinian's *Digest* on mistake.[72] This was quite in character from a judge who was quite prepared to utilise Civilian sources.[73] Pollock treated *Kennedy* v. *Panama* as a case on mistake.[74] Anson disagreed. In his third edition he labelled Pollock's treatment misleading.[75] MacMillan, who also puts the decision in context, argues that it turned on

[67] (1857) 2 H & N 564, 565–6. [68] 27 LJ Ex 117, 119.

[69] MacMillan suggests that Bramwell B's judgment may amount to an 'unattributed, possibly even unconscious, borrowing' from Pothier on mistakes of identity, see MacMillan, *Mistakes*, p. 218. She comes to this conclusion on the basis of the Weekly Report version of the case.

[70] (1867) LR 2 QB 580. [71] *Ibid.*, p. 588.

[72] The texts were taken from Paul and Ulpian: D.18.1.9, 10, 11.

[73] In the leading case on frustration, *Taylor* v. *Caldwell* (1863) 3 B & S 826, Blackburn J. made extensive references to Pothier and the Civil law; for a discussion, see Catharine MacMillan, 'Taylor v. Caldwell (1863)', in Charles Mitchell and Paul Mitchell (eds.), *Landmark Cases in the Law of Contract* (Oxford: Hart, 2008), pp. 167–203.

[74] Pollock, *Contract*, p. 386. [75] Anson, *Contract*, 3rd edn, p. 122.

failure of consideration and the reluctance of the court to grant rescission of a contract in the face of an innocent or negligent misrepresentation made to a purchaser of shares.[76]

In common with the earlier decisions, *Smith* v. *Hughes*[77] was not a particularly strong authority on mistake, although it too was soon treated as one.[78] The leading judgment by Cockburn C.J. was based on the principle of *caveat emptor* rather than mistake. Nevertheless, in a significant respect the decision was a breakthrough. Passages in the judgments of Blackburn J. and Hannen J. can be attributed to Judah Benjamin's *A Treatise on the Law of Sale of Personal Property*. Benjamin in turn was heavily influenced by Pothier in so far as he regarded a contract as formed by mutual assent and viewed a mistake as something preventing assent from taking place.[79]

A doctrine of contractual mistake developed over the course of the middle decades of the nineteenth century. It provides perhaps the clearest illustration of the influence of the Will Theory on English law. Mistake could be explained using Pothier's central thesis that contracts were formed by assent.[80] In the presence of a mistake the necessary assent was missing. Its simplicity was one obvious attraction for home-grown legal writers of this theory. Another was the way in which it provided an explanation for all categories of mistake. A third advantage of this approach was its superficial similarity with the existing way of doing things. The notion that the parties lacked assent was not very different from the traditional question under the general issue, namely, whether there was an agreement. The influence of legal writers was sometimes very direct. There are good grounds to believe that in *Smith* v. *Hughes*, Blackburn J. and Hannen J. were borrowing from Benjamin's treatise. But in the long run, perhaps the role played by legal writers in a more indirect way was more important. In their hands a series of decisions which at best were tangentially related to mistake began to be treated as leading authorities on mistake. Out of this apparently unpromising material, a whole edifice of contractual mistake was created. The lack of history was an advantage. It allowed Will Theory to be

[76] MacMillan, *Mistakes*, pp. 190–213.

[77] (1871) LR 6 QB 597, 40 LJQB 221, 19 WR 1059. For detailed discussion, see MacMillan, *Mistakes*, pp. 207–13; John Phillips, 'Smith v. Hughes (1871)', in Mitchell and Mitchell, *Landmark Cases in Contract*, pp. 205–21.

[78] J.P. Benjamin, *A Treatise on the Law of Sale of Personal Property*, 2nd edn (London: Henry Sweet, 1873), pp. 387–9; Pollock, *Contract*, p. 395; Anson, *Contract*, pp. 125–6.

[79] MacMillan, *Mistakes*, pp. 123–32.

[80] Pothier, *Obligations*, 1.1.1.3 § 1.

used in an undiluted form. In the process contractual mistake became a fixture of the Common law. The topic appeared on the Oxford syllabus in the 1870s. In the examination of 1877, candidates were asked, 'How far does a mistake on the part either of (a) the promisor, or of (b) the promisee affect the validity of a contract?'[81] By the 1870s contractual mistake was locked securely in place. It never looked back. The dubious origins of the doctrine were forgotten and it has largely remained uncontroversial into modern times.

Restructuring Equitable intervention in contract law

Eighteenth century judges were prepared to protect against the exploitation of one contracting party by another on the basis that they were protecting against fraud. Fraud covered a wide range of different situations beyond actual fraud. Other than grouping these cases under the head of fraud, no attempt was made to develop a coherent framework for equitable intervention. Lord Hardwicke recognised that it was more important to retain flexibility; only then could new kinds of fraud be tackled as they arose. Nineteenth century writers on Equity had a different agenda. They were not just concerned with practical solutions, but also with providing a systematic exposition. Fraud nevertheless cast a long shadow.

Joseph Story's *Commentaries on Equity Jurisprudence as Administered in England and America* was first published in England in 1839.[82] An American edition had appeared in 1835. Story had extensive knowledge of English law. He thought that Natural law provided an explanation for the binding force of contracts[83] and was at the heart of Equity[84] along with 'artificial modifications' of those principles.[85] Fraud was retained, but in a new form. Alongside 'actual' or 'positive' fraud, Story introduced 'constructive fraud',[86] which was little more than a convenient label for a range of public policy matters.[87] Public policy was very firmly tied into morality and found expression in the argument that those in another's

[81] The paper is reproduced in F.H. Lawson, *The Oxford Law School 1850–1965* (Oxford: Oxford University Press, 1968), Appendix II.

[82] 2nd edn, 2 vols. (Boston: Little & Brown, 1839).

[83] John Hogan, 'Joseph Story on the Law of Contract' (1957–1958) 12 *Rutgers Law Review* 366, 368. Hogan reproduces Story's entry on contract published anonymously in the *Encyclopedia Americana* in 1830.

[84] Story, *Commentaries*, p. vii. [85] *Ibid.*, p. vii. [86] *Ibid.*, pp. 261–422.

[87] *Ibid.*, pp. 213–14.

confidence should not exploit that position for their own advantage.[88] Natural law ideas were evident in the general principle: 'in regard to acts done or contracts made by parties, affecting their rights and interests . . . there must be a free and full consent.'[89] Edmund Snell, in his *The Principles of Equity Intended for the Use of Students and the Profession*,[90] also combined fraud and consent. A contract required full and free consent in order to bind the parties;[91] when advantage was taken of the absence of free and full consent, a fraud was perpetrated.[92]

Fraud remained the standard justification for Equity's intervention in cases of exploitation.[93] Story and Snell were both edging towards a version of vitiating factors which also included consent. But it was a long way from the full blown Will Theory favoured by the contract authors. Consensual analysis was equally weak outside cases of exploitation, for example in Snell's treatment of mistake.[94] On the other hand, consent was more prominent in George Jeremy's *A Treatise on the Equity Jurisdiction of the High Court of Chancery*.[95] Jeremy made a distinction between the potential for influence and a relationship of confidence. Agreements between a husband and wife, parent and child, and ward and guardian, were 'influence' cases.[96] Agreements between those in a fiduciary relationship were 'confidence' cases.[97] An agreement with a solicitor or attorney fell within both descriptions.[98] When a party entered into an agreement under 'influence', he was said not to be a free agent[99] in contrast to relationships of 'confidence', where the opportunity for fraud was 'not attributable so much to want of free agency as to the existence of a degree of confidence between the parties, which may enable the one to obtain an advantage at the expense or to the injury of the other'.[100] When legal writers came to address the problems of classification and justification the sorts of ideas associated with the Will Theory were further in the background than elsewhere. In the courts, undue influence took a long time before emerging as a ground for relief in its own right, and when it did so judges were slow to agree on its scope.[101]

[88] *Ibid.*, pp. 248–9. [89] *Ibid.*, p. 186. [90] (London: Stevens & Haynes, 1868).
[91] Snell, *Equity*, p. 368. [92] Snell, *Equity*, p. 368.
[93] Henry Maddock, *A Treatise on the Principles and Practice of the High Court of Chancery*, 2nd edn, 2 vols. (London: J. Clarke, 1820), vol. I, pp. 256–330.
[94] Snell, *Equity*, pp. 345–58. [95] (London: J. Clarke, 1828).
[96] Jeremy, *Equity*, p. 393. [97] *Ibid.*, p. 394. [98] *Ibid.*, p. 395. [99] *Ibid.*, p. 393.
[100] *Ibid.*, p. 394.
[101] For a more detailed discussion, see Michael Lobban, 'Contract', in William Cornish, Stuart Anderson, Raymond Cocks, Michael Lobban, Patrick Polden and Keith Smith,

Undue influence first appeared alongside an allegation of fraud in eighteenth century Chancery bills.[102] Even when undue influence was more explicitly the reason for the decision, there was a tendency to throw in a range of other factors including a weakness of mind,[103] the inadequacy of the bargain,[104] poverty,[105] and abuse of a position of trust.[106] The characteristics of undue influence were identified in the 1790s, when Lord Loughborough L.C. highlighted an un-free mind and improper pressure: 'Undue influence which necessarily implies a degree of weakness at the time, and *quoad* that instrument, making it not an instrument arising from fair bias of his own mind, but from the exercise of that improper influence'.[107]

The doctrine of undue influence began to develop fully after *Huguenin* v. *Baseley*.[108] The decision concerned a settlement between a widow and a clergyman rather than a contract, but the principles were the same. Sir Samuel Romilly for the plaintiff argued that those agreements between guardian and ward, and solicitor and client, were two examples of a more general principle of undue influence.[109] Having conceded that Equity had not previously set aside an agreement between a parishioner and clergymen,[110] support for both the general principle and a specific example was found in Pothier's volume on gifts.[111] Lord Eldon rescinded the agreement, holding that it did not spring from 'the pure, voluntary,

The Oxford History of the Laws of England, Vol. XII 1820–1914: Private Law (Oxford: Oxford University Press, 2010), pp. 402–9.

102 *Morris* v. *Burroughs* (1737) 1 Atk 399; *Bennet* v. *Vade* (1742) 2 Atk 324; *Debenham* v. *Ox* (1749) 1 Ves Sen 276; *Cocking* v. *Pratt* (1749–1750) 1 Ves Sen 400; *Wycherley* v. *Wycherley* (1763) 2 Eden 175; *Kinchant* v. *Kinchant* (1784) 1 Bro CC 369; *Welles* v. *Middleton* (1784) 1 Cox 112.

103 *Osmond* v. *Fitzroy* (1731) 3 P Wms 129.

104 *Clarkson* v. *Hanway* (1723) 2 P Wms 203.

105 *Cox* v. *Lamplugh* (1769) Dick 411.

106 *Osmond* v. *Fitzroy* (1731) 3 P Wms 129.

107 *Bates* v. *Graves* (1793) 2 Ves Jun 287, 288–9, per Lord Loughborough L.C.

108 (1807) 14 Ves Jun 273.

109 His argument was to be as influential as Lord Eldon's actual judgment. *Dent* v. *Bennett* (1839) 4 My & Cr 269, 277; Frederick White and Owen Tudor, *A Selection of Leading Cases in Equity*, 2 vols. (London: W. Maxwell, 1849–1850), vol. II, p. 430; Pollock, *Contract*, p. 516 was scarcely exaggerating when he wrote that Romilly's argument had been given 'repeated judicial approval' so that it had been 'given a weight scarcely if at all inferior to the decision itself'.

110 This was not strictly true; in *Norton* v. *Relly* (1764) 2 Eden 286 a similar agreement was set aside on the basis of public policy, fraud and misrepresentation. It was described as an unquestionable authority in *Nottidge* v. *Prince* (1860) 2 Giff 246, 263.

111 *Traité des Donations entre-Vifs* in *Oeuvres Complète de Pothier* (Paris, 1821), vol. XXIII, 1.2 § 8. The passage was later cited with approval in *Nottidge* v. *Prince* (1860) 2 Giff 246, 270.

well understood, acts of her mind'.[112] He also referred to the general principle of advantage-taking:

> The question is, not, whether she knew what she was doing, had done, or proposed to do, but how that intention was produced: whether all that care and providence was placed round her, as against those, who advised her, which, from their situation and relation with respect to her, they were bound to exert on her behalf.[113]

In the aftermath of *Huguenin* v. *Baseley*, the courts were slow to develop a single justification for undue influence. Some judges stressed public policy,[114] others free will,[115] and yet others advantage-taking.[116] Although judges were never wholly happy with a single explanation,[117] by the 1830s advantage-taking was becoming the most popular rationale. In *Hunter* v. *Atkins*,[118] Lord Brougham made a distinction between, on the one hand, an agreement between an attorney and client, or between guardian and ward, or between trustee and beneficiary, in which the onus was on the defendant to prove that he did not take advantage of that position, and, on the other, that of a stranger, where the burden of proving advantage-taking was on the plaintiff who was seeking to have the agreement set aside.

By the 1850s the jurisdiction in undue influence was a broad and flexible one. Sir George Turner V.C. remarked at this time:

> No part of the jurisdiction of the Court is more useful than that which it exercises in watching and controlling transactions between persons standing in relations of confidence to each other; and in my opinion this part of the jurisdiction of the Court cannot be too freely applied, either as to the persons between whom, or the circumstances in which, it is applied.[119]

In *Hunter* v. *Atkins*, Lord Brougham had suggested that particular types of relationship reversed the burden of proving an undue influence. Doctors and patients were added to the existing categories,[120] but the

[112] 14 Ves Jun 273, 296. For a later decision emphasising this aspect of the reasoning, see *Nicol* v. *Vaughan* (1832) 6 Bligh NS 104, 115.

[113] 14 Ves Jun 273, 300. [114] *Harris* v. *Tremenheere* (1808) 15 Ves Jun 34.

[115] *Griffiths* v. *Robins* (1818) 3 Madd 191; *Pratt* v. *Barker* (1826) 1 Sim 1 (1828) 4 Russ 507.

[116] *Lord Selsey* v. *Rhoades* (1824) 2 Sim & St 41.

[117] *Hayward* v. *Purssey* (1849) 3 De G & Sm 399, 404; *Williams* v. *Bayley* (1866) 1 LR HL 200, 216, per Lord Westbury.

[118] (1834) 3 My & K 131. [119] *Billage* v. *Southee* (1852) 9 Hare 534, 540.

[120] *Dent* v. *Bennett* (1839) 4 My & Cr 269.

list was not exhaustive.[121] The key lay in whether the parties were in a relationship of confidence, which was soon characterised as one in which one party exerted power and control over the other.[122]

Floating around the edges of these cases was a much broader principle, under which a recipient of a benefit, through a voluntary donation which was to the prejudice of the donor, was required to prove that the 'donor voluntarily and deliberately performed the act, knowing its nature and effect'.[123] In the first edition of his treatise, Pollock offered his support, claiming that it 'considerably modifies (it would be hardly too much to say overrides) the doctrine of *Hunter* v. *Atkins*'[124] but it did not apply when the recipient provided valuable consideration[125] and, by the second edition of his textbook, he was forced to concede that 'the present writer has reason to know that [the doctrine] cannot be relied on in practice'.[126]

In *Allcard* v. *Skinner*, Lindley L.J. observed that 'As no Court has ever attempted to define fraud so no Court has ever attempted to define undue influence, which includes one of its many varieties'.[127] Consensual analysis was beginning to come through in the nineteenth century, but it was never able to dominate. Will Theory was most prominent in Pollock's treatise. In the presence of undue influence, any consent was un-free[128] because the undue influence precluded 'free and deliberate judgment'.[129] 'The question', wrote Pollock, 'to be decided in each case is whether the party was a free and voluntary agent.'[130] Fraud remained important. These two elements of undue influence were never completely reconciled. Anson wrote that undue influence arose where 'one of the parties may from circumstances be morally incapable of resisting the will of the other, so that his consent is no real expression of intention',[131] yet at the same time stressed that there was 'taking of . . .

[121] (1839) 4 My & Cr 269, 276–7. This uncertainty was the source of annoyance to Pollock, *Contract*, p. 507.

[122] *Allcard* v. *Skinner* (1887) 36 Ch D 145; Charlotte Smith, 'Allcard v. Skinner (1887)', in Charles Mitchell and Paul Mitchell (eds.), *Landmark Cases in the Law of Restitution* (Oxford: Hart, 2006), pp. 183–211.

[123] *Cooke* v. *Lamotte* (1851) 15 Beav 234, 240; *Hoghton* v. *Hoghton* (1852) 15 Beav 278, 298–9.

[124] Pollock, *Contract*, p. 507. [125] *Blackie* v. *Clark* (1852) 15 Beav 595, 600.

[126] Frederick Pollock, *Principles of Contract at Law and in Equity*, 2nd edn (London: Stevens & Sons, 1878), p. 528. Pollock's scepticism was shared by White and Tudor, *Equity*, vol. II, p. 437.

[127] (1887) 36 Ch D 145, 183. [128] Pollock, *Contract*, pp. vii, 500. [129] *Ibid.*, p. 503.

[130] *Ibid.*, p. 503. [131] Anson, *Contract*, pp. 115–16.

an unfair advantage'.[132] The tension at the heart of undue influence continues to the present day.[133]

Consideration, privity and the classical law of contract

The continued survival of the doctrine of consideration after 1850 can in a large part be explained by the fact that its role was much diminished. Provided that a contract was seriously intended, it was difficult to argue that consideration was absent. As Leake explained, 'The object of [consideration] is to avoid the risk of giving binding effect to promises made inadvertently, and without an obligatory intention'.[134] In Leake's analysis, consideration no longer mattered in itself. It was merely a device for ascertaining whether there was an obligatory intention. Pollock's treatment was different. In the first edition of his treatise he argued that 'Notwithstanding these differences it seems very possible that the English Consideration may be directly descended from the Roman Causa'.[135] Pollock would later reject this view as historically unsound and treat consideration as a purely home-grown doctrine.[136] The fact that a parallel with *causa* was even drawn may reflect the extent to which consideration was seen as evidence of a contract seriously intended by this time.[137]

In the 1840s the requirement of reciprocity in consideration was stretched almost to breaking point. The boundaries of consideration were further loosened in the 1850s and 1860s. In *Shadwell* v. *Shadwell*,[138] an uncle promised to pay his nephew £150 a year on his marriage. The majority held that by marrying, the nephew had provided consideration for his uncle's promise. The finding of consideration was justified using the traditional formula that the nephew suffered a loss by marrying at the uncle's request and the uncle gained a benefit because the marriage was 'an object of interest to a near relative'.[139] Analysed in

132 *Ibid.*, p. 156.

133 Peter Birks and Chin Nyuk Yin, 'On the Nature of Undue Influence', in Jack Beatson and Daniel Friedmann (eds.), *Good Faith and Contract Law* (Oxford: Oxford University Press, 1995), pp. 57–97.

134 Leake, *Contracts*, p. 310. 135 Pollock, *Contract*, p. 149.

136 For a discussion, see Duxbury, *Pollock*, pp. 205–6.

137 The idea that *causa* has some role in the history of consideration is not completely without foundation, though Pollock placed too much weight on the relationship, A.W. Brian Simpson, *A History of the Common Law of Contract: The Rise of the Action of Assumpsit*, pbk edn (Oxford: Oxford University Press, 1987), pp. 402–4.

138 (1860) 9 CB NS 159. 139 *Ibid.*, p. 174.

terms of reciprocity, this outcome seems unconvincing. A better explanation can be found in the application of the same rule in a very different, commercial, context. In *Scotson* v. *Pegg*,[140] Wilde B. argued that 'if a person chooses to promise to pay a sum of money in order to induce another to perform what he has already contracted with a third person to do, I confess I cannot see why such a promise should not be binding'.[141] In short, where both parties intended a binding agreement, and both acted in reliance upon it, then the courts would not put obstacles in the way of a finding of consideration.

An exception to the rule in *Stilk* v. *Myrick*[142] also emerged in the 1850s. In *Hartley* v. *Ponsonby*,[143] a ship became short-handed part way through a voyage and the Master agreed to increase the wages of the remaining sailors. It was held that the new contract was supported by consideration. If this was an exception, it was a narrow one.[144] Any obligations the sailors had to the ship were discharged once the crew fell below a level which meant that the ship was no longer seaworthy. Where the crew were not placed in danger, there could be no consideration.[145] Contracts with sailors remained a special category governed by special rules,[146] but in a small way they also figured in the weakening of consideration.

For a period it looked as though *Cumber* v. *Wane*[147] would meet the same fate as other restrictions placed on consideration. In *Goddard* v. *O'Brien*,[148] Huddleson B. observed that 'The doctrine of *Cumber* v. *Wane* if not actually overruled, has been very much qualified'. It was difficult to square with other developments. Martin B. remarked in *Cooper* v. *Parker* that 'I shall always be ready to concur in such a judgment as tends to allow parties to contract for themselves what engagements they please'.[149] By this period judges were usually reluctant to allow consideration to defeat the parties' intentions. In this spirit, Pollock, in the first edition of his treatise, went as far as describing the rule as an 'absurdity',[150] pointing out that although a peppercorn was

140 (1861) 6 H & N 295, 3 LT 753. 141 (1861) 6 H & N 295, 300.

142 (1809) 2 Camp 317, 6 Esp 129. 143 (1857) 7 El & Bl 872.

144 Peter Luther, 'Campbell, Espinasse and the Sailors: Text and Context in the Common Law' (1999) 19 *Legal Studies* 526, 548–9. Luther also suggests that the Common law was following the Admiralty Court, citing *The Araminta* (1854) 1 Sp Ecc & Ad 224.

145 *Harris* v. *Carter* (1854) 3 El & Bl 559.

146 The form of these contracts was still governed by statute: *Frazer* v. *Hatton* (1857) 2 CB NS 512.

147 (1719) 11 Mod 342, 1 Stra 426. 148 (1882) LR 9 QBD 37, 39.

149 (1855) 15 CB 822, 828. 150 Pollock, *Contract*, p. 160.

valid consideration, £99 did not discharge a £100 debt. The rule was also abandoned in India.

Not every commentator was as hostile as Pollock. Anson regarded the rule that payment of a smaller sum could not amount to satisfaction of a larger one as 'a necessary result of the doctrine of consideration'.[151] But given developments elsewhere, it was perhaps a little surprising that the restrictive approach of *Cumber* v. *Wane* was upheld by the House of Lords in *Foakes* v. *Beer*.[152] Pollock was reluctantly forced to modify his treatment in the next edition of his treatise.[153] Others remained unhappy about the restriction. Lord Blackburn concurred with his fellow judges, but his speech was nearer to a dissent than a ringing endorsement. The American scholar James Barr Ames was a particularly vociferous critic, believing that the rule was not well founded in authority.[154] Ames argued that in cases like *Foakes* v. *Beer*, counter-promises were sufficient consideration in themselves. This view failed to attract support in England. Pollock responded that where the promisor was already bound to perform there could be no benefit to the promisee or detriment to the promisor.[155] Even now the courts remain reluctant to find consideration in cases of this sort despite the passage of more than a century, during which the rigidity of the doctrine has been further relaxed and it has declined in importance.[156]

Although it was long established that mutual promises were consideration for each other, the idea was not free from difficulty. Viewed broadly, any promises seriously intended might amount to sufficient consideration. In the first edition of his treatise, Pollock blandly stated that mutual promises could be consideration for one another.[157] Later on

151 Anson, *Contract*, p. 77.

152 (1883–1884) 9 App Cas 605; Michael Lobban, 'Foakes v. Beer (1884)', in Mitchell and Mitchell (eds.), *Landmark Cases in Contract*, pp. 223–67.

153 In the fourth edition of his treatise, published in 1885, p. 180, he described *Pinnel's Case* as 'paradoxically not anomalous'. In a short note on the case, (1885) 1 *Law Quarterly Review* 134, Pollock wrote that: 'The fact that the House of Lords did affirm the doctrine laid down in *Pinnel's Case* is as striking proof as can be found of the weight wisely given by the English courts to authority.' Even so, in the fifth edition of his treatise, Frederick Pollock still felt compelled to castigate the rule as an 'absurdity': *Principles of Contract*, 5th edn (London: Stevens & Sons, 1889), p. 179.

154 J.B. Ames, 'Two Theories of Consideration' (1898–1899) 12 *Harvard Law Review* 515, 522–3.

155 Frederick Pollock, *Principles of Contract at Law and in Equity*, 7th edn (London: Stevens & Sons, 1902), p. 189.

156 *Re Selectmove* [1995] 1 WLR 374; Janet O'Sullivan, 'In Defence of Foakes v. Beer' (1996) 55 *Cambridge Law Journal* 219.

157 Pollock, *Contract*, p. 152.

he would admit that there were some problems with this view.[158] By 1914, he was describing this rule as one of the 'secret paradoxes of the Common law' founded on history rather than logic.[159] Some regarded the whole notion as circular. The topic was a favourite one in the new university-based law journals in the United States and many of the leading contract scholars of the time had their say.[160] The subject was attractive to those engaged in the sort of formalistic reasoning so prevalent in American legal scholarship in an era before legal realism became fashionable.[161]

The most realistic view on the state of consideration at the end of the nineteenth century can be found in William Markby's *Elements of Law*,[162] where he states that:

> The result that I have derived from a perusal of the decisions of English judges upon the question of consideration is that it is impossible to apply it as a test of legal liability with consistency and with justice: that it is in truth not a test but an indication only, amongst many others, that the parties entering into a transaction had in contemplation their legal relations to each other.[163]

From the perspective of the late nineteenth century, *Foakes* v. *Beer* was a reminder of the continued importance of consideration in English contract law. Contract law was nevertheless continuing to evolve, and sometimes quite quickly. The question of the rights of a third party under a contract provides a good illustration. Throughout the eighteenth century the subject was largely ignored. Early nineteenth century legal writers

158 Cases where the promisor was already under a subsisting contract with a third party to perform were particularly awkward. In these cases the promisor does not suffer a detriment. Frederick Pollock, 'Afterthoughts on Consideration' (1901) 17 *Law Quarterly Review* 415 at 419, 'such cases are not frequent'.

159 Pollock made these remarks in a book review, 'The Student's Summary of the Law of Contract' (1914) 30 *Law Quarterly Review* 128, 129. For a discussion of Pollock's views, see Duxbury, *Pollock*, pp. 208–15.

160 Ames, 'Two Theories of Consideration'; C.C. Langdell, 'Mutual Promises as a Consideration for Each Other' (1900–1901) 14 *Harvard Law Review* 496; Henry Ballantine, 'Is the Doctrine of Consideration Senseless and Illogical' (1913) 11 *Michigan Law Review* 423; Henry Ballantine, 'Mutuality and Consideration' (1914–1915) 28 *Harvard Law Review* 121; Samuel Williston, 'Consideration in Bilateral Contracts' (1913–1914) 27 *Harvard Law Review* 503. For a discussion of the debate, see Richard Bronaugh, 'A Secret Paradox of the Common Law' (1983) 2 *Law & Philosophy* 193.

161 Neil Duxbury, *Patterns of American Jurisprudence* (Oxford: Oxford University Press, 2001), pp. 11–64.

162 3rd edn (Oxford: Oxford University Press, 1885).

163 *Ibid.*, para. 647.

continued to use the traditional formulation of the rule that 'the plaintiff must not be a stranger to the consideration',[164] others that the 'consideration must move from the plaintiff'.[165] The issue was not seen as sufficiently important to merit inclusion in the first edition of Chitty's treatise. The fact that it appeared in the second edition[166] can be attributed to *Price* v. *Easton*.[167] Lord Denman C.J. rejected the plaintiff's action on the grounds that 'I think the declaration cannot be supported, as it does not shew any consideration for the promise moving from the plaintiff to the defendant'.[168] In another report of the case his objections seem to be purely formal: 'The declaration does not allege any promise by the defendant to the plaintiff.'[169] Alongside the consideration rule, a separate parties-only rule began to emerge in the cases. Littledale J. purported to follow *Crow* v. *Rogers*, the leading authority on consideration, but he was also the first to use the language of privity when he said that 'No privity is shewn between the plaintiff and the defendant. This case is precisely like *Crow* v. *Rogers* and must be governed by it.'[170] His reasons for dismissing the action fit, if anything, more comfortably with the parties-only principle than consideration: 'It is consistent with all the matter alleged in the declaration, that the plaintiff may have been entirely ignorant of the arrangement between William Price and the defendant.'[171] The judgment of Patteson J. turns on the wholly formal ground that the plaintiff failed to declare himself as promisee:

> After verdict, the court can only intend that all matters were proved which were requisite to support the allegations in the declaration, or what

164 Colebrooke, *Obligations*, pp. 41–2; Charles Petersdorff, *A Practical and Elementary Abridgement of the Common Law*, 5 vols. (London: Stevens & Norton, 1843), vol. III, p. 40.

165 William Selwyn, *An Abridgement of the law of Nisi Prius*, 2 vols. (London: W. Clarke, 1808), vol. I, p. 45; Samuel Comyn, *The Law of Contracts and Promises*, 2nd edn (London: A. Strahan, 1824), p. 21; C.G. Addison, *A Treatise on the Law of Contracts and Rights and Liabilities Ex-Contractu* (London: W. Benning, 1847), p. 246.

166 Chitty, *Contracts*, pp. 46–7.

167 (1833) 4 B & Ad 433, 1 N & M 303, LJKB 51. The latter report omits Lord Denman's judgment. Vernon Palmer, *The Paths to Privity* (Clark, N.J.: The Lawbook Exchange, 2006), pp. 164–5 regards this decision as turning on consideration which is indeed how it is described by counsel in *Tipper* v. *Bicknell* (1837) 3 Bing NC 710, 715 and *Tweddle* v. *Atkinson* (1861) 1 B & S 393, 395.

168 (1833) 4 B & Ad 433, 434. 169 (1833) LJKB 51, 52.

170 (1833) 4 B & Ad 433, 434. In 1 N & M 303, 307 the reference to privity was omitted. Littledale J. may simply be using the term loosely without intending it to be seen as a separate doctrine, see Robert Flannigan, 'Privity – The End of an Era (Error)' (1987) 103 *Law Quarterly Review* 564, 568.

171 (1833) 4 B & Ad 433, 435.

> is necessarily to be implied from them. Now it is quite clear that the allegations in the declaration are not sufficient to shew a right of action in the plaintiff. There is no promise to the plaintiff alleged.[172]

Taunton J., the final judge, did not mention consideration at all.

Even Littledale J.'s judgment was some way from an unequivocal endorsement of the parties-only principle in contract. In these cases a restriction based on consideration was still dominant. It was a different story in actions on the case in tort, where the consideration objection was unavailable. *Winterbottom* v. *Wright* fell on the boundary between contract and tort.[173] The plaintiff sued the defendant coachbuilder after he was injured by a wheel falling from a defective coach owned by the post office. The basis of his action in tort was a contractual duty between the coachbuilder and the post office. In finding against the plaintiff, the court were attempting to draw lines between contract and tort, but were also mindful of placing an unreasonable burden on manufacturers.[174] Lord Abinger stressed the absence of privity between the parties.[175] The same judge had referred to privity three years earlier in an action of trover.[176] If nothing else, these authorities show that judges were familiar with the doctrine of privity and the idea that a duty between A and B could not generate a duty in favour of C, but it was some time yet before it was a feature of mainstream contract claims.

A parties-only rule also featured in Pothier's *Traité des Obligations*:

> When I stipulate with you for a third person the agreement is void: for by this agreement you do not contract any obligation in favour of either of such third person or myself. It is evident that you do not contract any in favour of the third person: for it is a principle that agreements can have no effect except between the contracting parties, and consequently that they cannot acquire any right to a third person who is not a party to them . . . By this agreement you do not contract any civil obligation in my favour; for, what I have stipulated in favour of the third person, not being any thing in which I have an interest capable of pecuniary appreciation,

172 *Ibid.*

173 (1842) 10 M & W 109; Palmer, *Privity*, pp. 205–12; Vernon Palmer, 'Why Privity Entered Tort: An Historical Re-examination of Winterbottom v. Wright' (1983) 27 *American Journal of Legal History* 85.

174 David Ibbetson, *A Historical Introduction to the Law of Obligations* (Oxford: Oxford University Press, 1999), p. 174; David Ibbetson, 'The Tort of Negligence in the Common Law in the Nineteenth and Twentieth Centuries', in Eltjo Schrage (ed.), *Negligence: The Comparative Legal History of the Law of Torts* (Berlin: Dunker & Humblot, 2001), p. 254.

175 (1842) 10 M & W 109, 114–15.

176 *Tollit* v. *Sherstone* (1839) 5 M & W 283, 288.

> no damages can result to me from a failure in the performance of your promise.[177]

This may be one situation in which Civilian learning trumped Pothier's central premise that contracts are formed by a meeting of wills. Strictly applied, provided both parties assented, there ought to be no difficulty in agreeing to give a third party a right of action under a contract. In Roman law on the other hand, subject to exceptions,[178] a contract could neither impose liability on a third party,[179] nor could it give the third party rights.[180]

Whilst Pothier may have influenced aspects of nineteenth century contract law, more convincing explanations for the emergence of a doctrine of privity can be found elsewhere. With the emergence of a unified law of contract the boundaries between different actions were less rigid and distinct than before. As a result, consideration-based reasoning seeps across into actions based on sealed documents, and reasoning based on a parties-only principle seeps across into actions of assumpsit. In *Barford* v. *Stuckey*, an action based on covenant under seal, Dallas C.J. disallowed the beneficiary's action, in part on the fact that the consideration did not move from her.[181] Bosanquet and Puller's note on *Pigott* v. *Thompson*[182] moves seamlessly from the decision relating to a sealed document in *Gilby* v. *Copley*[183] into a discussion of the action of assumpsit.

The instability of the law relating to third parties is visible in the treatment of the subject by Charles Addison in his treatise on contract. In the first edition, published in 1847, sealed contracts are placed firmly within the parties-only principle.[184] The section dealing with informal

177 Pothier, *Obligations*, 1.1.5 § 1.

178 F.H. Lawson (ed.), W.W. Buckland and Arnold McNair, *Roman Law and Common Law* (Cambridge: Cambridge University Press, 1952), pp. 214–17; Barry Nicholas, *An Introduction to Roman Law* (Oxford: Oxford University Press, 1969), pp. 199–204; Reinhard Zimmermann, *The Law of Obligations: Roman Foundations of the Civilian Tradition* (Oxford: Oxford University Press, 1996), pp. 34–40; Jan Hallebeek, 'Ius Questitum Tertio in Medieval Roman Law', in Eltjo Schrage (ed.), *Ius Quaesitum Tertio* (Berlin: Duncker & Humblot, 2008), pp. 7–20; Jan Hallebeck and Harry Dondorp, *Contracts for the Third-Party Beneficiary* (Leiden: Martinus Nijhoff, 2008), pp. 61–107.

179 Watson, *Justinian*, 45.1.83 pr.

180 F. De Zulueta (trans.), *The Institutes of Gaius* (Oxford: Oxford University Press, 1946), 3.103.

181 (1820) 2 Br & B 333, 335; the point is also made in argument by Lens Stj., see also *Lord Southampton* v. *Brown* (1827) 6 B & C 718, 5 LJKB 253.

182 (1802) 3 B & P 147, 149. 183 (1683) 3 Lev 138. 184 Addison, *Contracts*, p. 244.

contracts contains a stark denial of the parties-only principle. Addison suggests that a third party can enforce a contract made for his benefit.[185] The wide general statement is qualified by the rule that a stranger to the consideration cannot sue, but the qualification is not treated as a significant restriction. It is said that very little evidence is needed to link the promise and the consideration.[186] Where a promise is made to one person, the law can be stretched to interpret the consideration as having been provided by that person. Addison seems to hint that the limitation based on consideration does not provide much of a bar. By the fourth edition of 1856, the statement about consideration is strengthened. A non-party can only bring an action provided consideration moves from him.[187] The fifth edition of 1862 retains the principle that a non-party who provided consideration had a right of action, but the examples are very restricted indeed: an agent contracting on behalf of an undisclosed principal, and a holder of a bill of exchange or promissory note.[188] The statement that the law required little evidence to link the promise and the consideration had disappeared.

Tweddle v. *Atkinson*[189] is sometimes portrayed as the origin of a general parties-only restriction in the law of contract.[190] In a manner not dissimilar to the landmark cases on mistake, its iconic status is due to the way in which the decision came to be interpreted rather more than anything that was actually said in any of the judgments. The plaintiff was the son of John Tweddle (deceased). He married the daughter of William Guy (deceased). Prior to the marriage, both fathers had promised to give the plaintiff a marriage portion. This verbal agreement remained unperformed. The two fathers subsequently entered into a written agreement:

> Whereas it is mutually agreed that the said William Guy shall and will pay the sum of £200 to William Tweddle, his son-in-law; and the said John Tweddle, father to the aforesaid William Tweddle, shall and will pay £100 to the said William Tweddle, each and severally the said sums on or before the 21st day of August 1855. And it is hereby further agreed by William Guy and the said John Tweddle that William Tweddle has full

[185] *Ibid.*, p. 244. [186] *Ibid.*, p. 245.

[187] C.G. Addison, *A Treatise on the Law of Contracts and Rights and Liabilities Ex-Contractu*, 4th edn (London: Stevens & Norton, 1856), p. 940.

[188] C.G. Addison, *A Treatise on the Law of Contracts and Rights and Liabilities Ex-Contractu*, 5th edn (London: Stevens, 1862), pp. 948–9.

[189] (1861) 1 B & S 393, 30 LJQB 265, 4 LT 468, 9 WR 781.

[190] *Gandy* v. *Gandy* (1885) 30 Ch D 57, 69. For a contrary view, see *Darlington BC* v. *Wiltshire Northern Ltd* [1995] 1 WLR 68, 76.

> power to sue the said parties in any court of law or equity for the aforesaid sums hereby promised and specified.

The £200 due from Guy remained unpaid at his death and William Tweddle brought an action against his executor.

The terms of the written agreement left no room for doubt that the contract had been made between the two fathers and that William Tweddle was not a party to it; secondly, even though William Tweddle was not a party, it was clearly and expressly the intention of the fathers that he should be able to sue; and thirdly, the facts stood on all fours with *Dutton* v. *Poole*. George Mellish Q.C., as counsel for the plaintiff, rested his argument on the last point. The Queen's Bench refused to follow *Dutton* v. *Poole*, holding that family cases of this type were not exceptions to the general rule. The issue at the heart of *Tweddle* v. *Atkinson* was therefore how the general rule should be formulated. The precise grounds on which Edward James, for the defence, argued the case vary according to the report: the plaintiff could not sue because he was a stranger to the consideration;[191] the plaintiff could not sue because he was a stranger to the agreement and consideration did not move from him;[192] the plaintiff was a stranger to the contract and the consideration, and there was no privity between him and the defendant;[193] there was no privity between the plaintiff and the defendant's testator.[194]

All three of the judges rejected the claim, but their reasons are difficult to disentangle. In one report, Wightman J. appears to decide the case solely on the consideration doctrine, stating, 'But there is no modern case in which the proposition has been supported. On the contrary, it is now established that no stranger to the consideration can take advantage of a contract, although made for his benefit.'[195] In another report he stated the rule that no stranger to the consideration can sue on it,[196] but was also concerned that the consideration was the intended marriage and that it was past consideration for the agreement on which the plaintiff brought his action.[197] As a result, 'Here there is no consideration moving from the plaintiff, for the marriage was before the contract sued on, and according to the modern cases the plaintiff cannot sue'.[198] In the

191 (1861) 4 LT 468, 469. 192 (1861) 1 B & S 393, 395. 193 (1861) 30 LJQB 265, 266.
194 (1861) 9 WR 781. 195 (1861) 1 B & S 393, 398. 196 (1861) 4 LT 468, 469.
197 Nor was there an allegation of request to take the case outside the rule against past consideration.
198 (1861) 4 LT 468, 469.

final report, Wightman J. used both consideration and privity in order to deny the action:

> But no modern case can be found to support such a proposition and on the contrary, it has always been held that no stranger can take advantage of a contract made with another person ... It is admitted that if the plaintiff was a mere stranger he could not maintain the action; and I think that as no consideration ran from him, and, that being no party to the contract, he cannot recover.[199]

The reasons of Crompton J. are equally unclear from the reports. In one report he used the parties-only principle to defeat the claim:

> It would be monstrous to hold that a man was a party to the contract for one purpose and not for another so that he might be able to sue, without being liable to be sued. It is said that he becomes a party to the agreement, but if so, he must be liable to be sued.[200]

He is reported to have intervened during the course of argument in similar terms.[201] The other reports are not so clear cut:

> The modern cases have, in effect, overruled the old decisions; they shew that the consideration must move from the party entitled to sue upon the contract. It would be a monstrous proposition to say that a person was a party to the contract for the purpose of suing upon it for his own advantage, and not a party to it for the purpose of being sued.[202]
>
> It is now clear law that the consideration must move from the party entitled to sue on the contract. It would be a monstrous proposition to make a child party to the contract for one purpose, viz to sue for his own advantage, and not for another, to bear the liability.[203]

The judgment of Blackburn J. is more consistently reported. He does not deal with the third-party problem, but simply refused the action on the grounds that there was no good consideration for the promise.[204]

199 (1861) 30 LJQB 265, 257. 200 *Ibid.*, p. 267.

201 *Ibid.*, p. 266: '[An] action cannot be brought by the person with whom the contract is not made.'

202 (1861) 1 B & S 393, 398. Cf. (1861) 9 WR 781, 782: 'The consideration must move from the party who sues.'

203 (1861) 4 LT 468, 469.

204 (1861) 1 B & S 393, 399, 30 LJQB 265, 268. In both these reports he said that he was agreeing with Mellish's description of the general rule, but only in the 1 B & S 393, 395 report did Mellish formulate the rule in exactly that way, and there Mellish was merely agreeing with James's version of the rule. In 30 LJQB 265, 266 Mellish did not set out the form of the rule nor say that he agreed with James.

Tweddle v. *Atkinson* is hardly a ringing endorsement of the principle that only parties to a contract have a right of action.[205] Some writers continued to prefer an objection framed in the form of the rule that consideration must move from the promisee. In the sixth edition of Addison's treatise in 1869, *Tweddle* v. *Atkinson* was justified on the basis that the 'husband not being a party to the agreement could not sue upon it',[206] but it still appeared in a section headed 'strangers to consideration'. Successive editors of Chitty continued to classify *Tweddle* v. *Atkinson* as a consideration case.[207]

Other contemporaries fastened on to the parties-only principle.[208] The authors of the *Law Students Examination Chronicle*, published in the same year as *Tweddle* v. *Atkinson*, probably had the case in mind when they asked a question on the meaning of privity of contract.[209] The model answer given the following year was telling: 'The term "privity of contract" is used in various senses; thus it is said that in order to maintain assumpsit there must be a privity between the parties meaning a privity of contract.'[210] The status of *Tweddle* v. *Atkinson* as the source of the doctrine of privity is largely a consequence of the decision of the majority of textbook writers to treat the case as authority for the parties-only principle. The trend was begun by Leake six years after the decision, when he wrote that: 'The legal effect of a contract is, as a general rule, confined to the parties to it. A contract cannot create a right or a liability in a person who is not a party to it.'[211]

There was still some uncertainty about the impact of *Tweddle* v. *Atkinson*. There was no discussion of privity of contract in the Indian Contract Commission's report in the late 1860s, despite an analysis largely built around the Will Theory. Any such restriction was absent from the Indian Contract Act 1872. The Act shows that a parties-only principle was not an inevitable consequence of adopting the Will Theory. It may have been well into the 1870s before it was generally accepted that *Tweddle* v. *Atkinson* introduced a parties-only principle into the law

205 Palmer, *Privity*, pp. 165–6, 173–5.

206 Lewis Cave (ed.), C.G. Addison, *A Treatise on Law of Contracts*, 6th edn (London: Stevens & Sons, 1869), p. 1039.

207 Starting with John Russell (ed.), Joseph Chitty, *A Practical Treatise on the Law of Contracts*, 7th edn (London: H. Sweet, 1863), pp. 52–5. It was not until the twenty-second edition, edited by John Morris and published in 1961, that privity replaced consideration.

208 Palmer, *Privity*, pp. 174–5. 209 (1861), vol. I, p. 224. 210 (1862), vol. II, p. 5.

211 Leake, *Contracts*, p. 221. Leake cited *Crow* v. *Rogers* and *Price* v. *Easton* in support.

relating to unsealed contracts. That this became the standard interpretation may be largely down to the fact that it appeared in Pollock's treatise of 1876 and in Anson's book of 1879:

> However the rule is now distinctly established, so far as the common law right of action is concerned, that a third person cannot sue on a contract made by others for his benefit even if the contracting parties have agreed that he may, and that near relationship makes no difference. This was decided by the Court of Queen's Bench in *Tweddle* v. *Atkinson*.[212]

It was at one time thought that if a person who was to take a benefit under the contract was nearly related by blood to the promisee, a right of action would rest in him. But this doctrine was finally laid to rest in the case of *Tweddle* v. *Atkinson* by the Court of Queen's Bench.[213]

Lawyers, legal writers and the emergence of contract doctrine

It is always going to be difficult, if not impossible, to demonstrate a conclusive link between legal writers and the development of legal doctrine. One thing can be said with a degree of confidence. For a period from around 1850 to the end of the century, legal writers exerted more influence than before and probably since. Sometimes this influence went right to the centre of how contract law was perceived. In *Foster* v. *Wheeler*,[214] Kekewich J. said that 'Definitions of contract are to be found in the text-books, and I have consulted several of them . . . They are all founded on, and many of them simply adopt, the definition given by Pothier'. He also made specific reference to Pollock and the American writer Theophilus Parsons.[215] Pollock was something of a judicial favourite. Sometimes the debt was attributed and at other times not.[216] In comparison with modern times, the legal profession remained relatively small and relatively homogeneous. It was still possible for someone like Pollock to play a role in legal development. As well as his contract treatise, Pollock was also editor of, and a leading contributor towards, the *Law Quarterly Review*.[217] All the same, Pollock did not always get his

212 Pollock, *Contract*, pp. 190–1. 213 Anson, *Contract*, p. 200.

214 (1887) 36 Ch D 695, 698.

215 Theophilius Parsons, *The Law of Contracts* (Boston: Little, Brown & Co., 1853). It is somewhat ironic that within a short space of time Kekewich J. should turn his face against citing from textbooks, see Neil Duxbury, *Jurists and Judges* (Oxford: Hart, 2001), pp. 63–4.

216 Duxbury, *Pollock*, p. 207. 217 *Ibid.*, pp. 309–22.

own way, as his criticism of the rule in *Cumber* v. *Wane* would show. Collectively legal writers had an even more powerful role. Mistake developed as it did, not because of the case law, but in spite of it. It was the legal writers rather than the judges who were its handmaiden.

The authors of legal treatises created an even more important legacy than specific contract doctrines. A small group of contract authors comprised a small club of mutual admiration. In the 1880s, Pollock, describing his philosophy of legal education, stressed that the most important thing was to help the student to 'fix in his mind that there are such things as general principles of law; that the multitude of particulars in which he must inevitably be versed . . . are not really a chaos'.[218] Superficially at least, the law of contract is particularly well suited to this sort of analysis. The life of the contract has a clear beginning, middle and end. Some no doubt still believe in this analysis.[219] The emergence of law degrees also had a part to play. The first Oxford University contract law exam of 1877 was a demanding one. Question five asked candidates 'what are the essential characteristics of every contract valid by the law of England?' And there were more specific questions on topics such as consideration, mistake, agency, contract formation, fraud and incapacity. The idea that the law was founded on principle was evident from the title of the paper: 'Principles of the Law of Contract'. The term principle also came up repeatedly in the questions.[220]

Those who taught on these courses needed to justify their existence, earn their salaries, and cement their position. It is unsurprising therefore that these writers were seeking to separate themselves from legal practitioners and present law as an academic discipline.[221] The argument that contract law was capable of systematic and principled analysis suited their purposes admirably. This type of thinking led Dicey to compare works by Smith, Chitty and Addison unfavourably with Anson's treatise as writers who have 'learnt law without mastering its principles'.[222] The

218 Frederick Pollock, 'Oxford Law Studies' (1886) 2 *Law Quarterly Review* 453, 454–5.

219 Of course, the law of contract in practice is not necessarily the law of contract in the books. A literature advancing this view has grown since the seminal Stuart Macaulay, 'Non-Contractual Relations in Business: A Preliminary Study' (1963) 28 *American Sociological Review* 1.

220 The paper is reproduced in F.H. Lawson, *The Oxford Law School 1850–1965* (Oxford: Oxford University Press, 1968), Appendix II.

221 The same holds today, Fiona Cownie, *Legal Academics* (Oxford: Hart, 2004), pp. 35–7.

222 A.V. Dicey, *Can English Law be Taught at the Universities?* (London: Macmillan, 1883), p. 14.

distinction was recognised by practitioners themselves. Writing just after Pollock's death, Lord Wright claimed that 'Leake's book was for practitioners, while Pollock's book was for students of principles and legal thinkers'.[223]

Legal fashions may come and go but, while they last, intellectual fashions are remarkably durable.[224] Their legacy can last for generations. Students of law eventually become lawyers. Some are raised to the Bench. Methods of thought acquired when young can be difficult to shed. Whilst Joseph Story may have required his undergraduates at Harvard to consult a remarkably cosmopolitan range of literature,[225] the reality for most nineteenth century students of contract was rather more likely to begin and end with Anson's treatise. Less careful readers of Anson and Pollock could even be forgiven for thinking that contract law could be slotted into a logical framework. Some aspects of contract law were particularly poorly suited to this sort of analysis. Public policy was particularly troublesome.

[223] Lord Wright, 'In Memoriam' (1937) 53 *Law Quarterly Review* 151, 154.

[224] Dogma-driven teaching in law schools still exists, it is just that the dogma has changed. Modern law students, particularly in some provincial English universities, are taught to worship at the shrine of the meretricious Human Rights legislation with unthinking devotion. As Karl Popper once correctly observed: 'The fashionable thinker is, in the main, a prisoner of his fashion.' See M.A. Notturno (ed.), Karl Popper, *The Myth of the Framework* (London: Routledge, 1997), p. ix.

[225] *Report of the Select Committee on Legal Education* (1846) [686] PP vol. X, 1, p. 363.

10

Contract law, illegality and public policy

Frederick Pollock was perhaps more ill at ease in his discussion of public policy than any of the other many subjects that he considered in his contract treatise. In part this was a result of the difficulties of classification. Having distinguished between agreements that were illegal, immoral or contrary to public policy,[1] he conceded that:

> But like all classifications it is only approximate: and here more especially, where there is perhaps a wider field for judicial discretion than in any other part of the law, one must expect to find many cases which may nearly or quite as well be assigned to one place as another.[2]

Outside the authorities derived from the application of statutes, Pollock wrote, there was a 'clustered group of analogies rather than a linear chain of authority'.[3] Agreements contrary to public policy were particularly problematic because, 'it is doubtful whether these can be completely reduced to any general description, and how far judicial discretion may go in novel cases'.[4] Anson's treatment was no less hesitant. He began with a threefold classification of contracts prohibited by statute, Common law and public policy.[5] The two last categories, it was claimed, were 'not always very easy to distinguish'.[6] This was because 'certain matters of public policy have caused tolerably definite and express rules to grow up; and these are in effect rules of Common law'.[7]

Pollock noted that 'the general principle is, of course, that an unlawful agreement cannot be enforced'.[8] But even if there was an overarching or general principle, it was more difficult to present the application of the principle as, in itself, principled. For writers like Pollock and Anson, who

[1] Frederick Pollock, *Principles of Contract at Law and in Equity* (London: Stevens & Sons, 1876), pp. 218–20.

[2] *Ibid.*, p. 220. [3] Pollock, *Contract*, p. 221. [4] Pollock, *Contract*, p. 219.

[5] William Anson, *Principles of the English Law of Contract* (Oxford: Oxford University Press, 1879), p. 163.

[6] Anson, *Contract*, p. 164. [7] *Ibid.*

[8] Pollock, *Contract*, p. 292, see Stephen Waddams, *Principle and Policy in Contract Law* (Cambridge: Cambridge University Press, 2011), p. 154.

were so anxious to present the law of contract as systematic and logical, public policy was potentially inconvenient. Whilst some instances were 'tolerably definite', others were not. At first glance the previous generation of legal writers were rather less anxious about allowing contracts to be set aside on grounds of public policy. Samuel Comyn simply states that 'all contracts and agreements, which have for their object any thing contrary to the principles of sound policy, are void by the common law'.[9] Henry Colebrooke expressed himself in equally expansive terms:

> When the object or the consideration of the contract is against the law, against its policy and its provisions, against the principles of justice, against the rules and claims of decency and the dictates of morality, the agreement is void in law and equity.[10]

Behind the rhetoric Comyn confined public policy under rigid headings.[11] Most early nineteenth century writers were also keen to characterise these contracts as illegal rather than contrary to 'sound policy',[12] which was a potentially much broader idea. Even those like Joseph Chitty who were willing to discuss public policy more openly, did so in relatively cautious terms:

> A doubtful matter of public policy, is not sufficient to invalidate a contract. An agreement is not void on this ground, unless it expressly and unquestionably contravene public policy and be injurious, beyond all doubt, to the interests of the State.[13]

William Fox, writing in the 1840s, agreed. In questions of public policy he argued, 'doubtful questions . . . are to be decided by the legislature, and not by the courts of law, which have sometimes gone much further than they were warranted in such matters'.[14] Some indication of the difficulties of articulating any underlying features of these cases can be gleaned from the way in which Charles Addison gave up grouping the authorities under a separate heading; rather, they appear throughout his

9 Samuel Comyn, *A Treatise of the Law Relative to Contracts and Agreements not Under Seal*, 2 vols. (London: A. Strahan, 1807), p. 32.

10 H.T. Colebrooke, *Treatise on Obligations and Contracts* (London, 1818), p. 58.

11 Comyn, *Contracts*, pp. 30–46.

12 Colebrooke, *Contracts*, p. 63; Stephen Leake, *The Elements of the Law of Contract* (London: Stevens & Sons, 1867), pp. 376–412.

13 Joseph Chitty, *A Practical Treatise on the Law of Contracts not Under Seal* (London: S. Sweet, 1826), p. 217.

14 William Fox, *A Treatise on Simple Contracts and the Action of Assumpsit* (London: Stevens & Norton, 1842), p. 80.

treatise.[15] One of the most important categories, and one which Pollock argued led to public policy continuing as an 'assertion in a general form in modern times',[16] concerned wagers.

Wagers, the French ambassador and the law

In Tobias Smollett's novel *The Adventures of Ferdinand Count Fathom*, the Count describes a visit to a London gaming house:

> In one corner of the room might be heard a pair of lordlings running their grandmothers against each other, that is, betting sums on the longest liver; in another, the success of the wager depended upon the sex of the landlady's next child; and one of the waiter's happening to drop down in apoplectic fit, a certain noble peer exclaimed 'Dead, for a thousand pounds!' The challenge was immediately accepted; and when the master of the house sent for a surgeon to attempt the cure, the nobleman who set the price upon the patient's head, insisted upon his being left to the efforts of nature alone, otherwise the wager should be void.[17]

Wagering was a popular pastime amongst all social classes in eighteenth century England.[18] The wagers witnessed by Count Fathom were of a common type,[19] but wagers came in almost infinite varieties. An anecdote from 1709 recalls how four Members of Parliament raced their hats in a river and 'ran halloing after them; and he that won the prize was in greater rapture than if he carried the most dangerous point in Parliament'.[20] It was said that wagers 'very frequently ... originate

[15] C.G. Addison, *A Treatise on the Law of Contracts and Rights and Liabilities Ex-Contractu* (London: W. Benning, 1847).

[16] Pollock, *Contract*, p. 252.

[17] Tobias Smollett, *The Adventures of Ferdinand Count Fathom* (London, 1753), p. 126.

[18] Anon, *An Essay on Gaming* (London, 1761), p. 2; W.S. Lewis (ed.), Horace Walpole, *Horace Walpole's Correspondence*, 48 vols. (Oxford: Oxford University Press, 1967), vol. XXIV, p. 55, 11 November 1774 to Sir Horace Mann. For later accounts, see John Ashton, *The History of Gambling in England* (London: Duckworth, 1898), pp. 150–72; Paul Langford, *A Polite and Commercial People* (Oxford: Oxford University Press, 1992), pp. 571–4.

[19] Geoffrey Clark, *Betting on Lives: The Culture of Life Insurance in England 1695–1775* (Manchester: Manchester University Press, 1999), pp. 50–1. Clarke took a sample from the betting book of White's Club in London between 1743 to 1752: 35 per cent of wagers related to death, 17 per cent to birth and 10 per cent to marriage.

[20] James Malcolm, *Anecdotes of the Manners and Customs of London During the Eighteenth Century* (London: Longman, 1808), p. 132. To which the only sensible response is 'plus ça change, plus c'est la même chose'.

over the bottle or porter pot',[21] two possible examples of which were recorded by *The Spectator* in 1711. The first wager was that the Isle of White is a peninsula, the second that the World is round.[22]

In his defence of the practice, one anonymous author observed that there was a 'clamour against gaming'.[23] Gaming was said by an opponent, to be 'an inlet to drinking and debauchery'.[24] If some writers were to be believed, those who gambled could also expect more unpleasant consequences. The essayist Richard Hey listed more than fifty, ranging from financial ruin, to loss of interest in the opposite sex, impaired health, madness and suicide.[25] But his seemingly comprehensive list was incomplete. He omitted to mention the possibility that wagering might lead to legal proceedings.

In the early 1770s, rumours began to circulate that the French Ambassador, the Chevalier d'Eon, was female,[26] a fact that generated 'much noise among the knaves and fools of the metropolis'.[27] The topic

[21] Malcolm, *Anecdotes*, p. 161.

[22] Donald Bond (ed.), *The Spectator*, 5 vols. (Oxford: Oxford University Press, 1965), vol. II, p. 145 dated 16 August 1711.

[23] Anon, *A Modest Defence of Gaming* (London, 1754), p. 5; Justine Rosenberg-Orsini, *Moral and Sentimental Essays* (London, 1785), p. 43, 'much has been said and written against gaming'. For examples of attacks on gaming, see William De Britaine, *Humane Prudence*, 9th edn (London, 1702), p. 134; Josiah Woodward, *A Disswasive from Gaming* (London, 1718); John Brown, *On the Pursuit of False Pleasure, and the Mischiefs of Immoderate Gaming* (London, 1752); L.M. Stretch, *The Beauties of History; or, Pictures of Virtue and Vice, Drawn from Real Life*, 2 vols. (London, 1770), vol. I, p. 294; William Dodd, *Sermons to Young Men*, 3 vols. (London, 1771), vol. II, p. 262; William Penn, *The Selected Works of William Penn*, 3rd edn, 5 vols. (London, 1782), vol. IV, p. 32; John Fallowfield, *Miscellaneous Essays Divine and Moral* (Whitehaven, 1788), p. 35; Thomas Rennell, *The Consequences of the Vice of Gaming* (London, 1794); Anon, *Tales for Youth, or the High Road to Renown, Through the Paths of Pleasure* (London, 1797), p. 104.

[24] Jeremy Collier, *Essay Upon Gaming* (London, 1713), p. 36.

[25] *A Dissertation on the Pernicious Effects of Gaming* (Cambridge, 1783). Richard Hey was a well known essayist of the period and at the time a Fellow of Magdalene College Cambridge, see R.A. Anderson, rev. R. Mills, 'Hey, Richard', *Oxford Dictionary of National Biography*. The observation that gaming led to suicide was a common one: Addison (pseud.), *Interesting Anecdotes, Memoirs, Allegories, Essays, and Poetical Fragments*, 5 vols. (London, 1794), vol. V, p. 55; Anon, *An Essay on Gaming* (London, 1761), p. 2.

[26] *The London Magazine 1777* (London, 1777), p. 445 dated the beginning of the rumours as the winter of 1770. For examples of press speculation on the subject, see *Public Advertiser*, 12 March 1771; *Gazetteer and New Daily Advertiser*, 11 March 1771; *London Evening Post*, 12 March 1771.

[27] *The British Magazine and General Review* (London, 1772), vol. I, p. 258.

soon began to interest gamblers as well as gossips.[28] These wagers were depicted in cartoons. In one, d'Eon stands in front of a table containing a document on which is written 'A policy of 25 PCt On the Ch'D'Eon Man or Woman'; in another, headed 'A Deputation from Jonathan's[29] and the Freemasons',[30] stockbrokers hold up a piece of paper containing the words 'Petition from the Bulls and Bears in Change Alley'.[31] An advertisement in the *Westminster Gazette* gives some idea of the sort of wagers that were on offer:

> The gentleman declares d'Eon (alias the Chevalier d'Eon) a woman ... [T]his declaration he supports with a bet of any sum of money from one to five thousand guineas. Or, he proposes to anyone, who will deposit five hundred guineas in the hands of his banker, to pay ten thousand pounds if d'Eon proves herself either a man, hermaphrodite, or any other animal than a woman.[32]

The *London Magazine* described payments of ten to fifteen guineas in return for one hundred guineas should d'Eon prove to be female.[33] According to Horace Walpole, 'very great sums were wagered on the question'.[34] In 1771 it was estimated that £60,000 had been waged on d'Eon's gender.[35] By early 1777 that figure had risen to £120,000.[36] Given the size of individual wagers, the total sums involved may have been even higher.[37] John Wesket would later claim that the wagers led to the bankruptcy of a number of underwriters.[38]

[28] W.S. Lewis (ed.), Horace Walpole, *Horace Walpole's Correspondence*, 48 vols. (Oxford: Oxford University Press, 1939), vol. IV, pp. 493–4, 14 December 1770 from Madame du Deffand.

[29] Jonathan's Coffee House was a meeting place for brokers which became the London Stock Exchange: Ranald Michie, *The London Stock Exchange: A History* (Oxford: Oxford University Press, 2001), p. 20; Ellis Markman, *The Coffee House: A Cultural History* (London: Weidenfeld & Nicholson, 2004), pp. 166–84.

[30] D'Eon was a prominent Freemason. The Freemasons were becoming an influential body in England during the mid-eighteenth century, see Margaret Jacob, *Living the Enlightenment: Freemasonry and Politics in Eighteenth Century Europe* (New York: Oxford University Press, 1991), pp. 52–72.

[31] Change Alley was the location for Jonathan's Coffee House.

[32] *Westminster Gazette*, 10 September 1776. [33] *London Magazine*, p. 444.

[34] Walpole, *Correspondence*, vol. IV, p. 329: 'very great sums were wagered on the question'.

[35] *London Evening Post*, 14 May 1771. [36] *London Chronicle*, 5 May 1777.

[37] According to one report, £75,000 would remain in the country which would otherwise have been transmitted to Monsieur Panchard in Paris, see *Morning Chronicle*, 3 February 1778.

[38] John Wesket, *A Complete Digest of the Theory, Laws, and Practice of Insurance* (London, 1781), p. 584.

Whilst there is no evidence, despite speculation to the contrary, that d'Eon had a financial interest in the outcome of the wagers, others were less scrupulous in their actions. Anxious to secure the return of his grandfather's secret papers still in d'Eon's possession, Louis XVI sent Pierre-Augustin Caron de Beaumarchais to negotiate with d'Eon.[39] He was assisted by Charles-Claude Théveneau de Morande, a French journalist, blackmailer and spy living in London.[40] Armed with the knowledge that the King was prepared to allow d'Eon to live as a woman on his return to France, both men saw the opportunity to profit from the wagers.[41] Morande offered d'Eon large sums of money to cooperate.[42] Having refused, d'Eon challenged Morande to a duel. Morande's response was to conduct a campaign against d'Eon in the newspapers.[43] D'Eon retaliated with a libel action against one of the newspapers and Morande. The case was lost in November 1776,[44] after Lord Mansfield dismissed the action with an abrupt, 'Let the rule be discharged'. It nevertheless helped to bring matters to a head over the wagers. The *Westminster Gazette* reported that the quarrel 'is the only thing that could have made known for a certainty' the sex of d'Eon.[45] Those with policies started to become anxious.[46] Fearing that d'Eon was about to return to France with the question of his gender still to be settled, lawyers were engaged. At the same time, some of the brokers attempted to cut their losses by entering into agreements to pay up to 70 per cent of the value of the wagers in return for an agreement to have the wagers cancelled.[47]

Three actions to enforce the wagers were commenced in early 1777 and it was said that 'most first rate counsel are retained on one side

[39] Beaumarchais was perhaps best known as a playwright who wrote *The Barber of Seville* and *The Marriage of Figaro*.

[40] S. Burrows, 'Théveneau de Morande, Charles-Claude', *Oxford Dictionary of National Biography*; Simon Burrows, 'A Literary Low-Life Reassessed: Charles Théveneau de Morande in London, 1769–1791' (1998) 22 *Eighteenth Century Life* 76.

[41] Gary Kates, *Monsieur D'Eon is a Woman* (Baltimore: Johns Hopkins University Press, 2001), p. 231 suggests that the two men were involved in bets totalling £100,000, some of which was bet on behalf of Paris financiers.

[42] Kates, *Monsieur D'Eon*, p. 241. [43] For further examples, see *ibid.*, p. 243.

[44] *Public Ledger*, 25 November 1776; *Public Advertiser*, 29 November 1776.

[45] *Westminster Gazette*, 12 August 1776.

[46] For example, a letter signed a 'Policy Loser' appeared in the *Morning Post*, 27 August 1776: 'It is but common justice to the public so long imposed upon by this female adventurer that her dupes should give a summary of the most interesting particulars of her infamous transactions, by these means they would essentially serve the world at large, and particularly oblige your humble servant.'

[47] *London Chronicle*, 5 May 1777.

or the other'.[48] The first of the trio, the unreported *Hayes* v. *Jacques*, described by *The Gentleman's Magazine* of 1777 as 'the most extraordinary case that perhaps, ever happened in this or any other country',[49] came on before Lord Mansfield in July.[50] The court room was packed for the occasion with an audience eager to hear the salacious details and, no doubt, some who had entered into wagers.[51] Mr Jacques, a surgeon, had entered into an agreement with Mr Hayes, an under-writer. Like many wagers of the period, the contract resembled an ordinary insurance policy. Jacques had paid Hayes premiums of fifteen guineas for a number of years. Hayes agreed to match each premium with one hundred guineas should d'Eon prove to be a woman.

Francis Buller[52] claimed that he would prove that d'Eon was a woman, which the *Morning Chronicle* reported 'occasioned a good laugh'. D'Eon's former physician then swore that to his 'certain knowledge', d'Eon was a woman. D'Eon was particularly incensed in what he saw as breach of trust by his doctors.[53] It would be difficult to imagine anyone less impartial than the next witness, d'Eon's old enemy Morande. Morande may, at least to begin with, have genuinely believed that d'Eon was a woman.[54] He also stood to gain financially from the wagers,[55] and therefore it was in his interests to convince the jury that d'Eon was female. What his testimony lacked in veracity it made up for in impact:

> That she [d'Eon] had even proceeded so far as to display her bosom on the occasion . . . and had exhibited the contents of her female wardrobe, which consisted of sacques,[56] petticoats, and other habiliments calculated for feminine use . . . and then permitted him to have manual proof of her being in truth a woman.

48 *Ibid.* 49 *The Gentleman's Magazine* (London, 1777), p. 346.

50 *London Magazine*, pp. 378–9; *The Gentleman's Magazine* (London, 1777), pp. 346–7; *Morning Chronicle*, 2 July 1777.

51 *Morning Chronicle*, *ibid*., D'Eon himself observed that 'half the world' seemed to be there, see Kates, *Monsieur D'Eon*, p. 248.

52 The plaintiff was also represented by James Wallace who later became Attorney-General, see G.M. Ditchfield, 'Wallace, James', *Oxford Dictionary of National Biography*.

53 Gary Kates (ed.), Chevalier d'Eon, *The Maiden of Tonnerre: The Vicissitudes of the Chevalier and Chevaliére d'Eon de Beaumont* (Baltimore: Johns Hopkins University Press, 2001), p. 27. As d'Eon himself conceded, his physicians had kept their own counsel until they were subpoenaed as witnesses.

54 *Ibid*., p. 215. 55 For details of these potential gains, see *ibid*., pp. 230–4.

56 A sacque is a woman's hip-length jacket.

James Mansfield, counsel for Jacques and later Chief Justice of the Common Pleas,[57] began his argument for the defence by questioning whether this was a proper action to bring before that Court on the grounds that it 'was one of those gambling, indecent, and unnecessary cases that ought never to be permitted to come into a court of justice'. Instead of presenting witnesses prepared to deny that d'Eon was female, Mansfield argued that, because the plaintiff had greater knowledge that d'Eon was female, he was at an unfair advantage. This was a bold move given that outside a narrow range of situations, even Equity was not prepared to set aside bargained-for agreements on the grounds of unfair advantage. Perhaps predictably, the argument was not well received by Lord Mansfield, who responded with an anecdote told in a 'facetious and pointed manner' about two men who entered into a wager about the dimensions of a statue of Venus at which the Court once more descended into laughter.

When Lord Mansfield came to address the jury, he 'expressed his abhorrence of the transaction' and 'wished it had been in his power in concurrence with the jury, to have made both parties lose'. He was forced to concede all the same, that it was not an illegal contract, nor was it indecent. In consequence, it was binding. If the plaintiff could discharge the difficult burden of proving that d'Eon was a woman, then he could recover. Lord Mansfield seems to have accepted the evidence of the plaintiff's witnesses at face value, remarking that any other interpretation would mean that they had committed perjury. Unsurprisingly, given Lord Mansfield's direction, the jury took just two minutes to reach a verdict in favour of the plaintiff. Hayes recovered £700 by way of damages.

Da Costa v. *Jones* came on before Lord Mansfield and a jury in December 1777.[58] The declaration stated that, on the 4th of October 1771, in consideration that the plaintiff would pay 75 guineas, the defendant promised to pay £300 should d'Eon prove to be female. Morande was again the leading witness for the plaintiff. Buller also called three new witnesses.[59] The defence counsel, Bearcroft and Cowper, had

[57] M. Davis, 'Mansfield, James Sir', *Oxford Dictionary of National Biography*.

[58] The proceedings are reported in the *Daily Advertiser*, 17 December 1777; *Gazetteer*, 18 December 1777. Lord Mansfield's trial notes are reproduced in James Oldham, *The Mansfield Manuscripts and the Growth of English Law in the Eighteenth Century*, 2 vols. (Chapel Hill: University of North Carolina Press, 1992), vol. I, p. 534.

[59] In addition to de Morande and d'Eon's doctors, the court also heard testimony from Elizabeth Lautum who was the wife of d'Eon's landlord, friend and wine merchant. Mary Christie, a former servant of d'Eon, also gave evidence. The third witness, Elizabeth Coutans, is described in one report as a lady living in Tavistock Street. Lord Mansfield

not appeared in the earlier trial and they tried a different tactic. For the first time witnesses were called to testify that d'Eon was a man. The first witness, a naval Lieutenant, said that he had lodged with d'Eon and had 'seen him with his waistcoat and stockings off' and had 'always imagined him to be a man'. Two fellow Freemasons also testified that d'Eon would not have been admitted to the Lodge had he been female. But the reports of the case suggest that all three lacked the conviction of the plaintiff's witnesses who 'positively' asserted that d'Eon was female. Once more the jury found in the plaintiff's favour, awarding damages of £225. In *Roebuck* v. *Hammerton*, the third case on wagers, a verdict was again given for the plaintiff.[60] There matters rested until early the following year when both actions were heard before the court sitting in banc, giving Lord Mansfield an opportunity to examine the legal status of wagers.

The legal status of wagering contracts

Several old authorities suggested that wagers constituted valid contracts.[61] As Buller J. later observed, 'Till the case of *Da Costa* v. *Jones* the question was never agitated, or the mischievous consequences of sustaining such actions discussed'.[62] The matter was given greater impetus in the eighteenth century because many wagers took the form of insurance contracts. One critic of this type of wagering contract suggested that they were detrimental to the national interest:

> They render insurance suspected, foreigners apprehensive, the security of commerce precarious, contaminate probity, create ill will, as amongst other gamblers, produce lame ducks, and may in time introduce at Lloyds as well as Jonathan's such apposite and polite appellations as Bull and Bear.[63]

Statute intervened to prevent wagering by marine insurance.[64] A desire to prevent the work that he had done to develop the law of insurance

took the unusual step of striking her evidence out in his trial notes, see Oldham, *Mansfield Manuscripts*, vol. I, p. 534.

60 Oldham, *Mansfield Manuscripts*, vol. I, p. 539.

61 For older authority on the enforcement of a wager see: *Andrews* v. *Herne* (1661) 1 Lev 33; *Walcot* v. *Tappin* (1661) 1 Keb 56; A.W. Brian Simpson, *A History of the Common Law of Contract: The Rise of the Action of Assumpsit*, pbk edn (Oxford: Oxford University Press, 1987), pp. 534–5; J.H. Baker, *The Oxford History of the Law of England Volume VI 1483–1558* (Oxford: Oxford University Press, 2003), pp. 820, 859.

62 *Good* v. *Elliott* (1790) 3 TR 693, 697.

63 Wesket, *Digest*, p. lvi. For a similar view, see James Park, *System of the Law of Marine Insurance*, 2nd edn (London, 1790), p. 262.

64 (1746) 19 Geo 2 c. 37. On the application of the statute, see *Kent* v. *Bird* (1777) 2 Cowp 583; *Grant* v. *Parkinson* (1781) 3 Doug 16.

from unravelling perhaps lay behind the distinction drawn by Lord Mansfield between insurance and wagering:

> There are two sorts of policies of insurance; mercantile and gaming policies. The first sort are contracts of indemnity, and indemnity only . . . The second sort may be in the same form; but in them there is no contract of indemnity, because there is no interest on which a loss can accrue.[65]

As Lord Mansfield pointed out when applying the statute, 'the use of it [insurance] was perverted by its being turned into a wager'.[66] The same distinction can be found in another statute prohibiting wagering by insurance, which provided that 'no insurance shall be made . . . on the life or lives of any persons, or any other event or events whatsoever, wherein the person . . . shall have no interest whatsoever'.[67] *Roebuck* v. *Hammerton*[68] showed that some of the wagers on the gender of d'Eon could be caught under the statute.

The position of wagers entered into prior to the statutes or otherwise excluded was more complicated. In *Jones* v. *Randall*,[69] four years before *Da Costa* v. *Jones*,[70] Lord Mansfield had demonstrated that he was prepared to adopt a flexible view when it came to the validity of wagering contracts:

> But it is argued, and rightly, that notwithstanding it is not prohibited by any positive law, nor adjudged illegal by any precedents, yet it may be decided to be so upon principles; and the law of England would be a strange science indeed if it were decided on precedents only . . . The question then is, whether this wager is against principles? If it be contrary to any, it must be contrary either to principles of morality, for the law of England prohibits every thing which is *contra bonos mores*; or it must be against principles of sound policy; for many contracts which are not against morality, are still void as being against the maxims of sound policy.[71]

The wager in *Jones* v. *Randall* concerned the outcome of litigation in which plaintiff and defendant were also involved. It was nevertheless held to be valid. Lord Mansfield's admission during the course of argument in *Da Costa* v. *Jones* that, 'Never was a question more doubtful how it would be decided till it was actually determined',[72] showed that by

65 *Lowry* v. *Bourdieu* (1780) 2 Doug 468, 470; *Kent* v. *Bird* (1777) 2 Cowp 583, 585.
66 *Kent* v. *Bird* (1777) 2 Cowp 583, 585. 67 (1774) 14 Geo III c. 48.
68 (1778) 2 Cowp 737. 69 (1774) 1 Cowp 37. 70 (1778) 2 Cowp 729.
71 (1774) 1 Cowp 37, 39. 72 (1778) 2 Cowp 729, 733.

resorting to principle rather than precedent, the outcome of litigation could sometimes be hard to predict. But the fact that Lord Mansfield was so open about the importance of public policy and morality in wagering cases is further evidence that wagering contracts, even in the form of insurance contracts, were seen as a class apart from ordinary commercial contracts, and special considerations needed to be applied to their enforcement. Lord Mansfield had already made clear during the trial of *Da Costa* v. *Jones* that he was unhappy about these wagers coming before the Courts,[73] but he once more reiterated that, 'Indifferent wagers upon indifferent matters, without interest to either of the parties, are certainly allowed by the law of this country, in so far as they have not been restrained by particular Acts of Parliament'.[74]

The wager in *Da Costa* v. *Jones* was not covered by statute and the defendant was required to demonstrate that the wager ought not to be enforced on other grounds. Bearcroft and Cowper put forward two main arguments. The first was that such a wager should be struck down because it tended to introduce indecent evidence. Lord Mansfield rejected this submission, 'For indecency of the evidence is no objection to its being received, where it is necessary to the decision of a civil or criminal right'.[75] A second argument, that the wager 'affects the peace and comfort of a third person, and, as such the peace of society', was more favourably received:

> Here is a person who appears to all the world to be a man; is stated upon the record to be 'Monsieur Le Chevalier D'Eon'; has acted in that character in a variety of capacities; and has his reasons and advantages in so appearing. Shall two indifferent people, by a wager between themselves, injure him so, as to try in an action upon that wager, whether ... he is a cheat and impostor; or, shew that he is a woman, and be allowed to subpoena all his intimate friends, and confidential attendants, to give evidence that will expose him all over Europe? It is monstrous to state. It is a disgrace to judicature.[76]

A wager about a third person could be perfectly valid at Common law. In *Earl of March* v. *Pigott*,[77] two young men entered into a wager about whose father would live longest. Such a wager, being 'no reflection or injury'[78] to the third party, was upheld. *Da Costa* v. *Jones* was different. Because the wager was 'manifestly a gross injury to a third person'[79] it

[73] *Daily Advertiser*, 17 December 1777. [74] (1778) 2 Cowp 729, 734. [75] *Ibid.*
[76] *Ibid.*, pp. 735–6. [77] (1771) 5 Burr 2802. [78] (1778) 2 Cowp 729, 736.
[79] *Ibid.*, p. 736.

could not be enforced. The wager in *Earl of March* v. *Pigott* brought no discredit on either of the fathers.

Da Costa v. *Jones* was not the only wager to be declared invalid. A wager on the outcome of an election[80] between two voters was set aside because:

> One of the principal foundations of this constitution depends on the proper exercise of this franchise, that the election of members of Parliament should be free, and particularly that every voter should be free from pecuniary influence in giving his vote.[81]

One of the ironies of *Da Costa* v. *Jones* was that, despite Lord Mansfield's frequently expressed dislike of wagers, the decision also offered some comfort for those wanting to enforce wagers because Lord Mansfield re-stated the rule that wagers were *prima facie* enforceable. To be invalid, a wager needed to be contrary to statute, public policy or morality.

The statutory restrictions on wagering were something of a hotchpotch. In addition to insurance cases, an earlier statute had outlawed wagers on the War of Spanish Succession.[82] The impact of the statutes on wagering in practice is difficult to assess. There was certainly a perception that statutory regulation on gaming was widely flouted.[83] As was pointed out in *Roebuck* v. *Hammerton*,[84] the statutes were only designed to stop wagering in the form of insurance. The Common law was more difficult to predict. In *Atherfold* v. *Beard*,[85] Ashhurst J. was candid, 'In my opinion the Courts have gone far enough in encouraging impertinent wagers. Perhaps it would have been better for the public, if the Courts had originally determined that no action to enforce the payment of wagers should be permitted.'[86] A wager speculating on the amount to be collected though duties on hops was said to be 'against sound policy'.[87] Buller J. went even further, 'I do not find that it has ever been established as a position of law, that a wager between two persons, not interested in the subject-matter, is legal'.[88]

[80] There is a long history of gambling on the outcomes of elections, see Graeme Orr, 'Betting on Elections: Its History, Law and Risks' (2014) 42 *Federal Law Review* (forthcoming).

[81] *Allen* v. *Hearn* (1785) 1 TR 56, 59. [82] (1708) 7 Ann c. 16.

[83] Country Justice of the Peace, *Serious thoughts in regard to the publick disorders, with several proposals for remedying the same* (London, 1750), p. 10; Thomas Erskine, *Reflections on Gaming, Annuities and Usurious Contracts* (London, 1776), pp. 10–11.

[84] (1778) 2 Cowp 737. [85] (1788) 2 TR 610. [86] *Ibid.*, p. 615. [87] *Ibid.*, p. 615.

[88] *Ibid.*, p. 616.

Good v. *Elliott*[89] involved a wager on whether a third party had bought a wagon. Grose J. pointed out that were it the case that all wagers were void, there would have been no need for 'the elaborate opinion delivered by Lord Mansfield'[90] in *Da Costa* v. *Jones*. In his opinion, 'We may take the rule to be that those wagers are bad, which by injuring a third person disturb the peace of society, or which militate against the morality or sound policy of the kingdom'.[91] The way in which Grose J. justified *Da Costa* v. *Jones* was perhaps narrower than Lord Mansfield intended. The wager was bad not merely because it injured a third person, but also because the injury to d'Eon disturbed the peace of society.[92] He also stressed that the recent statute was not designed to invalidate all wagers, but only those in the form of insurance.[93] Ashhurst J. and Lord Kenyon delivered broadly similar opinions. It is implicit in both judgments that the stress on an injury to a third party was designed to catch those wagers which damaged the reputation of the third party.[94] Buller J. favoured a more radical solution. He argued that the wager fell within the third party exception, which he took to mean that a wager about a third party or his property was void.[95] He also suggested that all wagers should be outlawed.[96] The statute was also said to prohibit all wagers in which the parties had no interest.[97] Buller J. was not the only late eighteenth century judge who was antagonistic towards wagering contracts.[98] Writing in the early nineteenth century, Joseph Chitty detected judicial hostility towards wagers:

> And some judges at Nisi Prius have exercised a very extended discretion, in refusing to try actions on wagers, which, although not strictly illegal, have raised questions in which the parties have no interest, and have been of trifling, ridiculous, or contemptible nature.[99]

Chitty provided a list of authorities to back up his claim that, more often than not, judges were striking down wagers.[100] Oliphant disagreed. In his

[89] (1790) 3 TR 693. [90] *Ibid.*, p. 694. [91] *Ibid.*, p. 695.

[92] *Ibid.* There is some ambiguity on this point in *Da Costa* v. *Jones*, see (1778) 2 Cowp 729, 735.

[93] (1790) 3 TR 693, 696.

[94] *Ibid.*, pp. 703 (Ashhurst J.), 704 (Lord Kenyon). Lord Kenyon's relatively liberal line is slightly surprising given his well-known dislike of gaming, see G.T. Kenyon, *The Life of Lloyd, First Lord Kenyon: Lord Chief Justice of England* (London: Longmans, 1873), pp. 356–7.

[95] (1790) 3 TR 693, 699–700. [96] *Ibid.*, p. 697. [97] *Ibid.*, p. 702.

[98] *Brown* v. *Leeson* (1792) 2 H Bla 43, 46 (Lord Loughborough). Park, *Insurance*, p. 260 also thought that the courts were hostile towards wagers.

[99] Chitty, *Contracts*, pp. 155–6.

[100] *Shirley* v. *Sankey* (1800) 2 B & P 130; *Hartley* v. *Rice* (1808) 10 East 22; *Henkin* v. *Guerss* (1810) 12 East 247.

opinion, nineteenth century judges 'began to look more favourably on sporting transaction'.[101] The decision closest to *Da Costa* v. *Jones* concerns another remarkable figure, the prophetess Joanna Southcott.[102] A wager that she would shortly give birth to a boy was held invalid.[103] Judges had a considerable amount of discretion when it came to striking down wagers, but the rule remained that a wager was valid unless it fell under a statute or one of the Common law exceptions.[104] But the demise of wagering contracts was not far off. In 1845, statute intervened once more, but unlike earlier provisions, it provided an almost total prohibition on wagering contracts:

> All contracts or agreements whether by parole or in writing by way of gaming or wagering shall be null and void; and that no suit shall be brought or maintained in any court of Law or Equity for recovering any sum of money or valuable thing alleged to be won upon any wager.[105]

Unsurprisingly the legislation did not put a stop to gaming.[106] So-called 'p.p.i. policies' of insurance entered into by commercial parties were caught by the legislation, but continued to be honoured even though they were not strictly legally enforceable.[107] Some of the frustration that the Common law judges must have felt was expressed by Lord Campbell in an Indian appeal a few years later when he said, 'I look with concern and almost with shame, on the subterfuges and contrivances and evasions to which the Judges in England long resorted ... and I rejoice that it is at last constitutionally abrogated by the Legislature'.[108] Lord Campbell was discussing wagers, but his remarks had wider resonance by the nineteenth century.

[101] George Oliphant, *The Law Concerning Horses, Racing, Wager and Gaming* (London: S. Sweet, 1847), p. 188.

[102] S. Bowerbank, 'Southcott, Joanna', *Oxford Dictionary of National Biography*. In 1814 a number of her followers believed that she was pregnant with the new Messiah. She was nearly sixty-five at the time.

[103] *Ditchburn* v. *Goldsmith* (1815) 4 Camp 152.

[104] *Hussey* v. *Crickitt* (1811) 3 Camp 168, 173 (Heath J.).

[105] (1845) 8 & 9 Vict c. 109. For the application of the statute, see Pollock, *Contract*, pp. 241–2.

[106] David Miers, *Regulating Commercial Gambling* (Oxford: Oxford University Press, 2004), pp. 61–87; Ross McKibbin, 'Working-Class Gambling in Britain 1880–1939' (1979) 82 *Past and Present* 147.

[107] Michael Lobban, 'Commercial Law', in William Cornish, Stuart Anderson, Raymond Cocks, Michael Lobban, Patrick Polden and Keith Smith, *The Oxford History of the Laws of England Volume XII 1820–1914: Private Law* (Oxford: Oxford University Press, 2010), p. 680.

[108] *Ramloll Thackoorseydass* v. *Soojumnull Dhondmull* (1848) 6 Moo PC 300, 310.

Public policy, judges and the legislature

In *Jones* v. *Randall*, Lord Mansfield said that he was prepared to set aside a contract which was 'against the maxims of sound policy'.[109] His remarks suggest that eighteenth century judges wielded a broad discretion when it came to vitiating contracts on the grounds of public policy. Lord Mansfield had certainly recognised the role of public policy on other occasions,[110] but his statement should also be viewed in the context in which it was made. Wagering transactions were at best of doubtful social utility and attracted a great deal of criticism. Other judges were quite prepared to argue that wagers should be outlawed altogether. Even if the courts had the power to strike down agreements on the explicit basis of public policy, it was a power that was used sparingly. Instead of an overarching public policy doctrine, public policy was a doctrine that was largely confined to specific types of transaction, even in the eighteenth century. Even those categories which look potentially wide-ranging, such as contracts contrary to morals and good manners, turn out to be fairly self-contained. As Pollock pointed out, 'sexual immorality ... is the only or almost only kind of immorality [of] which the common law takes notice as such'.[111] Just as, if not more, important was the way in which public policy existed in the shadows. Used in this way, it had less to do with setting aside certain types of transaction than promoting certain outcomes. By its nature this is difficult to quantify, but the repeated desire to ensure that the law reflected the needs of commerce was one obvious example. Nor need the application of legal doctrine be divorced from public policy. It is more probable than not that *Stilk* v. *Myrick*[112] was motivated by public policy concerns, whether these were expressly articulated as in one report, or hidden beneath the skirts of the doctrine of consideration as in another.

The role of public policy was both less intrusive and less widespread in the eighteenth century than sometimes supposed. But by the nineteenth century there was undoubtedly a change in tone. The role of public policy in judging was beginning to be questioned:

> I am not much disposed to yield to the arguments of public policy: I think the courts of Westminster-Hall ... have gone much further than they

109 (1774) 1 Cowp 37, 39. 110 Waddams, *Principle and Policy*, pp. 148–50.

111 Pollock, *Contract*, p. 243. The authorities are concerned with so-called co-habitation agreements: *Walker* v. *Perkins* (1764) 3 Burr 1568.

112 (1809) 1 Esp 129, 2 Camp 317.

> were warranted in going into questions of policy: they have taken on themselves, sometimes, to decide doubtful questions of policy and they are always in danger of so doing, because courts of law look only at the particular case, and have not the means of bringing before them all those considerations which ought to enter into the judgment of those who decide on questions of policy.[113]
>
> I for one, protest as my Lord has done, against arguing too strongly upon public policy – it is a very unruly horse, and when once you get astride it you never know where it will carry you. It may lead you from the sound law. It is never argued at all but when other points fail.[114]

The first passage is taken from the judgment of Best C.J. A mere two years later the same judge showed that he continued to recognise the value of public policy. It was something that could be taken into consideration, 'if there be any doubts what is the law, judges solve such doubts by considering what will be the good or bad effects of their decision'.[115] Alternatively public policy was sometimes used as a means of justifying a long held custom.[116] The extent to which judges had 'taken it on themselves, sometimes, to decide doubtful questions of policy' should not be overstated, at least in the context of contract actions. But clearly it was not just legal writers who were anxious about the role of public policy. The subject was debated again in *Egerton* v. *Brownlow*,[117] which although not a contract case, was described by Pollock as 'the leading modern authority on "public policy"'.[118] There was a marked difference of emphasis between those who heard the case. Parke B. stated that:

> It is the province of the judge to expound the law only; the written from the statutes, the unwritten or common law from the decisions of our predecessors and of our existing courts, from text writers of acknowledged authority, and upon principles to be clearly deduced from them by sound reason and just inference; not to speculate upon what is best, in his opinion for the advance of the community.[119]

113 *Richardson* v. *Mellish* (1824) 2 Bing 229, 242 (Best C.J.).

114 (1824) 2 Bing 229, 252 (Burrough J.).

115 *Fletcher* v. *Lord Sondes* (1826) 3 Bing 501, 590 per Best C.J.

116 *Gifford* v. *Lord Yarborough* (1828) 5 Bing 163, 166.

117 (1853) 4 HLC 1; Percy Winfield, 'Public Policy and the English Common Law' (1928–1929) 42 *Harvard Law Review* 76, 88–90; Dennis Lloyd, *Public Policy: A Comparative Study in English and French Law* (London: Athlone Press, 1953), pp. 112–13.

118 Pollock, *Contract*, p. 253.

119 (1853) 4 HLC 1, 123. 4 HLC 1, 100, Wightman J. and Earle J. both concurred.

Alderson B. agreed, describing public policy as the 'prevailing opinion, from time to time, of wise men' it was he said that whilst it was an 'excellent principle, no doubt, for legislators to adopt' it was 'a most dangerous one for Judges'.[120] Pollock C.B. was less hostile towards public policy. He thought it was necessary to consider what he called 'public welfare' in 'a new and unprecedented case'.[121] Lord Lyndhurst responded to those who were sceptical about public policy by referring to the doctrine of restraint of trade. He suggested that those who argued that the doctrine was based on a principle of law missed the point. Its origins were in public policy, or as he added rhetorically, 'Does any man doubt that it was founded upon public policy?'[122]

The growing importance of the legislature perhaps made it less necessary for the courts to intervene in contract on the grounds of public policy. The Gaming Act is one good example. If public policy had not entirely disappeared, then it was left rather marginalised. Sometimes this process was very conscious, as in the way in which Pollock progressively downgraded *Egerton* v. *Brownlow* in successive editions of his treatise.[123] But it was not just public policy in a broad general sense which began to be eroded. Parke B., whilst cautious about the role of public policy, conceded that it continued to have a role in those contracts where one party was seeking to restrict the economic activities of another.[124] Even here the role of public policy began to change.

Restraint of trade was only established in its modern form during the early part of the eighteenth century.[125] Until the 1830s, judges were quite comfortable with emphasising public policy. Best C.J. even claimed that 'the first object of the law is to promote the public interest; the second to preserve the rights of individuals'.[126] In *Horner* v. *Graves*,[127] Tindal C.J. was still discussing public interest, but it was now seen as relevant to whether or not the restraint was reasonable and not whether the agreement was unenforceable outright:

> And we do not see how a better test can be applied to the question whether reasonable or not, than by considering whether the restraint is such only as to afford a fair protection to the interests of the party in

[120] *Ibid.*, p. 106. [121] *Ibid.*, p. 149. [122] *Ibid.*, p. 240.
[123] Waddams, *Principle and Policy*, p. 157. [124] (1853) 4 HLC 1, 122–4.
[125] J.D. Heydon, *The Restraint of Trade Doctrine*, 3rd edn (Sydney: Butterworths, 2008), pp. 1–32; *Mitchell* v. *Reynolds* (1711) 1 P Wms 181, Fort 295, 10 Mod 130. Though in one form or another restraint of trade was much older, see M.J. Trebilcock, *The Common Law of Restraint of Trade* (Toronto: Carswell, 1986), pp. 3–10.
[126] *Homer* v. *Ashford* (1825) 3 Bing 322. [127] (1831) 7 Bing 735.

> favour of whom it is given, and not so large as to interfere with the interests of the public. Whatever restraint is larger than the necessary protection of the party, can be of no benefit to either, it can only be oppressive; and if oppressive, it is, in the eye of the law, unreasonable. Whatever is injurious to the interests of the public is void, on the grounds of public policy.[128]

Only six years later in *Hitchcock* v. *Coker*,[129] Denman C.J. was much more reticent about using the public interest in the context of a restraint of trade, warning that, 'great difficulty may attend the application of that test from the variety of opinions that may exist on the question of interferences with the public interest which the law ought to permit'.[130] Instead he preferred to consider whether the agreement was necessary for the protection of the promisee. Public policy continued to be mentioned in restraint of trade cases until the 1840s,[131] but perhaps inevitably, as the reasonableness of the restraint came to be seen as the critical factor, the courts began to behave as though they could operate some kind of objective test divorced from public policy. This new position comes across most vividly in Pollock's textbook, 'at all events the restriction must in the particular case be reasonable, and this is a question not of fact but of law'.[132] As if to stress his argument, the factors relevant to reasonableness, namely, the extent of the restriction in space and time and the nature of the trade, were set out in a table.[133]

Writing in the 1870s, Frederick Pollock observed somewhat wistfully in regard to public policy that, 'The general tendency of modern ideas is no doubt against the continuation of such a jurisdiction. On the other hand there is a good deal of modern and even recent authority which makes it difficult to deny its continued existence.'[134] William Anson agreed before adding that the courts 'have tended to limit the sphere' within which public policy was exercised.[135] The cases on restraint of trade are less a demonstration of judicial antagonism to public policy as such, than a belief that its boundaries of the doctrine should be clearly defined. This increasingly formalistic type of reasoning was not confined to public policy. It was very evident elsewhere, as questions which in the past fell to the jury began to be better defined. It also fitted closely within the agenda of legal writers like Pollock who advocated coherence and order. But there was no golden age of judges imposing public policy on

[128] *Ibid.*, p. 743. [129] (1837) 6 Ad & El 438. [130] *Ibid.*, p. 445.
[131] *Sainter* v. *Ferguson* (1849) 7 CB 716, 729 (Cresswell J.), 730 (Vaughan Williams J.).
[132] Pollock, *Contract*, p. 289. [133] *Ibid.*, pp. 290–1. [134] *Ibid.*, p. 251.
[135] Anson, *Contract*, p. 175.

contracting parties any more than there was a dark age where public policy was entirely abandoned. The relationship between policy and other elements of reasoning like principles, 'are complex, and they run in both directions'.[136] Attempts to isolate public policy in judicial decision-making in any era are always going to come to grief one way or another,[137] or worse still, to collapse into an argument that all law is policy.[138] In one of its guises, public policy might have been increasingly marginalised, in another it was increasingly felt, and that was through the medium of legislation.

136 Waddams, *Principle and Policy*, p. 170. This is not to say that decision-making is restricted to policy and principles. Other values such as pragmatism may also play a role.

137 For a recent discussion in the context of a critique of Ronald Dworkin, see E.W. Thomas, *The Judicial Process* (Cambridge: Cambridge University Press, 2005), pp. 184–216.

138 Which is what Legal Realists and the Critical Legal Studies movement would have us believe.

11

Contract law and statute law

Hale's[1] and Blackstone's[2] accounts of statute law were brief if not actually hostile.[3] They could afford to be succinct when the volume of legislation remained relatively slight.[4] Unsurprisingly, statutes barely feature in most histories of the law of contract before 1800.[5] Some important statutes relating to contract were passed nevertheless. Rather than a sudden explosion of statutes in the nineteenth century, the change to more statutory involvement in contracting was gradual. Some, such as the Promissory Notes Act of 1704, were designed to facilitate contracting. Others aimed to prohibit certain types of contract. In the modern law the process of contracting is highly regulated.[6] Yet the principle is nothing new. The Statute of Frauds[7] is the most obvious example. The regulations imposed on pawnbrokers throw some light on the difficulties of statutory regulation and the problems of balancing protection for borrowers with the demands of lenders.

By the late eighteenth century Jeremy Bentham and others began to put the case for codification. Despite much discussion, the kind of large scale codification which began to be seen on the Continent failed to take

[1] Charles Gray (ed.), Matthew Hale, *The History of the Common Law of England* (Chicago: University of Chicago Press, 1971), pp. 3–15.

[2] William Blackstone, *Commentaries on the Laws of England*, 4 vols. (Oxford, 1765), vol. I, p. 89; William Blackstone, *Commentaries on the Laws of England*, 4 vols. (Oxford, 1768), vol. III, p. 328.

[3] H.G. Hanbury, 'Blackstone in Retrospect' (1950) 66 *Law Quarterly Review* 318, 322–3.

[4] Sheila Lambert, *Bills and Acts: Legislative Procedure in Eighteenth Century England* (Cambridge: Cambridge University Press, 1971), p. 52.

[5] P.S. Atiyah, *The Rise and Fall of Freedom of Contract* (Oxford: Oxford University Press, 1979), pp. 91–5.

[6] Modern illustrations include the Consumer Credit Act 1974, the Unfair Contract Terms Act 1977 and the Unfair Terms in Consumer Contract Regulations 1999.

[7] (1677) 29 Car II c. 3. For detailed discussion, see A.W. Brian Simpson, *A History of the Common Law of Contract: The Rise of the Action of Assumpsit*, pbk edn (Oxford: Oxford University Press, 1987), pp. 599–620.

hold. There was to be no contract code in England. In India, the most prized colony of the British Empire, a contract code was enacted. A very different set of circumstances were present here, but the process, which involved leading English lawyers, sheds some light on mid-nineteenth century thinking about contract doctrine and the role of Will Theory as well as codification.

Pawnbroking and statutory regulation

In an action of slander brought by a pawnbroker, Holt C.J. admitted that, 'The trade of a broker is an honest lawful trade, though it lies under suspicions'.[8] One late seventeenth century writer was more brutal:

> An unconscionable pawn-broker, I say, is Pluto's Factor, Old Nick's Warehouse-keeper, and English Jew that lives and grows fat on Fraud and Oppression, as Toads on Filth and Venome; whose Practice out-vies Usury, as much as Incest simple Fornication; and to call him a Tradesman, must be by the same Figure that Pickpockets stile their Legerdemain an Art and Mystery. His Shop, like Hellgates, is always open, where he sits at the Receipt of Custom, like Cacus in his Den, ready to devour.[9]

In addition to their supposed immorality,[10] pawnbrokers were variously accused of dealing in stolen goods,[11] deliberately understating the value of pawned goods,[12] wearing clothes that were pledged,[13] selling off pledges before they could be redeemed,[14] and charging above the permitted rate of interest.[15]

[8] *Anon* (1699) 12 Mod 344.

[9] Anon, *Four for a Penny: Or, Poor Robin's Character of an Unconscionable Pawn-broker* (London, 1678), p. 3. For a discussion of the public perceptions of pawnbrokers, see Alannah Tomkins, *The Experience of Urban Poverty* (Manchester: Manchester University Press, 2006), pp. 205–10.

[10] William Hogarth's portrayal of a wealthy pawnbroker benefiting from the gin craze remains a powerful image: Mark Hallett and Christine Riding, *Hogarth* (London: Tate, 2006), pp. 190–1.

[11] This was a common complaint: Anon, *Pawnbrokers Detected and Dissected* (London, 1809), p. 4.

[12] Anon, *The Devil and Broker or a character of a Pawnbroker in a Merry Dialogue* (London, 1677), p. 2; Peeping Tim (pseud.), *The Honest London Spy* (Dublin, 1793), pp. 72–3.

[13] Humphrey Humdrum (pseud.), *Mother Midnight's Comical Book* (London, 1753), p. 32.

[14] *Ibid.*

[15] Anon, *Pawnbrokers Detected*, p. 4. Interest rates were limited by the usury laws. For examples of pawnbroking and usury, see *R* v. *Walker* (1669) 2 Keb 531; *Bosanquet* v. *Earl of Westmoreland* (1738) West Temp Hard 598.

By the early eighteenth century the nature of money lending was changing. 'Specialised and capital-intensive'[16] commercial pawnbrokers spread from London to the port cities and finally to other urban centres.[17] Although it was said that this sort of lending 'mainly torments the poor',[18] for those whose earnings remained low, whose employment was often seasonal and were at the mercy of local employment markets and economic instability,[19] pawnbrokers provided a vital source of credit when times were hard.

Regulation of money lending has a long history. The usury laws[20] were widely flouted by pawnbrokers.[21] An excess of lawful interest could be recovered using money had and received, though the trouble and expense must have made it a rarity.[22] Specific legislation targeted at pawnbrokers is not as old but still venerable. An Act of 1603[23] responded to the perception that pawnbrokers were receivers of stolen property. More comprehensive legislation began to appear from 1757. As a result, pawnbrokers were required to keep proper records of goods received as pawn and sums advanced on the pledge.[24] Where the security was realised and the pledge was sold for a sum of more than £2, the details of the sale had to be recorded.[25] It was also made easier for the pledgor to recover compensation if the pledge was damaged 'through the default, neglect or wilful misbehaviour' by simply appearing before a Justice of the Peace.[26] The Act

[16] Beverly Lemire, 'From Petty Pawns and Informal Lending: Gender and the Transformation of Small Scale Credit in England, circa 1600–1800', in Kristine Bruland and Patrick O'Brien (eds.), *From Family Firms to Corporate Capitalism: Essays in Business and Industrial History in Honour of Peter Mathias* (Oxford: Oxford University Press, 1998), p. 129. A fair amount of capital was needed to set up in business: Peter Earle, *The Making of the English Middle Class* (London: Methuen, 1989), p. 107.

[17] Kenneth Hudson, *Pawnbroking: An Aspect of British Social History* (London: The Bodley Head, 1982), p. 31.

[18] Anon, *Four For a Penny*, p. 4.

[19] Keith Wrightson, *Earthly Necessities* (London: Penguin, 2002), pp. 305–20.

[20] (1713) 12 Ann st 2 c. 16 which set lawful interest at 5 per cent.

[21] Some of whom were charging 30 per cent per annum or more, Anon, *An Apology*, p. 15; Anon, *A Plain Answer to a Late Pamphlet, intitled, the Business of Pawnbroking Stated* (London, 1745), p. 18.

[22] Those who had been driven to pawn their goods were unlikely to have the resources to pursue money had and received. For a famous example, see *Astley* v. *Reynolds* (1731) 2 Stra 915. In pawnbroking terms the loan was a large one for £20, which suggests that the plate was worth considerably more.

[23] (1603) 1 Jac I c. 21. [24] *Ibid.*, s. 4. [25] *Ibid.*, s. 12.

[26] *Ibid.*, s. 4. This was not a lower standard than at Common law: *Syred* v. *Carruthers* (1858) El, Bl & El 469.

also tried to discourage pawning of stolen goods or clothes that were deposited for washing or mending by imposing criminal sanctions on the pledgor.[27]

A Bill of 1745, heavily promoted by the pawnbroking interest, proposed the introduction of a sliding scale of permitted charges. A similar scheme became law in 1784.[28] Loans of less than £10 were taken outside the usury laws.[29] Rates were calculated by the number of calendar months that the pledge remained in pawn and the size of the loan, up to a maximum of £10, above which the normal usury laws applied.[30] A pawnbroker was permitted up to half a penny on the smallest loans, defined as 2s 6d or less.[31] This amounted to 20 per cent per annum. The percentage allowed on larger loans was lower.[32] Given the small size of the average loan,[33] this change must have benefited most pawnbrokers. A system of licensing which came into existence the following year probably favoured the larger pawnbrokers at the expense of their smaller rivals, for whom the annual fee was more of a burden.[34]

An Act of 1800[35] set a new standard in the statutory regulation of money lending. Lord Cottenham claimed that the legislation benefited borrowers.[36] One leading pawnbroker, Alfred Hardaker, agreed:

> The regulations were as stringent and drastic as they could well be made, the Act itself being crowded with pains, penalties, and pitfalls, that one is lost in amazement that so numerous a body of intelligent tradesmen, could, for nearly three quarters of a century, endure its intolerable thraldom.[37]

[27] *Ibid.*, s. 6. [28] (1784) 24 Geo III c. 42. [29] *Ibid.*, s. 1. [30] *Ibid.*, s. 1.
[31] *Ibid.*, s. 1. [32] *Ibid.*, s. 1.
[33] Alanna Tomkins, 'Pawnbroking and Survival Strategies of the Urban Poor in 1770s York', in Steven King and Alanna Tomkins (eds.), *The Poor in England 1700–1850* (Manchester: Manchester University Press, 2003), p. 180. This remained the case in the nineteenth century. In his evidence to the Select Committee, *Report from the Select Committee on Pawnbrokers; together with the proceedings of the committee, minutes of evidence, and appendix*, (1870) [377] PP 391 vol. VIII q. 129, Alfred Hardaker estimated that more than half the annual pledges in Liverpool at the time were for 2s or less.
[34] (1785) 25 Geo III c. 47. The cost of a licence in London was £10. For the rest of the country a fee of £5 was payable. The licence fees were raised by (1815) 55 Geo III c. 184 to £15 in London and £7 10s for the rest of the country.
[35] (1800) 39 & 40 Geo III c. 99. [36] *Fitch* v. *Rochfort* (1849) 1 Hall & Twells 255, 262.
[37] Alfred Hardaker, *A Brief History of Pawnbroking* (London: Jackson, Ruston & Keeson, 1892), p. 41.

He went on to note the 'petty detail', 'prolixity and exactitude' of the legislation.[38] Aspects of the Act were certainly burdensome.[39] Prescriptive and detailed rules about record keeping and the issuing of pawn tickets were particularly arduous.[40] The obligation to record the pledgor's name and address put the pawnbroker to further trouble without reducing the trade in stolen goods.[41] Non-compliance could result in a fine of up to £10. Prosecutions depended on informers, which until the rules were changed, were entitled to half of the fine, thereby giving birth to a group of professional informers reporting trivial breaches.[42]

There was also some truth in Hardaker's assertion that the 'conditions under which Pawnbrokers carried on business ... were uncertain, unsafe and almost intolerable'.[43] Pawnbrokers stood accused of undervaluing pledges,[44] but were also the target of swindlers. 'Duffers' made a living by inflating the value of pledges.[45] If the pledge had been stolen, pawnbrokers were vulnerable to a claim from the genuine owner.[46] The procedures for asserting ownership were also relaxed. It was no longer necessary to resort to the slow and expensive action of trover. The owner simply needed to swear an oath of ownership before a magistrate.[47] Pawnbrokers could take some consolation from the fact that by the mid-nineteenth century, they were less vulnerable to a claim by a purchaser when an unredeemed but stolen pledge

[38] For an overview of this legislation, see C.G. Addison, *A Treatise on the Law of Contracts and Rights and Liabilities Ex-Contractu*, 2nd edn, 2 vols. (London: W. Benning, 1849), vol. I, pp. 382–7.

[39] Especially when combined with other legislative restrictions, for example (1846) 9 & 10 Vict c. 98, which limited opening hours of pawn shops.

[40] (1800) 39 & 40 Geo III c. 99 s. 6. Under the legislation pawnbrokers were unable to charge for a ticket where the sum lent was less than 5s. After 1860, ½d could be charged: Pawnbrokers Act (1860) 23 & 24 Vict c. 21 s. 1.

[41] Many honest customers may have given a false name and address because of the stigma attached to pawning, see *Select Committee on Pawnbrokers*, q. 76, 80, 81.

[42] Michael Lobban, 'Commercial Law', in William Cornish, Stuart Anderson, Raymond Cocks, Michael Lobban, Patrick Polden and Keith Smith, *The Oxford History of the Laws of England, Vol. XII 1820–1914: Private Law* (Oxford: Oxford University Press, 2010), p. 855.

[43] Hardaker, *Pawnbroking*, p. 57.

[44] Rosemary O'Day and David Englander (eds.), Henry Mayhew, *London Labour and London Poor* (London: Wordsworth Classics, 2008), p. 381, evidence from a coal-whipper. Coal-whippers were employed to unload coal from ships.

[45] Melanie Tebbutt, *Making Ends Meet: pawnbroking and working-class credit* (London: Methuen, 1984), pp. 83–7.

[46] Lobban, 'Commercial Law', pp. 853, 857.

[47] (1800) 39 & 40 Geo III c. 99 s. 13.

was sold.[48] Nor when a pledge was handed over on presentation of a ticket were pawnbrokers liable to the original owner.[49] A pawnbroker was even protected when the ticket had been lost or stolen[50] – a significant concession when tickets could be bought and sold and may have passed through many hands.[51] A true holder did not lose out either. When he wished to recover his goods he was entitled to ask the pawnbroker for a duplicate ticket and satisfy a magistrate that he was the owner of the pledge.[52]

Pawnbrokers were not averse to a spot of sharp practice themselves. One popular ruse was to make out tickets inflating the value of the pledge. These were then sold or dropped by an agent. When the finder came to redeem the item, thinking that they had secured a bargain, the actual cost of redemption was higher than the pledge was worth.[53] Pledges were often redeemed quite quickly.[54] It was common for the same item to be pledged many times over.[55] When the pledge was not redeemed after a year, it was forfeited and could be sold.[56] Contrary to popular perception, this was not particularly profitable for pawnbrokers, especially given that pledges worth more than 10s were required to be sold at public auction.[57]

48 Though by the mid-nineteenth century it was made clear that pawnbrokers only warrant the item to be the subject of a pledge the time for which had expired rather than a full warranty of good title: Lobban, 'Commercial Law', p. 853 citing *Morley* v. *Attenborough* (1849) 3 Exch 500; *Eicholz* v. *Bannister* (1864) 17 CB NS 708, 722. This was one of the exceptions to the general rule, see Addison, *Contracts*, vol. I, p. 317.

49 Francis Turner, *The contract of pawn: as it exists at common law, and as modified by the pawnbrokers' acts, the factors' acts, and other statutes* (London: Stevens, 1866), pp. 118–19. Unless they were asked to retain the goods by the true owner or had notice that they were stolen: (1800) 39 & 40 Geo III c. 99 s. 15.

50 (1800) 39 & 40 Geo III c. 99 s. 15.

51 On the trade in tickets, see Tebbutt, *Making Ends Meet*, p. 87.

52 (1800) 39 & 40 Geo III c. 99 s. 16. On the operation of this section, see *Burslem* v. *Attenborough* (1873) LR 8 CP 122.

53 Tebbutt, *Making Ends Meet*, p. 88. This was used as a way of getting a higher price for a forfeited pledge than a conventional sale.

54 Tomkins, 'Pawnbroking and Survival Strategies', pp. 178–80; *Select Committee on Pawnbrokers*, q. 203 (Hardaker) suggested that 80 per cent redeemed within three months.

55 Because many items were pawned and redeemed many times in the course of a year, the actual interest paid over a year could be quite considerable. A small loan redeemed week by week throughout the year would attract an APR of 260 per cent: Paul Johnson, *Saving and Spending: The Working Class Economy in Britain 1870–1939* (Oxford: Oxford University Press, 1985), p. 166.

56 (1800) 39 & 40 Geo III c. 99 s. 17. Reduced from two years under the earlier legislation.

57 (1800) 39 & 40 Geo III c. 99 s. 17; Tomkins, *Urban Poverty*, p. 217; *Select Committee on Pawnbrokers*, q. 451 (Dicker). The perception that pawned goods were worth many

The provisions on authorised profits were the biggest source of discontent amongst pawnbrokers. The 1800 Act required the display of a table of authorised profits 'painted or printed, in large legible characters'.[58] Rates were not always easy to understand.[59] Sometimes they were worked out as a fraction of a coin.[60] Pawnbrokers continued to argue that rates were too low.[61] The Irish lawyer and economist William Hancock claimed that in England licensed pawnbrokers were unwilling to lend less than 2s 6d.[62] The owners of unregulated 'dolly shops' or 'leaving shops' escaped regulation[63] by disguising pawn transactions as sales. These loans were supposedly brought within the remit of the legislation after 1856, but many such lenders continued to operate with blatant indifference to the legislation.[64] After the Usury Act in 1854, there were no longer any restrictions on interest on pawnbroking loans above £10, and these loans were increasingly profitable.[65]

As might be expected, the pawnbrokers who gave evidence to the Select Committee on Pawnbrokers in 1870 stressed that their trade was unprofitable and that the permitted rates had not kept pace with rising costs.[66] The possibility of further deregulation was discussed. Sir Thomas Henry, a magistrate, explained in his evidence to the committee, that were true

times more than the value of the loan may also have worked in the pawnbroker's favour when it came to the sale of forfeited goods: Tebbutt, *Making Ends Meet*, p. 89. Pawnbrokers often carried out a parallel business of buying and selling goods, see *Select Committee on Pawnbrokers*, q. 303 (Hardaker).

58 (1800) 39 & 40 Geo III c. 99 s. 22.

59 Even by pawnbrokers themselves, *Select Committee on Pawnbrokers*, q. 514 (Dicker), q. 735 (Attenborough). Tables were published for this purpose, R. Cole, *The Pawnbroker's Ready Reckoner or Book of Rates* (Plymouth: John Congdon, 1816).

60 (1800) 39 & 40 Geo III c. 99 s. 5; *Select Committee on Pawnbrokers*, q. 16, 17 (Hardaker).

61 Though cf., *Swire* v. *Leach* (1868) 18 CB NS 479, 492, Earle C.J. described the 'high rate of interest allowed by the statute'.

62 William Hancock, 'The Usury Laws and the Trade of Lending Money to the Poor in Ireland' (1850–1851) 13 *Law Review and Quarterly Journal British Foreign Jurisprudence* 88, 89. Figures in Appendix 9 of the *Committee on Pawnbrokers* from 1869 in Liverpool suggest that there was in fact a considerable amount of lending below 2s 6d.

63 Tebbutt, *Making Ends Meet*, pp. 121–3. For a description of a dolly shop, see Charles Dickens, *Our Mutual Friend* (London: Penguin, 1985), p. 408: 'It was a wretched little shop, with a roof that any man standing in it could touch with his hand; little better than a cellar or cave, down three steps.'

64 (1856) 19 & 20 Vict c. 27. In *Select Committee on Pawnbrokers* q. 2529 (Walter) it was claimed that such transactions were outside the legislation, stating that his customers 'sign their names and they agree to that arrangement ... [N]o court would say that I ought to give up that property.'

65 (1854) 17 & 18 Vict c. 90. The legislation did not apply to loans of less than £10.

66 *Select Committee on Pawnbrokers*, q. 436 (Dicker), q. 847 (Telfer), q. 892 (Nathan).

freedom of contract to be allowed then 'the pawnbroker would take advantage of the necessities of the poor';[67] a position that even the *laissez faire* supporting Dicey accepted in the context of money lending more generally.[68] Some pawnbrokers rejected complete freedom of contract as well.[69] This may owe less to conviction than to an unwillingness to give further ground to those who wished to see pawnbroking outlawed altogether.

The Pawnbrokers Act 1872 is sometimes seen as a compromise. Hawkins J. explained that the Act 'was passed – partly for the protection of pawnbrokers, partly also for the protection of pawners and owners of property pledged'.[70] The main beneficiaries of the new legislation were undoubtedly the licensed pawnbrokers. A determined attempt was made to bring the unlicensed lenders under the legislation.[71] At the same time, if the loan exceeded 40s then the parties were permitted to enter into a special contract which took the transaction outside the regulations on profits altogether.[72] Nevertheless, the standard form for contracting in Schedule 3 did not allow some other obligations to be omitted. Permissible profits on smaller loans also increased.[73]

Parliamentary regulation of the process of contracting in a way that is both comprehensive and intrusive, is not a recent development. Its limits were equally obvious when unlicensed pawnbrokers were able to operate with such blatant disregard for the rules. By the end of the nineteenth century, if not earlier, the influence of a powerful commercial body such as pawnbrokers was also apparent. Although pawnbrokers lacked a national association until the 1890s, there were powerful local organisations[74] which together formed a powerful lobby,[75] not least before the Select Committee. A Fabian Society pamphlet of 1899 argued that all the legislation after 1603 had improved the position of the pawnbroker at

[67] *Select Committee on Pawnbrokers*, q. 3579.

[68] A.V. Dicey, *Lectures on the Relation Between Law and Public Opinion in England* (London: Macmillan, 1963), pp. 152–3.

[69] *Select Committee on Pawnbrokers*, q. 437 (Dicker). For a contrary view see q. 859 (Telfer). The opposition to complete deregulation may have been tactical from pawnbrokers who feared that their trade might be outlawed altogether.

[70] *Singer Manufacturing Company* v. *Clark* (1879–80) LR 5 Ex D 37, 43.

[71] *The Times*, 27 December 1872.

[72] (1872) 35 & 36 Vict c. 93 s. 24. Other aspects of the legislation could also be varied, see C. Attenborough, *The Law of Pawnbroking* (London: Jackson, Ruston & Keeson, 1897), p. 101.

[73] (1872) 35 & 36 Vict c. 93 s. 10.

[74] Hudson, *Pawnbroking*, p. 71.

[75] *Hansard* HL vol. 213, col. 545 (6 August 1872).

the expense of the pawner,[76] and the 'Pawnbrokers' Act, 1872 . . . in every sense justifies its title'.

Codifying contract law

One eminent comparative legal historian has argued that 'If common law stands for anything, it is absence of codes, and likewise civil law stands for codification'. He continues, 'through a variety of political circumstances the English mind has come to associate codes with all that is abhorrent'.[77] Apart from a brief period around the time of the English Civil War,[78] support for codification in England before the nineteenth century was largely confined to mavericks like Thomas More[79] and Gerrard Winstanley.[80] From the late eighteenth century the cause of codification was taken up by another radical thinker, Jeremy Bentham. Bentham associated codification with 'utility, notoriety, completeness, manifest reasonableness'.[81] He proposed a code of civil law, penal and constitutional codes, alongside codes dealing with legal procedure and the legal system.[82] Bentham was only too well aware of the likely opposition that a code would face from what he called 'sinister interests'[83] in England. The greater legal certainty that he envisaged would flow from codification would benefit the public but not the

[76] Fabian Society, *Fabian Tract No. 91 Municipal Pawnshops* (London: Fabian Society, 1899), p. 2.

[77] R.C. Van Caenegem, *Judges, Legislators and Professors* (Cambridge: Cambridge University Press, 1993), pp. 39, 49.

[78] Barbara Shapiro, 'Codification of the Laws in Seventeenth Century England' [1974] *Wisconsin Law Review* 428. The debate about the merits of codification took place against the backdrop of a wider law reform movement, see Donald Veall, *The Popular Movement for Law Reform* (Oxford: Oxford University Press, 1970); Barbara Shapiro, 'Law Reform in Seventeenth Century England' (1975) 19 *American Journal of Legal History* 280.

[79] Paul Turner (ed.), Thomas More, *Utopia* (London: Penguin, 1965), p. 106.

[80] J.C. Davis, *Utopia and the Ideal Society: A Study in English Utopian Writing 1516–1700* (Cambridge: Cambridge University Press, 1983), pp. 169–203. For an account of Winstanley and the Levellers, see Christopher Hill, *The World Turned Upside Down* (London: Penguin, 1991), pp. 107–50.

[81] Phillip Schofield and Jonathan Harris (eds.), Jeremy Bentham, *'Legislator of the World' Writings on Codification, Law and Education* (Oxford: Oxford University Press, 1998), p. 168.

[82] The precise details changed over time, J.R. Dinwiddy, *Bentham* (Oxford: Oxford University Press, 1989), p. 60.

[83] Phillip Schofield, *Utility and Democracy* (Oxford: Oxford University Press, 2009), pp. 109–36.

lawyers, or as he put it, 'say that a lawyer has no interest in the uncertainty of the law, as well might you say, that a gunpowder maker has no interest in war, or a glazier in the breaking of windows'.[84] Like More, Bentham hoped that once the law was made accessible to the average lay man, lawyers would no longer be needed.[85]

Various foreign governments failed to take up Bentham's offer to produce a law code.[86] Meanwhile, in England, in the spring of 1808, he tried to persuade Samuel Romilly and Francis Horner to take up his cause in the House of Commons. Although sympathetic, they refused to do so on the grounds that he had failed to produce a complete code.[87] In the 1820s, Bentham took up the cause of English codification with renewed enthusiasm by circulating his *Petition for Codification*.[88] His proposals were widely discussed in newspapers and periodicals.[89] This time he also found a willing advocate in Parliament in the person of Daniel O'Connell, but in the end the result was just the same.[90]

By this time other English lawyers were beginning to take an interest in codification. Some, like John Austin, were influenced by Bentham.[91] Others found inspiration elsewhere. James Humphrey's *Observations on the actual state of the English laws of Real Property with the Outlines of a Code* appeared in 1826, and was based on the Napoleonic Code.[92] The mere use of the term 'code' could be relied upon to raise strong passions. Edward Sugden, the future Lord Chancellor, would even claim that 'a greater calamity could not befall the country' than the implementation of

[84] Phillip Schofield, 'Jeremy Bentham: Legislator of the World' (1998) 51 *Current Legal Problems* 115, 133.

[85] This was a reflection of Bentham's wider belief in the importance of informing the public, see David Liberman, 'Economy and Polity in Bentham's Science of Legislation', in Stefan Collini, Richard Whatmore and B.W. Young (eds.), *Economy, Polity and Society: British Intellectual History 1750–1950* (Cambridge: Cambridge University Press, 2000), p. 124.

[86] Schofield and Harris, *Legislator of the World*, pp. xii–xxxv.

[87] Schofield, *Utility and Democracy*, p. 244.

[88] As well as his *Codification Proposal*, reproduced in Schofield and Harris, *Legislator of the World*, pp. 244–372 and dating from 1821–2.

[89] J.R. Dinwiddy, *Radicalism and Reform in Britain, 1780–1850* (London: Hambledon, 1992), p. 348.

[90] Schofield, *Utility*, pp. 319–20.

[91] W.L. Morison, *John Austin* (London: Arnold, 1982), pp. 38–48.

[92] Bernard Rudden, 'A Code Too Soon. The 1826 Property Code of James Humphreys: English Rejection, American Reception, English Acceptance', in Peter Wallington and Robert Merkin (eds.), *Essays in Memory of F.H. Lawson* (London: Butterworths, 1986), p. 101.

Humphrey's code.[93] A Real Property Commission began work in 1828, but the reform proposals were modest.[94] A Criminal Law Commission was set up in 1833 but, in the face of Parliamentary and legal opposition, the outcome was the same.[95] Two years before Bentham's death in 1832, the *Law Magazine* had already announced that 'Codification ... has become a dead letter in England'.[96] If the outlook for codification in England was not altogether promising, in India the situation was very different.

The codification movement in India

Speaking in the House of Commons in 1833, Thomas Macaulay argued that, 'I believe that no country ever stood so much in need of a code of law as India, and I believe that there never was a country in which the want might be so easily supplied.'[97] The following March, Macaulay sailed for India in order to take up the post of Law Member of the Governor General's Council.[98] He was one of a number of influential Indian administrators who were sympathetic to some of Bentham's ideas.[99] Codification in India can also be seen as part of the growing Anglicisation of Indian society,[100] reflected in an ideological commitment to the imposition of

93 *Ibid.*, p. 103.

94 Stuart Anderson, 'Property', in William Cornish, Stuart Anderson, Raymond Cocks, Michael Lobban, Patrick Polden and Keith Smith, *The Oxford History of the Laws of England, Vol. XII 1820–1914: Private Law* (Oxford: Oxford University Press, 2010), pp. 49–78.

95 Lindsay Falmer, 'Reconstructing the English Codification Debate: The Criminal Law Commissioners, 1833–45' (2000) 18 *Law and History Review* 397; Keith Smith, 'Criminal Law', in William Cornish, Stuart Anderson, Raymond Cocks, Michael Lobban, Patrick Polden and Keith Smith, *The Oxford History of the Laws of England, Vol. XIII 1820–1914: Fields of Development* (Oxford: Oxford University Press, 2010), pp. 193–205.

96 Anon, 'Events of the Quarter' (1830) 4 *Law Magazine* 237, 244 cited by Smith, *ibid.*, p. 192.

97 (1833) 19 HC Deb 479, 531.

98 For his role in India, see John Clive, *Macaulay: The Shaping of the Historian* (London: Secker & Warburg, 1973), pp. 289–341. For Macaulay's political philosophy, see Joseph Hamburger, *Macaulay and the Whig Tradition* (London: University of Chicago Press, 1976).

99 Eric Stokes, *The English Utilitarians and India* (Oxford: Oxford University Press, 1959).

100 D.A. Washbrook, 'India, 1818–1860', in Andrew Porter (ed.), *The Oxford History of the British Empire: The Nineteenth Century* (Oxford: Oxford University Press, 1999), pp. 415–19.

English concepts of the rule of law.[101] Lawyers and officials out in India complained of the impracticalities of the *status quo*.[102] The Indian Law Commission, appointed in 1833, was the focus of these pressures. It was given a remit to implement a programme of codification. A Penal Code was quickly drafted. Macaulay also advocated reform of civil law by quoting an Indian judge of his acquaintance on the state of commercial law: 'He told me that it was a mere lottery. He knew how he should himself decide them. But he knew nothing more.'[103] Following Macaulay's return to England, the momentum for codification was lost for several decades. The Penal Code was not enacted until 1861.[104]

Since the days of the East India Company, different bodies of law had, in theory at least, applied to different sections of the Indian population.[105] The charters that created a Supreme Court in Calcutta and Recorders' Courts in Madras and Bombay, the other Presidency towns, decreed that Muslim and Hindu residents would continue to be governed by their own laws of contract.[106] In the absence of indigenous judges or barristers, native law officers provided opinions on points of Hindu and Muslim law. The reality may have been different. Sir Francis Macnaghten claimed that in his experience, he 'never knew or heard of an instance in which the Supreme Court was called upon in a case of contract, to decide by Hindu laws and usages'.[107] Writing in 1860, William Macpherson called the 'privilege, if it can be so called, of little value', and continued that, 'English Law is generally found to supply just

101 Thomas Metcalf, *Ideologies of the Raj* (Cambridge: Cambridge University Press, 1994), p. 37.

102 Whitley Stokes believed that the origins of the reform movement could be traced to correspondence in the 1820s between Sir Charles Metcalfe, a colonial governor, and the judges of Bengal, see Whitley Stokes, *The Anglo-Indian Codes*, 2 vols. (Oxford: Oxford University Press, 1887), vol. I, p. x.

103 (1833) 19 HC Deb 479, 532.

104 K.J.M. Smith, 'Macaulay's "Utilitarian" Indian Penal Code: An Illustration of the Accidental Function of Time, Place and Personalities in Law Making', in W.M. Gordon and T.D. Fergus (eds.), *Legal History in the Making* (London: Hambledon Press, 1991), pp. 145–64.

105 Bernard Cohn, *Colonialism and its Forms of Knowledge* (Princeton: Princeton University Press, 1996), pp. 57–75; Bernard Cohn, 'From Indian Status to British Contract' (1961) 21 *Journal of Economic History* 613.

106 (1781) 21 Geo III c. 70 s. 17; (1797) 37 Geo III c. 142 s. 13. For details on the operation of the courts, see M.P. Jain, *Indian Legal History*, 2nd edn (Bombay: Tripathi, 1966).

107 Francis Macnaghten, *Considerations on the Hindoo Law, as is current in Bengal* (Serampore: Mission Press, 1824), p. 403.

principles'.[108] A careful study of the case law suggests that indigenous law played a sporadic role at best in contract disputes in the Charter courts.[109] In cases of contracts between Europeans, the English Common law, with some allowance for local conditions, applied.[110]

There was more scope for indigenous law outside the Charter Courts.[111] Judges were often not legally trained. Henry Maine complained:

> The inferior judges, when they were applying some half-remembered legal rule learnt in boyhood, or culling a proposition of law from a half-understood English textbook, no doubt honestly thought in many cases that they were following the rule prescribed for them, to decide, 'by equity and good conscience' wherever no native law or usage was discoverable.[112]

The formula 'equity and good conscience' allowed a good deal of flexibility.[113] In this respect, these courts were not much different from the Courts of Conscience in England. In a minute produced in his capacity as the legal member of the Governor-General's Council in 1867, Henry Maine[114] argued that 'justice, equity and good conscience have of late years been much affected, as a fact, by the English law of contract'.[115] Macpherson claimed that judges 'generally avoided any wide departure from its [the Common law] principles except in cases affected by some of the special features of oriental life and transactions'. These remarks may be true of the 1860s, but in earlier decades a combination of indigenous law and common sense informed judgments rather more than the

[108] William Macpherson, *Outlines of the Law of Contract as administered in the Courts of British India* (London: R.C. Lepage, 1860).

[109] Stelios Tofaris, *A Historical Study of the Indian Contract Act 1872* (unpublished PhD, University of Cambridge, 2011), pp. 5–87.

[110] *Ibid.*, pp. 23–30.

[111] For a discussion of these courts, see *Copies of the Special Reports of the Indian Law Commissioners* (1842) [585] PP vol. XXX, 227.

[112] Henry Maine, *Village-Communities In the East and West*, 3rd edn (London: J. Murray, 1876), p. 299. For similar remarks by a Bengal barrister in 1868, see IOR/L/PJ/5/15 (Money).

[113] IOR/L/PJ/5/15 (Superintendent of Stamps, Fort St George).

[114] For the life of Maine, see George Feaver, *From Status to Contract: A Biography of Sir Henry Maine 1822–1888* (London: Longmans, 1969); R.C.J. Cocks, *Sir Henry Maine: A Study in Victorian Jurisprudence* (Cambridge: Cambridge University Press, 2004). On his role as Law Member, see Gordon Johnson, 'India and Henry Maine', in Alan Diamond, *The Victorian Achievement of Sir Henry Maine* (Cambridge: Cambridge University Press, 1991), pp. 376–88.

[115] 'Statement of Objects and Reasons', 9 July 1867, *Copies of papers showing the present position of the question of a contract law for India* (1867–8) [239] PP vol. XLIX, 86.

Common law.[116] As time passed the role of indigenous law diminished even in these courts. Anglo-Indian writers from Sir William Jones onwards began to produce digests and other works on Hindu and Muslim law.[117] These heavily Anglicised versions came to be relied on by judges at the expense of the native law officers. These same men were often at pains to stress the similarities between the Common law of contract and the indigenous laws.[118] Irrespective of the value of such comparisons, they expressed a mind-set in which codification of contract became a realistic proposition.

Codifying Indian contract law: the Second Report

The Third Indian Law Commission was appointed in 1861. Work on a report on contract law began in 1864 and was finished by 1866. Three of the six Commissioners were judges[119] headed by the Master of the Rolls John Romilly, the son of Bentham's close friend Samuel Romilly.[120] Sir Edward Ryan, a former Chief Justice of India and author of Ryan and Moody's law reports, was a long time supporter of codification.[121] The final judge, Sir William James, was Vice Chancellor of Chancery at the time and later a Lord Justice of Appeal. James had a special interest in India.[122] They were joined by Sir John Macleod, a civil servant, who had been a member of the Indian Law Commission since its inception,[123]

[116] George Rankin, *Background to Indian Law* (Cambridge: Cambridge University Press, 1946), p. 90.

[117] For a useful general discussion, see Tofaris, *A Historical Study*, pp. 49–56. For Jones, see David Ibbetson, 'Sir William Jones as a Comparative Lawyer', in Alexander Murray (ed.), *Sir William Jones 1746–94: A Commemoration* (Oxford: Oxford University Press, 1998), pp. 17–42. These works included: W. Jones, *Institutes of Hindu Law* (Calcutta, 1794); H. Colebrooke, *A Digest of Hindu Law on Contracts and Successions* (Calcutta, 1798); Thomas Strange, *Elements of Hindu Law* (London: Payne & Foss, 1825).

[118] Macnaughten, *Hindoo Law*, p. 403.

[119] The Commission responsible for contract was appointed in 1864, when two of the members of the Third Commission appointed in 1861, Willes J. and Sir William Earle, retired. See *Commissions and Appointments in India*, IOR/H/25.

[120] J.A. Hamilton, rev., Patrick Polden, 'Romilly, John', *Oxford Dictionary of National Biography*. Romilly was Master of the Rolls between 1851 and 1873.

[121] Ryan was Chief Justice between 1833 and 1843, see Katherine Prior, 'Ryan, Sir Edward', *Oxford Dictionary of National Biography*.

[122] He wrote a book on the history of India, *The British in India* (London: Macmillan, 1882), which was edited by his daughter, Mary Schwabe. It was written between 1864 and 1869 and published posthumously.

[123] In a letter to his friend Thomas Ellis, Macaulay described Macleod as 'the cleverest man that I have found in India by many degrees': Thomas Pinney (ed.), *The Letters of*

Robert Lowe, later Chancellor of the Exchequer and Home Secretary,[124] and John Henderson,[125] a barrister. The secretary to the Commission, William Macpherson, was an expert on Indian contract law, having published his *Outlines of the Law of Contract as Administered in the Courts of British India* a few years before.

The doyen of nineteenth century contract scholars, Sir Frederick Pollock, claimed that the 1866 report was 'an elementary statement of the effect of common law and equitable doctrine as understood about forty years ago'.[126] But as the report's authors admitted, 'we have deemed it expedient to depart, more or less, from the English law in several particulars'.[127] It would have been difficult for the Commissioners to have ignored the Common law altogether. The Commissioners were too steeped in its values. The Common law was also too well established in India. At the same time, the nature of their remit afforded them much more room for manoeuvre than they would have had, had they been drawing up a domestic code. Certain aspects of the proposed code would prove to be controversial all the same. There were some major departures from the current Common law and the process also raised questions about contract law, public policy and local conditions.

The Second Report is, in many respects, a surprising document. In some respects it runs counter to some of the received wisdom about the attitude of English lawyers, both to codification and reform of the law of contract. The code departed from English law in some major and minor ways. The Third Commission was prepared to borrow quite directly from Civil law.[128] In the draft code, a contract was defined as 'an agreement between parties whereby a party engages to do a thing or engages not to do a thing'.[129] This closely mirrors the French Civil Code[130] and

Thomas Babington Macaulay, 6 vols. (Cambridge: Cambridge University Press, 1976), vol. III, p. 201.

124 James Winter, *Robert Lowe* (Toronto: University of Toronto Press, 1976).

125 On his death Henderson was replaced by Sir Robert Lush the judge: J.A. Hamilton, rev., Hugh Mooney, 'Lush, Sir Robert', *Oxford Dictionary of National Biography*. Lush was immortalised in a 'Spy' caricature in *Vanity Fair* with the title 'A little Lush'. The title might be thought to refer to a fondness for drink. The text which accompanies the 'Spy' print in possession of the author offers a different explanation: 'When told that the mess-toast had been changed from "Women and Wine" to "Lush and Shea" he wisely and modestly said, "A spell of sobriety will do the Bar no harm" and "a little lush may do the Bench some good".'

126 Frederick Pollock and Dinshah Mulla, *The Indian Contract Act with a Commentary, Critical and Explanatory* (Oxford: Oxford University Press, 1905), p. v.

127 *Contract Law for India*, p. 3.

128 For example, *ibid.*, p. 5.

129 In clause 1.

130 *Code Civil*, book 3,3,1 § 1101.

Pothier's treatise.[131] The description of contract as an agreement was hardly unfamiliar in England, but the difference was that in Civilian sources this principle informed the way that the subject was structured. This was not really true in England at this time. Section 10 of the Indian Contract Act is as explicit a statement of Will Theory as it is possible to find outside mainland Europe: 'All agreements are contracts if they are made by the free consent of parties competent to contract, for lawful consideration and with a lawful object, and are not hereby expressly declared to be void.' The Act goes on to define 'free consent' before analysing coercion, undue influence, fraud and misrepresentation in terms of its absence. A few English writers, including Colebrooke and Jeremy, had already experimented with versions of this approach,[132] but it only reached full fruition in Pollock's textbook of 1876.[133] So close was the Indian Contract Act in methodology to Pollock's own, that he added an appendix containing the relevant provisions of the legislation.[134]

The Second Report was ahead of English law in other significant ways as well, particularly in its treatment of mistake. Clause 7 states that 'where both parties to an engagement by contract are under a mistake as to a matter of fact essential to the engagement, the engagement is void', and is pure Pothier.[135] That the Commission turned to Pothier was not a matter of chance. The secretary to the Commission, William Macpherson, had specifically praised Pothier's analysis of mistake in his treatise.[136] A well-defined doctrine of mistake had not even emerged in England by the time the report was published and arguably when it did so, it could not be described as satisfactory.

The attitude of the Commission towards well-established doctrine was even more radical. By this time in England, consideration was a very different doctrine from the century before. But in appearance at least, it remained little changed. It was still at the heart of English contract law. Having weighed up but rejected the possibility of abolishing the requirement of consideration altogether, the Commission proceeded to modify its application in ways that were unthinkable in England. Clause 10

[131] William Evans (trans.), R. Pothier, *A Treatise on the Law of Obligations or Contracts*, 2 vols. (London: A. Strahan, 1806), 1.1.1 § 1.

[132] Colebrooke, *Contracts*; George Jeremy, *A Treatise on the Equity Jurisdiction of the High Court of Chancery* (London: J. Clarke, 1828).

[133] Frederick Pollock, *Principles of Contract at Law and in Equity* (London: Stevens & Sons, 1876).

[134] Pollock, *Contract*, pp. 542–55.

[135] Pothier, *Obligations*, 1.1.3.1 §§ 17–18.

[136] MacPherson, *Contract*, p. xi.

removed the need for consideration when the agreement was in writing and the contract was registered. Minus the registration requirement, Lord Mansfield and Wilmot J. had tried and failed to introduce something similar in the mid-eighteenth century.[137] The importance of a second reform, the proposal that a promise to pay a pre-existing debt amounted to good consideration, would only become fully apparent nearly two decades later following *Foakes* v. *Beer*,[138] in which the House of Lords held that a promise to pay a pre-existing debt was not good consideration.[139] The rule that consideration must move from the promisee was also abandoned. The provisions on recovery of money paid or services rendered were more liberal than in England where liability for money had and received was tightly restrained.[140]

Reaction to the Second Report and the Indian Contract Act 1872

Having been referred to a select committee, the draft Bill was circulated amongst lawyers and government officials in India. The reaction was neither wholly favourable nor consistent. One Indian judge argued that judges were left with too little discretion,[141] another that they were left with too much.[142] A few provisions attracted the majority of adverse comment. The decision of the Commission to omit an Indian equivalent to the Statute of Frauds was, wrote one respondent, likely to 'cause much baseless litigation'.[143] In England, drawing a distinction between a penalty and a liquidated damages clause had often proved difficult.[144] The Commission thought that the best solution was to abolish the distinction altogether. Whilst this would have simplified matters, a judge in the Bombay Small Causes Court thought it would also 'afford greater facilities to the grasping money lender to impose upon the ignorant borrower'.[145] The measure was also described as a 'retrograde step',[146] one that caused

[137] In *Pillans* v. *Van Mierop* (1765) 3 Burr 1663. [138] (1884) 9 App Cas 605.

[139] Michael Lobban, 'Foakes v. Beer (1884)', in Charles Mitchell and Paul Mitchell (eds.), *Landmark Cases in the Law of Contract* (Oxford: Hart, 2008), pp. 223–67.

[140] This was noted by a respondent to the Bill, IOR/L/PJ/5/15 (Pitt-Kennedy).

[141] IOR/L/PJ/5/15 (Belli). [142] IOR/L/PJ/5/15 (West).

[143] IOR/L/PJ/5/15 (Pitt-Kennedy). For other criticism, see IOR/L/PJ/5/15 (Cochrane).

[144] Lobban, 'Contract', pp. 523–9.

[145] IOR/L/PJ/5/15 (Canoba). For similar remarks, see IOR/L/PJ/5/15 (Deputy Commissioner, Delhi) who argued that 'the people of this country need to be protected against the results of their own rashness in entering into over-reaching contracts'.

[146] IOR/L/PJ/5/15 (Coghlan).

'grave apprehensions'[147] and was 'regrettable'.[148] Another judge of the Small Causes Court put the opposite point of view, when he argued that:

> The penalty of a contract is, in my opinion, always intended, in fact, as a device to ensure the punctual and exact performance of a contract; and whether it be in the nature of a punishment, or only by way of fixing definitely beforehand by mutual consent the amount of damage consequent on a breach appears to me to be wholly immaterial, so long as both parties with their eyes open have consented.[149]

The Act combined both approaches by allowing the parties to stipulate the level of damages in advance without needing to resort to the actual loss, but restricting recovery to a proportionate amount.[150] The debate over two other clauses would have wider consequences. The proposal that a *bona fide* purchaser took good title even where the seller lacked title was contrary to the traditional Common law rule of *nemo dat quod non habet*. Some of the respondents also thought that it would encourage theft of cattle.[151] In the original version of the Contract Bill, the Indian Law Commission had added a series of clauses introducing specific performance as a remedy in contract disputes.[152] The remedy was not to apply to agreements to cultivate land in a particular manner or to grow particular crops.[153] This limitation was inserted for a reason. Tensions between the indigenous growers of indigo (ryots) and European planters had caused problems, including civil unrest, for decades.[154] The ryots argued that they were being exploited by the planters; the planters that the ryots, having received advance payment, were refusing to perform their contracts. Henry Maine, as Law Member of the Governor General's Council, produced a series of minutes on the subject.[155] His main objection, that the proper place for specific performance was a code of procedure rather than of substance, masked wider misgivings. John Lawrence, the Governor General, was in favour of the clauses but decided that it was

[147] IOR/L/PJ/5/15 (Turner). [148] IOR/L/PJ/5/15 (Ráo).

[149] IOR/L/PJ/5/15 (Fagan).

[150] H.S. Cunningham and H.H. Shepherd, *The Indian Contract Act of 1872*, 3rd edn (Calcutta: Thacker, 1878), p. xlviii, s. 74. This approach was championed by one of the respondents, see IOR/L/PJ/5/15 (Cochrane).

[151] IOR/L/PJ/5/15 (Fitzpatrick), (Baden-Powell), (Oliphant). [152] Cll. 51–5.

[153] Cl. 52.

[154] For an interesting account, see Blair Kling, *The Blue Mutiny: The Indigo Disturbances in Bengal 1859–1862* (Philadelphia: University of Pennsylvania Press, 1966).

[155] *Contract Law for India*, pp. 86–9, 91–2, 94–5, 95–6, 97–8, 99–100.

expedient to omit them and refer the matter to the Secretary of State.[156] When he in turn referred the matter back to the Indian Law Commissioners, they stood by their original recommendations.[157]

At this point relations between the various interested parties began to deteriorate. A select committee of the Indian legislature drew up their own draft Bill which reinstated the *nemo dat* rule.[158] The Duke of Argyll, the new Secretary of State India, sided with the Indian Law Commission.[159] This left Maine in a difficult position. His defence of the Indian legislature in a Minute of April 1868 stressed the need to take account of local conditions:

> I have striven to prevail on the Legislature to sanction the Commissioner's drafts with the minimum of change; and they will believe me when I say that, in making this effort, I have often had to contend against criticisms which were at least plausible, and to struggle with difficulties which however slightly they may be believed at home, are still real and substantial, and not in the less real and substantial because they assume a form somewhat unlike that which impede legislation in England.[160]

Both sides became increasingly intransigent. In the spring of 1870, the Indian Government reiterated their support for the position adopted by the Select Committee on the *nemo dat* rule, and stressed that it was not for the Secretary of State to impose a bill in the teeth of objections by the Indian legislature. In July of the same year, the Indian Law Commission resigned, complaining that despite much 'time and labour' their proposals had still not been implemented.[161] An Indian Office minute noted rather dryly that such delays were not unusual.[162] The Commissioners could not be persuaded to reconsider. Their final letter to the Secretary of State concluded rather bitterly:

> We must repeat that no information which has reached the Commissioners does in our opinion explain the inaction of the legislature to which we adverted in our former letter, and which we have been obliged to consider as systematic and persistent.[163]

[156] *Ibid.*, pp. 92–3, 96, 101. [157] *Ibid.*, pp. 101–3.
[158] *Report of the Select Committee on the Bill to Define and Amend the Law Relating to Contracts* (1868) IOR/L/PJ/5/15.
[159] Rankin, *Indian Law*, p. 84.
[160] Henry Maine, *Minutes by the Honourable Sir H.S. Maine (1862–9)* (Calcutta: Government of India, 1890), p. 134.
[161] Cited by C. Ilbert, 'Indian Codification' (1889) 5 *Law Quarterly Review* 347, 351–2.
[162] IOR/L/PJ/5/438 July 1870. [163] Cited by Ilbert, 'Codification', p. 352.

In the meantime, Henry Maine had returned to England in order to take up the post of Corpus Professor of Jurisprudence at Oxford.[164] He was replaced by James Fitzjames Stephen.[165] Stephen admitted that whilst the Law Commission remained in place, 'there was the difficulty of altering their work to any considerable extent'. With their departure, the Secretary of State also conceded defeat and ordered the Indian legislature to deal with the matter as they saw fit.[166]

Stephen was now free to make further amendments. Of all the contentious clauses in the original bill, only that omitting the Statute of Frauds remained unscathed.[167] The impact of the reform of consideration was also reduced in the final Act. A written agreement that was registered was only binding where it was made 'on account of natural love and affection between the parties standing in near relation to each other',[168] the exact opposite of Lord Mansfield's position in *Pillans* v. *Van Mierop*.[169] The Act cleared up any ambiguity about another long established rule: consideration need not move from the promisee.[170]

Stephen complained that the first part of the original Bill was 'arranged in a very obscure and confused manner'.[171] His changes to its structure and the addition of a new definitional section[172] did not meet with general approval. James Bryce complained that Stephen's 'capacity for the work of drafting was deemed not equal to his fondness

[164] On Maine's departure and his part in securing Stephen's succession, see Feaver, *Status to Contract*, pp. 106–7.

[165] For Stephen's role in codification in India, see K.J.M. Smith, *James Fitzjames Stephen* (Cambridge: Cambridge University Press, 2002), pp. 126–32; C. Ilbert, 'Sir James FitzJames Stephen as a Legislator' (1894) 10 *Law Quarterly* Review 222.

[166] *Abstracts of the Proceedings of the Council of the Governor-General of India 1871*, p. 757; IOR/V/9/11–12.

[167] This was welcome by some: Frederick Pollock and Dinshah Mulla, *The Indian Contract Act with a Commentary, Critical and Explanatory*, 2nd edn (Oxford: Oxford University Press, 1909), p. 377 described the Statute of Frauds as 'happily not in force in British India'.

[168] S. 25(1).

[169] (1765) 3 Burr 1663. In the same case Wilmot J. had suggested a wider exception not limited to commercial parties where an agreement was in writing. The only evidence that this was ever supported is the unreported case of *Williamson* v. *Losh* (1774) noted in Joseph Chitty, *A Practical Treatise on Bills of Exchange*, 5th edn (London: S. Brooke, 1818), pp. 93–4.

[170] S. 2(d). Whether it was possible for a third party to sue on another's contract remained unclear.

[171] IOR/L/PJ/5/438. [172] S. 2.

for it'.[173] Pollock took exception to the definitional section, which was described as 'in a wholly different style and not altogether in harmony with the body of the work'.[174] Stephen admitted that he had relied on David Dudley Field's New York Civil Code[175] when drafting the legislation, much to the displeasure of Pollock and others.[176]

Codification in England and India

The nineteenth century was sandwiched between two major civil codes, the French Code Civil and the German BGB.[177] Nothing resembling either was ever remotely likely to come to fruition in England. Nevertheless, a series of statutes taken together could be regarded as a code of commercial contract law. This legislation covered bills of exchange, partnership, sale of goods and marine insurance.[178] With the exception of the Partnership Act, which was drafted by Frederick Pollock, these Acts were the creations of one man, Mackenzie Chalmers.[179] Chalmers would claim that the idea of codification was suggested to him by the Indian Codes.[180] He also had a strong ideological commitment to the exercise,[181] combined with a belief that codification gave businessmen greater certainty.[182]

173 James Bryce, *Studies in History and Jurisprudence* (Oxford: Oxford University Press, 1901), p. 129.

174 Pollock and Mulla, *Indian Contract Act*, p. v.

175 Field may have influenced the direction of the legislation all the way back to the Law Commission's original bill, see Ilbert, 'James Fitzjames Stephen', p. 223; IOR/L/PJ/5/15 (C.D. Field in 1868). Field was strongly influenced by Civilian ideas, see D. Clark, 'The Civil Law Influence on David Dudley Field's Code of Civil Procedure', in Mathias Reimann (ed.), *The Reception of Continental Ideas in the Common Law World 1820–1920* (Berlin: Duncker & Humblot, 1993), pp. 63–87.

176 Ilbert, 'James Fitzjames Stephen', p. 223; Pollock and Mulla, *Indian Contract Act*, 2nd edn, pp. vii, 164.

177 Tony Weir (trans.), Franz Wieacker, *A History of Private Law in Europe* (Oxford: Oxford University Press, 2003), pp. 269–75, 371–86.

178 Bills of Exchange Act 1882; Partnership Act 1890; Sale of Goods Act 1893; Marine Insurance Act 1906.

179 Steve Hedley, 'Chalmers, Sir Mackenzie Dalzell', *Oxford Dictionary of National Biography*.

180 M.D. Chalmers, 'Codification of Mercantile Law' (1903) 19 *Law Quarterly Review* 10, 11. From 1896 to 1899, Chalmers served as the Law Officer on the Governor General's Council.

181 R.B. Ferguson, 'Legal Ideology and Commercial Interests: The Social Origins of the Commercial Law Codes' (1977) 4 *British Journal of Law and Society* 18.

182 Chalmers, 'Codification', pp. 14–15.

Commercial interests also played an important role, particularly, but not exclusively, in relation to the Partnership Act.[183]

This legislation was not the work of cranks or Benthamite zealots. Pollock and Chalmers were respected lawyers who had produced digests on partnership,[184] bills of exchange and insurance.[185] Chalmers' views on Bentham are unknown, but Pollock was, at best, an 'ambivalent admirer'.[186] At least some mainstream lawyers, businessmen and politicians were prepared to come out in favour of legislation of this sort. But there were limits. This was not the sort of general code advocated by Bentham. Attempts to introduce a much wider mercantile code which would apply to both England and Scotland came to nothing.[187] At the same time, Pollock praised the Indian Contract Act in the preface to his contract treatise as 'the most instructive example of what can be done to consolidate and simplify English case law'.[188]

Writing the year after the Indian Contract Act came into force, Sheldon Amos warned of the dangers of those anxious to advance the cause of codification in England, drawing too close an analogy with events in India.[189] If anything, the Indian legislation shows the limits of the codification. This was not codification in the grand manner envisaged by Bentham. It was not informed by 'utility, notoriety, completeness, manifest reasonableness'. It was not legislation from first principles. Such principles as there were came from the Will Theory, but these were blended with the existing Common law of contract then in force in India. There was no clean break with the past. Some doctrines like consideration, which remained contrary to Will Theory, were retained. The whole process was built on compromise. Bentham's

183 Ferguson, 'Legal Ideology', pp. 26–7. So too was the Bills of Exchange Act, see M.D. Chalmers, 'An Experiment in Codification' (1886) 2 *Law Quarterly Review* 125.

184 Frederick Pollock, *A Digest of the Law of Partnership* (London: Stevens & Sons, 1877).

185 M.D. Chalmers, *A Digest of the Law of Bills of Exchange, Promissory Notes and Cheques* (London: Stevens & Sons, 1878); M.D. Chalmers, *A Digest of the Law of Marine Insurance* (London: Clowes & Sons, 1901).

186 Duxbury, *Pollock*, p. 104.

187 Lord Rodger, 'The Codification of Commercial Law in Victorian Britain' (1991) 80 *Proceedings of the British Academy* 149 reproduced in (1992) 108 *Law Quarterly Review* 570. For a contemporary account, see Anon, 'The Proposed Mercantile Code' (1885) 29 *Journal of Jurisprudence* 186.

188 Pollock, *Contract*, p. viii.

189 Sheldon Amos, *An English Code, Its Difficulties and Modes of Overcoming them* (London: Strahan, 1873), pp. 86–94.

dream of a code that could be understood by the lay man would not be realised in India. P.K. Nambyar, an advocate of the High Court of Madras, remarked in 1879 that:

> The Indian Contract Act, surely requires schools for its explanation, and casuists (as Bentham puts it) to unravel its subtleties. It does not speak a language familiar to everybody. The Indian Contract Act is not distinguished from other books by its great simplicity and clearness. And so if Bentham were alive to see the Indian Contract Act, he would emphatically say, that the measure is an imperfect one.[190]

The Act did not reduce the need for judges. It was not exhaustive. There were too many problems of interpretation. These were resolved with reference to the English Common law.[191] Other factors worked against a Benthamite contract code in India. There are always going to be frictions when a remote body of experts come against local conditions. In a letter to his friend Grant Duff, Henry Maine, having criticised the Indian Law Commission as ‘a perfectly irresponsible body’ with little recent experience of India, continued:

> I am greatly afraid that the law commissioners have formed a radically false notion of the India of the present day. I admit that . . . on the subject of the first Code, the Penal Code, there is much to countenance an impression that India is a field for the application of a diluted Benthamism . . . As to the Penal Code, nobody cares about criminal law except theorists and habitual criminals . . . [A] substantive Civil Law applying to everybody and cutting across every transaction of everyday life, is a very different matter.[192]

The principal objections to the proposed Indian code were practical rather than based on doctrinal purity. But the process was not ideologically or politically neutral.[193] The pre-legislation system was presented as inefficient. At the same time, the differences between the indigenous and the Common law were downplayed. This was not an accident. The fate of Dudley Field’s code demonstrated that without the political will,

190 P.K. Nambyar, *The Principles of the Indian Law of Contract* (Madras: Vyjayanti Press, 1897), p. 111.

191 R.N. Gooderson, ‘English Contract Problems in Indian Code and Case Law’ (1958) 16 *Cambridge Law Journal* 67.

192 Reproduced in Feaver, *Status to Contract*, pp. 101–3.

193 For a discussion of the politics of codification more generally in the nineteenth century, see Peter van den Berg, *The Politics of European Codification* (Groningen: Europa Law Publishing, 2007).

no code, however well drafted, could hope to prosper.[194] The participants in the project were prepared to face the political realities by accepting that the legislation would have to take account of local conditions. They disagreed on the extent of the compromise that was necessary. The fate of codification in India in the nineteenth century was not only determined by the political conditions in India and England. The role of large personalities such as Macaulay, Maine and Stephen, in determining the speed and direction of codification, was crucial.

In India, the codification project was bound up in the ideology of the Raj in its pomp.[195] Even here the task of codification was far from easy. It generated strong feelings. One Bengal barrister went as far as to label the original Bill 'a painful and cruel infliction'.[196] The starkest lesson of the whole episode is captured in Amos's remarks that, 'No one who has practically tried his hand at the Codification of the English Law can be unaware of the extraordinary difficulties by which the task is beset'.[197] In England itself, the hurdles were all that much higher.

[194] For an account of these events, see Mathias Reimann, 'The Historical School of Codification: Savigny, Carter and the Defeat of the New York Civil Code' (1989) 37 *American Journal of Comparative Law* 95.

[195] Which has been described as 'the late Victorian unified sub-continental British Raj, with its arrogant ... elite bureaucracy', see B. Lenman, 'Britain and India', in H. T. Dickinson (ed.), *A Companion to Eighteenth Century Britain* (Oxford: Blackwell, 2002), p. 472.

[196] The barrister in question was J.B. Money, an Assistant Secretary in Bengal. He was writing in 1868, IOR L/PJ/5/15.

[197] Amos, *English Code*, p. 1.

12

The law of contract: stability and change

> By its nature, of course, genius defies easy understanding or simple elucidation. This is particularly so with the common law; its reputed genius is much vaunted but little explained. However, the common law's peculiar forte is seen to lie in its capacity to allow for change and innovation in an overall process that emphasizes the importance of continuity and stability.[1]

The history of the law of contract between 1670 and 1870 involved a combination of continuity and change. The strongest element of continuity was the legal system itself. Those traditional elements of Common law contract litigation in the superior courts including the forms of action, pleading and the civil jury trial, remained in place throughout the period covered by this book. Yet none of these things were totally static. The civil jury in 1670 was not the same body as the civil jury in 1770 or 1870. By the mid-eighteenth century, specialist juries of merchants were increasingly common in some cases. The long process of judges wrestling control from jurors was beginning. In nineteenth century England, the old order, as reflected by the traditional rules of pleading and procedure or the jury trial, was seen as unsatisfactory. Writing in 1859 in *The Dark Side of Trial by Jury*, Joseph Brown complained that, 'The time has at length arrived when the trial by jury must itself be tried . . . I accuse it of incapacity, of ignorance, of partiality, of cumbersomeness, of barbarism'.[2] Brown gives a good flavour of the dissatisfaction that some undoubtedly felt. Reform in these areas was still painfully slow. There were a series of false starts and dead ends.[3] Not

[1] Allan C. Hutchinson, *Evolution and the Common Law* (Cambridge: Cambridge University Press, 2005), p. 1.

[2] (London: William Maxwell, 1859), p. 7.

[3] For an account of some of these, see Patrick Polden, 'The Superior Courts of Common Law', in William Cornish, Stuart Anderson, Raymond Cocks, Michael Lobban, Patrick Polden and Keith Smith, *The Oxford History of the Laws of England, Volume XI 1820–1914: English Legal System* (Oxford: Oxford University Press, 2010), pp. 569–630.

everyone was unhappy with the *status quo*. There were those who even venerated the complex rules of pleading.[4] The civil jury continued in a diminished form into the twentieth century,[5] and the forms of action would continue to have a hold over lawyers long after the Common Law Procedure Act 1852.[6] Institutions of all types are complex. Short of revolution, invasion or social collapse, such change as occurs within them tends to be a process that takes place bit by bit, year by year.[7] Much the same is true of the substantive law itself. It has been said that, 'Law is largely backward-looking and heavily inertial: it stays the same unless and until it is changed; energy has to be expended in the deliberate introduction of any change and scholarly reformulations are sterile until and unless they become part of the legal fabric.'[8]

The law of contract and the realm of ideas

The impact of the Enlightenment is still being felt today.[9] The extent to which the Enlightenment really heralded an age of reason is a matter of debate, but it was undoubtedly a time during which ideas were becoming more important. This was evident in the law as elsewhere. It is not necessary to look too hard in order to find references to Roman law, Civil law and even Natural law in the eighteenth century legal authorities. At the same time, this sort of borrowing was never very systematic or frequent. This is not to say that such ideas had no impact,[10] although it must sometimes be the case that they were used to add lustre to a

4 Michael Lobban, *The Common Law and English Jurisprudence* (Oxford: Oxford University Press, 1991), pp. 61–7.

5 Michael Lobban, 'The Strange Life of the English Civil Jury, 1837–1914', in John Cairns and Grant McLeod (eds.), *The Dearest Birth Right of the People of England* (Oxford: Hart, 2002), pp. 173–209.

6 A.H. Chaytor and W.J. Whittaker (eds.), F.W. Maitland, *The Forms of Action at Common Law* (Cambridge: Cambridge University Press, 1948), p. 2; *United Australia Ltd* v. *Barclays Bank Ltd* [1941] AC 1, 29 (Lord Atkin).

7 Even then the new tends to include at least some elements of the old. The division between the Anglo-Norman legal system and the Anglo-Saxon legal system was never as absolute as it is sometimes supposed to be: Patrick Wormald, *Legal Culture in the Early Medieval West* (London: Hambledon, 1999), p. 304.

8 David Ibbetson, 'Comparative Legal History: A Methodology', in Anthony Musson and Chantal Stebbings (eds.), *Making Legal History* (Cambridge: Cambridge University Press, 2012), p. 140.

9 Anthony Pagden, *The Enlightenment and Why It Still Matters* (Oxford: Oxford University Press, 2013).

10 D. Ibbetson, 'Natural Law and Common Law' (2001) 5 *Edinburgh Law Review* 4.

pre-determined outcome. More broadly, the relationship between English law and that on mainland Europe was always more complicated than captured in the idea of isolation, and such legal borrowing was not entirely novel.[11]

The eighteenth century saw the first serious attempts to impose some order on the law of contract.[12] The Civilian writers had a methodology of their own. For those outside this tradition, it was more difficult. The fact that Ballow relied so heavily on Natural law ideas says something about the lack of a home-grown alternative.[13] There was an obvious tension at the heart of the whole exercise. Reconciling the messy reality of English law within the neat lines of Natural law theory was always going to be impossible. Ballow, and also Gilbert in his unpublished work, were genuine pioneers. It was another seventy-five years before this sort of project was attempted again when Henry Colebrooke published his *A Treatise on Obligations and Contracts*.[14] As with Ballow, there was an obvious inspiration. In Colebrooke's case it was the work of the French writer Robert Pothier, which was by then available in an English translation. Colebrooke's book was still not typical. Unlike most of his contemporaries, he was not writing for practitioners. Pothier may have had some influence on those who were as well. At least a trace of his ideas can be found in the writings of practical men like Joseph Chitty. But the influence of the Will Theory should not be exaggerated. It was particularly convenient where there were gaps in the substantive law. The law of contractual mistake and damages is testimony to this. Much of nineteenth century contract law was not new at all. Sometimes the ideas that were emerging from Will Theory may have helped to shape existing doctrine. This can be seen in the way that the requirement of reciprocity was eroded in the doctrine of consideration. Other doctrines like the parties-only principle survived unscathed and unaltered. It is only necessary to compare the Indian Contract Act 1872 to see what a law of contract built on Will Theory might look like. And even here the final Act could not be described as a pure version of Will Theory.

[11] David Ibbetson, *Common Law and Ius Commune* (London: Selden Society, 2001).

[12] Which is not to suggest that there were no early attempts to systematise the law as a whole, see David J. Siepp, 'The Structure of English Common Law in the Seventeenth Century', in W.M. Gordon and T.D. Fergus (eds.), *Legal History in the Making* (London: Hambledon, 1991), pp. 61–83.

[13] Henry Ballow, *Treatise of Equity* (London, 1737).

[14] (London, 1818).

In a candid letter which was enclosed with a copy of his treatise and sent to his friend, the judge Thesiger L.J., Sir William Anson admitted that:

> Writing as I have done for students and beginners I have ventured on a definitiveness of statement as to the results of the cases which would have been presumptuous in a book of practice. I took a great deal of trouble to arrange the various parts of the subject in due proportion & order . . . Some parts of the subject are very interesting, and here and there it seems, though I may be wrong, that the law is still unsettled even on rudimentary points, and in such matters one feels the excitement of an explorer.[15]

What Anson doesn't go on to say is that, like Pollock, he was not above manipulating the case law in order to produce a neat fit. Will Theory doesn't stand up to very close scrutiny. The role of promises is particularly troublesome for one thing.[16] The roots of Will Theory can be traced into Natural law and beyond, but no real attempt is ever made to explain why, in the mature theory, a meeting of wills justified imposing a contract. This does not seem to have worried anyone overmuch at the time.[17] In the longer term, the way in which contract law was presented in the books was more significant than any deep theoretical concerns. It is still remarkable how durable the idea that all contracts can be reduced to a set of universal principles has proved to be. Despite differences of content, the way that most contract textbooks are structured has not significantly altered since the nineteenth century.[18] The sense of coherence, that the same law was applied in the same way irrespective of the status of the parties or subject-matter of the contract, was always something of a myth.

[15] The letter dated 20 March 1879 is reproduced in Stephen Waddams, *Principle and Policy in Contract Law* (Cambridge: Cambridge University Press, 2011), p. 212.

[16] Warren Swain, 'Contract as Promise: The Role of Promising in the Law of Contract. An Historical Account' (2013) 17 *Edinburgh Law Review* 1, 15–19.

[17] Because of the often witless attempts at theorising, or 'research' in modern universities, it is often easy to forget that the law worked perfectly well without either university academics or their theories and could do so again. For much the same point, see Steve Hedley, 'Is Private Law Meaningless?' (2011) 64 *Current Legal Problems* 89, 94: 'The common law has survived for most of its history without any deep elaborated theory.'

[18] Bearing in mind that contract law is often taught to first-year law students, the division of a contractual relationship into creation, terms, vitiation, and remedies has a certain pedagogical appeal.

A healthy dose of scepticism is required before assuming that judges were, and are, widely influenced by legal literature. Modern studies show that the impact of legal literature on judges is rather sporadic.[19] Some judges will be more receptive to these sorts of influences than others. There are a number of examples in the eighteenth and nineteenth century case law of some judges drawing on a wide range of sources outside the earlier authorities. There were certainly occasions when legal literature could shape counsel's argument and ultimately, when accepted, lead to a change in the law. Sir Samuel Romilly's argument as counsel, which drew on the writing of Pothier, made a significant contribution towards the emergence of undue influence in the nineteenth century, as was acknowledged at the time.[20] The influence of legal writing may be more subtle and less direct. Those who were brought up as students on Anson and Pollock are likely to perceive the law of contract in a particular way thereafter.

Lawyers, judges and controlling change

In 1865, *The Spectator* asserted that, 'The Bar is essentially a conservative body. Its traditions, its rules of etiquette, and the training of its members are to a great extent opposed to originality of thought.'[21] There is some truth in this view. At the same time, reluctance to reform need not necessarily be a bad thing. A legal system in a constant state of upheaval would be unsettling to lawyers and litigants alike. The fact that Holt C.J. proceeded with caution when faced with attempts to enforce promissory notes at Common law, was less an example of pig-headed resistance to innovation – he was quite prepared to allow actions formulated as bills of exchange – than a recognition that left unchecked, promissory notes had the potential to undermine the doctrine of consideration, and with it one of the major pillars of contract law as it then stood.

[19] Alan Paterson, *The Law Lords* (London: Macmillan, 1982), pp. 14–20; Neil Duxbury, *Jurists and Judges* (Oxford: Hart, 2001), pp. 17–22; Alan Paterson, *Final Judgment* (Oxford: Hart, 2013), pp. 213–21. For a more positive view, see Lord Rodger, 'Judges and Academics in the United Kingdom' (2010) 29 *University of Queensland Law Journal* 29; Jack Beatson, 'Legal Academics: Forgotten Players or Interlopers?', in Andrew Burrows, David Johnson and Reinhard Zimmermann (eds.), *Judge and Jurist: Essays in Memory of Lord Rodger of Earlsferry* (Oxford: Oxford University Press, 2013), pp. 523–41.

[20] *Huguenin* v. *Baseley* (1807) 14 Ves Jun 273.

[21] *The Spectator Vol. 38* (London: John Campbell, 1865), p. 773.

Lawyers, in common with the other professions, were a popular target for satirists.[22] The idea of the judge as a remote, arrogant or even somnolent figure as portrayed by Hogarth,[23] was always slightly unfair. Eighteenth and nineteenth century judges often had very wide experience outside their court rooms in politics and in wider society.[24] The decisions in contract cases were informed by a number of factors which included the needs of commercial litigants, the dictates of contemporary morality, and the requirements of public policy. Judges were of course a product of their class. Even some of those who were self-made men built up large fortunes in legal practice.[25] In these circumstances, it was perhaps not surprising that heirs were afforded protection from money lenders. It would be a mistake nevertheless to assume that judges were only motivated by class interest. Sailors after all also received special treatment. There was a genuine concern about usury which went beyond a desire to protect the landed gentry. Contract law was always more nuanced. It would have made a very inefficient tool of class oppression if that had ever been the aim.[26]

Eighteenth and nineteenth century contract judgments are often rich, innovative and thoughtful. Legal reasoning was more open textured than it later became. Writing about America, Morton Horwitz has argued that 'Contract law provides another excellent illustration of the deep pressure towards formalism in the nineteenth century'.[27] English law witnessed some of the same pressures. In relation to the doctrine of restraint of trade for example, public policy began to be pushed to the margins. But however much someone like Pollock may have desired it, public policy, as he freely admitted, never entirely fell away from contract judgments. Even in the years around 1870, formalistic reasoning never completely

[22] Penelope Corfield, *Power and the Professions in Britain 1700–1850* (London: Routledge, 1995), pp. 42–69.

[23] William Hogarth's painting 'The Bench' completed in 1754, contains caricatures of Willes C.J., Bathurst J., the Hon. William Noel and Sir Edward Clive. It resides at the Fitzwilliam Museum, Cambridge.

[24] Daniel Duman, *The Judicial Bench in England 1727–1875* (London: Royal Historical Society, 1982), pp. 72–104.

[25] *Ibid.*, pp. 142–3.

[26] There is an extensive debate about whether the criminal law in the eighteenth century was a ruling class conspiracy against the poor: Douglas Hay, Peter Linebaugh, John G. Rule, E.P. Thompson and Cal Winslow, *Albion's Fatal Tree* (New York: Pantheon Books, 1975); John Langbein, 'Albion's Fatal Flaws' (1983) 98 *Past and Present* 96.

[27] Morton Horwitz, 'The Rise of Legal Formalism' (1975) 19 *American Journal of Legal History* 251, 259.

triumphed. Even reasoning which might appear formalistic on the surface can disguise more complex patterns of reasoning. Formalistically the doctrine of consideration required a benefit or detriment, but beneath the surface what that actually meant began to change as the requirement of reciprocity wore increasingly thin in the nineteenth century.

Following a recent revival of interest in judicial biography,[28] it is respectable once again to ascribe legal change to individual judges. The precise role played by an individual is nevertheless almost impossible to quantify. Before the nineteenth century, when precedent was less rigid than it later became, judges were left with considerable scope to influence the direction of contract law. This is particularly true during the formative stages of doctrinal development. Some judges were more conservative than others. The various attempts to reform consideration came to grief because there was no agreement on the need for change, at least not by such a direct route. Judicial idiosyncrasies were capable of taking the law in new directions. At a time when the Bench remained small and cohesive, before the late nineteenth century,[29] the pull of tradition was very strong. When the consensus was challenged, as occurred when Lord Mansfield began drawing on equitable ideas in order to develop the Common law, some of his colleagues reacted unfavourably. Sometimes there was a genuine opportunity to develop the law because there was a gap in the law. Contracts of insurance and negotiable instruments were allowed to evolve in line with commercial expectations. But once the law was settled, the virtues of certainty and predictability were emphasised.

Individual views might very well change over time. Some of Lord Mansfield's later judgments were far from radical, particularly when he regarded a doctrine as well settled.[30] His attempt to rein in the action of money had and received is one obvious example. The generation of

[28] This is one of the better ideas to cross the Atlantic from the United States of America in recent decades. For details of the major Legal Biography project at the London School of Economics see: www.lse.ac.uk/collections/law/projects/legalbiog/lbp.htm.

[29] Duman, *Judicial Bench*, p. 17. In 1727 there were a mere seventeen judges in the central courts combined.

[30] This aspect of Lord Mansfield is almost entirely ignored. For one exception which perhaps goes too far in the other direction, see A.W.B. Simpson, 'Innovation in Nineteenth Century Contract Law' (1975) 91 *Law Quarterly Review* 247, 'the innovating judge . . . has become part of the folklore of the profession, incongruously typified by that arch conservative Lord Mansfield'.

judges who followed Lord Mansfield were to some extent involved in working out the limits of previous developments. But attempts to change contract law did not end with the death of Lord Mansfield. There were further outbreaks of reform too. The attempt to introduce moral consideration, although short lived, was as radical as anything proposed fifty years before.

Contract law and complexity

One of the problems with some accounts of eighteenth and nineteenth century contract law is that they fail to recognise the extent to which legal evolution was a product of the legal system itself. Lawyers, judges, legal writers, and of course litigants themselves, all played a part. The process of change was complex, if not always conscious or even obvious. It ebbed and flowed. An account of contract law between 1670 and 1870 which viewed the legal system in isolation from wider society is also incomplete. It is impossible to draw very firm or very broad conclusions about the relationship between law and society. Attempts to do so risk accusations of over simplifying or peddling a particular political agenda.[31] A clear pattern is rarely present. So for example, some judges were anxious to prohibit contracts of gaming altogether, whereas others appeared more concerned with the effect of gaming contracts on the contracts of insurance. Wider society was equally divided. While moralists attacked gambling, many affluent and influential people were enthusiastic participants at the gaming tables. The same is true of money lending. Pawnbrokers and usurers were widely reviled, but they fulfilled a necessary function. The extent to which judges were influenced by commercial considerations is also difficult to pin down. In part, this is because there were so many sources of mercantile practice beyond the evidence of merchants themselves, through lawyers, mercantile juries and mercantile literature. Most judges, including Lord Mansfield, were reluctant to allow commercial considerations to completely overturn established rules. A compromise was often required. Negotiable instruments were such a success because they were part of the Common law, but not of it.

Anyone looking for easy or glib explanations about the formative period of modern contract law will need to look elsewhere. Even when law is changing it remains deeply rooted in the past, not just in matters of

[31] A Critical Legal Theorist would no doubt respond that my own account is no more than Conservative legal history. I do not regard this as an insult.

doctrine, but in the way that lawyers and judges think. Lawyers are not always capable of adjusting to new ways of thinking.[32] However, a legal system that failed to adapt would not last very long.[33] Undoubtedly some periods see more reform than others. At times, changes in contract doctrine have taken place quite quickly. English contract law, however, remains a work in progress. A doctrine of contractual mistake was put in place in little more than a quarter of a century, but it still took a further century before it was settled that there was no separate doctrine of equitable mistake.[34] A final word can usefully be left to the great English Marxist historian E.P. Thompson, whose remarks apply very aptly to the history of the law of contract between 1670 and 1870: 'minds which thirst for a tidy platonism very soon become impatient with actual history.'[35]

[32] This is of course not to say that a legal system cannot adapt rapidly when the conditions are right, see Lawrence Friedman, *The Legal System: A Social Science Perspective* (New York: Russell Sage, 1987), pp. 155–6.

[33] Hence once there was a sufficient momentum behind changes in the way that the legal system operated, it proved difficult to stop despite some hostility within the legal profession.

[34] *Great Peace Shipping Ltd* v. *Tsavliris Salvage (International) Ltd (The Great Peace)* [2003] QB 679.

[35] E.P. Thompson, 'The Peculiarities of the English' (1965) *Socialist Register* 311.

BIBLIOGRAPHY

Primary sources

Parliamentary papers and reports

Report From The Committee Appointed To Take Into Consideration The Laws now in being against Usury, And The present Practice of purchasing Annuities for the Life of the Grantor (London, 1777)

Select Committee on the Usury Laws (1818) [376] PP vol. VI, 137

Commissions and Appointments in India (1827–1862) IOR/H/25

2nd Report into the Practice and Proceedings of the Superior Courts of Common Law (1830) [123] PP vol. XI, 547

Copies of the Special Reports of the Indian Law Commissioners (1842) [585] PP vol. XXX, 227

1st Report of Her Majesty's Commissioners for Inquiring into the Process, Practice, and System of Pleading in the Superior Courts of Common Law (1851) [1389] PP vol. XXII, 567

Report of the Select Committee on Legal Education (1846) [686] PP vol. X, 1

Copies of papers showing the present position of the question of a contract law for India (1867–68) [239] PP vol. XLIX, 86

Report from the Select Committee on Pawnbrokers; together with the proceedings of the committee, minutes of evidence, and appendix (1870) [377] PP vol. VIII, 391

Legislative Council Proceedings (Debates) 1871–1872, vols. 10–11, IOR/V/9/11–12

File on Resignation of Third Indian Law Commission (1870) IOR/L/PJ/5/438

Government of India Bills and Acts (1872) IOR/L/PJ/5/15

Books

Abbot, Charles, *A Treatise of the Law Relative to Merchant Ships and Seaman* (London: E. Brooke, 1802)

Abbot, Charles, *A Treatise of the Law Relative to Merchant Ships and Seamen*, 5th edn (London: Butterworth, 1827)

Addison (pseud.), *Interesting Anecdotes, Memoirs, Allegories, Essays, and Poetical Fragments*, 5 vols. (London, 1794)

Addison, C.G., *A Treatise on Contracts and Liabilities Ex-Contractu* (London: W. Benning, 1847)

Addison, C.G., *A Treatise on the Law of Contracts and Rights and Liabilities Ex-Contractu*, 4th edn (London: Stevens & Norton, 1856)

Addison, C.G., *A Treatise on the Law of Contracts and Rights and Liabilities Ex-Contractu*, 5th edn (London: Stevens, 1862)

Amos, Sheldon, *An English Code, Its Difficulties and Modes of Overcoming them* (London: Strahan, 1873)

Anon, *The death of usury* (Cambridge, 1594)

Anon, *A Brief Survey of the Growth of Usury in England* (London, 1671)

Anon, *The Devil and Broker or a character of a Pawnbroker in a Merry Dialogue* (London, 1677)

Anon, *Four for a Penny: Or, Poor Robin's Character of an Unconscionable Pawnbroker* (London, 1678)

Anon, *Arbitrium Redivivum: Or The Law of Arbitration* (London, 1694)

Anon, *A Gentleman's Assistant*, 2nd edn (London, 1709)

Anon, *A Common Law Treatise of Usury* (London, 1710)

Anon, *A true state of publick credit* (London, 1721)

Anon, *Law quibbles. Or, a treatise of the evasions, tricks, turns and quibbles, commonly used in the profession of the law, to the prejudice of clients, and others* (London, 1724)

Anon, *The Inconsolable: or the contented cuckold. A dramatic farce in three Acts* (London, 1738)

Anon, *A Compendious Library of the Law* (London, 1740)

Anon, *A Plain Answer to a Late Pamphlet, intitled, the Business of Pawnbroking Stated* (London, 1745)

Anon, *A Modest Defence of Gaming* (London, 1754)

Anon, *An Essay on Gaming* (London, 1761)

Anon, *An address to the purchasers or subscribers to the General and complete abridgment of law and equity, by Charles Viner* (London, 1767)

Anon, *Obscurities and Defects of the Mercantile Law Considered, in an Essay on Bills of Exchange* (London, 1769)

Anon, *Reflections on Usury* (London, 1783)

Anon, *The Advantages of Settling Disputes by Arbitration* (Carlisle, 1795)

Anon, *A Treatise on the Study of the Law* (London, 1797)

Anon, *Tales for Youth, or the High Road to Renown, Through the Paths of Pleasure* (London, 1797)

Anon, *Pawnbrokers Detected and Dissected* (London, 1809)

Anson, William, *Principles of the English Law of Contract* (Oxford: Clarendon Press, 1879)

Archbold, John, *The Practice of the Court of King's Bench*, 2 vols. (London: J. Butterworth, 1819)

Attenborough, C., *The Law of Pawnbroking* (London: Jackson, Ruston & Keeson, 1897)

Austin, John, *The Province of Jurisprudence Determined*, 3 vols. (London: John Murray, 1861–1863)

Babington, Richard, *A Treatise on the Law of Auctions* (London: Henry Butterworth, 1826)

Bacon, Matthew, *A New Abridgment of the Law*, 5 vols. (London, 1736)

Ballantine, William, *Some Experiences of a Barristers Life* (New York: Henry Holt, 1882)

Ballow, Henry, *Treatise of Equity* (London, 1737)

Bankton, *An Institute of the Laws of Scotland 1751* (Edinburgh: Stair Society, 1993)

Barrister, A., *Legal Recreations or Popular Amusements*, 2 vols. (London, 1792)

Basile, Mary, Bestor, Jane, Coquillette, Daniel and Donahue, Charles (eds.), *Lex Mercatoria and Legal Pluralism: A Late Thirteenth-Century Treatise and Its Afterlife* (Cambridge, Mass.: Ames Foundation, 1998)

Bateman, J., *A Practical Treatise on the Law of Auctions* (London: A. Maxwell, 1838)

Baxton, John, *The English vsurer; or Vsury condemned, by the most learned and famous diuines of the Church of England* (London, 1634)

Bayley, John, *A Short Treatise on the Laws of Bills of Exchange, Cash Bills and Promissory Notes* (London, 1789)

Beale, Hugh (ed.), *Chitty on Contracts*, 31st edn, 2 vols. (London: Sweet & Maxwell, 2012)

Beatson, J., *Anson's Law of Contract*, 27th edn (Oxford: Oxford University Press, 1998)

Beawes, Wydham, *Lex Mercatoria Rediviva or the Merchant's Directory* (London, 1751)

Beawes, Wydham, *Lex Mercatoria Rediviva or the Merchant's Directory*, 5th edn (London, 1792)

Bellott, Hugh and Willis, James R., *The Law Relating to Unconscionable Bargains with Money Lenders* (London: Stevens & Hayes, 1897)

Benbrigge, John, *Usura Accommodata* (London, 1646)

Benjamin, J.P., *Treatise on the Law of Sale of Personal Property* (London: Henry Sweet, 1868)

Bentham, Jeremy, *Defence of Usury; Shewing the Impolicy of the Present Legal Restraints on the terms of Pecuniary Bargains* (London, 1787)

Bentham, Jeremy, *Rationale of Judicial Evidence*, 5 vols. (London: Hunt & Clark, 1827)

Blackburn, Colin, *A Treatise on the Effect of the Contract of Sale on the Legal Rights of Property and Possession in Goods, Wares and Merchandise* (London: William Benning, 1846)

Blackstone, William, *Analysis of The Laws of England* (Oxford, 1756)

Blackstone, William, *Commentaries on the Laws of England*, 4 vols. (Oxford, 1765–1769)

Blencowe, R.W. and Lowe, M.A. (eds.), Thomas Turner, *The Diary of a Georgian Shopkeeper* (Oxford: Oxford University Press, 1979)

Bohun, William, *The Practising Attorney: or Lawyer's Office* (London, 1724)

Bond, Donald (ed.), *The Spectator*, 5 vols. (Oxford: Oxford University Press, 1965)

Boote, Richard, *An Historical Treatise of an Action or Suit at Law* (London, 1766)

Bracken, Henry, *Ten Minutes Advice to Every Purchaser of a Horse out of a Dealer, jockey or groom's stable* (London, 1774)

Brent, Charles, *Money essay'd or the time value of it tryed* (London, 1728)

Brown, Arthur, *A Compendious View of the Civil Law*, 2 vols. (London, 1798)

Brown, John, *On the Pursuit of False Pleasure, and the Mischiefs of Immoderate Gaming* (London, 1752)

Brown, Joseph, *The Dark Side of Trial by Jury* (London: William Maxwell, 1859)

Brownsword, Roger, *Contract Law: Themes for the Twenty-First Century*, 2nd edn (Oxford: Oxford University Press, 2006)

Bryce, James, *Studies in History and Jurisprudence* (Oxford: Oxford University Press, 1901)

Buller, Francis, *An Introduction to the Law Relative to Trials at Nisi Prius* (London, 1767)

Burrell, Lady Sophie, *Poems Dedicated to the Right Honourable The Earl of Mansfield* (London, 1793)

Burrows, Andrew, *Understanding the Law of Obligations* (Oxford: Hart, 1998)

Byles, John, *A Practical Treatise on the Law of Bills of Exchange, Promissory Notes, Bank-Notes, Bankers' Cash-Notes and Checks*, 2nd edn (London: S. Sweet, 1834)

Cam, Helen (ed.), *Year Books of Edward II* (London: Selden Society, 1969)

Campbell, David (ed.), Ian MacNeil, *The Relational Theory of Contract* (London: Sweet & Maxwell, 2001)

Campbell, John, *The Lives of the Chief Justices of England*, 3 vols. (London: John Murray, 1849)

Campbell, R., *The London Tradesman* (London, 1747)

Campbell, Robert (ed.), John Austin, *Lectures on Jurisprudence or the Philosophy of Positive Law*, 2 vols. (London: John Murray, 1869)

Cannon, Garland (ed.), *The Letters of Sir William Jones* (Oxford: Oxford University Press, 1970)

Cannon, John (ed.), *The Letters of Junius* (Oxford: Oxford University Press, 1978)

Cave, Lewis (ed.), C.G. Addison, *A Treatise on Law of Contracts*, 6th edn (London: Stevens & Sons, 1869)

Chalmers, M.D., *A Digest of the Law of Bills of Exchange, Promissory Notes and Cheques* (London: Stevens & Sons, 1878)

Chalmers, M.D., *A Digest of the Law of Marine Insurance* (London: Clowes & Sons, 1901)

Chaytor, A.H. and W.J. Whittaker (eds.), F.W. Maitland, *The Forms of Action at Common Law* (Cambridge: Cambridge University Press, 1948)

Child, Josiah, *Brief Observations Concerning Trade and Interest of Money* (London, 1668)

Child, Josiah, *A Discourse about Trade* (London, 1690)

Chitty, Joseph, *A Treatise on the Law of Bills of Exchange, Checks on Bankers, Promissory Notes, Bankers' Cash Notes and Banknotes* (London, 1799)

Chitty, Joseph, *A Treatise on the Parties to Actions, the Forms of Action and on Pleading*, 2 vols. (London: J. Butterworth & W. Clark, 1809)

Chitty, Joseph, *A Practical Treatise on Bills of Exchange, Checks on Bankers, Promissory Notes, Bankers' Cash Notes and Bank Notes*, 3rd edn (London: W. Clark, 1809)

Chitty, Joseph, *A Practical Treatise on Bills of Exchange, Checks on Bankers, Promissory Notes, Bankers' Cash Notes and Bank Notes*, 5th edn (London: S. Brooke, 1818)

Chitty, Joseph, *A Treatise on the Laws of Commerce and Manufacturers and the Contracts Relating Thereto*, 2 vols. (London: J. Butterworth, 1824)

Chitty, Joseph, *A Practical Treatise on the Law of Contracts Not Under Seal* (London: S. Sweet, 1826)

Chitty, Joseph, *A Practical Treatise on the Law of Contracts Not Under Seal*, 2nd edn (London: S. Sweet, 1834)

Chitty, Joseph, *The Practice of the Law in all its Departments*, 2nd edn, 2 vols. (London: S. Sweet, 1834)

Chitty, Joseph, *A Treatise on the Parties to Actions, the Forms of Actions and on Pleading*, 6th edn, 2 vols. (London: W. Clark, 1836)

Chitty, T., Denning, A.T. and Harvey, C.P., *A Selection of Leading Cases*, 13th edn (London: Sweet & Maxwell, 1929)

Christian, Edward (ed.), William Blackstone, *Commentaries on the Laws of England*, 13th edn, 4 vols. (London: A. Strahan, 1800)

Coke, Edward, *Institutes of the Laws of England*, 4 vols. (London, 1644)

Cole, R., *The Pawnbroker's Ready Reckoner or Book of Rates* (Plymouth: John Congdon, 1816)

Colebrooke, H., *A Digest of Hindu Law on Contracts and Successions* (Calcutta, 1798)

Colebrooke, H.T., *A Treatise on Obligations and Contracts* (London, 1818)

Colebrooke, Thomas, *The Life of H.T. Colebrooke* (London: Trüber, 1873)

Collier, Jeremy, *Essay Upon Gaming* (London, 1713)

Collins, Hugh, *The Law of Contract*, 4th edn (London: Lexis Nexis, 2003)

Comyn, Robert, *A Treatise on the Law of Usury* (London: R. Pheney, 1817)

Comyn, Samuel, *A Treatise of the Law Relative to Contracts and Agreements not Under Seal*, 2 vols. (London: A. Strahan, 1807)

Comyn, Samuel, *The Law of Contracts and Promises*, 2nd edn (London: A. Strahan, 1824)

Croake, James, *Curiosities of Law and Lawyers* (London: Sampson Low, 1882)

Crooke, George, *The Merchant, Tradesman and Farmer's Director* (Lincoln, 1778)

Culpeper, Thomas, *A tract against the high rate of usury* (London, 1668)

Culpeper, Thomas, *A Short Appendix to the Late Treatise Concerning the Abatement of Usury* (London, 1668)

Cunningham, H.S. and Shepherd, H.H., *The Indian Contract Act of 1872*, 3rd edn (Calcutta: Thacker, 1878)

Cunningham, Timothy, *The Law of Bills of Exchange, Promissory Notes, Bank-Notes, and Insurances* (London, 1760)

Curley, Thomas (ed.), Robert Chambers, *A Course of Lectures on English Law Delivered at the University of Oxford 1767–73*, 2 vols. (Oxford: Oxford University Press, 1986)

Cushing, L.S. (trans.), R.J. Pothier, *Treatise on the Contract of Sale* (Boston: Little & Brown, 1839)

Da Costa, Anthony, *The case of Mr Da Costa with Mr Monmartel, relating to a bill of exchange* (London, 1736)

De Britaine, William, *Humane Prudence*, 9th edn (London, 1702)

De Zulueta, F. (trans.), *The Institutes of Gaius* (Oxford: Oxford University Press, 1946)

Defoe, Daniel, *The Complete English Tradesman in Familiar Letters* (London, 1726)

Defoe, Daniel, *The Complete English Tradesman*, 2 vols. (London, 1727)

Dicey, A.V., *Can English Law be Taught at the Universities?* (London: Macmillan, 1883)

Dicey, A.V., *Lectures on the Relation Between Law and Public Opinion in England* (London: Macmillan, 1963)

Dickens, Charles, *Our Mutual Friend* (London: Penguin, 1985)

Dodd,William, *Sermons to Young Men*, 3 vols. (London, 1771)

Erskine, Thomas, *Reflections on gaming, annuities, and usurious contracts* (London, 1776)

Espinasse, Isaac, *A Digest of the Law of Actions at Nisi Prius*, 2 vols. (Dublin, 1790)

Evans, William, *Essays: On the Action for Money Had and Received, on the Law of Insurances, and on the Law of Bills of Exchange and Promissory Notes* (Liverpool: Merritt & Wright, 1802)

Evans, William (trans.), R. Pothier, *A Treatise on the Law of Obligations or Contracts*, 2 vols. (London: A. Strahan, 1806)

Fabian Society, *Fabian Tract No. 91 Municipal Pawnshops* (London: Fabian Society, 1899)

Fallowfield, John, *Miscellaneous Essays Divine and Moral* (Whitehaven, 1788)

Fenton, Roger, *A Treatise of Usurie* (London, 1611)

Filmer, Robert, *Quæstio quod liberica* (London, 1653)
Finch, Henry, *English Law, or, A Discourse Thereof* (London, 1627)
Fonblanque, John (ed.), Henry Ballow, *A Treatise of Equity*, 2 vols. (London, 1793–1794)
Fonblanque, John (ed.), Henry Ballow, *A Treatise of Equity*, 5th edn (London: Clarke, 1820)
Forbes, William, *A Methodical Treatise Concerning Bills of Exchange* (Edinburgh, 1718)
Forsyth, William, *History of Trial by Jury* (London: John Parker, 1852)
Foss, Edward, *The Judges of England*, 9 vols. (London: John Murray, 1864)
Fox, William, *A Treatise on Simple Contracts and the Action of Assumpsit* (London: Stevens, 1842)
Friedman, Arthur (ed.), Oliver Goldsmith, *The Vicar of Wakefield* (Oxford: Oxford University Press, 2006)
G.F., *The Secretary's Guide* (London, 1705)
Gane, Percival (ed.), Joannes Voet, *The Selective Voet Being the Commentary on the Pandects* (Durban: Butterworth, 1957)
Gaskin, J.C.A. (ed.), Thomas Hobbes, *The Elements of Law* (Oxford: Oxford University Press, 1999)
Gent, E.R., *The Experienc'd Farrier or Farring Completed*, 4th edn (London, 1720)
Gibbon, Edward, *Memoirs of My Life* (London: Penguin, 1990)
Giles, Jacob, *Every Man his own Lawyer or, a Summary of the Laws of England in a New Instructive Method*, 7th edn (London, 1772)
Grant, James, *The Bench and the Bar*, 2 vols. (London: Henry Colburn, 1837)
Gray, Charles (ed.), Matthew Hale, *The History of the Common Law of England* (Chicago: University of Chicago Press, 1971)
Gregor, Mary (ed.), Immanuel Kant, *The Metaphysics of Morals* (Cambridge: Cambridge University Press, 1996)
Grotius, H, *Of the Rights of War and Peace*, 3 vols. (London, 1715)
Guest, A.G. (ed.), William Anson, *Principles of the English Law of Contract*, 24th edn (Oxford: Oxford University Press, 1975)
Guest, A.G. (ed.), William Anson, *Principles of the English Law of Contract*, 25th edn (Oxford: Oxford University Press, 1979)
Hale, Matthew, *The Analysis of the Law* (London, 1713)
Hall, G.D.G. (ed.), *The Treatise on the Laws and Customs of the Realm of England Commonly Called Glanvill* (Oxford: Oxford University Press, 1965)
Hannay, Robert, *Defence of the Usury Laws* (Edinburgh: William Blackwood, 1823)
Hardaker, Alfred, *A Brief History of Pawnbroking* (London: Jackson, Ruston & Keeson, 1892)
Hargrave, Francis, *Collectanea Juridica*, 2 vols. (London: E. Brooke, 1840)
Hawles, John, *The English-mans right a dialogue between a barrister at law and a jury-man* (London, 1680)

Hey, Richard, *A Dissertation on the Pernicious Effects of Gaming* (Cambridge, 1783)

Holliday, John, *A Life of William Late Earl of Mansfield* (London, 1797)

Holt, Francis, *A System of the Shipping and Navigation Laws*, 2nd edn (London: Butterworth, 1824)

Howard, Sylvanus, *Every tradesman his own lawyer* (London, 1794)

Howe, Mark De Wolf (ed.), *The Pollock–Holmes Letters*, 2 vols. (Cambridge: Cambridge University Press, 1942)

Humdrum, Humphrey (pseud.), *Mother Midnight's Comical Book* (London, 1753)

Hutton, William, *Courts of Requests: Their Nature, Utility and Powers Described* (Birmingham, 1787)

Hutton, William, *A Dissertation on Juries* (Birmingham, 1789)

Ibbetson, David (ed.), William Jones, *An Essay on the Law of Bailments* (Bangor: Welsh Legal History Society, 2004)

Jacob, Giles, *Lex Mercatoria or the Merchant's Companion* (London, 1718)

Jeremy, George, *A Treatise on the Equitable Jurisdiction of the High Court of Chancery* (London: Clarke, 1828)

Jeremy, Henry, *The Laws Relating to Horses* (London: J. Clarke, 1825)

Jervis, John, *All the New Rules in Relation to Pleading and Practice* (London: S. Sweet, 1839)

Jones, W., *Institutes of Hindu Law* (Calcutta, 1794)

Lord Kames, *Principles of Equity*, 2nd edn (Edinburgh, 1767)

Kates, Gary (ed.), Chevalier d'Eon, *The Maiden of Tonnerre: The Vicissitudes of the Chevalier and Chevaliére d'Eon de Beaumont* (Baltimore: Johns Hopkins University Press, 2001)

Keener, William, *Treatise on the Law of Quasi-Contracts* (New York: Baker Voorhis, 1893)

Kelsey, F. (trans.), Hugo Grotius, *The Rights of War and Peace (1646 edn)* (Oxford: Oxford University Press, 1925)

Kent, James, *Commentaries on American Law*, 9th edn, 4 vols. (Boston: Little, Brown & Co., 1858)

Kenyon, G.T., *The Life of Lloyd, First Lord Kenyon: Lord Chief Justice of England* (London: Longmans, 1873)

King, Charles, *The British Merchant; or, Commerce Preserv'd*, 3 vols. (London, 1721)

Kyd, Stewart, *A Treatise on the Law of Bills of Exchange and Promissory Notes* (London, 1790)

Lawes, Edward, *A Practical Treatise on Pleading in Assumpsit* (London: W. Reed, 1810)

Lawrence, John, *A Philosophical and Practical Treatise on Horses*, 2 vols. (London, 1796–1798)

Leake, Stephen, *The Elements of the Law of Contracts* (London: Stevens & Sons, 1867)

Lee, R.W. (trans.), Hugo Grotius, *Introduction to the Jurisprudence of Holland* (Oxford: Oxford University Press, 1926)

Lely, J.M. and Geary, Neville (eds.), Joseph Chitty, *A Treatise on the Law of Contracts*, 12th edn (London: Sweet & Maxwell, 1890)

Lewis, W.S. (ed.), Horace Walpole, *Horace Walpole's Correspondence*, 48 vols. (Oxford: Oxford University Press, 1967)

Lincoln, Anthony, and McEwen, Robert (eds.), *Lord Eldon's Anecdote Book* (London: Stevens & Sons, 1960)

Lodge, Thomas, *An alarum against vsurers* (London, 1584)

Lustig, Irma and Pottle, Frederick (eds.), James Boswell, *Boswell: The English Experiment, 1785–1789* (London: Heinemann, 1986)

Mackeldey, Ferdinand, *Lehrbuch der Institutionen des heutigen Römischen Privatrechts* (Leipzig: Giessen, 1814)

Macnaghten, Francis, *Considerations on the Hindoo Law, as is current in Bengal* (Serampore: Mission Press, 1824)

Macpherson, William, *Outlines of the Law of Contracts as Administered in the Courts of British India* (London: R.C. Lepage, 1860)

Maddock, Henry, *A Treatise on the Principles and Practice of the High Court of Chancery*, 2nd edn, 2 vols. (London: J. Clarke, 1820)

Magens, Nicholas, *An Essay on Insurances*, 2 vols. (London, 1755)

Maine, Henry, *Ancient Law* (London: Dent, 1861)

Maine, Henry, *Village-Communities In the East and West*, 3rd edn (London: J. Murray, 1876)

Maine, Henry, *Minutes by the Honourable Sir H.S. Maine (1862–69)* (Calcutta: Government of India, 1890)

Malcolm, James, *Anecdotes of the Manners and Customs of London During the Eighteenth Century* (London: Longman, 1808)

Malynes, Gerard, *The center of the circle of commerce* (London, 1623)

Malynes, Gerard, *Lex Mercatoria* (London, 1686)

Marius, John, *Advice Concerning Bills of Exchange*, 2nd edn (London, 1655)

Marius, John, *Advice Concerning Bills of Exchange*, 3rd edn (London, 1674)

Martin, Francois-Xavier (trans.), R. Pothier, *A Treatise on Obligations Considered in a Moral and Legal View* (Newbern: Martin & Ogden, 1802)

Matthews, William (ed.), *The Diary of Dudley Ryder 1715–1716* (London: Methuen, 1939)

McCulloch, J.R., *Early English Tracts on Commerce* (Cambridge: Economic History Society, 1952)

Meek, Ronald, Raphael, D.D. and Stein, Peter (eds.), Adam Smith, *Lectures on Jurisprudence* (Oxford: Oxford University Press, 1978)

Miller, John, *Elements of the Law of Insurance* (Edinburgh, 1787)

Mitchell, Catherine, *Interpretation of Contracts* (Abingdon: Routledge-Cavendish, 2007)

Morgan, John, *Essays Upon the Law of Evidence, New Trials, Special Verdicts, Trials at Bar and Repleaders*, 3 vols. (London, 1789)

Mosse, Miles, *The Arraignment and Conviction of Usurie* (London, 1595)

Muir, Kenneth (ed.), William Shakespeare, *Othello* (London: Penguin, 1968)

Mulcahy, Linda and Wheeler, Sally (eds.), *Feminist Perspectives on Contract Law* (London: Cavendish, 2005)

Nambyar, P.K., *The Principles of the Indian Law of Contract* (Madras: Vyjayanti Press, 1897)

Newland, John, *Treatise on Contracts within the Jurisdiction of Courts of Equity* (London: Butterworth, 1806)

North, Roger, *A Discourse on the Study of the Laws* (London: C. Baldwyn, 1824)

Notturno, M.A. (ed.), Karl Popper, *The Myth of the Framework* (London: Routledge, 1997)

O'Day, Rosemary and Englander, David (eds.), Henry Mayhew, *London Labour and London Poor* (London: Wordsworth Classics, 2008)

Oldfather, Charles and Oldfather, William (trans.), Samuel Pufendorf, *Of the Law of Nature and Nations (1688 edn)* (Oxford: Oxford University Press, 1934)

Oldham, James, *The Mansfield Manuscripts and the Growth of English Law in the Eighteenth Century*, 2 vols. (Chapel Hill: University of North Carolina Press, 1992)

Oldham, James (ed.), *Case Notes of Sir Soulden Lawrence* (London: Selden Society, 2013)

Oliphant, George, *The Law Concerning Horses, Racing, Wager and Gambling* (London: S. Sweet, 1847)

Ord, Mark, *Essay on the Law of Usury* (London, 1797)

Ord, Mark, *Essay on the Law of Usury*, 2nd edn (London: W. Clark, 1804)

Paley, William, *The Principles of Moral and Political Philosophy* (London, 1785)

Palmer, N. (ed.), *Palmer on Bailment*, 3rd edn (London: Sweet & Maxwell, 2009)

Park, James, *A System of the Law of Marine Insurances*, 2nd edn (London, 1790)

Parker, Thomas, *The laws of shipping and insurance* (London, 1775)

Parsons, Theophilius, *The Law of Contracts* (Boston: Little, Brown & Co., 1853)

Peel, Edwin (ed.), *Treitel The Law of Contract*, 13th edn (London: Sweet & Maxwell, 2011)

Penn, William, *The Selected Works of William Penn*, 3rd edn, 5 vols. (London, 1782)

Petersdorff, Charles, *A Practical and Elementary Abridgement of the Common Law*, 5 vols. (London: Stevens & Norton, 1843)

Petyt, William, *Britannia Languens, or A Discourse of Trade* (London, 1680)

Pinney, Thomas (ed.), *The Letters of Thomas Babington Macaulay*, 6 vols. (Cambridge: Cambridge University Press, 1976)

Plowden, Francis, *A Treatise Upon the Law of Usury and Annuities* (London, 1797)

Plucknett, T.F.T and Barton, J.L. (eds.), *St German's Doctor and Student* (London: Selden Society, 1974)

Pollock, Frederick, *Principles of Contract at Law and in Equity* (London: Stevens & Sons, 1876)

Pollock, Frederick, *Principles of Contract at Law and in Equity*, 3rd edn (London: Stevens & Sons, 1881)

Pollock, Frederick, *Principles of Contract at Law and in Equity*, 5th edn (London: Stevens & Sons, 1889)

Pollock, Frederick, *Principles of Contract at Law and in Equity*, 7th edn (London: Stevens & Sons, 1902)

Pollock, Frederick, *A Digest of the Law of Partnership* (London: Stevens & Sons, 1877)

Pollock, Frederick and Mulla, Dinshah, *The Indian Contract Act with a Commentary, Critical and Explanatory* (Oxford: Oxford University Press, 1905)

Pollock, Frederick and Mulla, Dinshah, *The Indian Contract Act with a Commentary, Critical and Explanatory*, 2nd edn (Oxford: Oxford University Press, 1909)

Polson, Archer, *Law and Lawyers: A Sketch Book of Legal Biography, Gossip, and Anecdote* (London: Routledge, 1858)

Pothier, Robert Joseph, *Traité des Donations entre-Vifs* (Paris, 1821)

Powell, Edmund, *The Principles and Practice of the Law of Evidence*, 2nd edn (London: John Crockford, 1859)

Powell, Joseph John, *Essay Upon the Law of Contracts and Agreements*, 2 vols. (London, 1790)

Prest, W. (ed.), *The Letters of Sir William Blackstone* (London: Selden Society, 2005)

Price, Jacob, *Joshua Johnson's Letterbook, 1771–1774* (London: London Record Society, 1979)

Prichard, M.J. and Yale, D.E.C. (eds.), *Hale and Fleetwood on Admiralty Jurisdiction* (London: Selden Society, 1993)

Priestley, Joseph, *An Essay on the Course of Liberal Education* (London, 1765)

Pufendorf, Samuel, *Of the Law of Nature and Nations* (Oxford, 1703)

Pulteney, William, *The honest jury or Caleb triumphant. A new ballad* (London, 1729)

Rede, Leman, *Strictures on the Lives and Characters of the Most Eminent Lawyers of the Present Day* (London, 1790)

Rennell, Thomas, *The Consequences of the Vice of Gaming* (London, 1794)

Roberts, S.C. (trans.), F. De La Rochefoucauld, *A Frenchman in England 1700–1850* (Cambridge: Cambridge University Press, 1933)

Rogers, Pat (ed.), Daniel Defoe, *A Tour Through the Whole Island of Great Britain* (London: Penguin, 1986)

Rolle, Henry, *Un Abridgement des plusieurs cases et resolutions del Common Ley* (London, 1668)

Rosenberg-Orsini, Justine, *Moral and Sentimental Essays* (London, 1785)
Russell, John (ed.), Joseph Chitty, *A Treatise on the Law of Contracts*, 5th edn (London: H. Sweet, 1853)
Russell, John (ed.), Joseph Chitty, *A Treatise on the Law of Contracts*, 6th edn (London: H. Sweet, 1857)
Russell, John (ed.), Joseph Chitty, *A Practical Treatise on the Law of Contracts*, 7th edn (London: H. Sweet, 1863)
Russell, John (ed.), Joseph Chitty, *A Treatise on the Law of Contracts*, 8th edn (London: H. Sweet, 1868)
Salmon, T., *A Critical Essay Concerning Marriage* (London, 1794)
Sandars, Thomas (trans.), *The Institutes of Justinian* (London: Longmans, 1948)
Sayer, Joseph, *The Law of Damages* (London, 1770)
Schofield, Phillip and Harris, Jonathan (eds.), Jeremy Bentham, *'Legislator of the World' Writings on Codification, Law and Education* (Oxford: Oxford University Press, 1998)
Schwabe, Mary (ed.), William James, *The British in India* (London: Macmillan, 1882)
Sedgwick, Theodore, *A treatise on the measure of damages, or, An inquiry into the principles which govern the amount of compensation recovered in suits at law*, 2nd edn (New York: John Voorhies, 1852)
Sellon, B.J., *The Practice of the Courts of King's Bench and Common Pleas*, 2 vols. (London, 1792)
Sheppard, William, *Actions Upon the Case for Deeds viz Contracts, Assumpsits, Deceits, Nuisances, Trover and Conversion*, 2nd edn (London, 1675)
Simpson, Joseph, *Reflections on the Natural and Acquired Endowments Requisite for the Study of Law* (London, 1764)
Smith, John, *An Elementary View of the Proceedings in an Action at Law* (London: Saunders & Benning, 1835)
Smith, John, *A Selection of Leading Cases on Various Branches of the Law*, 2 vols. (London: A. Maxwell, 1837–1840)
Smith, John, *The Law of Contracts* (London: William Benning, 1847)
Smollett, Tobias, *The Adventures of Ferdinand Count Fathom* (London, 1753)
Stephen, George, *The Adventures of a Gentleman in Search of a Horse* (London: Longmans, 1835)
Stephen, George, *The Juryman's Guide* (London: Charles Knight, 1845)
Stephen, Henry, *A Treatise on Pleading in Civil Actions* (London: Butterworth, 1824)
Stokes, Whitley, *The Anglo-Indian Codes*, 2 vols. (Oxford: Oxford University Press, 1887)
Story, Joseph, *Commentaries on Equity Jurisprudence as Administered in England and America*, 2nd edn, 2 vols. (Boston: Little & Brown, 1839)
Strahan, William (trans.), Jean Domat, *The Civil Law in its Natural Order* (London, 1722)

Strange, Thomas, *Elements of Hindu Law* (London: Payne & Foss, 1825)

Stretch, L.M., *The Beauties of History; or, Pictures of Virtue and Vice, Drawn from Real Life*, 2 vols. (London, 1770)

Surtees, Robert, *The Horseman's Manuel* (London: A. Miller, 1831)

T.P., *The case of usury further debated* (London, 1684)

Tancock, Leonard (trans.), Voltaire, *Letters on England* (London: Penguin, 2005)

Taplin, William, *The gentleman's stable directory: or, modern system of farriery* (London, 1788)

Tawney, R.H. (ed.), Thomas Wilson, *A Discourse Upon Usury 1572* (London: Bell & Sons, 1925)

Thorne, S. (ed.), *Bracton On the Laws and Customs of England*, 4 vols. (Cambridge, Mass.: Harvard University Press, 1968)

Tidd, William, *The practice of the Court of King's Bench in personal actions*, 2 vols. (London, 1790)

Tim, Peeping (pseud.), *The Honest London Spy* (Dublin, 1793)

Treitel, G.H., *The Law of Contract* (London: Stevens & Sons, 1962)

Tuck, Richard (ed.), Thomas Hobbes, *Leviathan* (Cambridge: Cambridge University Press, 1991)

Turner, Francis, *The Contract of Pawn* (London: Stevens, 1866)

Turner, Paul (ed.), Thomas More, *Utopia* (London: Penguin, 1965)

Viner, Charles, *A General Abridgement of Law and Equity* (Aldershot, 1741–1758)

Von Savigny, Friedrich, *System des heutigen römischen Rechts*, 9 vols. (Berlin: Veit und Comp, 1840)

Waingrow, Marshall, Redford, Bruce and Goldring, Elizabeth (eds.), James Boswell, *The Life of Samuel Johnson*, 4 vols. (Edinburgh: Edinburgh University Press, 1999)

Walker, D.M. (ed.), Viscount Stair, *The Institution of the Law of Scotland* (Edinburgh: University of Edinburgh and Glasgow Press, 1981)

Warnkoenig, L., *Commentarii Juris Romani Privati* (Leiden: Leodii, 1825–1829)

Warren, Samuel, *A Popular and Practical Introduction to Law Studies*, 2nd edn (London: Maxwell, 1845)

Watson, A. (trans.), *The Digest of Justinian* (Philadelphia: University of Pennsylvania Press, 1985)

Wentworth, John, *A complete system of pleading: comprehending the most approved precedents and forms of practice*, 10 vols. (London, 1797–1799)

Wesket, John, *A Complete Digest of the Theory, Laws, and Practice of Insurance* (London, 1781)

White, Frederick and Tudor, Owen, *A Selection of Leading Cases in Equity*, 2 vols. (London: W. Maxwell, 1849)

White, Henry (ed.), R. Roper, *A Treatise on the Law of Legacies*, 3rd edn, 2 vols. (London: Butterworth, 1828)

Willes, John and Keating, Henry (eds.), John Smith, *A Selection of Leading Cases on Various Branches of the Law*, 4th edn, 2 vols. (London: William Maxwell, 1856)

Williams, Edward, *A Treatise on the Law of Executors and Administrators*, 3rd edn, 2 vols. (London: Saunders & Benning, 1841)

Wilmot, John, *Memories of the Life of The Right Honourable Sir John Eardley Wilmot Knt. Late Lord Chief Justice of the Court of Common Pleas*, 2nd edn (London: J. Nicholls, 1811)

Winfield, Percy, *The Province of the Law of Tort* (Cambridge: Cambridge University Press, 1931)

Winfield, Percy (ed.), Frederick Pollock, *Pollock's Principles of Contract*, 12th edn (London: Stevens & Sons, 1946)

Winfield, Percy, *The Law of Quasi-Contract* (Cambridge: Cambridge University Press, 1952)

Wiseman, Robert, *The Law of Laws, or The Excellency of the Civil Law Above All Humane Laws Whatsoever* (London, 1654)

Withy, Robert, *A Practical Treatise Upon The Law of Annuities* (London: Butterworth, 1800)

Wood, Allen (ed.), Georg Hegel, *Elements of the Philosophy of Right* (Cambridge: Cambridge University Press, 1991)

Wood, Thomas, *A New Institute of Imperial or Civil Law* (London, 1704)

Wood, Thomas, *An Institute of the Laws of England in their Natural Order*, 2 vols. (London, 1720)

Wooddeson, Richard, *Elements of Jurisprudence Treated of in the Preliminary Part of a Course of Lectures on the Laws of England* (London, 1783)

Wooddeson, Richard, *A Systematical View of the Laws of England as Treated of in a Course of Vinerian Lectures*, 3 vols. (London, 1792–1793)

Woodward, Edward, *The Law of Quasi-Contract* (Boston: Little, Brown & Co., 1913)

Woodward, Josiah, *A Disswasive from Gaming* (London, 1718)

Yale, D.E.C., *Lord Nottingham's Chancery Cases Vol. I* (London: Selden Society, 1954)

Yale, D.E.C., *Lord Nottingham's Chancery Cases Vol. II* (London: Selden Society, 1961)

Yale, D.E.C. (ed.), *Lord Nottingham's Manual of Chancery Practice and Prolegomena of Chancery and Equity* (Cambridge: Cambridge University Press, 1965)

Yorke, Phillip, *The Life and Correspondence of Philip Yorke, Earl of Hardwicke*, 3 vols. (Cambridge: Cambridge University Press, 1913)

Articles and book chapters

Anon, 'Treatise on the Law of Obligation or Contracts by M. Pothier' (1807) 3 *Law Journal* 297

Anon, 'Review of Bentham, Rationale of Judicial Evidence' (1828) *The Edinburgh Review* 457

Anon, 'Sale and Warranty of Horses' (1828–1829) 1 *Law Magazine* 318
Anon, 'Events of the Quarter' (1830) 4 *Law Magazine* 237
Anon, 'My contemporaries from the note book of a retired barrister' (1832) 6 *Fraser's Magazine* 220
Anon, 'Of the Distinction between Law and Fact' (1844) 1 *Law Review* 37
Anon, 'Of the function of the judge as distinguished from those of the jury' (1845) 2 *Law Review* 27
Anon, 'The Law of Contracts' (1846) 5 *Law Magazine or Quarterly Review of Jurisprudence* 256
Anon, 'Addison's Treatise on Contracts' (1847) 6 *Law Magazine or Quarterly Review of Jurisprudence* 210
Anon, 'The Proposed Mercantile Code' (1885) 29 *Journal of Jurisprudence* 186
Anson, W, 'Stephen Martin Leake' (1894) 10 *Law Quarterly Review* 2
Ballantine, Henry, 'Is the Doctrine of Consideration Senseless and Illogical' (1913) 11 *Michigan Law Review* 423
Ballantine, Henry, 'Mutuality and Consideration' (1914–1915) 28 *Harvard Law Review* 121
Chalmers, M.D., 'An Experiment in Codification' (1886) 2 *Law Quarterly Review* 125
Chalmers, M.D., 'Codification of Mercantile Law' (1903) 19 *Law Quarterly Review* 10
Dodds, C.E., 'Lectures to the Incorporated Law Society' (1835–1836) 11 *Legal Observer* 233, 329, 331, 409, 501; (1836) 12 *Legal Observer* 161, 341, 345, 347, 425; (1836–1837) 13 *Legal Observer* 161, 241, 339; (1836) 11 *Legal Observer* 505
Hanbury, H.G., 'The Recovery of Money' (1924) 40 *Law Quarterly Review* 31
Hancock, William, 'The Usury Laws and the Trade of Lending Money to the Poor in Ireland' (1850–1851) 13 *Law Review and Quarterly Journal British Foreign Jurisprudence* 88
Ilbert, C., 'Indian Codification' (1889) 5 *Law Quarterly Review* 347
Ilbert, C., 'Sir James Fitzjames Stephen as a Legislator' (1894) 10 *Law Quarterly Review* 222
Langdell, C.C., 'Mutual Promises as a Consideration for Each Other' (1900–1901) 14 *Harvard Law Review* 496
Macaulay, Stuart, 'Non-Contractual Relations in Business: A Preliminary Study' (1963) 28 *American Sociological Review* 1
Pollock, Frederick, 'Notes on Current Cases' (1885) 1 *Law Quarterly Review* 134
Pollock, Frederick, 'Oxford Law Studies' (1886) 2 *Law Quarterly Review* 453
Pollock, Frederick, 'Afterthoughts on Consideration' (1901) 17 *Law Quarterly Review* 415
Pollock, Frederick, 'The Student's Summary of the Law of Contract' (1914) 30 *Law Quarterly Review* 128
Smollett, Tobias, 'The Frederician Code' (1762) 13 *The Critical Review Series I*, 1, 3
Williston, Samuel, 'Consideration in Bilateral Contracts' (1913–1914) 27 *Harvard Law Review* 503

Lord Wright, 'In Memoriam' (1937) 53 *Law Quarterly Review* 151, 154

Manuscripts

BL MS Hargrave 265, 266
All Souls MS 300 vol. 18 (unfol.)

Secondary sources

Books

Alexander, Gilchrist, *The Temple of the Nineties* (London: William Hodge, 1938)

Allen, C.J.W., *The Law of Evidence in Victorian England* (Cambridge: Cambridge University Press, 1997)

Allen, Carleton Kemp, *Law in the Making*, 4th edn (Oxford: Oxford University Press, 1946)

Appleby, Joyce, *Economic Thought and Ideology in Seventeenth-Century England* (Princeton: Princeton University Press, 1980)

Arthurs, H.W., *Without the Law* (Toronto: University of Toronto Press, 1985)

Ashton, John, *The History of Gambling in England* (London: Duckworth, 1898)

Ashton, T.S., *An Economic History of England: The 18th Century* (London: Methuen, 1959)

Atiyah, P.S., *The Rise and Fall of Freedom of Contract* (Oxford: Oxford University Press, 1979)

Atiyah, P.S., *Promises, Morals, And Law* (Oxford: Oxford University Press, 1981)

Atiyah, P.S., *Essays on Contract* (Oxford: Oxford University Press, 1986)

Backscheider, Paula, *Daniel Defoe: His Life* (Baltimore: Johns Hopkins University Press, 1989)

Baker, J.H., *English Legal Manuscripts*, 2 vols. (London: Inter Documentation Co., 1978)

Baker, J.H., *English Legal Manuscripts in the United States of America: A Descriptive List*, 2 vols. (London: Selden Society, 1985)

Baker, J.H., *The Common Law Tradition* (London: Hambledon, 2000)

Baker, J.H., *The Law's Two Bodies* (Oxford: Oxford University Press, 2001)

Baker, J.H., *An Introduction to English Legal History*, 4th edn (London: Butterworths, 2002)

Baker, J.H., *The Oxford History of the Laws of England Volume VI 1483–1558* (Oxford: Oxford University Press, 2003)

Baker, J.H., *Baker and Milsom Sources of English Legal History: Private Law to 1750*, 2nd edn (Oxford: Oxford University Press, 2010)

Balen, Malcolm, *A Very English Deceit: The South Sea Bubble and the World's First Great Financial Scandal* (London: Fourth Estate, 2002)

Baloch, Tariq, *Unjust Enrichment and Contract* (Oxford: Hart, 2009)

Bellamy, Liz, *Commerce, Morality and the Eighteenth-Century Novel* (Cambridge: Cambridge University Press, 1998)
Bennett, W.P., *The History and Present Position of the Bill of Lading as a Document of Title to Goods* (Cambridge: Cambridge University Press, 1914)
Berg, Maxine, *Luxury and Pleasure in Eighteenth Century Britain* (Oxford: Oxford University Press, 2005)
Brooks, Christopher, *Lawyers, Litigation and English Society since 1450* (London: Hambledon Press, 1998)
Brooks, C., *Pettyfoggers and Vipers of the Commonwealth: The 'Lower Branch' of the Legal Profession in Early Modern England* (Cambridge: Cambridge University Press, 2004)
Buckland, W.W., *Equity in Roman Law* (London: University of London Press, 1911)
Carr, E.H., *What Is History?*, 2nd edn (London: Penguin, 1988)
Carswell, John, *The South Sea Bubble* (London: Cresset Press, 1960)
Clark, Geoffrey, *Betting on Lives: The Culture of Life Insurance in England, 1695–1775* (Manchester: Manchester University Press, 1999)
Clark, J.C.D., *English Society 1660–1832* (Cambridge: Cambridge University Press, 2000)
Clay, C.G.A., *Economic Expansion and Social Change: England 1500–1700, II, Industry, Trade and Government* (Cambridge: Cambridge University Press, 1984)
Clive, John, *Macaulay: The Shaping of the Historian* (London: Secker & Warburg, 1973)
Cocks, Raymond, *Foundations of the Modern Bar* (London: Sweet & Maxwell, 1983)
Cocks, R.C.J., *Sir Henry Maine: A Study in Victorian Jurisprudence* (Cambridge: Cambridge University Press, 2004)
Cohn, Bernard, *Colonialism and its Forms of Knowledge* (Princeton: Princeton University Press, 1996)
Colley, Linda, *Britons Forging the Nation 1707–1837* (London: Pimlico, 1994)
Coquillette, Daniel, *The Civilian Writers of Doctors' Commons* (Berlin: Duncker & Humblot, 1988)
Corfield, Penelope, *Power and the Professions in Britain 1700–1850* (London: Routledge, 1995)
Cornish, W.R., and Clark, G. de N, *Law and Society in England 1750–1850* (London: Sweet & Maxwell, 1989)
Cornish, William, Anderson, Stuart, Cocks, Raymond, Lobban, Michael, Polden, Patrick and Smith, Keith, *The Oxford History of the Laws of England, Volume XI 1820–1914: English Legal System* (Oxford: Oxford University Press, 2010)
Cornish, William, Anderson, Stuart, Cocks, Raymond, Lobban, Michael, Polden, Patrick and Smith, Keith, *The Oxford History of the Laws of*

England, Vol. XII 1820–1914: Private Law (Oxford: Oxford University Press, 2010)

Cowan, Brian, *The Social Life of Coffee: The Emergence of the British Coffee House* (New Haven, Conn: Yale University Press, 2005)

Cownie, Fiona, *Legal Academics* (Oxford: Hart, 2004)

Crafts, N.F.R, *British Economic Growth During the Industrial Revolution* (Oxford: Oxford University Press, 1985)

Curley, Thomas, *Sir Robert Chambers Law, Literature, and Empire in the Age of Johnson* (Madison, Wis.: University of Wisconsin Press, 1998)

Davis, J.C., *Utopia and the Ideal Society: A Study in English Utopian Writing 1516–1700* (Cambridge: Cambridge University Press, 1983)

Dawson, John, *Unjust Enrichment: A Comparative Analysis* (Boston: Little, Brown & Co., 1951)

Lord Denning, *Borrowing from Scotland* (Glasgow: Jackson, 1963)

Dickson, P.G.M., *The Sun Insurance Office* (Oxford: Oxford University Press, 1960)

Dinwiddy, J.R., *Bentham* (Oxford: Oxford University Press, 1989)

Duman, Daniel, *The Judicial Bench in England 1727–1875* (London: Royal Historical Society, 1982)

Duxbury, Neil, *Patterns of American Jurisprudence* (Oxford: Oxford University Press, 2001)

Duxbury, Neil, *Jurists and Judges* (Oxford: Hart, 2001)

Duxbury, Neil, *Frederick Pollock and the English Juristic Tradition* (Oxford: Oxford University Press, 2004)

Duxbury, Neil, *The Nature and Authority of Precedent* (Cambridge: Cambridge University Press, 2008)

Dworkin, Ronald, *Justice in Robes* (Cambridge, Mass.: Harvard University Press, 2006)

Earle, Peter, *The Making of the English Middle Class* (London: Methuen, 1991)

Earle, Peter, *Sailors: English Merchant Seamen 1650–1775* (London: Methuen, 2007)

Ellegård, Alvar, *Who Was Junius?* (Stockholm: Almquist & Wiksell, 1962)

Evans, Richard, *In Defence of History* (London: Granta, 1997)

Feaver, George, *From Status to Contract: A Biography of Sir Henry Maine 1822–1888* (London: Longmans, 1969)

Fifoot, C.H.S., *Lord Mansfield* (Oxford: Oxford University Press, 1938)

Fifoot, C.H.S., *History and Sources of the Common Law* (London: Stevens & Sons, 1949)

Fifoot, C.H.S., *Judge and Jurist in the Reign of Victoria* (London: Sweet & Maxwell, 1959)

Finn, Margot, *The Character of Credit* (Cambridge: Cambridge University Press, 2003)

Franklin, Michael, *Orientalist Jones* (Oxford: Oxford University Press, 2011)

Friedman, Lawrence, *The Legal System: A Social Science Perspective* (New York: Russell Sage, 1987)

Gilmore, Grant, *The Death of Contract* (Columbus: Ohio State University Press, 1974)

Gordley, James, *The Philosophical Origins of Modern Contract Doctrine* (Oxford: Oxford University Press, 1991)

Gordley, James, *Foundations of Private Law* (Oxford: Oxford University Press, 2006)

Grassby, Richard, *The Business Community of Seventeenth-Century England* (Cambridge: Cambridge University Press, 2002)

Greig, Hannah, *The Beau Monde* (Oxford: Oxford University Press, 2013)

Griffin, Dustin, *Patriotism and Poetry in Eighteenth Century Britain* (Cambridge: Cambridge University Press, 2002)

Haakonssen, Knud, *Natural Law and Moral Philosophy* (Cambridge: Cambridge University Press, 1996)

Hallebeek, Jan, *The Concept of Unjust Enrichment in Late Scholasticism* (Nijmegen: Gerard Noodt Instituut, 1996)

Hallebeek, Jan and Dondorp, Harry, *Contracts for the Third-Party Beneficiary* (Leiden: Martinus Nijhoff, 2008)

Hallett, Mark and Riding, Christine, *Hogarth* (London: Tate, 2006)

Hamburger, Joseph, *Macaulay and the Whig Tradition* (London: University of Chicago Press, 1976)

Hanbury, Harold, *The Vinerian Chair and Legal Education* (Oxford: Blackwell, 1958)

Hardcastle, M.S., *Life of John, Lord Campbell*, 2 vols. (London: John Murray, 1881)

Harris, Robin, *Not For Turning: The Life of Margaret Thatcher* (London: Bantam Press, 2013)

Hay, Douglas, Linebaugh, Peter, Rule, John G., Thompson, E.P. and Winslow, Cal, *Albion's Fatal Tree* (New York: Pantheon Books, 1975)

Helmholz, R.H., *The Oxford History of the Laws of England Vol. I The Canon Law and Ecclesiastical Jurisdiction from 597 to the 1640s* (Oxford: Oxford University Press, 2004)

Heward, Edmund, *Lord Mansfield* (London: Barry Rose, 1979)

Heydon, J.D., *The Restraint of Trade Doctrine*, 2nd edn (Sydney: Butterworths, 1999)

Hill, Christopher, *The World Turned Upside Down* (London: Penguin, 1991)

Hochstrasser, T.J., *Natural Law Theories in the Early Enlightenment* (Cambridge: Cambridge University Press, 2000)

Hoeflich, M.H., *Roman and Civil Law and the Development of Anglo-American Jurisprudence in the Nineteenth Century* (Athens, Ga: University of Georgia Press, 1997)

Hoeflich, Michael, *Legal Publishing in Antebellum America* (New York: Cambridge University Press, 2010)

Hogg, Martin, *Promises and Contract Law* (Cambridge: Cambridge University Press, 2011)

Hoggart, Richard, *The Uses of Literacy* (London: Penguin, 2009)

Holden, J. Milnes, *The History of Negotiable Instruments in English Law* (London: Athlone Press, 1955)

Holdsworth, W.S., *A History of English Law*, 17 vols. (London: Methuen, 1922–1972)

Holdsworth, W.S., *Sources and Literature of English Law* (Oxford: Oxford University Press, 1925)

Holmes, Richard, *The Age of Wonder* (London: Harper Collins, 2008)

Hoppit, Julian, *A Land of Liberty? England 1689–1727* (Oxford: Oxford University Press, 2000)

Horwitz, Morton, *The Transformation of American Law 1870–1960* (Oxford: Oxford University Press, 1992)

Hudson, Kenneth, *Pawnbroking: An Aspect of British Social History* (London: The Bodley Head, 1982)

Hunt, Edwin, *A History of Business 1200–1550* (Cambridge: Cambridge University Press, 1999)

Hurst, James Willard, *Law and Economic Growth: The Legal History of the Lumber Industry in Wisconsin 1836–1915* (Cambridge, Mass.: Harvard University Press, 1964)

Hutchinson, Allan C., *Evolution and the Common Law* (Cambridge: Cambridge University Press, 2005)

Ibbetson, David, *An Historical Introduction to the Law of Obligations* (Oxford: Oxford University Press, 1999)

Jackson, Gordon, *Hull in the Eighteenth Century: A Study in Economic and Social History* (Oxford: Oxford University Press, 1972)

Jackson, R.M., *The History of Quasi-Contract in English Law* (Cambridge: Cambridge University Press, 1936)

Jacob, Margaret, *Living the Enlightenment: Freemasonry and Politics in Eighteenth Century Europe* (New York: Oxford University Press, 1991)

Jain, J.P., *Indian Legal History*, 2nd edn (Bombay: Tripathi, 1966)

Johnson, Paul, *Saving and Spending: The Working Class Economy in Britain 1870–1939* (Oxford: Oxford University Press, 1985)

Jones, Norman, *God and the Moneylenders* (Oxford: Basil Blackwell, 1989)

Karsten, Peter, *Heart versus Head: Judge-Made Law in Nineteenth-Century America* (Chapel Hill: University of North Carolina Press, 1997)

Kates, Gary, *Monsieur D'Eon is a Woman* (Baltimore: Johns Hopkins University Press, 2001)

Kennedy, Duncan, *The Rise and Fall of Classical Legal Thought* (Washington D.C.: Beard Books, 2006)

King, Blair, *The Blue Mutiny: The Indigo Disturbances in Bengal 1859–1862* (Philadelphia: University of Pennsylvania Press, 1966)

Klinck, Dennis, *Conscience, Equity and the Court of Chancery in Early Modern England* (Farnham: Ashgate Publishing, 2010)

Knowles, Dudley, *Routledge Philosophy Guidebook to Hegel and the Philosophy of Right* (London: Routledge, 2002)

Kreitner, Roy, *Calculating Promises* (Stanford, Calif.: Stanford University Press, 2007)

Lambert, Sheila, *Bills and Acts: Legislative Procedure in Eighteenth Century England* (Cambridge: Cambridge University Press, 1971)

Langford, Paul, *A Polite and Commercial People* (Oxford: Oxford University Press, 1992)

Langford, Paul, *Public Life and the Propertied Englishman 1689–1798* (Oxford: Oxford University Press, 1994)

Lawson, F.H. (ed.), W.W. Buckland and Arnold McNair, *Roman Law and Common Law* (Cambridge: Cambridge University Press, 1952)

Lawson, F.H., *The Oxford Law School 1850–1965* (Oxford: Oxford University Press, 1968)

Le Mahieu, D.L., *The Mind of William Paley* (Lincoln, Nebr.: University of Nebraska Press, 1976)

Lemmings, David, *Gentlemen and Barristers* (Oxford: Oxford University Press, 1990)

Lemmings, David, *Professors of the Law* (Oxford: Oxford University Press, 2000)

Letwin, William, *The Origins of Scientific Economics* (London: Routledge, 2003)

Lewin, C.G., *Pensions and Insurance Before 1800* (East Linton: Tuckwell Press, 2003)

Lieberman, David, *The Province of Legislation Determined: Legal Theory in Eighteenth Century Britain* (Cambridge: Cambridge University Press, 1989)

Lloyd, Dennis, *Public Policy: A Comparative Study in English and French Law* (London: Athlone Press, 1953)

Lobban, Michael, *The Common Law and English Jurisprudence 1760–1850* (Oxford: Oxford University Press, 1991)

Mackie, Erin, *The Commerce of Everyday Life* (London: Palgrave, 1998)

MacMillan, Catharine, *Mistakes in Contract Law* (Oxford: Hart, 2009)

McVeigh, John, *Tradefull Merchants* (London: Routledge, 1981)

Manchester, A.H., *Modern Legal History* (London: Butterworths, 1980)

Markman, Ellis, *The Coffee House: A Cultural History* (London: Weidenfeld & Nicholson, 2004)

Martin, Frederick, *The History of Lloyd's and of Marine Insurance in Great Britain* (London: Macmillan, 1876)

Mathias, Peter, *The First Industrial Nation*, 2nd edn (London: Methuen, 1995)

Melikan, Rose, *John Scott, Lord Eldon, 1751–1838: The Duty of Loyalty* (Cambridge: Cambridge University Press, 1999)

Metcalf, Thomas, *Ideologies of the Raj* (Cambridge: Cambridge University Press, 1994)

Michie, Ranald, *The London Stock Exchange: A History* (Oxford: Oxford University Press, 2001)

Miers, David, *Regulating Commercial Gambling* (Oxford: Oxford University Press, 2004)

Milsom, S.F.C., *The Legal Framework of English Feudalism* (Cambridge: Cambridge University Press, 1976)

Milsom, S.F.C., *The Natural History of the Common Law* (New York: Columbia University Press, 2003)

Mitchell, B.R., *Abstract of British Historical Statistics* (Cambridge: Cambridge University Press, 1962)

Mitchell, B.R., *European Historical Statistics 1750–1975*, 2nd edn (London: Macmillan, 1981)

Morison, W.L., *John Austin* (London: Arnold, 1982)

Muldrew, Craig, *The Economy of Obligation* (Basingstoke: Macmillan, 1998)

Murray, Alexander (ed.), *Sir William Jones 1746–94: A Commemoration* (Oxford: Oxford University Press, 1998)

Nicholas, Barry, *An Introduction to Roman Law* (Oxford: Oxford University Press, 1969)

Ogilvie, R.M., *Latin and Greek: A History of the Influence of Classics on English Life from 1600 to 1918* (London: Routledge & Kegan Paul, 1964)

Oldham, James, *English Common Law in the Age of Mansfield* (Chapel Hill: University of North Carolina Press, 2004)

Oldham, James, *The Varied Life of the Self-Informing Jury* (London: Selden Society, 2005)

Pagden, Anthony, *The Enlightenment and Why It Still Matters* (Oxford: Oxford University Press, 2013)

Palmer, Vernon, *The Paths to Privity* (Clark, N.J.: The Lawbook Exchange, 2006)

Paterson, Alan, *The Law Lords* (London: Macmillan, 1982)

Paterson, Alan, *Final Judgment* (Oxford: Hart, 2013)

Pocock, J.G.A., *The Ancient Constitution and the Feudal Law: A Study of English Historical Thought in the Seventeenth Century*, 2nd edn (Cambridge: Cambridge University Press, 1987)

Polden, Patrick, *A History of the County Court, 1846–1971* (Cambridge: Cambridge University Press, 1999)

Pollock, Frederick and Maitland, Frederic, *The History of English Law Before the Time of Edward I*, 2nd edn, 2 vols. (Cambridge: Cambridge University Press, 1968)

Porter, Roy, *Enlightenment* (London: Penguin, 2000)

Postan, M., *Medieval Trade and Finance* (Cambridge: Cambridge University Press, 1973)

Prest, Wilfrid, *William Blackstone: Law and Letters in the Eighteenth Century* (Oxford: Oxford University Press, 2008)

Pugh, L.P., *From Farriery to Veterinary Medicine 1785–1795* (Cambridge: Heffer, 1962)

Rankin, George, *Background to Indian Law* (Cambridge: Cambridge University Press, 1946)

Raven, James, *Judging New Wealth* (Oxford: Oxford University Press, 1992)

Raynes, Harold, *A History of British Assurance*, 2nd edn (London: Pitman, 1964)

Rich, E.E. and Wilson, C.H. (eds.), *The Cambridge Economic History of Europe*, 8 vols. (Cambridge: Cambridge University Press, 1977)

Rocher, Rosane and Rocher, Ludo, *The Making of Western Indology* (Abingdon: Routledge, 2012)

Rogers, James, *The Early History of the Law of Bills and Notes* (Cambridge: Cambridge University Press, 1995)

Roscoe, Edward, *A History of the English Prize Court* (London: Lloyds, 1924)

Rule, John, *The Vital Century* (London: Longman, 1995)

Schofield, Phillip, *Utility and Democracy* (Oxford: Oxford University Press, 2009)

Schulz, Fritz, *Classical Roman Law* (Oxford: Oxford University Press, 1951)

Seabourne, Gwen, *Royal Regulation of Loans and Sales in Medieval England* (Woodbridge: The Boydell Press, 2003)

Shapiro, Barbara, *A Culture of Fact: England 1550–1720* (Ithaca: Cornell University Press, 2003)

Sheridan, L.A., *Fraud in Equity: A Study in English and Irish Law* (London: Pitman, 1957)

Simpson, A.W.B., *A History of the Land Law*, 2nd edn (Oxford: Oxford University Press, 1986)

Simpson, A.W. Brian, *A History of the Common Law of Contract: The Rise of the Action of Assumpsit*, pbk edn (Oxford: Oxford University Press, 1987)

Simpson, A.W. Brian, *Reflections on the Concept of Law* (Oxford: Oxford University Press, 2011)

Smith, K.J.M., *James Fitzjames Stephen* (Cambridge: Cambridge University Press, 2002)

Smith, Stephen, *Contract Theory* (Oxford: Oxford University Press, 2004)

Starkey, David, *British Privateering Enterprise in the Eighteenth Century* (Exeter: University of Exeter Press, 1990)

Stein, Peter (ed.), W.W. Buckland, *A Textbook of Roman Law from Augustus to Justinian*, 3rd edn (Cambridge: Cambridge University Press, 1963)

Stein, P.G., *The Character and Influence of the Roman Civil Law* (London: Hambledon, 1988)

Steinberg, S.H., *Five Hundred Years of Printing*, 3rd edn (London: Penguin, 1974)

Stewart, Robert, *H. Brougham 1778–1868: His Public Career* (London: The Bodley Head, 1985)

Stokes, Eric, *The English Utilitarians and India* (Oxford: Oxford University Press, 1959)

Stoljar, S.J., *A History of Contract at Common Law* (Canberra: Australian National University Press, 1975)

Stone, Lawrence, *The Crisis of the Aristocracy 1558–1641* (Oxford: Oxford University Press, 1965)

Supple, Barry, The Royal Exchange Insurance (Cambridge: Cambridge University Press, 1970)

Sutherland, Lucy, *A London Merchant 1695–1774* (London: Frank Cass, 1962)

Tebbutt, Melanie, *Making Ends Meet: Pawnbroking and Working-Class Credit* (London: Methuen, 1984)

Teeven, Kevin, *A History of the Anglo-American Common Law of Contract* (New York: Greenwood Press, 1990)

Teeven, Kevin, *Promises on Prior Obligations at Common Law* (Westport: Greenwood, 1998)

Thomas, E.W., *The Judicial Process* (Cambridge: Cambridge University Press, 2005)

Trebilcock, M.J., *The Common Law of Restraint of Trade* (Toronto: Carswell, 1986)

Van Caenegem, R.C., *Judges, Legislators and Professors* (Cambridge: Cambridge University Press, 1993)

Van den Berg, Peter, *The Politics of European Codification* (Groningen: Europa Law Publishing, 2007)

Veall, Donald, *The Popular Movement for Law Reform* (Oxford: Oxford University Press, 1970)

Waddams, Stephen, *Principle and Policy in Contract Law* (Cambridge: Cambridge University Press, 2011)

Weiner, Martin, *English Culture and the Decline of the Industrial Spirit 1850–1980*, 2nd edn (Cambridge: Cambridge University Press, 2004)

Weir, Tony (trans.), Franz Wieacker, *A History of Private Law in Europe* (Oxford: Oxford University Press, 2003)

Winter, James, *Robert Lowe* (Toronto: University of Toronto Press, 1976)

Wiswall, F., *The Development of Admiralty Jurisdiction and Practice since 1800* (Cambridge: Cambridge University Press, 1970)

Wood, Diane, *Medieval Economic Thought* (Cambridge: Cambridge University Press, 2002)

Wormald, Patrick, *Legal Culture in the Early Medieval West* (London: Hambledon, 1999)

Wrightson, Keith, *Earthly Necessities* (London: Penguin, 2002)

Zimmermann, Reinhard, *The Law of Obligations: Roman Foundations of the Civilian Tradition* (Oxford: Oxford University Press, 1996)

Articles and book chapters

Ames, J.B., 'Two Theories of Consideration' (1898–1899) 12 *Harvard Law Review* 515

Anderson, B.L., 'Money and the Structure of Credit in the Eighteenth Century' (1970) 12 *Business History* 85

Anderson, R.A., rev. R. Mills, 'Hey, Richard', *Oxford Dictionary of National Biography*

Arnold, Morris, 'Law and Fact in the Medieval Jury Trial: Out of Sight, Out of Mind' (1974) 18 *American Journal of Legal History* 267

Arthurs, H.W., 'Without the Law: Courts of Local and Special Jurisdiction in Nineteenth Century England' (1984) 5 *Journal of Legal History* 130

Ashton, T.S., 'The Bill of Exchange and Private Banks 1790–1830' (1945) 15 *Economic History Review* 25

Atiyah, Patrick, 'An Autobiographical Fragment', in Geoffrey Wilson (ed.), *Frontiers of Legal Scholarship* (Chichester: Wiley, 1995), pp. 34–46

Baker, J.H., 'New Light on Slade's Case' (1971) 29 *Cambridge Law Journal* 51

Baker, J.H., 'University College and Legal Education 1826–1976' (1977) 30 *Current Legal Problems* 1

Baker, J.H., 'The Law Merchant and the Common Law Before 1700' (1979) 38 *Cambridge Law Journal* 295

Baker, J.H., 'Review of P.S. Atiyah, Rise and Fall of Freedom of Contract' (1980) 43 *Modern Law Review* 467

Baker, J.H., 'Origins of the "Doctrine" of Consideration, 1535–1585', in Morris Arnold *et al.* (eds.), *On the Laws and Customs of England: Essays in Honor of Samuel E. Thorne* (Chapel Hill: University of North Carolina Press, 1981), pp. 336–58

Baker, J.H., 'Records, Reports and the Origins of Case-Law in England', in John Baker (ed.), *Judicial Records, Law Reports, and the Growth of Case Law* (Berlin: Duncker & Humblot, 1989), pp. 15–46

Baker, J.H., 'Custom and Usage', in *Halsbury's Laws of England* (London: Butterworths, 1998), vol. XII (I)

Baker, J.H., 'The Use of Assumpsit for Restitutionary Money Claims 1600–1800', in Eltjo Schrage (ed.), *Unjust Enrichment: The Comparative Legal History of the Law of Restitution* (Berlin: Duncker & Humblot, 1995), pp. 31–57

Baker, J.H., 'The Law Merchant as a Source of English Law', in William Swadling and Gareth Jones, *The Search for Principle: Essays for Lord Goff of Chieveley* (Oxford: Oxford University Press, 2000), pp. 79–96

Baker, John, 'Privity of Contract in the Common Law before 1680', in Eltjo Schrage (ed.), *Ius Quaesitum Tertio* (Berlin: Duncker & Humblot, 2008), pp. 35–60

Baloch, Tariq, 'Law Booksellers and Printers as Agents of Unchange' (2007) 66 *Cambridge Law Journal* 389

Barton, J.L., 'Review of AWB Simpson, A History of the Common Law of Contract' (1977) 27 *University of Toronto Law Journal* 373

Barton, J.L., 'Contract and Quantum Meruit: The Antecedents of Cutter v. Powell' (1987) 8 *Journal of Legal History* 48

Barton, J.L., 'Contractual Damages and the Rise of Industry' (1987) 7 *Oxford Journal of Legal Studies* 40

Barton, J.L., 'The Enforcement of Hard Bargains' (1987) 103 *Law Quarterly Review* 118

Barton, J.L., 'Redhibition, Error and Implied Warranty in English Law' (1994) 62 *Tijdschrift voor Rechtsgeschiedenis* 317

Beatson, Jack, 'Restitution and Contract: Non-Cumul?' (2001) 1 *Theoretical Inquiries in Law* 83

Beatson, Jack, 'Legal Academics: Forgotten Players or Interlopers?', in Andrew Burrows, David Johnson and Reinhard Zimmermann (eds.), *Judge and Jurist: Essays in Memory of Lord Rodger of Earlsferry* (Oxford: Oxford University Press, 2013), pp. 523–41

Benke, N., '"No Inefficacy Arises Merely from the Naked Promise" Bermerkungen zu Consideration und Versprechen in Pillans v. Van Mierop (1765)' (1987) 14 *Ius Commune* 1

Berg, Maxine and Hudson, Pat, 'Rehabilitating the Industrial Revolution' (1992) 45 *Economic History Review (NS)* 24

Berman, Harold and Reid, Charles, 'The Transformation of English Legal Science from Hale to Blackstone' (1996) 45 *Emory Law Journal* 437

Birks, Peter, 'English and Roman Learning in Moses v. Macferlan' (1984) 37 *Current Legal Problems* 1

Birks, Peter and MacLeod, Grant, 'The Implied Contract Theory of Quasi-Contract: Civilian Opinion Current in the Century Before Blackstone' (1986) 6 *Oxford Journal of Legal Studies* 46

Birks, Peter and Yin, Chin Nyuk, 'On the Nature of Undue Influence', in Jack Beatson and Daniel Friedmann (eds.), *Good Faith and Contract Law* (Oxford: Oxford University Press, 1995), pp. 57–97

Birks, Peter, 'Comparative Unjust Enrichment', in Peter Birks and Arienna Pretto (eds.), *Themes in Comparative Law* (Oxford: Oxford University Press, 2002), pp. 137–51

Borsay, Peter, 'The Culture of Improvement', in Paul Langford (ed.), *The Eighteenth Century* (Oxford: Oxford University Press, 2002), pp. 183–212

Bowerbank, S., 'Southcott, Joanna', *Oxford Dictionary of National Biography*

Bronaugh, Richard, 'A Secret Paradox of the Common Law' (1983) 2 *Law & Philosophy* 193

Burrows, S., 'Théveneau de Morande, Charles-Claude', *Oxford Dictionary of National Biography*

Burrows, Simon, 'A Literary Low-Life Reassessed: Charles Théveneau de Morande in London, 1769–1791' (1998) 22 *Eighteenth Century Life* 76

Cairns, John, 'Eighteenth Century Professorial Classification of English Common Law' (1987–1988) 33 *McGill Law Journal* 226

Cairns, John, 'Legal Theory', in Alexander Broadie (ed.), *The Cambridge Companion to the Scottish Enlightenment* (Cambridge: Cambridge University Press, 2003), pp. 222–42

Cairns, John, 'Famous as a School for Law, as Edinburgh . . . for Medicine: Legal Education in Glasgow, 1761–1801', in Andrew Hook and Richard Sher (eds.), *The Glasgow Enlightenment* (East Linton: Tuckwell Press, 1995), pp. 133–59

Campbell, Sybil, 'Usury and Annuities of the Eighteenth Century' (1928) 44 *Law Quarterly Review* 473

Campbell, Sybil, 'The Economic and Social Effect of the Usury Laws in the Eighteenth Century' (1933) 16 *Transactions of the Royal Historical Society 4th Series* 197

Cannadine, David, 'The Present and the Past in the English Industrial Revolution 1880–1980' (1984) 103 *Past and Present* 131

Clark, D., 'The Civil Law Influence on David Dudley Field's Code of Civil Procedure', in Mathias Reimann (ed.), *The Reception of Continental Ideas in the Common Law World 1820–1920* (Berlin: Duncker & Humblot, 1993), pp. 63–87

Clark, Gregory, 'Debt, Deficits, and Crowding Out: England, 1727–1840' (2001) 5 *European Review of Economic History* 403

Cocks, Ray, 'The Middle Temple in the 19th Century', in Richard Harvery (ed.), *History of the Middle Temple* (Oxford: Hart, 2011), pp. 287–336

Cohn, Bernard, 'From Indian Status to British Contract' (1961) 21 *Journal of Economic History* 613

Coquillette, Daniel, 'Legal Ideology and Incorporation IV: The Nature of Civilian Influence on Modern Anglo-American Commercial Law' (1987) 67 *Boston University Law Review* 877

Cordasco, Francesco, 'Junius', *Oxford Dictionary of National Biography*

Courtney, W.P., rev. Matthew Kilburn, 'Lee, Sir George', *Oxford Dictionary of National Biography*

Cranston, Ross, 'The Rise and Rise of Standard Form Contracts: International Commodity Sales 1800–1970', in Ross Cranston, Jan Ramberg and Jacob Zeigler (eds.), *Commercial Law Challenges in the Twenty First Century* (Stockholm: Iustus Forlag, 2007), pp. 11–71

Croft, Clyde, 'Lord Hardwick's Use of Precedent in Equity', in Thomas Watkin (ed.), *Legal Record and Historical Reality* (London: Hambledon, 1989), pp. 121–55

Cunnington, Ralph, 'Failure of Basis' [2004] *Lloyds Maritime and Commercial Law Quarterly* 234

Danzig, Richard, 'Hadley v. Baxendale: A Study in the Industrialization of the Law' (1975) 4 *Journal of Legal Studies* 249

Davis, M., 'Mansfield, James Sir', *Oxford Dictionary of National Biography*

Davis, Ralph, 'English Foreign Trade, 1660–1700' (1954) 7 *Economic History Review (NS)* 150

Devine, Dennis *et al.*, 'Jury Decision Making: 45 Years of Empirical Research on Deliberating Groups' (2001) 7 *Psychology, Public Policy and Law* 622

Dicey, A.V., 'Law-Teaching, Oral and Written', in Herbert Henson (ed.), *A Memoir of the Right Honourable Sir William Anson* (Oxford: Oxford University Press, 1920), pp. 84–102

Dinwiddy, J.R., 'Early Nineteenth Century Reactions to Benthamism' (1984) 34 *Transactions of the Royal Historical Society 5th Series* 47

Ditchfield, G.M., 'Wallace, James', *Oxford Dictionary of National Biography*

Dockray, Martin, 'Cutter v. Powell: A Trip Outside the Text' (2001) 117 *Law Quarterly Review* 664

Dwyer, Deidre, 'Expert Evidence in the English Civil Courts 1550–1800' (2007) 28 *Journal of Legal History* 93

Dylag, Matthew, 'The Negotiability of Promissory Notes and Bills of Exchange in the Time of Chief Justice Holt' (2010) 31 *Journal of Legal History* 149

Falmer, Lindsay, 'Reconstructing the English Codification Debate: The Criminal Law Commissioners, 1833–45' (2000) 18 *Law and History Review* 397

Faust, Florian, 'Hadley v. Baxendale: An Understandable Miscarriage of Justice' (1994) 15 *Journal of Legal History* 41

Feenstra, Robert, 'Grotius' Doctrine of Unjust Enrichment as a Source of Obligation: Its Origin and Its Influence in Roman-Dutch Law', in Eltjo Schrage (ed.), *Unjust Enrichment: The Comparative Legal History of the Law of Restitution* (Berlin: Duncker & Humblot, 1995), pp. 197–236

Ferguson, R.B., 'Legal Ideology and Commercial Interests: The Social Origins of the Commercial Law Codes' (1977) 4 *British Journal of Law and Society* 18

Finer, S.E., 'The Transmission of Benthamite Ideas 1820–50', in Gillian Sutherland (ed.), *Studies in the Growth of Nineteenth Century Government* (London: Routledge & Kegan Paul, 1972), pp. 11–32

Finn, Margot, 'Debt and Credit in Bath's Court of Requests 1829–39' (1994) 21 *Urban History* 211

Flannigan, Robert, 'Privity – The End of an Era (Error)' (1987) 103 *Law Quarterly Review* 564

Francis, Clinton, 'The Structure of Judicial Administration and the Development of Contract Law in Seventeenth-Century England' (1983) 83 *Columbia Law Review* 35

Francis, Clinton, 'Practice, Strategy, and Institution: Debt Collection in the English Common-Law Courts, 1740–1840' (1985–1986) 80 *Northwestern University Law Review* 807

Gardner, Simon, 'Trashing with Trollope: A Deconstruction of the Postal Rules in Contract' (1992) 12 *Oxford Journal of Legal Studies* 170

Gash, N., 'Surtees, Robert Smith', *Oxford Dictionary of National Biography*

Getzler, Joshua, 'The Fate of the Civil Jury in Late Victorian England: Malicious Prosecution as a Test Case', in John Cairns and Grant McLeod (eds.), *The Dearest Birth Right of the People of England* (Oxford: Hart, 2002), pp. 218–37

Gooderson, R.N., 'English Contract Problems in Indian Code and Case Law' (1958) 16 *Cambridge Law Journal* 67

Gordley, James, 'Contract, Property, and Will – The Civil Law and Common Law Tradition', in Harry Scheiber (ed.), *The State and Freedom of Contract* (Stanford, Calif.: Stanford University Press, 1998), pp. 66–88

Gordley, James, 'Good Faith in Contract Law in the Medieval Ius Commune', in Reinhard Zimmermann and Simon Whittaker (eds.), *Good Faith in European Contract Law* (Cambridge: Cambridge University Press, 2000), pp. 93–117

Gordon, Robert, 'Historicism in Legal Scholarship' (1980–1981) 90 *Yale Law Journal* 1017

Gordon, Robert, 'Critical Legal Histories' (1984) 36 *Stanford Law Review* 57

Grantham, Ross and Rickett, Charles, 'On the Subsidiarity of Unjust Enrichment' (2001) 117 *Law Quarterly Review* 273

Grover, Robinson, 'The Legal Origins of Thomas Hobbes's Doctrine of Contract' (1980) 18 *Journal of the History of Philosophy* 177

Hallebeek, Jan, 'Ius Questitum Tertio in Medieval Roman Law', in Eltjo Schrage (ed.), *Ius Quaesitum Tertio* (Berlin: Duncker & Humblot, 2008), pp. 7–20

Hamburger, Philip, 'The Development of the Nineteenth-Century Consensus Theory of Contract' (1989) 7 *Law and History Review* 241

Hamilton, J.A., rev., Hugh Mooney, 'Lush, Sir Robert', *Oxford Dictionary of National Biography*

Hamilton, J.A., rev., Patrick Polden, 'Romilly, John', *Oxford Dictionary of National Biography*

Hanbury, H.G., 'Blackstone in Retrospect' (1950) 66 *Law Quarterly Review* 318

Hanly, Conor, 'The Decline of Civil Jury Trial in Nineteenth-Century England' (2005) 26 *Journal of Legal History* 253

Hedley, Steve, 'Chalmers, Sir Mackenzie Dalzell', *Oxford Dictionary of National Biography*

Hedley, Stephen, 'Keeping Contract in its Place – Balfour v. Balfour and the Enforceability of Informal Agreements' (1985) 5 *Oxford Journal of Legal Studies* 391

Hedley, Steve, 'From Individualism to Communitarianism? The Case of Standard Forms', in Thomas Watkin (ed.), *Legal Record and Historical Reality* (London: Hambledon Press, 1989), pp. 229–42

Hedley, Steve, 'Is Private Law Meaningless?' (2011) 64 *Current Legal Problems* 89

Helmholz, R.H., 'Usury and the Medieval English Church Courts' (1986) 61 *Speculum* 364

Henderson, Edith, 'Relief from Bonds in the English Chancery: Mid-Sixteenth Century' (1974) *American Journal of Legal History* 298

Hogan, John, 'Joseph Story on the Law of Contract' (1957–1958) 12 *Rutgers Law Review* 366

Holdsworth, W.S., 'Early History of the Contract of Insurance' (1917) 17 *Columbia Law Review* 85

Holdsworth, W., 'New Rules of Pleading of the Hilary Term 1834' (1923) 1 *Cambridge Law Journal* 261

Holdsworth, W., 'Blackstone's Treatment of Equity' (1929–1930) 43 *Harvard Law Review* 1

Hoppit, Julian, 'Financial Crisis in Eighteenth Century England' (1986) 39 *Economic History Review* 39

Horwitz, Henry and Oldham, James, 'John Locke, Lord Mansfield, and Arbitration During the Eighteenth Century' (1993) 36 *Historical Journal* 137

Horwitz, Henry and Polden, Patrick, 'Continuity or Change in the Court of Chancery in the Seventeenth and Eighteenth Centuries?' (1996) 35 *Journal of British Studies* 24

Horwitz, Henry, 'The Nisi Prius Trial Notes of Lord Chancellor Hardwicke' (2002) 23 *Journal of Legal History* 152

Horwitz, Henry, 'Changes in the Law and Reform of the Legal Order: England (and Wales) 1689–1760' (2002) 21 *Parliamentary History* 301

Horwitz, Morton, 'The Conservative Tradition in the Writing of American Legal History' (1973) 17 *American Journal of Legal History* 275

Horwitz, Morton, 'The Rise of Legal Formalism' (1975) 19 *American Journal of Legal History* 251

Hostettler, J., 'Jeremy Bentham – Reformer Extraordinary' (1992) 156 *Justice of the Peace and Local Government Law* 668

Ibbetson, D., 'Natural Law and Common Law' (2001) 5 *Edinburgh Law Review* 4

Ibbetson, David, 'Assumpsit and Debt in the Early Sixteenth Century: The Origins of the Indebitatus Count' (1982) 41 *Cambridge Law Journal* 142

Ibbetson, David, 'Sixteenth Century Contract Law: Slade's Case in Context' (1984) 4 *Oxford Journal of Legal Studies* 295

Ibbetson, David, 'Implied Contracts and Restitution: History in the High Court of Australia' (1988) 8 *Oxford Journal of Legal Studies* 312

Ibbetson, David, 'Consideration and the Theory of Contract in the Sixteenth Century Common Law', in John Barton (ed.), *Towards a General Law of Contract* (Berlin: Duncker & Humblot, 1990), pp. 67–123

Ibbetson, David, 'Unjust Enrichment in England before 1600', in Eltjo Schrage (ed.), *Unjust Enrichment: The Comparative Legal History of the Law of Restitution* (Berlin: Duncker & Humblot, 1995), pp. 121–48

Ibbetson, David, 'Sir William Jones as a Comparative Lawyer', in Alexander Murray (ed.), *Sir William Jones 1746–94: A Commemoration* (Oxford: Oxford University Press, 1998), pp. 17–42

Ibbetson, David, 'The Tort of Negligence in the Common Law in the Nineteenth and Twentieth Centuries', in Eltjo Schrage (ed.), *Negligence: The*

Comparative Legal History of the Law of Torts (Berlin: Dunker & Humblot, 2001), pp. 229–71

Ibbetson, David, 'What Is Legal History a History of?', in Andrew Lewis and Michael Lobban (eds.), *Law and History* (Oxford: Oxford University Press, 2004), pp. 33–40

Ibbetson, David, 'Legal Periodicals in England 1820–1870' (2006) 28 *Zeitschrift für Neuere Rechtsgeschichte* 175

Ibbetson, David, 'Custom in Medieval Law', in Amanda Perreau-Saussine and James Murphy (eds.), *The Nature of Customary Law* (Cambridge: Cambridge University Press, 2007), pp. 151–75

Ibbetson, David and Swain, Warren, 'Third Party Beneficiaries in English Law: From Dutton v. Poole to Tweddle v. Atkinson', in Eltjo Schrage (ed.), *Ius Quaesitum Tertio* (Berlin: Duncker & Humblot, 2008), pp. 191–213

Ibbetson, David, 'Coggs v. Barnard (1703)', in Charles Mitchell and Paul Mitchell (eds.), *Landmark Cases in the Law of Contract* (Oxford: Hart, 2008)

Ibbetson, David, 'Law and Custom: Insurance in Sixteenth Century England' (2008) 29 *Journal of Legal History* 291

Ibbetson, David, 'Comparative Legal History: A Methodology', in Anthony Musson and Chantal Stebbings (eds.), *Making Legal History* (Cambridge: Cambridge University Press, 2012), pp. 131–45

Ibbetson, David, 'The Assessment of Contractual Damages at Common Law in the Late Sixteenth Century', in Matthew Dyson and David Ibbetson (eds.), *Law and the Legal Process* (Cambridge: Cambridge University Press, 2013), pp. 126–47

Jackson, R.M., 'The Scope of the Term "Contract"' (1937) 53 *Law Quarterly Review* 535

Jackson, R.M., 'The Incidence of Jury Trial During the Past Century' (1937–1938) 1 *Modern Law Review* 132

Johnson, Gordon, 'India and Henry Maine', in Alan Diamond (ed.), *The Victorian Achievement of Sir Henry Maine* (Cambridge: Cambridge University Press, 1991), pp. 376–88

Johnson, Paul, 'Small Debts and Economic Distress in England and Wales, 1857–1913' (1993) 46 *Economic History Review* 65

Jolowicz, H.F., 'Some English Civilians' (1949) 2 *Current Legal Problems* 139

Jones, Gareth, 'The Role of Equity in the English Law of Restitution', in Eltjo Schrage (ed.), *Unjust Enrichment: The Comparative Legal History of the Law of Restitution* (Berlin: Duncker & Humblot, 1995), pp. 149–69

Jones, Neil, 'Ballow (Bellewe), Henry', *Oxford Dictionary of National Biography*

Kadens, Emily, 'The Puzzle of Judicial Education: The Case of Chief Justice William De Grey' (2009–2010) 75 *Brooklyn Law Review* 143

Kennedy, Duncan, 'The Structure of Blackstone's Commentaries' (1979) 28 *Buffalo Law Review* 205

Kingston, Christopher, 'Marine Insurance in Britain and America 1720–1844: A Comparative Institutional Analysis' (2007) 67 *Journal of Economic History* 379

Klinck, Dennis, 'Lord Nottingham's "Certain Measures"' (2010) 28 *Law and History Review* 711

Kremer, Ben, 'The Action for Money Had and Received' (2001) 17 *Journal of Contract Law* 93

Landau, Peter, 'The Development of Law', in David Luscombe and Jonathan Riley-Smith (eds.), *The New Cambridge Medieval History IV*, 7 vols. (Cambridge: Cambridge University Press, 2004), vol. IV, pp. 113–47

Langbein, John, 'Albion's Fatal Flaws' (1983) 98 *Past and Present* 96

Langbein, John, 'Historical Foundations of the Law of Evidence: A View from the Ryder Sources' (1996) 96 *Columbia Law Review* 1168

Lehman, W., 'Some Observations on the Law Lectures of Professor Millar at the University of Glasgow (1761–1801)' (1970) 15 NS *Juridical Review* 56

Lemire, Beverly, 'From Petty Pawns and Informal Lending: Gender and the Transformation of Small Scale Credit in England, circa 1600–1800', in Kristine Bruland and Patrick O'Brien (eds.), *From Family Firms to Corporate Capitalism: Essays in Business and Industrial History in Honour of Peter Mathias* (Oxford: Oxford University Press, 1998), pp. 112–38

Lenman, B., 'Britain and India', in H.T. Dickinson (ed.), *A Companion to Eighteenth Century Britain* (Oxford: Blackwell, 2002), pp. 460–72

Lewis, A.D.E., 'The Background to Bentham on Evidence' (1990) 2 *Utilitas* 195

Lieberman, David, 'Property, Commerce, and the Common Law', in John Brewer and Susan Staves (eds.), *Early Modern Conceptions of Property* (London: Routledge, 1996), pp. 144–60

Lieberman, David, 'Contract before Freedom of Contract', in Harry Scheiber (ed.), *The State and Freedom of Contract* (Stanford, Calif.: Stanford University Press, 1998), pp. 89–121

Lieberman, David, 'Economy and Polity in Bentham's Science of Legislation', in Stefan Collini, Richard Whatmore and B.W. Young (eds.), *Economy, Polity and Society: British Intellectual History 1750–1950* (Cambridge: Cambridge University Press, 2000), pp. 107–34

Lieberman, David, 'Adam Smith on Justice, Rights and Law', in Knud Haakonssen (ed.), *The Cambridge Companion to Adam Smith* (Cambridge: Cambridge University Press, 2006), pp. 214–45

Lobban, M., 'Law, Edward', *Oxford Dictionary of National Biography*

Lobban, Michael, 'The English Legal Treatise and English Law in the Eighteenth Century' (1997) 13 *Iuris Scripta Historica* 69

Lobban, Michael, 'Contractual Fraud in Law and Equity' (1997) 17 *Oxford Journal of Legal Studies* 441

Lobban, Michael, 'Henry Brougham and Law Reform' (2000) 115 *The English Historical Review* 1184

Lobban, Michael, 'The Strange Life of the English Civil Jury, 1837–1914', in John Cairns and Grant McLeod (eds.), *The Dearest Birth Right of the People of England* (Oxford: Hart, 2002), pp. 173–209

Lobban, Michael, 'The Ambition of Lord Kame's Equity', in Andrew Lewis and Michael Lobban (eds.), *Law and History* (Oxford: Oxford University Press, 2003), pp. 97–121

Lobban, Michael, 'Preparing for Fusion: Reforming the Nineteenth Century Court of Chancery' (2004) 22 *Law and History Review* 389

Lobban, Michael, 'Foakes v. Beer (1884)', in Charles Mitchell and Paul Mitchell (eds.), *Landmark Cases in the Law of Contract* (Oxford: Hart, 2008), pp. 223–67

Lubbe, Gerhard, 'Formation of Contract', in Kenneth Reid and Reinhard Zimmermann (eds.), *A History of Private Law in Scotland*, 2 vols. (Oxford: Oxford University Press, 2000), vol. II, pp. 1–46

Lücke, Horst, 'Slade's Case and the Origins of the Common Counts' (1965) 81 *Law Quarterly Review* 422

Luther, Peter, 'Campbell, Espinasse and the Sailors: Text and Context in the Common Law' (1999) 19 *Legal Studies* 526

Macmillan, Catharine, 'Taylor v. Caldwell (1863)', in Charles Mitchell and Paul Mitchell (eds.), *Landmark Cases in the Law of Contract* (Oxford: Hart, 2008), pp. 167–203

Macmillan, Catharine, 'Stephen Martin Leake: A Victorian's View of the Common Law' (2011) 32 *Journal of Legal History* 3

Macnair, Michael, 'Sir Jeffrey Gilbert and His Treatises' (1994) 15 *Journal of Legal History* 252

Macnair, Mike, 'Equity and Conscience' (2007) 27 *Oxford Journal of Legal Studies* 659

MacNeil, William, 'Living on: Borderlines – Law/History' (1995) 6 *Law and Critique* 167

MacQueen, Hector and Sellar, W. David, 'Unjust Enrichment in Scots Law', in Eltjo Schrage (ed.), *Unjust Enrichment: The Comparative Legal History of the Law of Restitution* (Berlin: Duncker & Humblot, 1995), pp. 289–321

Mathews, Carol, 'A Model of the Old House Architecture in Blackstone's Life and Commentaries', in Wilfrid Prest (ed.), *Blackstone and His Commentaries* (Oxford: Hart, 2009), pp. 15–34

Mathias, Peter, 'The Lawyer as Businessman in Eighteenth-Century England', Peter Mathias and D.C. Coleman (eds.), *Enterprise and History* (Cambridge: Cambridge University Press, 1984), pp. 151–70

McGovern, William, 'Contract in Medieval England: The Necessity for Quid Pro Quo and a Sum Certain' (1969) 13 *American Journal of Legal History* 173

McIntosh, Marjorie, 'Money Lending on the Periphery of London' (1988) 20 *Albion* 557

McKibbin, Ross, 'Working-Class Gambling in Britain 1880–1939' (1979) 82 *Past and Present* 147

Miles, M., '"Eminent Practitioners": The New Visage of Country Attorneys c.1750–1800', in G.R. Rubin and David Sugarman (eds.), *Law, Economy and Society, 1750–1914: Essays in the History of English Law* (Abingdon: Professional Books, 1984), pp. 470–503

Milsom, S.F.C., 'The Past and the Future of Judge-Made Law' (1981–1982) 8 *Monash University Law Review* 1

Milsom, S.F.C., 'Pollock and Maitland: A Lawyer's Retrospective', in John Hudson (ed.), *The History of English Law: Centenary Essays on Pollock and Maitland* (Oxford: Oxford University Press, 1996), pp. 243–59

Mingay, G.E., 'The Agricultural Depression 1730–1750' (1956) 8 *Economic History Review* 323

Mitchell, Paul, 'The Development of Quality Obligations in Sale of Goods' (2001) 117 *Law Quarterly Review* 645

Mitchell, Paul and Phillips, John, 'The Contractual Nexus: Is Reliance Essential?' (2002) 22 *Oxford Journal of Legal Studies* 115

Mitchell, Paul, 'Patterns of Legal Change' (2012) 65 *Current Legal Problems* 177

Mitnick, John, 'From Neighbor-Witness to Judge of Proofs: The Transformation of the English Civil Juror' (1988) 32 *American Journal of Legal History* 201

Musson, Anthony, 'Arbitration and the Legal Profession in Late Medieval England', in Matthew Dyson and David Ibbetson (eds.), *Law and the Legal Process* (Cambridge: Cambridge University Press, 2013), pp. 56–76

Nicholas, Barry, 'Jurisprudence', in M.G. Brock and M.C. Curthoys (eds.), *The History of the University of Oxford*, 8 vols. (Oxford: Oxford University Press, 2000), vol. VII, pp. 385–96

O'Sullivan, Janet, 'In defence of Foakes v. Beer' (1996) 55 *Cambridge Law Journal* 219

Oldham, James, 'Buller, Sir Francis', *Oxford Dictionary of National Biography*

Oldham, James, 'Murray, William', *Oxford Dictionary of National Biography*

Oldham, James, 'The Origins of the Special Jury' (1983) 50 *University of Chicago Law Review* 137

Oldham, James, 'Reinterpretations of Eighteenth Century English Contract Theory: A View From Lord Mansfield's Trial Notes' (1988) 76 *Georgetown Law Journal* 1949

Oldham, James, 'Detecting Non-Fiction: Sleuthing among Manuscript Case Reports for What Was Really Said', in Chantal Stebbings (ed.), *Law Reporting in Britain* (London: Hambledon Press, 1995), pp. 133–68

Oldham, James, 'The Seventh Amendment Right to Jury Trial: Late Eighteenth Century Practice Reconsidered', in Katherine O'Donovan and Gerry Rubin (eds.), *Human Rights and Legal History: Essays in Honour of Brian Simpson* (Oxford: Oxford University Press, 2000), pp. 225–53

Oldham, James, 'Underreported and Underrated: The Court of Common Pleas in the Eighteenth Century', in Hendrik Hartog *et al.* (eds.), *Law as Culture and Culture as Law* (Madison, Wis.: Madison House, 2000), pp. 119–46

Oldham, James, 'Jury Research in the English Reports in CD-ROM', in John Cairns and Grant McLeod (eds.), *The Dearest Birth Right of the People of England: The Jury in the History of the Common Law* (Oxford: Hart, 2002), pp. 131–54

Oldham, James, 'Law Making at Nisi Prius in the Early 1800s' (2004) 25 *Journal of Legal History* 221

Orr, Graeme, 'Betting on Elections: Its History, Law and Risks' (2014) 42 *Federal Law Review* (forthcoming)

Palmer, Vernon, 'Why Privity Entered Tort: An Historical Re-examination of Winterbottom v. Wright' (1983) 27 *American Journal of Legal History* 85

Parker, Alice, 'Tobias Smollett and the Law' (1942) 39 *Studies in Philology* 545

Parry, R. Gwynedd, 'Is Legal Biography Really Legal Scholarship?' (2010) 30 *Legal Studies* 208

Perillo, Joseph, 'Robert J. Pothier's Influence on the Common Law of Contract' (2004–2005) 11 *Texas Wesleyan Law Review* 267

Phillips, John, 'Smith v. Hughes (1871)', in Charles Mitchell and Paul Mitchell (eds.), *Landmark Cases in the Law of Contract* (Oxford: Hart, 2008), pp. 205–21

Powell, Edward, 'Arbitration and the Law in England in the Late Middle Ages' (1983) 32 *5th Series Transactions of the Royal Historical Society* 49

Prest, Wilfrid, 'Dialectical Origins of Finch's Law' (1977) 36 *Cambridge Law Journal* 326

Prest, Wilfrid, 'The Experience of Litigation in Eighteenth-Century England', in David Lemmings (ed.), *The British and Their Laws in the Eighteenth Century* (Woodbridge: The Boydell Press, 2005), pp. 133–54

Prichard, M.J., 'Non-Suit: A Premature Obituary' (1960) 18 *Cambridge Law Journal* 88

Prior, Katherine, 'Ryan, Sir Edward', *Oxford Dictionary of National Biography*

Pugsley, David, 'The Facts of Hadley v. Baxendale' [1976] *New Law Journal* 420

Raven, James, 'The Book Trades', in Isabel Rivers (ed.), *Books and Their Readers in Eighteenth Century England: New Essays* (London: Continuum, 2001), pp. 1–34

Reid, Kenneth, 'From Text-Book to Book of Authority: The *Principles* of George Joseph Bell' (2011) 15 *Edinburgh Law Review* 6

Reimann, Mathias, 'The Historical School of Codification: Savigny, Carter and the Defeat of the New York Civil Code' (1989) 37 *American Journal of Comparative Law* 95

Reimann, Mathias, 'Nineteenth Century German Legal Science' (1989–1990) 31 *Boston College Law Review* 837

Roberts, David, 'Jeremy Bentham and the Victorian Administrative State', in Bhikhu Parekh (ed.) *Jeremy Bentham: Ten Critical Essays* (London: Cass, 1974), pp. 187–204

Robinson, Robert, 'A Study in Eighteenth Century Legal Scholarship' (1991) 35 *American Journal of Legal History* 432

Lord Rodger, 'The Codification of Commercial Law in Victorian Britain' (1991) 80 *Proceedings of the British Academy* 149

Lord Rodger, 'Judges and Academics in the United Kingdom' (2010) 29 *University of Queensland Law Journal* 29

Rogers, C.P., 'Continental Literature and the Development of the Common Law by the King's Bench: c.1750–1800', in Vito Piergiovanni (ed.), *Courts and the Development of Commercial Law* (Berlin: Duncker & Humblot, 1987), pp. 161–93

Rogers, James, 'The Myth of Negotiability' (1989–1990) 31 *Boston College Law Review* 265

Rudden, Bernard, 'A Code Too Soon. The 1826 Property Code of James Humphreys: English Rejection, American Reception, English Acceptance', in Peter Wallington and Robert Merkin (eds.), *Essays in Memory of F.H. Lawson* (London: Butterworths, 1986), pp. 101–16

Rudden, B., 'Pothier et la common law', in J. Monéger (ed.), *Robert-Joseph Pothier, d'hier à aujourd'hui* (Paris: Economica, 2001), p. 91–101

Rudolph, Julia, 'That "Blunderbuss of Law": Giles Jacob, Abridgment, and Print Culture' (2008) 37 *Studies in Eighteenth Century Culture* 197

Schofield, Phillip, 'Jeremy Bentham: Legislator of the World' (1998) 51 *Current Legal Problems* 115

Shapiro, Barbara, 'Law and Science in Seventeenth Century England' (1968–1969) 21 *Stanford Law Review* 727

Shapiro, Barbara, 'Codification of the Laws in Seventeenth Century England' [1974] *Wisconsin Law Review* 428

Shapiro, Barbara, 'Law Reform in Seventeenth Century England' (1975) 19 *American Journal of Legal History*, 280

Sheehan, Duncan, 'Natural Obligations in English Law' [2004] *Lloyds Maritime and Commercial Law Quarterly* 171

Siepp, David, 'Roman Legal Categories in the Early Common Law', in Thomas Watkin (ed.), *Legal Record and Historical Reality* (London: Hambledon Press, 1989), pp. 9–36

Siepp, David J, 'The Structure of English Common Law in the Seventeenth Century', in W.M. Gordon and T.D. Fergus (eds.), *Legal History in the Making* (London: Hambledon, 1991), pp. 61–83

Simpson, A.W.B., 'Innovation in Nineteenth Century Contract Law' (1975) 91 *Law Quarterly Review* 247

Simpson, A.W.B., 'The Horwitz Thesis and the History of Contracts' (1979) 46 *University of Chicago Law Review* 533

Simpson, A.W.B., 'The Rise and Fall of the Legal Treatise: Legal Principles and the Forms of Legal Literature' (1981) 48 *University of Chicago Law Review* 632

Simpson, A.W.B., 'Contract: The Twitching Corpse' (1981) 1 *Oxford Journal of Legal Studies* 265

Simpson, A.W.B., 'Contracts for Cotton to Arrive: The Case of the Two Ships Peerless' (1989–1990) 11 *Cardozo Law Review* 287

Slatter, Michele, 'The Norwich Court of Requests – A Tradition Continued' (1984) 5 *Journal of Legal History* 97

Smith, Charlotte, 'Allcard v. Skinner (1887)', in Charles Mitchell and Paul Mitchell (eds.), *Landmark Cases in the Law of Restitution* (Oxford: Hart, 2006), pp. 183–211

Smith, K.J.M., 'Macaulay's "Utilitarian" Indian Penal Code: An Illustration of the Accidental Function of Time, Place and Personalities in Law Making', in W.M. Gordon and T.D. Fergus (eds.), *Legal History in the Making* (London: Hambledon Press, 1991), pp. 145–64

Smith, K.J.M. and McLaren, J.P.S., 'History's Living Legacy: An Outline of Modern Historiography of the Common Law' (2001) 21 *Legal Studies* 251

Steckley, George, 'Litigious Mariners: Wage Cases in the Seventeenth Century Admiralty Court' (1999) 42 *Historical Journal* 315

Steckley, George, 'Collisions, Prohibitions and the Admiralty Court in Seventeenth Century London' (2003) 21 *Law and History Review* 41

Stern, Simon, 'The Case and the Exceptions: Creating Instrumental Texts in Law and Literature', in Laura Runge and Pat Rogers (eds.), *Producing the Eighteenth Century Book: Writers and Publishers in England 1650–1800* (Newark, Del.: University of Delaware Press, 2009), pp. 95–116

Stoljar, S., 'Dependent and Independent Promises' (1956–1958) 2 *Sydney Law Review* 217

Stoljar, Samuel, 'The Great Case of Cutter v. Powell' (1956) 34 *Canadian Bar Review* 288

Stoljar, Samuel, 'The Consideration of Forbearance' (1965–1967) 5 *Melbourne University Law Review* 34

Styles, John, 'Our Traitorous Money Makers: The Yorkshire Coiners and the Law, 1760–83', in John Brewer and John Styles (eds.), *An Ungovernable People* (London: Hutchinson, 1980), pp. 172–249

Sugarman, David, 'Great Beyond His Knowing: Morton Horwitz's Influence on Legal Education and Scholarship in England, Canada, and Australia', in Daniel Hamilton and Alfred Brophy (eds.), *Transformations in American Legal History Law, Ideology and Methods. Essays in Honor of Morton J. Horwitz*, 2 vols. (Cambridge, Mass.: Harvard University Press, 2010), vol. II, pp. 504–42

Sutherland, L.S., 'The Law Merchant in the Seventeenth and Eighteenth Centuries' (1934) 17 *4th Series, Transactions of the Royal Historical Society* 149

Swain, Warren, 'Cutter v. Powell and the Pleading of Claims of Unjust Enrichment' [2003] *Restitution Law Review* 46

Swain, Warren, 'The Changing Nature of the Doctrine of Consideration 1750–1850' (2005) 26 *Journal of Legal History* 55

Swain, Warren, 'The Classical Model of Contract: The Product of a Revolution in Legal Thought' (2010) 30 *Legal Studies* 513

Swain, Warren and Fairweather, Karen, 'The Legal Regulation of Pawnbroking in England, A Brief History', in James Devenney and Mel Kenny (eds.), *Consumer Credit, Debt and Investment in Europe* (Cambridge: Cambridge University Press, 2011), pp. 142–59

Swain, Warren, 'Contract as Promise: The Role of Promising in the Law of Contract. An Historical Account' (2013) 17 *Edinburgh Law Review* 1

Swain, Warren, 'Unjust Enrichment and the Role of Legal History in England and Australia' (2013) 36 *New South Wales Law Journal* 1030

Temin, Peter and Voth, Hans-Joachim, 'Banking as an Emerging Technology: Hoare's Bank, 1702–1742' (2006) 13 *Financial History Review* 149

Temin, Peter and Voth, Hans-Joachim, 'Interest Rate Restrictions in a Natural Experiment: Loan Allocation and the Change in the Usury Laws in 1714' (2008) 118 *The Economic Journal* 743

Tettenborn, Andrew, 'Subsisting Contract and Failure of Consideration – A Little Scepticism' [2002] *Restitution Law Review* 1

Thompson, E.P., 'The Peculiarities of the English' (1965) *Socialist Register* 311

Tomkins, Alanna, 'Pawnbroking and Survival Strategies of the Urban Poor in 1770s York', in Steven King and Alanna Tomkins (eds.), *The Poor in England 1700–1850* (Manchester: Manchester University Press, 2003), pp. 166–98

Treitel, G.H., 'Consideration: A Critical Analysis of Professor Atiyah's Fundamental Restatement' (1976) 50 *Australian Law Journal* 439

Tushnet, Mark, 'Perspectives on the Development of American Law: A Critical Review of Friedman's A History of American Law' [1977] *Wisconsin Law Review* 81

Tushnet, Mark, 'Critical Legal Studies: A Political History' (1991) 100 *Yale Law Journal* 1515

Virgo, Graham, 'Restitution Through the Looking Glass: Restitution Within Equity and Equity Within Restitution', in Joshua Getzler (ed.), *Rationalizing Property, Equity and Trust: Essays in Honour of Edward Burn* (London: Lexis/Nexis, 2003), pp. 82–110

Vogenauer, Stefan, 'Law Journals in Nineteenth-Century England' (2008) 12 *Edinburgh Law Review* 26

Waddams, Stephen, 'What Were the Principles of Nineteenth-Century Contract Law?', in Andrew Lewis, Paul Brand and Paul Mitchell (eds.), *Law in the City: Proceedings of the Seventeenth British Legal History Conference, London, 2005* (Dublin: Four Courts Press, 2007), pp. 305–18

Washbrook, D.A., 'India, 1818–1860', in Andrew Porter (ed.), *The Oxford History of the British Empire: The Nineteenth Century* (Oxford: Oxford University Press, 1999), pp. 395–421

Washington, George, 'Damages in Contract at Common Law' (1931) 47 *Law Quarterly Review* 345; (1932) 48 *Law Quarterly Review* 90

Watterson, Stephen, 'Carter v. Boehm (1766)', in Charles Mitchell and Paul Mitchell (eds.), *Landmark Cases in the Law of Contract* (Oxford: Hart, 2008)

Williams, Ian, 'Early-Modern Judges and the Practice of Precedent', in Paul Brand and Joshua Getzler (eds.), *Judges and Judging in the History of the Common Law and Civil Law* (Cambridge: Cambridge University Press, 2012), pp. 51–66

Williamson, Jeffrey, 'Why Was British Economic Growth So Slow During the Industrial Revolution' (1984) 44 *Journal of Economic History* 687

Winder, W.H.D., 'The Courts of Requests' (1936) 52 *Law Quarterly Review* 369

Winfield, Percy, 'Public Policy and the English Common Law' (1928–1929) 42 *Harvard Law Review* 76

Yale, D.E.C., 'A View of the Admiralty Jurisdiction: Sir Mathew Hale and the Civilians', in Dafydd Jenkins (ed.), *Legal History Studies 1972* (Cardiff: University of Wales Press, 1972), pp. 87–109

Young, P.W. and Gomez, A.A., 'The Status of Law Reports Produced in England Prior to 1865' (2013) 87 *Australian Law Journal* 844

Unpublished PhD

Tofaris, Stelios, *A Historical Study of the Indian Contract Act 1872* (unpublished PhD, University of Cambridge, 2011)

INDEX

www.ingramcontent.com/pod-product-compliance
Lightning Source LLC
LaVergne TN
LVHW011529200926
848484LV00001B/198

* 9 7 8 1 1 0 7 0 4 0 7 6 2 *